Business Law for People in Business

William H. Glover, Jr., J.D.
Daniel Adrian Doss, Ph.D.

Printed in the United States of America
ISBN 978-0-9990053-9-2

Authors

William "Bill" Glover, J.D. – William H. Glover drafts forms, legal digests, and legal summaries for U.S. Legal Forms. He received his B.B.A. degree from the University of Mississippi in 1973 and his J.D. degree from the University of Mississippi School of Law in 1976. He joined the firm of Wells Marble & Hurst in 1976 as an Associate and became a Partner in 1979. While at Wells, he supervised major real estate commercial loan transactions and employment law cases. His practice also involved estate administration and general commercial law. Mr. Glover joined the faculty of Belhaven University in Jackson, Mississippi in 1996 as Assistant Professor of Business Administration and University Attorney, where he taught business law and business ethics in the BBA and MBA programs until 2004, before a short stay at Wells Marble & Hurst, PLLC as General Counsel. Mr. Glover retired as a Colonel and Staff Judge Advocate for Headquarters of the Mississippi State Guard. He was called to active duty during Hurricanes Dennis, Katrina, and Gustav. He received the Magnolia Medal from the Mississippi Army National Guard in 2010.

Daniel Adrian Doss, Ph.D. – Dr. Doss's background includes Associate Professor, College of Business and Technology, University of West Alabama; Assistant Professor, Belhaven College; Adjunct Assistant Professor, Embry-Riddle Aeronautical University; and Chair of Graduate Business and Management, University of Phoenix (Memphis). His professional career consisted of software engineering and analytical positions in both the defense and commercial industries. Corporate entities included full-time and contract positions with Federal Express and uMonitor.com, and contract positions, via Data Management Consultants, with Loral Corporation (formerly IBM Federal Systems) and Lockheed-Martin. Additional credentials include Colonel, Mississippi State Guard, where he serves as an intelligence officer; graduate of the Lafayette County Law Enforcement Officer Training Academy (Mississippi); and graduate of the Law Enforcement Mobile Video Institute. He has also co-authored a variety of peer-reviewed journal articles and conference proceedings. His education consists of a D.Litt. et. Phil. in Police Science, University of South Africa; Ph.D. in Business Administration, Northcentral University; M.C.J. in Homeland Security, University of Mississippi; M.A. in Computer Resources and Information Management, Webster University; M.B.A., Embry-Riddle Aeronautical University; Graduate Certificate in Forensic Criminology, University of Massachusetts (Lowell); Graduate Certificate in Non-Profit Financial Management, University of Maryland (Adelphi); and a B.S. in Computer Science with a Mathematics minor, Mississippi State University. He is currently pursuing a third doctorate, in higher education administration, at Jackson State University.

Acknowledgements

To my Dad who taught me (by example) how to have the drive and courage to succeed and to my Mother who taught me not to run over people in the process.

—Bill Glover

Thanks to Almighty God for this publication opportunity. Micah 6:8 – "He hath shewed thee, O man, what is good; and what doth the Lord require of thee, but to do justly, and to love mercy, and to walk humbly with thy God?"

For my little girl, Caleigh – I love you! Now that Daddy is finished with this manuscript, we can play in the swimming pool all day!

Many years ago, during a professorship at the Memphis campus of Belhaven College, my boss suggested that I write a book of legal business definitions. In return for the idea, he requested that I include simply a "thank you" message at the front of the text. Well, I've not done all of that yet, but this manuscript is close … so … to keep a promise – ***THANKS, TOM!***

Thank you to my co-author, Dr. Bill Glover. Your participation and friendship are greatly appreciated, and I have thoroughly enjoyed this opportunity to collaborate with you.

—Adrian Doss

Contents

Contents

Chapter 1
INTRODUCTORY OVERVIEW

INTRODUCTION

Once upon a time, people in business could close a deal without worry that there would be any misunderstandings in the future and certainly no possibility of a lawsuit. Unfortunately, those days are long past. But does this mean someone in business always needs an attorney for every aspect of his or her business? That certainly would be cost prohibited. *Business Law for People in Business* discusses, in layman's terms, the most common legal issues that face today's small business owners.

Business law encompasses the law governing contracts, sales, agency, employment law, business organizations, property, and bailments. Other popular areas include insurance, wills and estate planning, and consumer and creditor protection. Business law may include issues such as starting, selling, or buying a small business, managing a business, dealing with employees, or dealing with contracts, as well as several other topics as you can see from the Table of Contents.

Commercial law includes all aspects of business, including advertising and marketing, collections and bankruptcy, banking, contracts, negotiable instruments. The Uniform Commercial Code (UCC), which governs sales and commercial paper, has been adopted in some form by almost all states. There are agencies at the state and federal level which administer the law in such issues such as employment affairs and consumer and credit protection. The laws aim to protect fair business practices and due process rights for aggrieved workers and others.

The following are the topics covered by this book:

- Definitions and sources of law
- Alternative means of dispute resolution
- Administrative agencies
- Government regulation of competition and prices
- International law and transactions
- Business crime and cyberlaw
- Tort and cyber torts
- Intellectual property rights
- Contract law
- Morals, ethics, and values
- Personal property and bailments
- Sales and leases of personal property
- Products liability and warranties
- Consumer protection
- Secured transactions in personal property
- Insurance
- Agency

- Laws governing labor-management relations
- Employment law
- Employment discrimination
- Overview of business organizations
- Introduction to corporation law
- Regulation of securities
- Management of the corporation
- Real property law
- Environmental law
- Wills, estates and trusts
- E-commerce
- Business sales
- Business ethics
- Corporations

Chapter 2
DEFINITIONS AND SOURCES OF LAW

LAW

Law consists of the body of principles that govern conduct and that can be enforced in Courts or by administrative agencies. In other words, conceptually, laws are enforceable rules. A right is the legal power to require someone else to do something or refrain from doing something. A duty is the legal obligation to do or not do something. The U.S. Constitution grants certain fundamental rights to persons, and these rights cannot be altered or eliminated by any statute, ordinance or judicial decision.

For example, Americans enjoy a fundamental right of privacy which guarantees the right to be protected from unreasonable governmental searches and seizures of property along with the right to be free from intrusion by the government and others into one's private affairs. The U.S. Supreme Court has held that the right of privacy is a constitutional right even though this is not specifically stated in the constitution. State constitutions as well as certain federal and state statutes also recognize this right.

SOURCES OF LAW usually refers to a statute passed by State Legislature or Congress. This term can also refer to Constitutional law, whether a State Constitution or the U.S. Constitution. Statutory laws are laws passed by a State Legislature or Congress. Ordinances are laws passed by a City (e.g., city council) or County (e.g., board of supervisors).

Administrative regulations are generally regulations written by National or State administrative agencies. For example, the Internal Revenue Service (IRS) passes Revenue Regulations. These Regulations generally have the force of law since Congress gives the IRS this authority to pass them with the force of law. Generally, such regulations are interpretations and specific rules about a statute in the Internal Revenue Code.

Sometimes regulations do not have the force of law, but are looked to in interpreting law by the Courts. The regulations passed by the Wage & Hour Department of the Department of Labor regarding the Fair Labor Standards Act might be an example. These regulations do not carry the same weight of authority as regulations passed by the IRS.

Case law involves principles expressed for first time in a court decision. For example, imagine a spectator attending a baseball game in 1890. The batter fouls the ball, which hits and injures a spectator. The spectator sues the team and the player who hit the ball for negligence. If the court, for the first time, held that a spectator **assumes the risk** of getting hit by a foul ball at a baseball game, this would establish the case law of **assumption of risk.** Old case law is often called **common law.**

Imagine that a spectator gets hit by a basketball while attending a basketball game. A court should use the **precedent** set by the baseball case to rule that the spectator assumed the risk of getting hit by a ball at a basketball game. The phrase ***stare decisis*** is Latin for **let the decision stand.** In other words, Courts should not change precedent.

Uniform State laws resulted from the work of the National Conference of Commissioners on Uniform State Laws. This Conference consisted of representatives from every State. They drafted statutes on various subjects for adoption by State legislatures. For example, the Uniform Commercial Code has been adopted in every State. This Code deals with such areas as the sale of goods and negotiable instruments (e.g., checks). A Uniform State Law is not binding in a state unless it is adopted by a state's legislature.

Substantive law is law that creates, defines, and regulates rights and liabilities, such as a law passed by Congress or a state's legislature. This term also includes case law. **Procedural law** is law that provides the guidelines in enforcing rights and liabilities given by substantive law. For example, the Federal Rules of Civil Procedure deals with procedures that must be followed in prosecuting a lawsuit in a Federal Court. Procedures are given on such areas as filing a complaint, answering the complaint, what motions are allowed, etc.

THE COURT SYSTEM AND ITS PERSONNEL

A **court** is a tribunal established by a government to decide controversies, provide a remedy for persons who have been wronged, punish wrongdoers, and prevent wrongs.

Courts can decide only certain types or classes of cases (lawsuits). **Jurisdiction** is the power to hear and decide cases. Courts may have:

- **Original jurisdiction** is the power to decide cases where the lawsuit is filed.
- **Appellate jurisdiction** is the power to review decisions of lower courts to determine if a lower court made a reversible error.
- **General or jurisdiction** is the power to decide most types of cases, whether civil or criminal,
- **Limited** (special) jurisdiction is the power to decide only certain types of cases.

Criminal or Civil Jurisdiction

Criminal courts can decide cases involving crimes, whereas **civil courts** can decide cases involving private wrongs and other civil disputes.

Courts with original jurisdiction are **trial courts,** and they render the initial judgment in civil and criminal cases. A reversible error ordinarily occurs when a lower court: (i) applies the wrong law in resolving the case; or (ii) incorrectly interprets or applies the law in resolving a case.

THE FEDERAL COURT SYSTEM

The federal court system consists of the following three levels of courts:

Federal district courts have original jurisdiction to decide most cases filed in federal court including: (i) civil suits in which the U.S. is a party; (ii) actions involving any federal law, such as the US. Constitution, federal statutes or administrative rules, or US treaties; and (iii) cases between parties who are residents of different states if $75,000 or more is involved. Other federal courts with limited jurisdiction include the federal bankruptcy court, Tax Court, US. Court of International Trade, US. Claims Court, and Court of Military Appeals.

A U.S. Courts of Appeals has only appellate jurisdiction and review judgments of federal district courts in their respective circuits. The decision of a U. S. Court of Appeals is final unless the Supreme Court hears an appeal of the case.

The **U.S. Supreme Court** is the highest federal court and has original jurisdiction over cases involving ambassadors, public ministers or consuls, and cases in which two or more states are involved. It has appellate jurisdiction over all cases brought in federal court and certain cases appealed from state supreme courts. Through the process of granting a **writ of certiorari,** the Court has the discretion to decide whether or not to hear an appeal.

STATE COURT SYSTEMS

The typical state court system consists of the following types of courts. A **general trial court** has general jurisdiction of criminal and civil cases. States may have courts with limited jurisdiction, such as **juvenile courts, probate courts,** and **family law courts.** Cities and counties may also have courts of limited jurisdiction such as **municipal courts, traffic courts,** and **small claims courts.** The highest court in most states is called the **state supreme court** and generally only has appellate jurisdiction. The decision of a state supreme court is typically final unless a writ of **certiorari** is filed with the U.S. Supreme Court.

THE PARTICIPANTS IN THE COURT SYSTEM

The **plaintiff** is the party who commences a **civil lawsuit** and the **prosecutor** is the party who brings a **criminal case** on behalf of the government. The d**efendant** is the party against whom a civil or criminal lawsuit is brought. The **judge** is the primary officer of the court, and the **jury** is a body of citizens who are appointed by a court to determine the facts and render a **verdict** in a case.

Someone working at a court may be an "employee" of the Court or an "officer" of the Court or both. The **judge** is the primary officer of a court. He or she may be elected or appointed. For example, federal judges are appointed. Many state court judges are elected (unless someone dies in office and a temporary appointment is made by the governor). **Attorneys** are considered to be officers of the Court. This is why a judge can appoint an attorney to represent an indigent defendant in a criminal case. Attorneys have to be sworn in by a court in order to practice in that type of court.

A **Clerk** of the court is sometimes elected (e.g., county clerks) and sometimes appointed (e.g. a federal court clerk).

The **sheriff** of a county not only has law enforcement duties, but court duties as well.
For example:

- Serving a summons (e.g., serving a civil complaint in a lawsuit);
- Serving a subpoena (on witnesses);
- Preserving Order in a court; and

- Carrying out judgments by taking possession of assets and selling them to satisfy a monetary judgment if necessary;

U.S. Marshals have similar duties in federal courts except they do not serve a summons or subpoenas except in rare situations.

Jurors are officers of the court. They are responsible for deciding on what the true facts are in a case (i.e., the finders of fact).

Steps in a Civil Lawsuit

Filing a Complaint or Petition
Any complaint or petition for relief in a court must be filed within the statutory time limit **(Statute of Limitations).** These statutes vary from state to state. These statutes also vary depending on what your cause of action is. For example, in many states, the statute of limitations regarding a cause of action for breach of contract is **three years,** while the cause of action for an intentional tort, like slander, is **one year.**

A **complaint** is a general statement of the plaintiff's claim. The complaint must describe the actions that led to the claim of a violation (i.e., violation of rights). The claim can be for money damages. It could also be a claim for equitable remedies like specific performance (*e.g.,* court forcing a party to abide by a contract) or an injunction (*e.g.,* stopping a person from doing something). The complaint must establish jurisdiction of the court in which it is filed. For example, if the complaint is filed in federal court, it must show **diversity of citizenship** or that a **federal statutory** or **constitutional** question is involved.

See Appendix 1 for a sample complaint.

Class actions are sometimes filed against large companies. A class action can occur when a group of plaintiffs have same cause of action against one defendant. For example, a group of consumers might sue a lender for failure to pay abide by federal truth-in-lending disclosures on their loan forms. One advantage in a class action is that legal expenses can be shared by a large group of plaintiffs. Class actions have been the subject of abuse. Oftentimes individual plaintiffs get a small amount, while their lawyers get a fee based on the total amount paid to all members of the class. This amount can be huge. This practice has led to some frivolous class action suits.

Service of Process generally involves attaching a copy of the complaint to a summons which is served on the defendant. The summons explains to the defendant what is going on and certain rights that that the defendant has. The summons explains:

- That the defendant is being sued;
- The name of the Court in which he is being sued;
- When he must file an answer; and
- The fact that a default judgment will be entered if no answer is filed.

The **summons** (or process) is delivered by an **officer of the court.** In many state courts, this can be a deputy sheriff or a professional process server. Deputy Marshals or process servers are used in federal court. Constables are used in justice of some states. In exceptional circumstances, when the defendant cannot be found, service may be made by publication in a newspaper. Generally, anyone above the age of eighteen (18) can be appointed to serve process,

The summons must normally be served on the individual defendant. Some states allow service on a member of defendant's household if the defendant is not available. A plaintiff must serve a corporate defendant by serving the registered agent or an appropriate officer of the corporation.

See Appendix 2 for a Sample Summons

The Answer

In the **answer,** the defendant tells his side of the story. He is supposed to admit facts that are true and deny allegations that are not true. This answer must be filed within a certain period of time which is usually stated on the summons. Failure to file an answer can result in a default judgment against the defendant. This is a judgment for failure to defend that is entered against the defendant just like there had been a trial.

The defendant can file a **counterclaim** against the plaintiff as part of his answer. The effect of the counterclaim is that the defendant is suing the plaintiff in the same action. The plaintiff must file an answer to the counterclaim or a default judgment will be taken against him.

See Appendix 3 for Sample Answer

Ending a Suit through Motions

Motions are formal requests for the court to take some sort of action. The pleadings generally will consist of the complaint, the answer, any counterclaim, and all motions. In a **motion for judgment on the pleadings,** the defendant is arguing that even if everything said in the complaint were true, plaintiff would still have no cause of action against defendant. For example, suppose you have a business partner who calls you a liar in a room where only you and your partner were present. You sue you partner for slander. He would be entitled to a judgment on the pleadings since there was no publication (verbally or in writing) of your slanderous remark. Only he heard it. If the court grants this motion, the case is over unless you appeal the judgment.

Another type of motion that is often filed is a **motion to dismiss.** Two common grounds for this motion are expiration of the appropriate statute of limitations or that the court lacks jurisdiction over the case. For example, courts of equity in some states have jurisdiction over disputes involving land. If such a dispute were filed in a circuit court, a motion to dismiss for lack of jurisdiction would be appropriate.

A **motion for summary judgment** is appropriate in situations where there are no important facts in dispute and the only dispute is how the law should be applied to the facts. If there is no dispute over the important facts of the case, there is nothing for a jury to determine since that is their job, to decide what the facts are based on the evidence presented at trial. The judge will therefore apply the law to the facts and render a judgment. That will be the end of the case unless there is an appeal. Generally, this motion is not made unless all discovery has been completed.

See Appendix 4 for Sample Motion

Discovery
The period allowed for discovery is when the plaintiff and defendant get information from each other and other people to use as evidence at trial. Discovery pleadings generally consist of the following:

- **Interrogatories** are written questions submitted (with the court's permission) by one party to a civil suit to the opposing party on any matter relevant to the case. The opposing party must answer in writing, under oath and within the period allowed by the court. The objective of the interrogatory process is to obtain admissions of the crucial facts of the opposing party's case.
- **Requests for Production of Documents:** These are written requests served on the opposing party's attorney requesting that documents relevant to the case be produced for inspection and copying.
- **Requests for Admission:** These are requests from one party to another to admit facts that are not in dispute so that the evidence produced at trial will basically include matters that are in dispute. Honest and complete responses can shorten the trial.
- **Depositions:** These are statements of the parties or potential witnesses taken under oath by a court reporter. Depositions are usually taken by a private court reporter (*i.e.,* one not employed by a court) in the office of one of the lawyers. Depositions are used to pin down the testimony of witnesses and to find out what witnesses are going to say at trial.

Courts are generally very liberal regarding what information is subject to discovery. It must be generally relevant in some way although, technically, courts will allow the parties to ask for **anything that is reasonably calculated to lead to discoverable evidence.**

Attorneys do not have to disclose **work product.** Work product consists of the thoughts, strategies and theories of the attorneys of the parties, whether it is in the form of memos, notes, letters or any similar document.

Pretrial Conferences always are required in Federal Courts and are being required more and more in some state courts. The following usually occur in pretrial conferences:

- The parties agree on the facts not in dispute.
- They tell each other whom their witnesses will be.
- They identify what their evidence will be and provide copies of documents that will be offered into evidence.

Each party will submit in writing the facts they intend to prove and the law or jury instructions that should be applied to the facts. The Judge will generally act somewhat as a mediator, at least in federal court, and try to get the parties to settle case.

The Trial

Facts have to be in dispute to make a trial necessary. The Trier of fact can either be a jury or a judge alone, unless a jury is required by law. A jury trial is generally required by Constitution if the amount in controversy exceeds $20. However, a jury trial is generally not required if it is an equitable issue like an injunction action. The right to a jury can be waived. There is an absolute right to a jury trial in criminal cases.

Prospective jurors are drawn at random from voting lists or other lists (like licensed drivers) and make up the pool from which the juries are picked. Some prospective jurors are excused, like mothers of small children or someone on whom serving would be a hardship like an accountant during tax season.

Voir dire is used to weed out jurors that may be biased in some way. The judge and the attorneys ask questions about a prospective juror's knowledge of the case, occupation, relationship to the attorneys or parties, and similar questions. Most states have jurors fill out a questionnaire on general topics to save time. Jurors can be challenged for cause. The argument would be that they were incapable of making an impartial decision. For example, they might be friends of one of the parties or one of the attorneys.

Attorneys can also use a limited number of **peremptory challenges** to remove potential jurors with whom they are uncomfortable. A peremptory challenge is a right to strike a juror with or without cause. However, the challenge can't be based on race or sex. In a personal injury action involving a big company, plaintiff attorneys sometimes will want jurors of limited education rather than business people. People with limited education are sometimes more likely to rule on emotion against a ***big rich insurance company***, for example.

In the **opening statement,** each party's attorney gives a summary of what he intends to prove and the evidence that will be used. Next, the plaintiff presents his evidence, which will primarily consist of the testimony of witnesses. The plaintiff has the burden of proof. The standard of proof is the **preponderance of evidence** in most civil cases. The standard in criminal cases is *beyond a* **reasonable doubt.** The standard in some civil cases, like in a suit charging fraud, is **clear and convincing evidence.** This standard is somewhere in between beyond a reasonable doubt and preponderance of evidence.

In **direct examination** of a witness, the attorney calling the witness will ask the questions. In the **cross-examination** of the witness, the opposing counsel asks questions. He will often try to discredit the witness. For example, if accident that is the subject of the suit occurred at night, the questioning might go something like this:

- You testified that you were 60 ft. from the accident, is that correct?
- The accident happened on August 15, is that correct?
- It was cloudy that night, wasn't it?
- It was dark, wasn't it?
- You couldn't see very well, could you?

A good cross-examiner will only ask questions that he knows the answer to and which will yield a yes or no answer. However, a witness has the right to explain his answer.

In **redirect examination**, the attorney who called the witness will try to undo any damage caused by the cross-examination. The opposing counsel will then have the right to *re-cross.* This is similar to cross-examination.

The witness must have personal knowledge of what he is testifying about. He must have direct or indirect contact with facts of case, *e.g.,* actually witnessed the accident in question or overheard the contract in dispute being negotiated. A witness must testify based on his personal knowledge. He generally cannot give his opinion unless it is based on his five senses. Examples:

- Looked dark.
- Smelled smoke.
- Saw the defendant take the item from the store.
- Felt pain.
- Heard the misrepresentations made by the salesman.

An expert witness can give opinions. For example, in a medical malpractice case involving a doctor, an expert witness (usually another doctor) will have to give an opinion that the defendant doctor's actions were negligent in that they were not in accordance with the standard of care of the medical community. In an eminent domain suit a main issue will be the fair market value of the real property that is to be condemned. Both parties will need to call an appraiser as an expert witness to give his opinion as to the fair market value of the property.

After the plaintiff presents all his evidence, he *rests* his case. In a jury trial, the plaintiff will ordinarily make a motion for a directed verdict. This motion is to be granted by the judge if the plaintiff has not made a *prima facie case.* The plaintiff must offer proof of each legal element of his claim. This is called making a *prima facie case.* For example, to prove fraud, you would normally have to prove:

- that a false statement had been made;
- that defendant knew it was false;
- that defendant made statement to deceive plaintiff;
- that plaintiff was deceived;
- resulting in damages to plaintiff.

Failure to offer proof on one of these elements could cause a motion for directed verdict to be sustained. That would be the end of the trial.

Next, the defendant (*i.e.,* the defendant's attorney) calls his witnesses and introduces his evidence. Evidence, other than testimony, that either party could introduce would be documents, like a contracts or a letter, or tangible items like a defective piece of equipment.

Hearsay evidence is testimony that is offered by a witness who does not have personal knowledge of the information being given but just heard it from someone else. This type of evidence is generally inadmissible. In a suit where the issue is whether or not a contract was breached, suppose that testimony is offered by a witness to the effect that the witness heard the defendant say that he had no intention of strictly abiding by the terms of the contract. Such evidence would be hearsay and generally not admissible. There are several exceptions to the hearsay rule.

In the **closing argument** each attorney summarizes what he has proven. Hopefully, each attorney will have proven what he promised to prove during his opening statement. Attorneys for each party will also try to point out defects in the case of the opposition.

In a jury trial jury instructions are given to the jury at the end of the case. These instructions are prepared by the attorneys of both parties and presented to the judge for approval. The instructions tell the jurors what the law is and how to apply the law to the facts that have been proven. Here are some possible samples of jury instructions in a case involving conversion (civil theft of personal property):

Instruction to Jury as to the Definition of Conversion: You are instructed that conversion consists in the exercise of dominion and control over property inconsistent with, and in denial of, the rights of the true owner or the party having the right of possession. It is the exercise of a wrongful claim of right or dominion over the property which assumes that the converter is entitled to its possession. This taking to oneself of another person's property is a conversion.

Instruction to Jury that Refusal to Deliver Goods after Demand and Tender of Freight and Storage Charges can Constitute Conversion: You are instructed that if you believe from the evidence that plaintiff was the owner of the property in question, and made proper demand and tender prior to this suit, but that defendant refused to deliver the property unless plaintiff paid freight and storage charges on other property not received or stored at the same time as the property in question, then such refusal of delivery by defendant constituted a conversion.

Instruction to Jury that Unauthorized Sale of Personal Property can Constitute Conversion: You are instructed that any assertion of title to, or any act of dominion over, personal property inconsistent with the rights of the owner, such as a sale of the property of one person by another, is a conversion. Therefore, if you find that the plaintiff was the owner of the *(describe personal property)* at the time of the alleged taking, and that the defendant sold it without the plaintiff's consent you should find for the plaintiff.

Instruction to Jury Regarding Compensatory Damages for Conversion: You are instructed that if, under the evidence and the instructions of the court, you find the defendant liable to the plaintiff for damages for conversion of the *(describe personal property),* then the measure of the plaintiff's damages will be the value of the property at the time and place of the conversion, with *(number)* percent interest since that date.

During jury deliberations, the jurors will decide on a **verdict.** A unanimous verdict is ordinarily not required in civil cases. In some states, only nine out of twelve of the jury must agree on a verdict. A **hung jury** occurs when the jury cannot agree on a verdict. The case must be tried over again or dismissed.

Post trial motions generally consist of the following:

- **Motion for a new trial.** Sample grounds would be if the jury misconstrued a jury instruction or the jury clearly should have found more damages.

- **Motion for a judgment notwithstanding the verdict** (JNOV). If the judge grants a JNOV, the judge reverses the decision of the jury and enters judgment for the other side because, for example, the jury's verdict clearly did not conform to the evidence. It is rare for a judge to grant a JNOV.

An **appeal** to a higher court can be made by the party who lost the case or if the party who won believes that damages do not conform to the evidence. There are time limits on appeal. The time in which a party has to file a notice of appeal depends on the court.

The appellate court makes its decision on selected portions to the transcript of the trial, legal briefs of the attorneys, and oral arguments of the attorneys, if permitted by court. No witnesses are heard or evidence is presented.

Appendix 1 – Sample Complaint

Complaint for Breach of Written Contract Seeking Damages and Attorney's Fees

IN THE *(Name of Court)* COURT OF *(Name of County), (Name of State)*

ACME, INC.	**PLAINTIFF**
V.	**CAUSE NO. 000,000**
JOHN DOE	**DEFENDANT**

COMPLAINT

COMES NOW Plaintiff ***Acme, Inc., (Acme)*** in the above-styled and numbered cause, by and through its attorneys, and files this its Complaint against Defendant, ***John Doe* (*Doe*),** and in support thereof would show unto the Court the following matters and facts:

1. ***Acme*** is a corporation organized and existing under the laws of the state of *(name of state),* with its principal office located at *(street address, city, county, state, zip code).*

2. Defendant ***Doe*** is an adult resident citizen of *(city, county, and state)*, and may be served with process and other writs of this Court at his place of residence located at *(street address, city, county, state, zip code).*

3. On or about *(date)* in *(location where parties entered into contract),* Plaintiff and Defendant entered into a written agreement, a copy of which is attached hereto as Exhibit A and made a part hereof. According to paragraph ____ of the contract, the Defendant promised to *(describe Defendant's promises).*

4. The consideration set forth in the agreement was fair and reasonable.

5. Plaintiff has performed all conditions, covenants, and promises required by it on its part to be performed in accordance with the terms and conditions of the contract.

6. On or about *(date)*, the Defendant breached the contract by *(describe circumstances of breach).*

7. By reason of Defendant's breach of the contract, the Plaintiff has suffered damages in the (*amount).*

8. By the terms of the contract, the Plaintiff is entitled to recover its reasonable attorney fees incurred in the enforcement of the provisions of the contract. By reason of the Defendant's breach, the Plaintiff has been forced to secure the services of (*name of firm or attorney)* to prosecute this lawsuit.

WHEREFORE, plaintiff prays judgment against Defendant as follows:

1. For compensatory damages in the sum of $ __________________;
2. For interest on the sum of $______________ from and after (*date)*, to date of judgment;
3. For reasonable attorney's fees according to proof;
4. For costs of suit herein incurred; and
5. For such other and further relief as the court may deem proper.

Respectfully submitted,

ACME, INC.

By: _________________________________
William H. Smith
State Bar No. _____________

One of Its Attorneys

Appendix 2 – Sample Summons

IN THE *(Name of Court)* COURT OF *(Name of County), (Name of State)*

THE STATE OF *(Name)*
COUNTY OF *(Name)*

TO: John Doe
(Street Address)
(City, State, Zip Code)

THE COMPLAINT WHICH IS ATTACHED TO THIS SUMMONS IS IMPORTANT AND YOU MUST TAKE IMMEDIATE ACTION TO PROTECT YOUR RIGHTS.
You are required to mail or hand deliver a copy of a written response to the Complaint to the attorney for the Plaintiff(s), whose post office address is *(Box Number)* and whose street address is *(street address, city, zip code)*. Your response must be mailed or delivered within thirty (30) days from the date of delivery of this summons and complaint or a judgment by default will be entered against you for the money or other things demanded in the complaint.

You must also file the original of your response with the Clerk of this Court within a reasonable time afterward.

Issued under my hand and the seal of said Court, this day of _______, 20____.

(Name), **Clerk of Court**

By: ______________________ D.C.

SEAL OF COURT

Appendix 3 – Sample Answer

General Form of an Answer by Defendant in a Civil Lawsuit

IN THE *(Name of Court)* COURT OF *(Name of County), (Name of State)*

ACME, INC.	**PLAINTIFF**
V.	**CAUSE NO. 000,000**
JOHN DOE	**DEFENDANT**

ANSWER AND AFFIRMATIVE DEFENSES

Comes now **John Doe,** Defendant herein, and submits his answer and affirmative defenses to the allegations contained in the Complaint filed against him herein.

FIRST DEFENSE
Defendant would show that the Complaint fails to state a claim or cause of action against him upon which any relief can be granted.

SECOND DEFENSE
And now, answering the allegations of the Complaint filed against him, paragraph by paragraph, Defendant would show the following:

I. Defendant admits the allegations of Paragraph 1 of the Complaint *[e.g. that*

II. *Defendant is an adult resident citizen of (street address, city, county, state, zip code)].*

III. Defendant admits the allegations of Paragraph 3 of the Complaint *[e.g. that Plaintiff is an adult resident citizen of (street address, city, county, state, zip code)].*

IV. Defendant denies the allegations of Paragraph 4 of the Complaint.

WHEREFORE, now having fully answered said Complaint, Defendant requests that said Complaint be dismissed with prejudice and that Defendant be awarded costs of this suit from Plaintiff.

Respectfully submitted,

____

JOHN DOE

CERTIFICATE OF SERVICE

I, ***John Doe,*** do hereby certify that a true and correct copy of the above and foregoing Answer and Affirmative Defenses has been sent, via first class mail, postage prepaid, to *(Name of Attorney for Plaintiff)* at *(street address, city, county, state, zip code).*

So certified, this the _____ day of _________, 20___.

____

JOHN DOE

Appendix 4 – Sample Motion

IN THE *(Name of Court)* COURT OF *(Name of County), (Name of State)*

ACME, INC. **PLAINTIFF**

V. **CAUSE NO. 000,000**

JOHN DOE **DEFENDANT**

Motion of Plaintiff

Comes now **JOHN DOE,** Defendant, in the above-captioned cause, moves the Court to ***(specify relief sought)*** on the grounds that ***(specify grounds for motion).***

Wherefore, Defendant, respectfully moves the Court to ***(specify relief sought).***

Respectfully submitted,

____

JOHN DOE

Certificate of Service

This is to certify that I, *(Name of Attorney),* attorney for Defendant **John Doe, X. Plaintiff,** have this date served a true and correct copy of the above and foregoing **Motion** by U.S. Mail, postage fully prepaid, to the following counsel of record for Plaintiff:

(Name of Attorney)
Post Office Box 0000
City, State, Zip Code

This the ____day of ________, 20___.

Respectfully Submitted,

____

(Name of Attorney)
State Bar No. _____
Attorney for Plaintiff

Notice of Motion

You are notified that on ***(date)***, at ***(time)***, or as soon thereafter as counsel can be heard, in Courtroom 000 of the *(Name of Court)* for *(Name of County), (Name of State),* at the *(Name of*

County) Courthouse at ***(street address, city, county, state, zip code)***, Defendant **John Doe, Plaintiff,** by and through his attorney, will bring on for hearing his **Motion** for the reasons stated in the above Motion.

Respectfully Submitted,

____
(Name of Attorney)
State Bar No. _____
Attorney for Plaintiff

Appendix 5
Interrogatories in Federal Court to Judgment Debtor in General and Regarding Property Available to Satisfy Judgment

IN THE UNITED STATES DISTRICT COURT
FOR THE *(NAME)* DISTRICT OF *(STATE)*
***(NAME)* DIVISION**

(Name of Plaintiff and Judgment Creditor) **Plaintiff**

v. **Civil Action No.** ________

(Name of Defendant and Judgment Debtor) **Defendant**

First Set of Interrogatories to Judgment Debtor

Theses Interrogatories are propounded to you as Judgment Debtor, in aid of the Judgment previously entered against you, and you are required to answer such Interrogatories under oath as provided by Rule 33 and Rule 69(a) of the Federal Rules of Civil Procedure.

1. Please state your present residence, how long have you lived there, and how much you pay for rent, board, services, etc.

2. What salary or income have you received since the Judgment against you in this action was secured? Please state the source, the amount of each payment to you, and the dates of payments.

3. Please describe any uncollected debts or other money coming to you, including the amounts of each and the name and address of each debtor.

4. What is your occupation?

5. Please state what money you have received within the last ninety days from any source, the name of each payor, the dates of receipt and amounts, and describe any disposition of such money, including the names of the payees, their addresses, the dates of payments and the amount of each payment.

6. Please state what back accounts you have, the name of the Bank for each account, when you made your last deposit in each account, and when drew your last check on each account.

7. Please state the money you have spent since the Judgment in this cause of action was entered against your, the names of the payees, the amounts of each payment and dates of each payment.

8. Have any payments been made on account for you by any third party within the last three years? If so, please state by what person, the names of the payees, the dates of payments and the amounts of payments.

9. Please list by address and legal description any real property or any interest in real property you or your spouse own or have in interest in, and specify with respect to each property its purchase or acquisition date, the amount of the purchase price, the source of the purchase price or the manner of the property's acquisition, and from whom it was acquired.

10. Please describe any interest you or your spouse have in any stocks, bonds, or other securities; promissory notes, drafts, bills of exchange, or other commercial papers; judgments; jewelry or antiques; stamp or coin collections; automobiles or trucks; patents, inventions, trade names, trademarks, or copyrights; and/or warehouse receipts, bills of lading, or other documents of title.

11 Please describe any interest you or your spouse have in any other property not inquired about in Interrogatory Numbers 9 and 10 and specify with respect to each property its purchase or acquisition date, the amount of the purchase price, the source of the purchase price or the manner of the property's acquisition, and from whom it was acquired.

12 If any of the property inquired about in Interrogatory Numbers 9,10 or 11 is mortgaged, pledged, encumbered, or subject to any conditional bill of sale, state the full detail the status of same as to the names and addresses of each mortgagee and/or pledgee and the amounts of each mortgage and/or pledge.

13. Please describe any checking or savings account or accounts, stating for each account, the name and address of the bank or savings institution where the account is maintained, the account number, and the amount of the balance in the account as of the date these Interrogatories were served on you.

14. Please give the name and address of each safe deposit box you or your spouse have.

15. Please identify any business you or your spouse own or have part ownership in, your interest in it, the name under which it operates, and whether it is a sole proprietorship, a partnership, limited liability company, limited partnership, limited liability partnership or a corporation.

16. Did you file federal or state income tax returns in the last three years? If so, please state whether or not you retained copies of the returns and where they are located.

17. Have you issued any financial statement in the past three years? If so, please state to whom, when, and for what reason.

18. State what books and records you keep, showing your receipts and disbursements for the last three years and the location of each such book and/or record.

19. Please indicate the full name of your spouse and, if employed, your spouse's occupation, her employer and the employer's address.

20. Please list by address and legal description any real properties you or your spouse have an ownership in within this state or outside of this state and specify with respect to each property its purchase or acquisition date, the amount of the purchase price, the source or the manner of its acquisition, and from whom it was acquired.

21. Please identify any property have you within this state, real or personal, that has not been previously identified, and as to each, list by address and legal description any such properties, and specify with respect to each property its purchase or acquisition date, the amount of the purchase price and the source or the manner of its acquisition and from whom it was acquired.

22. Have you made any transfers of real or personal property? If so, state to whom, the dates, and the names of the transferees.

23. Please identify any property have you outside of this state, real or personal, that has not been previously identified, and as to each, list by address and legal description any such properties and specify with respect to each property, state its purchase or acquisition date, the amount of the purchase price, the source or the manner of its acquisition, and from whom it was acquired.

24. What property did you have at the time when this judgment was secured? Trace the disposition of this property.

Respectfully submitted,

____
Signature of Plaintiff
Printed Name: _________________________

CERTIFICATE OF SERVICE

I, the undersigned, *(Name of Plaintiff),* the Plaintiff, do hereby certify that I have this day mailed, by United States mail, postage prepaid, a true and correct copy of the above and foregoing First Set of Interrogatories to Defendant at:

(Name of Defendant)
(Address of Defendant)

DATED, this the day of _______________, 20_____.

____
Printed Name and Signature of Plaintiff

Appendix 6

IN THE UNITED STATES DISTRICT COURT
FOR THE *(NAME)* DISTRICT OF *(STATE)*
***(NAME)* DIVISION**

Plaintiff

____
(Name of Plaintiff and Judgment Creditor)

v. **Civil Action No.** ________

Defendant

____
(Name of Defendant and Judgment Debtor)

First Set of Requests for Production of Documents to Judgment Debtor

These Requests for Production of Documents are propounded to you as Judgment Debtor, in aid of the Judgment previously entered against you, and you are required to answer such Interrogatories under oath as provided by Rule 34 and Rule 69(a) of the Federal Rules of Civil Procedure.

Pursuant to Rule 34 and Rule 69(a) of the Federal Rules of Civil Procedure, you are requested to produce for inspection and copying in the office of ________________________ ***(Name of Attorney)***, on __________________ ***(date)***, the following records and documents:

1. All documents that evidence or directly relate to your present residence, how long have you lived there, and/or how much you pay for rent, board, services, etc.

2. All documents that evidence or directly relate to the salary or income you have received since the Judgment against you in this action was secured on ______________________ ***(date)***.

3. All documents that evidence or directly relate to any uncollected debts or other money coming to you.

4. All documents that evidence or directly relate to proof of your occupation.

5. All documents that evidence or directly relate to the money you have received within the last _____ days from any source, the name of each payor, the dates of receipt and/or the amounts; and all documents that evidence or directly relate to any disposition of such money, including the names of the payees, their addresses, the dates of payments and/or the amount of each payment.

6. All documents that evidence or directly relate to back accounts you have, the name of the Bank for each account, when you made your last deposit in each account, and/or when drew your last check on each account.

7. All documents that evidence or directly relate to the money you have you spent since the Judgment in this cause of action was entered against you; and all documents that evidence or directly relate to the names of the payees, the amounts of each payment and/or the dates of each payment.

8. All documents that evidence or directly relate to or reflect any payments made on account for you by any third party within the last three year; and all documents that evidence or directly relate to name of the person, the names of the payees, the dates of payments and/or the amounts of payments.

9. All documents that evidence or directly relate to a legal description any real property or any interest in real property you or your spouse own or have in interest in.; and all documents that evidence or directly relate to, with respect to each property, its purchase or acquisition date, the amount of the purchase price, the source of the purchase price or the manner of the property's acquisition, and/or from whom it was acquired.

10. All documents that evidence or directly relate to any interest you or your spouse have in any stocks, bonds, or other securities; promissory notes, drafts, bills of exchange, or other commercial papers; judgments; jewelry or antiques; stamp or coin collections; automobiles or trucks; patents, inventions, trade names, trademarks, or copyrights; and/or warehouse receipts, bills of lading, and/or other documents of value.

11. All documents that evidence or directly relate to any interest you or your spouse have in any other property not inquired about in Interrogatory Numbers 9 and 10; and all documents that evidence or directly relate to, with respect to each property, its purchase or acquisition date, the amount of the purchase price, the source of the purchase price or the manner of the property's acquisition, and/or from whom it was acquired.

12. All documents that evidence or directly relate to any of the property inquired about in Numbers 9,10 or 11 that is mortgaged, pledged, encumbered, or subject to any conditional bill of sale; and all documents that evidence or directly relate to the full detail the status of said property as to the names and addresses of each mortgagee and/or pledgee and the amounts of each mortgage and/or pledge.

13. All documents that evidence or directly relate to any checking or savings account or accounts you or your wife have; and all documents that evidence or directly relate to each account, the name and address of the bank or savings institution where the account is maintained, the account number, and/or the amount of the balance in the account as of the date these Requests were served on you.

14. All documents that evidence or directly relate to the name and address of each safe deposit box you or your spouse have.

15. All documents that evidence or directly relate to any business you or your spouse own or have part ownership in, your interest in it, the name under which it operates, and/or whether it is a sole proprietorship, a partnership, limited liability company, limited partnership, limited liability partnership or a corporation.

16. Please produce true and correct copies of your file federal or state income tax returns in the last three years?

17. Please produce any financial statement you have given in the past three years, and all documents that evidence or directly relate to whom, when, and for what reason.

18. Please produce any books and records you keep, showing your receipts and disbursements for the last three years.

19. All documents that evidence or directly relate to the full name of your spouse and, if employed, your spouse's occupation, her employer and the employer's address.

20. All documents that evidence or directly relate to the address and legal description any real properties you or your spouse have an ownership in within this state or outside of this state; and all documents that evidence or directly relate to each property, its purchase or acquisition date, the amount of the purchase price, the source or the manner of its acquisition, and/or from whom it was acquired.

21. All documents that evidence or directly relate to any property you have within or outside of this state, real or personal, that has not been previously identified; and all documents that evidence or directly relate to the address and legal description of any such properties, its purchase or acquisition date, the amount of the purchase price and the source or the manner of its acquisition and/or from whom it was acquired.

22. All documents that evidence or directly relate to any transfers of real or personal property within the last two years?

23. All documents that evidence or directly relate to any property you have outside of this state, real or personal, that has not been previously identified; and all documents that evidence or directly relate to each, the address of each and the legal description of each as well as the address and legal description any such properties, the property's purchase or acquisition date, the amount of the purchase price, the source or the manner of its acquisition, and/or from whom it was acquired.

24. All documents that evidence or directly relate to what property you had at the time when this judgment was secured; and all documents that evidence or directly relate to the disposition of this property.

Respectfully submitted,

____
(Name of Plaintiff/Judgment Creditor)

By: _________________________________
(Name of Plaintiff's Attorney)
State Bar No. _____________

One of His Attorneys

CERTIFICATE OF SERVICE

I, the undersigned, ______________________ ***(Name of Plaintiff)***, the Plaintiff, do hereby certify that I have this day mailed, by United States mail, postage prepaid, a true and correct copy of the above and foregoing First Set of Requests for Production of Documents to Defendant at:

(Name of Defendant)
(Address of Defendant)

DATED, this the _____ day of ________________, 20_____.

By: _________________________________
(Name of Plaintiff's Attorney)
State Bar No. _____________

Appendix 7

UNITED STATES DISTRICT COURT
FOR THE EASTERN DISTRICT OF MICHIGAN
SOUTHERN DIVISION

JOHN SMITH, JR. **Plaintiff**

V. **No. 95-CV-74547-DT**

ACME & ASSOCIATES, INC.

PLAINTIFF'S FIRST SET OF REQUESTS FOR ADMISSIONS

John Smith, Jr., by his counsel, submits the following Requests for Admissions to Defendant Acme & Associates, Inc. pursuant to FRCivP Rule 36.

INSTRUCTIONS

If Acme & Associates, Inc. (hereafter the "Defendant") fails to respond or object to any request within 30 days of the service of the Requests, the matter shall be deemed admitted under Rule 36.

As is more fully set out in Rule 36(a), the Defendant must admit or deny each request, and, where necessary, specify the parts of each request to which it objects or cannot in good faith admit or deny. If the Defendant objects to only part of a Request, it must admit or deny the remainder of the Request. In the event that the Defendant objects to or denies any Request or portion of a Request, the Defendant must state the reasons for its objection or denial.

These Requests shall be deemed continuing and supplemental answers shall be required if you directly or indirectly obtain further information after your initial response as provided by FRCivP Rule 26(e).

Each Request solicits all information obtainable by Defendant Acme & Associates, Inc. from Defendant=s attorneys, investigators, agents, employees and representatives. If you answer a Request on the basis that you lack sufficient information to respond, describe any and all efforts you made to inform yourself of the facts and circumstances necessary to answer or respond.

DEFINITIONS

1. The word "or" is used herein in its inclusive sense unless the context clearly requires otherwise.

2. The term "document" means and includes without limitation all correspondence, memoranda, certificates, notes, books, manuals, pamphlets, brochures, advertisements, books of account, balance sheets, financial statements, profit and loss statements, working papers,

schedules, diaries, calendars, logs, time records, equipment records, microfilms, transcripts, recordings, tapes, telexes, telegrams, files, proposals, bids, offers, contracts, agreements, change orders, worksheets, drawings, blue prints, designs, specifications, time cards, compilations, graphs, charts, bills, statements, invoices, receipts, bills of lading, shipping records, confirmations, applications, purchase orders, checks, checkbooks and other checking records, photographs, formulae, prescriptions, studies, projections, reports, computer programs, information contained in computer banks, tapes, 3 cards, printouts and drafts to the extent they differ from the originals, and all other records and papers of any nature whatsoever.

3. Any reference to a specifically named person, corporation or other entity and any reference generally to "person" shall include the employees, agents, representatives and other persons acting on behalf thereof or through whom the referenced person acts. The term "person" means and includes natural persons, corporations, partnerships, joint ventures, sole proprietorships, associations, trusts, estates, firms and any other entity.

4. As used herein, "Plaintiff" means, unless otherwise indicated, JOHN SMITH, Jr.

5. As used herein, "Defendant", shall be deemed to include ACME & Associates, Inc., and Robert E. Johns, as well as their agents, attorneys, representatives or any other person acting on their behalf or on behalf of any one of them.

FIRST SET OF ADMISSIONS

First Set of Admissions, Request 1. Admit that for all time periods relevant to the complaint filed in this matter, Acme & Associates, Inc. was an enterprise engaged in commerce or in the production of goods for commerce within the meaning of Section 3(s)(1)(A) of the Fair Labor Standards Act, 29 U.S.C. '203(s)(1)(A).

First Set of Admissions, Request 2. Admit that Plaintiff was employed by Defendant from approximately 1978 until approximately 1987 and was treated as and characterized as an employee by Defendant during this time period.

First Set of Admissions, Request 3. Admit that the "agreement" signed in December 1993 by Plaintiff and Robert E. Johns and attached as **Exhibit A** was prepared by Defendant and not by Plaintiff.

First Set of Admissions, Request 4. Admit that the "agreement" signed in December 1993 by Plaintiff and Robert E. Johns and attached as **Exhibit A** was not presented to the Plaintiff at his request, but at the initiative of Defendant.

First Set of Admissions, Request 5. Admit that the "agreement" signed in December 1993 by Plaintiff and Robert E. Johns and attached as Exhibit A resulted in Plaintiff being treated as an independent contractor by Defendant for the period beginning in December 1993 and ending in May 1997.

First Set of Admissions, Request 6. Admit that for the period beginning in December 1993 and ending in May 1997 there was no other person performing services for the Defendant as a draftsman, senior draftsman, or structural draftsman being treated as an independent contractor on a non-temporary basis other than the Plaintiff.

First Set of Admissions, Request 7. Admit that for the period beginning in December 1993 and ending in May 1997 there were other persons performing services for the Defendant as a draftsman, senior draftsman, or structural draftsman and being treated as employees by the Defendant.

First Set of Admissions, Request 8. Admit that persons treated as employees by the Defendant during the period of Plaintiff's employment beginning in December 1993 and ending in May 1997 received fringe benefits, including health insurance and pension.

First Set of Admissions, Request 9. Admit that Defendant used a work week beginning on Monday and ending on Sunday and paid its employees and Plaintiff on the basis of such a work week.

First Set of Admissions, Request 10. Admit that persons treated as employees by the Defendant during the period of Plaintiff's employment beginning in December 1993 and ending in May 1997 received overtime premium pay for any hours worked over forty (40) hours in a work week.

Respectfully submitted,

____

William H. Glover
Wells Marble & Hurst
1018 laurel Drive
Flowood, MS 39232
555-555-5555

Attorney for JOHN SMITH, Jr.

Chapter 3

ALTERNATIVE MEANS OF DISPUTE RESOLUTION

Alternative Means of Dispute Resolution is known by the initials ADR. What is ADR? First, ADR deals with disputes. If you have no dispute, you do not need ADR. Second, ADR also deals with the resolution of disputes. And third, ADR deals with alternatives to the traditional means of dispute resolution.

What are the traditional means of dispute resolution? Basically, there are two, negotiation and litigation. Negotiation involves the two parties who are having the dispute trying to resolve the dispute by working things out between themselves. But if the parties are unable to resolve this dispute between themselves, then the only other traditional alternative left to them is litigation. The business community has been trying to institute ways of resolving disputes without litigation. The result of these efforts is ADR which can be defined as those processes and procedures used to resolve disputes without litigation. Because of the rising cost and delay of litigation, business people are beginning to more and more seek to resolve disputes out of Court.

We live in a very litigious society. People will file suit at the drop of a hat. It is not uncommon for suit to be filed by a person without even bothering to enter into serious negotiations. Advertising by personal injury lawyers have not helped matters either. Litigation is a serious matter, and should be seriously and soberly considered before being commenced. Lawsuits are often based on such things as anger, bitterness, greed, pride, and materialism. Once litigation is commenced, the parties can rapidly lose control over the process because other entities become involved, such as lawyers and the courts. Litigation will ultimately lead to a decision but it may or may not be a just decision. Litigation is not designed to produce reconciliation but rather a victory for one side and a loss for another. In litigation there is a winner and a loser. Sometimes neither party is happy at the end. ADR offers people, who have disputes where all communication has broken down, ways to resolve their disputes without having to resort to lawsuits.

ADR is usually much less expensive than litigation. Litigation is very expensive. Even a simple lawsuit can cost several thousands of dollars. A complicated lawsuit can cost tens of thousands of dollars to each party, and complicated lawsuits can run quickly run into six figures.

Many lawyer advertisements say that no charge will be made unless they collect for you, in other words, win the case and recover damages. That is basically true. But they receive anywhere from one-third to one-half of the amount recovered if suit is filed. The defendant usually has to pay an attorney on an hourly basis to defend him. This can range anywhere from $175 to $500 per hour in Mississippi. Therefore, even if the defendant wins, he's still out substantial, and frequently, tremendous legal expenses. If he loses, then he has to pay a judgment in addition to the legal expenses. What if it is a small dispute involving, say $5,000? Does it make any sense to pay $5,000 or more in legal fees and expenses, if you are lucky, to win $5,000? An ADR process can cost only hundreds instead of thousands of dollars.

ADR usually offers a quick resolution to a dispute. A typical lawsuit will last one to two years, and can drag on for four or five years. It drains the time, energies and emotions of the litigants. Frequently, they feel helpless about their ability to control the litigation, and they feel helpless because they usually are helpless. Our courts are so clogged with civil cases that it sometimes takes years to resolve a typical case. Not only are there too many civil suits, there are a huge number of criminal cases which can take priority over civil cases. An ADR process can resolve a dispute in a single day that could take two years to litigate. Even in a complex case, the time savings are substantial. The parties are able to set their own time frame, within their own schedules, and move the proceedings along as rapidly, or as deliberately, as they wish. ADR procedures are much more flexible than litigation procedures and the parties can dispense with a lot of the pre-trial procedures done in a litigation situation. The result is that the dispute is much more efficiently and quickly resolved with an ADR procedure than it is with litigation.

One of the greatest advantages of ADR procedures is that it offers the possibility of a mutually acceptable resolution. In mediation proceedings the parties are actively involved in the process. They are able to talk to each other, either directly or through a neutral third party. They are able to express their grievances and frustrations and state their positions directly to the other party, without everything being filtered through a set of attorneys. ADR does rest upon willingness of the parties involved to seek to resolve their differences, and if they are dealing in good faith, they will have to consider the merits and arguments of the other side. But by doing nothing more than talking the matter out, with some assistance from a neutral third party, often the parties can find a solution that is mutually acceptable.

Another strong advantage of ADR is that it provides a means whereby a broken relationship can be restored, or a strained relationship to be preserved. Litigation usually produces permanent alienation, and we should be concerned with finding ways that will lead to reconciliation.

There are other advantages to ADR. These would include a desire to keep the dispute private, and the results of the dispute confidential. Also, if the dispute involves a very complex or technical factual issue, the parties may prefer to have the dispute mediated or decided by experts, rather than entrusting the dispute to a judge or a jury who don't have the expertise necessary to deal with the dispute. If there is great uncertainty on both sides about the outcome of the dispute, ADR would provide them an opportunity to hammer out among themselves a certain result than to trust in an uncertain result at the hands of a judge and jury.

The main two types of are mediation and arbitration. **Mediation** is the ADR procedure closest to direct negotiations. Of all of the types of ADR procedures, mediation is the most flexible, informal, and provides the greatest hope of reconciliation. In the past, it has not been used as much as arbitration, but arbitration is so much like litigation that disillusionment with litigation has had an effect on arbitration. Today, mediation is the new kid on the block. In fact, mediation has been called the sleeping giant of ADR which is now awakening.

Mediation is nothing more than a process by which parties in a dispute negotiate a settlement of their claims against each other through the assistance of a trained, neutral mediator. It is a non-adversarial process. Mediation is entirely voluntary and non-binding. The mediator has no power to render a decision nor force the parties to accept a settlement. The mediator generally does not give an opinion or render an award. The mediator typically does not even have any knowledge of the case prior to mediation. On first glance, mediation would seem to be a very weak procedure, but its apparent weakness is in realty its strength.

Because it is voluntary and non-binding, it is attractive to parties who do not want to litigate, yet who cannot negotiate directly. It is considered to be non-threatening, and most people take a ***what have I got to lose*** attitude with mediation. Also, mediation gives significance to values such as trust, respect, patience and tolerance. A unique attribute of mediation is that it affords each party the opportunity to communicate confidentially to the mediator about what his or her true feelings and expectations are when the parties are unable or unwilling to communicate these things directly to the other party. The mediator acts as a go-between for the two parties. The parties retain full control of the outcome and may drop out of the proceeding at any time. In mediation, the participants attack the problem as joint problem solvers rather than attacking one another. It is adaptable to most any situation. Although the parties who enter mediation do not have to commit to finding a solution, they do have to commit to dealing with each other in good faith in an effort to try to find a solution.

Mediation can be very successful, depending a good deal on the ability of the mediator and the desire of the parties to reach an agreement out of court. However, it is not uncommon for parties to enter mediation believing that it will not work, only to emerge with a solution. One of the reasons for this is that the parties become involved in a search for a mutually acceptable outcome without having to determine which party's position is correct. I believe that mediation should always be the first ADR procedure considered.

Arbitration is an entirely different animal. Arbitration is a process in which the disputing parties choose a neutral third person, or arbitrator, who hears both sides of the dispute and then renders a decision. The big difference between mediation and arbitration is that a mediator helps the parties to fashion their own settlement, while an arbitrator decides the issue. An arbitrator is more like a judge than a mediator. The parties go into arbitration knowing that they will be bound by the decision. The parties go into mediation knowing that nothing will be decided unless and until they agree to it. Arbitration, however, is unlike litigation in that the parties choose the arbitrator, the proceedings are conducted in a private manner, and the rules of evidence and procedure are informal. Also, in arbitration, the arbitrators tend to be experts in the issues they are called on to decide. Arbitration has been the widest used ADR process in the business world, and would be especially desirable where the parties do not want to litigate an issue, but do want a binding decision. They can go into arbitration knowing that they can get a quick, and relatively inexpensive decision, which they agree they will be bound by. Mediation offers no guarantee of a decision. It is not uncommon to find arbitration provisions in business contracts.

Most arbitration is binding. However, it can be non-binding if that is what the parties desire. That kind of defeats the purpose of arbitration though. In any event, in both binding and non-binding arbitration, the arbitrator renders a decision much like a judge.

You can agree to a combination of mediation and arbitration where the parties agree in advance to try to resolve their differences through mediation if possible, but if no agreement is reached, they automatically go to arbitration. The mediator then becomes the arbitrator and renders a binding decision.

Sample Mediation. First you have to choose a mediator. There are several sources you can contact to get a mediator. The mediator is paid for his services.

Once the mediator has been retained, he or she will control the process. Typically, both parties will meet in a joint session with the mediator. If they are represented by attorneys, the attorneys can also come to the meeting, and the attorneys can, if the parties desire, speak for their clients. However, it is essential that the parties themselves get involved in the mediation process.

The mediator will begin by introducing himself, and he may ask the parties to introduce themselves. He will then begin the process of mediation. Typically, he should explain that he has no interest in the outcome, that he is neutral, that he is undertaking the mediation based on the understanding that the parties are sincerely interested in trying to resolve their dispute, and that they will deal in good faith with each other. He should tell the parties that he is not a judge, that he cannot force a decision, that he cannot order anything. He should tell them that they are not in a court of law, they will not be cross-examined, they will not be put under oath, and that they are not limited to traditional legal remedies. He might wish to tell them also that it is not necessary to establish right and wrong in this mediation, or to decide the truth. Finally, the parties should understand that during mediation they should use good manners, be civil and avoid offending one another. What is important is to find a solution to the dispute that is mutually agreeable to both sides, not to decide who is right and who is wrong.

Once the mediator has made his comments, then typically he will invite one side to state his case. Different mediators have different styles, but if I were mediating the case I would always suggest that the party speak to me and not to the other party. The other party will hear what is being said but all comments should be directed to me. Once the party has stated his case, then the mediator will ask the other party to state his case. If during the course of this opening session, the parties want to talk directly across the table to each other, I would permit it. But it is best to let one party fully state his case without interruption, and then the other party state his case.

Once the opening session is concluded, then the mediator goes into private sessions with the parties. The parties will be placed in different rooms and the mediator will shuttle back and forth between the parties. At these private sessions he will encourage the parties to state those things which they felt they could not say in open session, and he needs to assure them that what they say in these private sessions will be held confidential, unless they authorize him to release the information. This is where the real work of mediation is done. It is in these sessions that the mediator may have to be creative. Generally, he functions by asking questions, and he refrains from offering opinions, but he can offer suggestions. The balance of the mediation then is taken up with the mediator going back and forth and each time trying to narrow the issues and to find a common solution. The parties are guided by the mediator in fashioning their own solution. This is where compromise comes in, and give and take. This is where the mediator must identify the expectations of the parties, and try to find solutions that deal with their true grievances or their true interests. Money may not be important. It may be something else, such as offended feelings, or embarrassment or some other non-material need. If mediation is going to work, it will work during these private sessions that the mediator has with the parties. The longer the mediation lasts, the greater the risk that it will fail. The mediator might have to remind the parties of the consequences of an impasse, namely litigation.

If a solution is found, then the mediator should then bring the parties back into a closing session and bring the matter to a close by securing an agreement between the parties as to what has been decided. Typically, this will first be an informal memorandum, and then followed by a formal agreement which is signed by the parties.

SAMPLE MEDIATION AGREEMENT BETWEEN PRIVATE PARTIES

Mediation agreement made *(date)*, between *(name of first party)*, hereinafter called First Party, of *(address of first party)*, and *(name of second party)*, of *(address of second party),* hereinafter called *Second Party,* said *First Party* and *Second Party* being jointly referred to as the *Parties,* and *(name of first mediator)* of *(address of Mediator)* (the *Mediator*).

Whereas, the Parties have entered into mediation with the Mediator with the intention of reaching a consensual settlement of their dispute regarding *(set forth circumstances of dispute)*;

The Parties and the Mediator agree as follows:

1. Neutrality

The Mediator is a neutral facilitator who will assist the Parties to reach their own settlement. He will not make decisions about "right" or "wrong" or tell the Parties what to do.

2. No Legal Advice

The Mediator does not offer legal advice nor does he provide legal counsel. Each Party is advised to retain his or her own attorney in order to be properly counseled about his or her legal interests, rights and obligations.

3. Confidentiality

The Parties understand that in order for mediation to work, open and honest communications are essential. Accordingly, all written and oral communications, negotiations and statements made in the course of mediation will be treated as privileged settlement discussions and are absolutely confidential. To this end the parties agree that:

A. The Mediator will not reveal anything discussed in mediation without the permission of both Parties.

B. The Parties agree that they will not at any time, before, during, or after mediation, call the Mediator or anyone associated with the Mediator as witnesses in any legal or administrative proceeding concerning this dispute. To the extent that they may have a right to call the Mediator or anyone associated with the Mediator as witnesses, the Parties waive this right.

C. The Parties agree not to subpoena or demand the production of any records, notes, work product or the like of the Mediator in any legal or administrative proceeding concerning this dispute. To the extent that they may have a right to demand these documents, the Parties waive this right.

D. If, at a later time, either Party decides to subpoena the Mediator, the Mediator will move to quash the subpoena. That Party agrees to reimburse the Mediator for whatever expenses they incur in such an action (including attorney's fees) plus *(dollar amount)* per hour per Mediator for all the time that is taken by this matter.

E. The exception to the above is that this agreement to mediate and any written agreement made and signed by the Parties as a result of mediation may be used in any relevant proceeding, unless the Parties make a written agreement not to do so.

4. Full Disclosure

The Parties understand that full disclosure of all relevant and pertinent information is essential to the mediation process. Accordingly, there will be a complete and honest disclosure by each of the Parties to the other and to the Mediator of all relevant information and documents. This includes providing each other and the Mediator with all information and documentation that usually would be available through the discovery process in a legal proceeding. If either Party fails to make full disclosure, the agreement reached in mediation may be set aside.

5. Withdrawal

While both Parties intend to continue with mediation until a settlement agreement is reached, the Parties understand that either or both Parties may withdraw from mediation at any time. The Parties agree that if one or both Parties decide to withdraw from mediation, best efforts will be made to discuss this decision in the presence of both Parties and the Mediator.

6. Termination by Mediator

If the Mediator determines that it is not possible to resolve the issues through mediation, the process can be terminated once this has been conveyed to the Parties and confirmed in writing.

7. Memorandum of Understanding

When an agreement is reached, the Mediator will prepare a Memorandum of Understanding. Each Party is advised to review this with his or her own attorney before the agreement is placed in final form and signed.

8. Sharing of Costs

The Parties agree to share the cost of mediation.

9. Rules and Procedures

Additional rules and procedures for the mediation may be negotiated and agreed upon by the Mediator and the Parties at any time during the mediation process.

10. Governing Law

This Agreement shall be governed by, construed, and enforced in accordance with the laws of the State of __________.

Each party hereby declares:
I have read, understood and agreed to each provision of this agreement.

WITNESS our signatures as of the day and date first above stated.

___________________________	___________________________
(Printed name)	***(Printed name)***
(Signature of First Party)	***(Signature of Second Party)***

SAMPLE ARBITRATION AGREEMENT

Agreement to Arbitrate Employment Claims Between Employer and At-Will Employee

This Arbitration Agreement is made this the *(date)* between *(Name of Employer)*, a corporation organized and existing under the laws of the state of _____________, with its principal office located at *(street address, city, state, zip code)*, referred to herein as *Company, and (Name of Employee)* of *(street address, city, state, zip code)*, referred to herein as *Employee.*

For and in consideration of the mutual covenants contained in this Agreement, and other good and valuable consideration, the receipt and sufficiency of which is hereby acknowledged, the parties agree as follows:

1. Any dispute, controversy or claim arising out of or in relation to Employee's employment with Company or regarding the termination of employment (with the exception of claims for workers' compensation, unemployment insurance and any other matter within the jurisdiction of a state labor commissioner or an equivalent state official), shall be settled by binding arbitration in accordance with the rules and procedures promulgated by the American Arbitration Association.

2. Judgment on the award rendered by the arbitrator(s) may be entered in any court having jurisdiction.

3. The arbitration proceeding shall be held at a location mutually convenient to Employee and Company.

4. Civil discovery shall be permitted for production of documents and the taking of depositions. All discovery shall be governed by the *(Name of State)* Rules of Civil Procedure. All issues regarding compliance with discovery requests shall be decided by an arbitrator in accordance with the rules of the American Arbitration Association.

5. The arbitrator shall have the authority to award any remedy or relief that a *(Names of State)* court could order or grant, including but not limited to specific performance, a payment of damages, issuance of injunction, or the imposition of sanctions for abuse or frustration of the arbitration process.

6. This Agreement does not shorten time limits under which Employee may bring a claim to arbitration. The time limits under which a dispute, claim or controversy may be brought to arbitration will be governed by the applicable statutes of limitations as set forth in the *(Name of State)* Code of Civil Procedure.

7. Following a hearing conducted by the arbitrator, the arbitrator shall issue a written opinion and award that shall be signed and dated. The opinion and award shall decide all issues submitted and shall set forth the legal principles and findings of fact supporting each part of the opinion. The arbitrator shall be permitted to award only those remedies in law or equity which are requested by the parties and which the arbitrator determines to be supported by credible, relevant evidence.

8. Employee and Company agree that arbitration in accordance with the rules of the American Arbitration Association shall be the exclusive forum for resolving all disputes arising out of or involving Employee's employment with Company or the termination of that employment (with the exception of claims for workers' compensation, unemployment insurance and any matter within the jurisdiction of the state labor commissioner or equivalent state official). All arbitration awards shall be binding upon the parties to this Agreement.

9. All fees and costs associated with the retention of the arbitrator (including the fees charged by the arbitrator) shall be borne by Company. However, each party shall bear the expense of its own counsel, experts, witnesses and the preparation and presentation of evidence.

10. Nothing in this Agreement shall be construed as precluding any employee from filing a charge or complaint with the Equal Employment Opportunity Commission (EEOC), the National Labor Relations Board (NLRB) or any other similar state or federal agency seeking administrative resolution of a dispute or claim. However, any claim that cannot be resolved administratively through such an agency shall be subject to this arbitration policy.

11. Nothing contained in this agreement shall be deemed to alter or modify the Company's policy of at-will employment. Employment at the Company is at-will and can be terminated by either Employee or Company at any time, with or without cause or notice.

12. Employee and Company agree that this Arbitration Agreement shall survive the termination of Employee's employment with Company. Employee certifies that he is aware that by entering into this Agreement, he is waiving his right to have his claims against Company, if any, tried before a jury. Employee further certifies that he has had the opportunity to consult with legal counsel prior to executing this Arbitration Agreement.

13. The failure of either party to this Agreement to insist upon the performance of any of the terms and conditions of this Agreement, or the waiver of any breach of any of the terms and conditions of this Agreement, shall not be construed as subsequently waiving any such terms and conditions, but the same shall continue and remain in full force and effect as if no such forbearance or waiver had occurred.

14. This Agreement shall be governed by, construed, and enforced in accordance with the laws of the State of __________.

15. Any notice provided for or concerning this Agreement shall be in writing and shall be deemed sufficiently given when sent by certified or registered mail if sent to the respective address of each party as set forth at the beginning of this Agreement.

16. In this Agreement, any reference to a party includes that party's heirs, executors, administrators, successors and assigns, singular includes plural and masculine includes feminine.

WITNESS our signatures as of the day and date first above stated.

(Name of Company)

__________________________	By:__________________________
(Printed Name if Employee)	*(Printed Name & Office in Corporation)*
(Signature of Employee)	*(Signature of Officer)*

Chapter 4

ADMINISTRATIVE AGENCIES

Administrative agencies resulted from the inability of governments, federal, state and local, to effectively regulate many aspects of business as well as other aspects of laws affecting citizens. As life and business became more and more complicated, the administrative agency came into being. Law governing administrative agencies is known as **administrative law.**

Administrative agencies affect each of us every day in hundreds of ways. They have become the fourth branch of government. Supporters believe that they provide unique expertise in complex areas. Detractors regard them as unelected government run amok.

Many administrative agencies are familiar. The Federal Aviation Administration, which requires all airlines to ensure that your seats are upright before takeoff and landing, is an administrative agency. The Internal Revenue Service haunts us every April 15. The Environmental Protection Agency regulates the water quality of the river in your town. The Federal Trade Commission oversees the commercials from your television set.

Other agencies are less familiar. You may never have heard of the Bureau of Land Management, but if you go into the oil and gas industry, you will learn that this powerful agency has more control over your land than you do. If your software corporation wants to hire an Argentine expert on databases, you will get to know the complex workings of the Immigration and Naturalization Service: No one lawfully enters this country without its approval.

Administrative agencies use three kinds of power to do the work assigned to them: they make rules, investigate, and adjudicate.

One of the most important functions of an administrative agency is to make rules. In doing this, the agency attempts to establish fair and uniform behavior for all businesses in the affected area. To **create** a new rule is to **promulgate** it. Agencies promulgate two types of rules: legislative and interpretive.

These agency rules are much like statutes. For example, the Federal Communications Commission (FCC) promulgated a rule requiring all cable television systems with more than 3,500 subscribers to develop the capacity to carry at least 20 channels and to make some of those channels available to local community stations. This legislative rule has a heavy financial impact on many cable systems. As far as a cable company was concerned, it was more important than most statutes passed by Congress. Legislative rules can have the full effect of a statute.

These rules do not change the law. They are the agency's interpretation of what the law already requires. But they can still affect all of us.

In 1977, Congress passed the Clean Air Act in an attempt to reduce pollution from factories. The act required the Environmental Protection Agency (EPA) to impose emission standards on "stationary sources" of pollution. But what did "stationary source" mean? It was the EPA's job to define that term. Environmentalists wanted the term defined to include every smokestack in a factory so that the EPA could regulate each one. The EPA, however, developed the "bubble concept," ruling that "stationary source" meant an entire factory, but not the individual smokestacks. As a result, polluters could shift emission among smokestacks in a single factory to avoid EPA regulation. Environmentalists howled that this gutted the purpose of the statute, but to no avail. The agency had spoken, merely by interpreting a statute.

Agencies do an infinite variety of work and they need broad factual knowledge of the field they govern. Some companies cooperate with an agency, furnishing information and even voluntarily accepting agency recommendations. For example the United States Product Safety Commission investigates hundreds of consumer products every year and frequently urges companies to recall goods that the agency considers defective.

In addition to legislative authority, administrative agencies generally have the power to execute the regulations and bring proceedings against violators. Of course, this power is limited to matters within an agency's jurisdiction. The agency typically has the power to investigate possible violations, require people to appear as witnesses, and require witnesses to produce relevant papers and records. As previously mentioned, the agency has the authority to bring action against violators of the law and the regulations of the agency. Some companies refuse to turn over needed information. To force disclosure, agencies use **subpoenas** and searches. A subpoena is an order to appear at a particular time and place to provide evidence. A ***subpoena duces tecum*** requires the person to appear and bring specified documents. Many businesses and other organizations intensely dislike subpoenas and resent government agents plowing through records and questioning employees.

Facts: Under the Occupational Safety and Health Act of 1970, an employer may be ordered to eliminate or abate an unsafe working condition. If the employer fails to comply, a civil penalty may be assessed against it. Atlas Roofing was ordered to abate a specific working condition, and a penalty was assessed against it for failure to do so. It claimed that the procedure that had been followed violated the right to a jury trial declared by the Seventh Amendment of the federal Constitution: "In suits at common law, where the value in controversy shall exceed twenty dollars, the right of trial by jury shall be preserved . . . "

Decision: Judgment against Atlas Roofing. The constitutional provision means only that where a jury was required at common law, it must now be provided. The Constitutional provision has no application to new duties and liabilities created by statute that were unknown to the common law. Such new duties and liabilities may therefore be determined without a jury.[1]

---

[1] Atlas Roofing Company, Inc. v Occupational Safety and Health Review Commission, 430 US 442 (1977)

An administrative agency has only such powers as have been granted to the governmental agency that by law creating the agency. A contract must abide by a law declared by Congress as construed by the Courts, and also with the regulations and decisions of a governing administrative agency.

Because of the legislative, executive, and judicial powers of administrative agencies, there have been objections that the agencies do not act in an impartial manner. To counteract this, some agencies have separated their various functions. For example, the judicial function of the FTC is now performed by administrative law judges.

To provide a check on possible abuse, there are provisions in the law for public knowledge of the activities of administrative agencies. The Freedom of Information Act provides that information contained in the records of federal administrative agencies shall be made available upon proper request. Most of the meetings of the major administrative agencies are open to the public.

The Administrative Procedure Act, with certain exceptions, requires that every federal agency publish in the Federal Register a statement of the rules, principles, and procedures followed by the agency.

Typically, federal administrative agencies, prior to adopting regulations, invite public comment of both individuals and businesses which would be affected by the regulations. The opinions of individuals and such businesses are not binding on the administrative agency, but are taken into consideration. In fact, the APA, with certain exceptions, requires that a federal agency planning to adopt a new regulation must give public notice of this intent. The agency then must hold a hearing in which members of the public may be present to express their views and make suggestions.

As previously stated in order to inform the public of federal regulations, the **Federal Register Act** provides that an administrative regulation is not binding until it is printed in the Federal Register. This is a governmental publication that lists all administrative regulations.

The Occupational and Health Act of 1970 authorizes the secretary of labor to adopt job standards to protect workers from harmful substances. The secretary is directed by the statute to adopt that standard which most adequately assures, to the extent feasible, on the basis of the best available evidence that no employee will suffer material impairment of health. Acting under this authorization, the secretary adopted a Cotton Dust Standard to protect workers exposed to cotton dust. This dust causes serious lung disease that disables about one out of twelve cotton factory workers. The cotton industry attacked the validity of the Cotton Dust Standard on the ground that the secretary, in adopting the standard, had not considered the cost to the cotton industry of complying with the standard (a cost of $656.5 million). Was the Cotton Dust Standard valid? *Yes.* The statute directed the Secretary of Labor to adopt a standard that was feasible, meaning "capable of being done." Congress did not direct the secretary to weigh the costs of the standard against its benefits. The act directed the secretary to attain the benefits without directing that any consideration be given to the costs. Congress thus closed the door on consideration by the secretary of the costs of protecting the workers. Because Congress decided that as a matter of public policy, the workers were to be protected, the secretary could not be required by the court to change this policy determination. The Cotton Dust Standard adopted by the secretary without evaluation of the cost of compliance was therefore valid.

With regard to the investigative authority of an agency, a person has basically the same protection against unreasonable search and seizure by an administrative officer as that person would have against unreasonable search and seizure by a police officer. However, this general rule is subject to exceptions such as when the danger of concealment is great. In such a situation, the agency may make a warrantless inspection or search without advance notice. **Donovan v. Dewey** (U.S. 1981) was a case involving the inspection of mines and quarries pursuant to the Federal Mine Safety and Health Act. This Act allows government inspectors to make inspections of mines and quarries a specified number of times each year to see if the safety laws are being observed. Also, inspectors can make inspections, without a search warrant, to see if the safety laws are being observed. Also, inspectors can make inspections, without a search warrant, to see if prior violations have been corrected. When this power was challenged, the Supreme Court stated that the Federal Constitution does not prohibit all searches of property, but only unreasonable searches. In the case of business property, greater freedom to search may be allowed than in the case of a private home. To require advance notice of a particular inspection might defeat the purpose of the inspection which would be to find violations. The Court in this case pointed out that the purpose of the inspection was closely related to national health and safety.

The Fifth Amendment provides in part that a person shall not be compelled to be a witness against himself in any criminal case. However, this protection may not apply in a situation where the records being subpoenaed by the agency are required to be kept by the person or business subject to the administrative investigation.

An agency may be given the power to sit as a Court to determine whether or not there have been any violations of the law or of the agency's regulations. For example, the NLRB determines whether an unfair labor practice has occurred. The FTC acts as a Court to determine whether unfair competition has occurred.

Generally, either a private individual or the agency itself may file a complaint regarding violations of regulations. It is also generally necessary for an agency to give notice and hold a hearing at which all persons affected by the complaint may be present. There is no right of trial by jury. Also, some administrative agencies have the right to make an initial determination without holding a hearing. If the agency's conclusion is challenged, the agency will then hold a hearing.

Often, administrative agencies will inform a business of a violation (for example an OSHA violation) and give the business a chance to correct the violation before a formal complaint is made. Also, settlements may be made after the complaint and even during the formal hearing. Also, even after the hearing, and a decision has been made, a settlement still can be made if the agency believes that there is a chance that the decision may be overturned on appeal to a Court.

Some agencies have the power to impose a penalty and to issue orders that are binding on the person or business being regulated without an administrative proceeding. The only recourse for the penalized person or business is to appeal to a Court. For example, OSHA has the power to assess civil penalties against employers for failing to put an end to a dangerous working condition. Certain environmental protection statutes adopted by states give a state agency the power to fine violators of environmental protection regulations. The FTC can issue a cease and desist order to stop a business practice that it deems to be improper. This order to stop is binding unless it is reversed on an appeal to a Court.

An administrative agency may have the authority to require proof of compliance of companies, even though they are not being investigated or even though there is no complaint pending. For example, employers employing 100 people or more are required by law to file an EEO-1 Report which can be examined by the Equal Employment Opportunity Commission (EEOC) to determine the racial, sexual, and national origin makeup of the work force. The Wage and Hour Department may audit a particular business even if there has been no complaint against that business. This audit would be similar to an IRS audit in that the records of the company would be examined.

As previously stated, a law creating an administrative agency typically provides that an appeal can be taken from a decision of the agency to a particular Court. Of course, a person must have **standing** to appeal. In other words, the person appealing must have been the subject of the administrative action. For example, ABC Corporation could not appeal a decision of OSHA which was against XYZ Corporation.

It is generally very difficult to override a decision of a federal administrative agency on appeal. Basically, to override such a decision, you would have to show that the agency's decision was an incorrect application of the law or that the evidence was such that the agency should have made a different decision. Where a question of fact is involved, for example, who is telling the truth and who is not, the Court will normally accept the agency's determination.

Bell was employed by the Sinclair Radio Corporation. She was fired from her job and made a complaint to the National Labor Relations Board that she was fired because she belonged to a union. The examiner of the board held a hearing, at which Bell produced evidence of an antiunion attitude of the employer. The employer produced evidenced that Bell had been fired because she was chronically late and did poor work. The examiner and the Labor Relations Board concluded that Bell was fired because of her union membership. Sinclair appealed. The court reached the conclusion that, if the court had been the board, it would have held that the discharge of Bell was justified because it would not have believed the testimony of Bell's witnesses. Will the court reverse the decision of the National Labor Relations Board? *No.* When the question is who should have been believed, the court will not substitute its personal opinion for that of the agency and therefore will not reverse the decision of the agency merely because the agency believed one witness or group of witnesses and the court would have believed other witnesses. The decision of the agency as to the credibility of the witnesses is final and cannot be reversed on appeal. Therefore, the court will affirm the decision of the NLRB even though it actually disagrees with that decision.[2]

---

[2] 306 F.2d 569 (5th Cir. 1962)

Chapter 5

GOVERNMENT REGULATION OF COMPETITION AND PRICES

GOVERNMENT REGULATION OF COMPETITION AND PRICES

The **Sherman Antitrust Act** prohibits monopolies and restraint of trade. For example, several suppliers of widgets get together and agree they will all sell widgets for $1.00 to stores, and no less. This hurts competition. This Act prohibits: (1) a conspiracy by two or more persons to unreasonably restrain trade (i.e., to unreasonably limit competition; (2) an unlawful monopoly or an attempt to monopolize an industry; and (3) price fixing.

Price fixing is an agreement between participants on the same side in a market to buy or sell a product, service, or commodity only at a fixed price, or maintain the market conditions so that the price is maintained at a given level by controlling supply and demand. Two main types of price fixing between competitors is prohibited. This is called **horizontal price fixing. Vertical price fixing** is also prohibited. This is when a manufacturer and an independent retailer agree on a resale price of a product.

The Sherman Act does not regulate how big a company may get unless the company continues to buy up other companies in such a way as to:

- substantially lessen competition; and
- tend to create a monopoly.

The breakup of AT&T is an example of breaking up a monopoly in order to create more competition.

The **Robinson-Patman Act** prohibits price discrimination between buyers of a product if discrimination substantially hurts competition. For example, ABC, Inc., can't sell widgets to XYZ Corp. for $1.00 each and to Acme for $1.50 each if this drives Acme out of business. There are exceptions such as difference in quantity. For example, XYZ might get a favored price if it buys 1,000,000 widgets and Acme only buys 100,000.

The **Clayton Act** prohibits a corporation from acquiring an interest in the stock or assets of another corporation if doing so substantially lessens competition or may create a monopoly. A Federal Court may enter a **divestiture order** making the guilty party give up the property it acquired.

Mergers of large companies may have to be approved by FTC and Antitrust Division of U.S. Justice Department. (Hart-Scott-Rodino filing). You may see this when two airlines merge.

There must be some sort of interstate commerce for federal laws to apply. With regard to Sherman Act jurisdiction, you have a very broad standard. Even intrastate activities can be covered if they affect interstate commerce. Jurisdiction under the Clayton Act is about the same.

The Robinson-Patman Act has the strictest jurisdiction standards regarding the interstate activities necessary. Under this Act, the seller must actually be engaged in interstate commerce and the sales that are being complained about must be across state lines. Firms are not subject to this Act if they only sell to persons in the same state.

Horizontal restraints of trade are designed to lessen competition among a firm's competitors. For example, if Ford and GM get together and fix prices to drive Chrysler out of business, that would be a horizontal restraint of trade.

Monopolizing is prohibited by Section 2 of the Sherman Act. However, some monopolies are permitted. For example, newspapers can be a monopoly in a town that cannot support but one. Also, a monopoly which is the result of superior skill, foresight, and industry will be permitted. West Publishing Company had a monopoly for a long time regarding the publishing of legal opinions. They were the first publishing company, to my knowledge, to publish state and federal appellate court opinions on a large scale basis. They are still the best in the business, although they do have a little competition. The Internet is eventually going to hurt their business, since court opinions are now being put on the web.

The elements of monopolization are twofold:

- possession of monopoly power in a relevant market; and
- willfully acquiring or maintaining that power.

Monopoly power is the power to control prices or exclude competition in the relevant market. A court will examine a firm's market power to see whether or not the firm's product has an **inelastic demand curve,** i.e., people or not willing to take substitutes. This would be evidence of monopolization. An elastic demand curve means that there is significant competition. Also, a firm's percentage share of the market will be examined. There is no magic percentage. A court will also examine the relevant market to determine **market share.** This will involve both the geographic market as well as the product. As far as the geographic market, national sales of a product may be 50% while local sales may be only be 20% in an area. There would therefore be no monopoly in the local market. As far as the product is concerned, courts will look at the **cross-elasticity** of demand -- are customers willing to substitute goods? For example, will consumers substitute Hershey's chocolate chip cookies for Nestle's chocolate cookies. If so, this would be evidence that there was no monopoly. The decision on the relevant market can control whether there is monopolization. For example, if Saran Wrap has 75% of the clear plastic wrap market, but only 20% of the food wrap market (foil, wax paper, and plastic bags), they would not have a monopoly regarding food wrap.

In order to prove monopolization, one must show that the defendant did the acts in question on purpose. For example, you must show that the monopoly has resulted from something other than superior skill, foresight, and industry. Or you must show **predatory pricing** -- pricing below cost for a temporary period to drive others out. Or you must show **exclusionary conduct --** conduct that would prevent a competitor from entering the market. An example would be interfering with a competitor's purchase of a factory that would have promoted more competition.

The Sherman Act can be violated by attempts to monopolize. The plaintiff must show the dangerous probability of monopolization.

The Sherman Act prohibits price-fixing. This is some type of collaboration among competitors for the purpose of raising, depressing, fixing, or stabilizing the price of a commodity. Price fixing is a per se violation of the Sherman Act. This type of conduct is considered unreasonable and illegal, and there is no defense. Setting minimum prices is unlawful since it discourages competition even if the prices are reasonable. Setting maximum prices is also illegal since this has a tendency to stabilize prices. An agreement of competitors to use list prices as a guideline is an exchange of price information that hurts the market and is therefore unlawful.

Production limitations control supply, therefore control prices and is therefore illegal. Limitations on competitive bidding is a per se violation and illegal. An example would be where engineers agree not to bid on projects since low bidding can cause safety risks due to cost cutting. It is a per se violation of the Sherman Act for competitors to divide up markets since it lessens competition in the market that has been divided.

Another type of Sherman Act violation has to do with **group boycotts** and refusals by competitors to deal with certain buyers unless conditions are met. The boycotters may have the best intentions in the world, but such boycotts are still illegal. For example, garment manufacturers have boycotted buyers who sold knockoff goods.[3] These are goods that carry counterfeit trademarks. Such a boycott is a violation of the Sherman Act.

As far as antitrust considerations, courts follow the **rule of reason** standard. A joint venture is not unlawful per se. Courts will consider the benefits and detriments of the joint venture in determining its legality.

One exception to federal antitrust legislation is the **Noerr-Pennington** doctrine. This doctrine allows competitors to work together for governmental action such as lobbying and other political efforts. Due to First Amendment protection, Congress can't restrain this kind of activity. In a 1991 U.S. Supreme Court case, the court held that lobbying by a company that controlled the outdoor advertising market was still exempt from antitrust laws under this doctrine even though the company was trying to protect its market control.

The Local Government Antitrust Act exempts state and local governments from antitrust suits. The Joint Venture Trading Act allows joint ventures for international competition. However, prior approval of the Justice Department is required. The Shipping Act of 1984 allows joint ventures among shippers in order to promote better international competition.

The Clayton Act prohibits **interlocking directorates.** Directors of firms with one million dollars or more in capital are prohibited from being a director for a competitor. This law lessens the likelihood that anticompetitive information will be exchanged.

---

[3] Knock off goods are an identical unauthorized, but cheaper. copy of a patented, trademarked, or copyrighted product or work.

In a **consolidation** of two or more corporations, their separate existences cease, and a new corporation with the property and the assets of the old corporations comes into being. A **merger** is different from a consolidation in that when two corporations merge, one absorbs the other. One corporation preserves its original charter and identity and continues to exist. The other corporation disappears, and its corporate existence terminates.

Generally, the corporate entity which continues the business after a merger or a consolidation will succeed to all of the rights and property of the predecessors and will also be subject to all of the debts and liabilities of the predecessor corporations. For example, A merges into B. Suppose A had a contract with C. B did not. After the merger, B is liable to C on the contract.

A corporation may merely purchase the assets of another business. This would not be a merger or consolidation. In an acquisition, the purchaser does not become liable for the obligations of the business whose assets are being purchased.

Horizontal mergers are mergers between competitors. There is a presumption that such mergers are illegal. In other words, you have to disprove their illegality. Courts look at the market share of the companies involved and the surviving company to determine legality. There are basically two exceptions:

- **failing company doctrine** where the purpose of the merger is the asset acquisition; and
- **small company defense** where two small companies merge in order to compete better with larger firms.

Vertical restraints of trade involve parties in the chain of distribution, e.g., the manufacturer to the wholesaler to the retailer. One example of a vertical restraint of trade would be retail price maintenance. This would involve an attempt by a manufacturer to control the price that retailers charge for a product. This is a per se violation of section one of the Sherman Act. This would apply to minimum as well as maximum prices. It is also a violation to attempt to control retail prices through consignments. This would be where a manufacturer makes the retailer its agent for the sale of goods and gives the retailer a commission for each sale.

Suggested retail prices are not unlawful as long as the manufacturer or wholesaler does not try to enforce the suggested price in some. An example would be refusing to sell to a retailer unless the suggested price were used.

What about sole outlets and exclusive dealerships? This is where the manufacturer appoints a distributor or retailer as the exclusive outlet. This type of situation is not an automatic violation of the Sherman Act. The courts use a **rule of reason** test. The freedom of manufacturers to pick and choose dealers is protected as long as there is sufficient interbrand competition. For example, Coke can have exclusive distributors as long as there is sufficient competition from other soft drink manufacturers like Pepsi.

Another vertical restraint of trade involves customer and territorial restrictions. For example, a manufacturer might restrict by territory whom a dealer can sell to. The legality of such an arrangement is again subject to a rule of reason analysis. A court will consider the amount of interbrand competition. Having an exclusive Ford dealership in a tri-county might even cause interbrand competition to increase. GM and Chrysler dealerships might want to come in and compete with this one Ford dealership.

Courts will also look at the market power of the manufacturer. The more market power, the less interbrand competition you will have. In other words, the consumers will have fewer substitute goods to choose from. The more market power a manufacturer has, the more likely it is that a court will strike down this vertical type restraint.

Another vertical restraint involves **tying arrangements.** This involves requiring a buyer to buy an additional product in order to get a product it needs. An example is of requiring the buyer of a copier machine to buy the seller's paper when other brands of paper would be acceptable. The copier machine is the tying product and the paper is the tied product. Tying can be a violation of the Clayton Act regarding contracts for the sale of goods and the Sherman Act regarding the sale of services. What the courts look at is whether or not the tying product is unique. If it is, then there is an antitrust violation unless the sale comes within one of the two defenses that courts have recognized.

One defense is the **new industry defense.** This is where the tying product, let's say solar water heaters, is permitted to have a tied product, let's say certain plumbing, in order to provide quality control so that the new industry will succeed. The other defense is **quality control** for the protection goodwill. This would apply if the specifications for the tied goods were so complicated or unique that only the manufacturer could supply them.

Another type of vertical restraint of trade is an **exclusive dealing** or **requirements** contract. This is where a buyer agrees to only handle the seller's goods and will not carry those of the competition. Another example would be where the buyer agrees to buy all of its needs from the seller and no one else. Before this type of agreement would be declared illegal, it must involve a substantial share of the market.

As previously stated, price discrimination is prohibited by the Robinson-Patman Act, which is an amendment to the Clayton Act. Basically, this is selling the same product to different buyers at different prices. There are four elements that must be proven in a price discrimination case:

- interstate commerce;
- price discrimination between purchasers of the same goods;
- the goods have to be of like grade and quality; and
- competition must be harmed in some way.

First, the seller must be actually engaged in interstate commerce in the sense that one of the transactions in question must actually be across state lines.

Second, there must be an actual purchase involved. Leases and consignments are not included. Also the purchases must occur at about the same time. The price discrimination can come from indirect charges like charging one purchaser more for shipping than another.

Third, the goods sold must be of like grade or quality. For example, the sale of one shipment of hamburger meat at $1.00 per pound would be ok even if another buyer paid $.75 per pound if the cheaper meat was of inferior quality to the more expensive meat.

Finally, the sales must hurt competition. This can be proven by showing that there is a substantial price cut in a certain area with the effect of injuring a smaller competitor. Predator pricing is illegal. This is pricing below cost for a temporary period in order to drive others out of the market.

There are defenses to price discrimination. One is that a seller may charge less in one market than in another in order to meet the competition in that market. Another defense is where there are cost differences that must be offset such as different shipping costs in one market than in another. The last defense deals with market changes, inflation and material costs. The seller must simply establish that a price change was initiated in response to one of these factors.

Because the level of international competition has increased, the U.S. now allows joint ventures in international markets that would not be permitted within the U.S. The reason such joint ventures are now allowed is obviously to help U.S. firms compete with foreign firms. For example, General Mills was allowed to purchase Nabisco's cold cereal business in the United Kingdom and in the U.S. so it could compete more effectively in North American and European Markets.

The U.S. probably has the most stringent antitrust laws in the world. This puts U.S. countries at a disadvantage when competing in world markets. While normally the U.S. is not allowed to prosecute international cartels like OPEC, because of sovereign immunity, it can prosecute foreign companies that engage in commerce in the U.S.

Chapter 6
ETHICS

BUSINESS ETHICS

The performing and conducting of business involve considerations of wheeling, dealing, and getting results effectively and efficiently. Among capitalistic, free-markets, successful results are highly met with corresponding rewards. In other words, regardless of one's investment, an expectation of some future reward exists in due time. Fair returns are anticipated as exchanges for expended amounts of labor, skill, and time that produce goods and services. Despite much effort that may accompany such endeavors and exchanges, all such activity must be ethical and legal.

Ethics are the guides and standards that influence decisions. Although some may view ethics as some form of conscience wherein notions of right versus wrong influence behavior, others may consider ethics to be some type of expressed or unexpressed code whereby adherence is mandatory. Ethical indoctrination and conceptual reinforcement may occur via relations and experiences with religion and faith, culture, society, traditions, law, or accepted norms. Certainly, personal experience and belief affect one's ethical perspectives.

A variety of ethical considerations affect organizations. Examples range from the duties and rights that exist within the employer-employee relationship to the obligations of agency with respect to the stakeholders of the organization. Notably, the scandalous incidents involving Enron, HealthSouth, and Worldcom represented heinous ethical transgressions. Any organization will experience some type of ethical issues regardless of its purpose or mission. Generally, ethical issues arise in the areas of social responsibility, organizational governance, corporate espionage, confidentiality, and several others.

ETHICAL ISSUES

Ethical issues may originate from the fashioning of business relationships, specific transactions, or the performing of duties. Ethical issues typically involve questioning moral considerations of some issues with respect to a contemplated decision and respective courses of action. Individuals, groups, and organizations are all subject to the wiles of ethical issues. Honesty and integrity are primary considerations of many ethical issues. A variety of scenarios exist regarding such issues: falsification of records, bribery, favoritism, lying, and use of organizational resources. Examples of specific issues may be lying about sick days or accomplishments for a promotion; fabricating time-card records; and so forth.

MORALS, ETHICS, AND VALUES

Ethics are related to morals and values. Individuals, groups, and organizations are affected by ethics, morals, and values. For the most part, within a specific society, morals, values, and ethics are fairly and generally static. However, they tend to change somewhat through time as generations come and go and as cultural attributes change through time. Within the U.S., the years of Prohibition are certainly testaments to such societal change.

Morals, ethics, and values are engrained among legal systems globally. Morals represent the foundational beliefs of right versus wrong within a society. Around the world, morals may vary whereby acts and concepts that are completely moral in one society may be deemed completely immoral in another society.

Ethics are derived from morals societally. Ethics represent the guiding principle and rules that influence human behaviors. A variety of ethics exist – religious, professional, vocational, individual, and so forth. Attorneys adhere to a code of ethics. For instance, the Code of Professional Responsibility of the American Bar Association was adopted in 1969. It was amended several times since its adoption.

Values represent those things that may be cherished societally in conjunction with morals and ethics. Within this context, values represent moral beliefs, principles, and ethics of people, groups, or organizations. For instance, a society may value its freedoms and liberties.

ETHICAL CODES

A variety of ethical codes exist among various professions, vocations, and occupations. They exist for attorneys, judges, law enforcement personnel, security personnel, counselors, medical professionals, and so forth. Regardless of one corresponding occupation, adhering to one's respective ethical codes involves considerations lifestyle conformance to the prescribed code of ethics. For instance, physicians adhere to a medical code of ethics, and realtors also must adhere to their respective ethical codes. Law and ethical codes are different. Law is established and set by legislative entities whereas ethical codes are crafted by organizational boards or memberships.

Although ethical codes may differ among organizations, professions, vocations, and occupations, they generally all accommodate some common areas: 1) gratuities and gifts, 2) contributions and monies, 3) business relationships, 4) behaviors that may be shady or criminal, and 5) individual conduct and personal behavior.

CRIME AND ETHICS

The notions and concepts of morals, values, and ethics are also apparent within the definition of crime. Specifically, crime is anything society says it is via the legislative process, codified and expressed, and finally made enforceable by governmental authority. For instance, crimes of moral turpitude, such as murder, have corresponding underpinnings of morals, ethics, and values societally. From a long-term, societal perspective, this definition of crime provides the opportunity for change. In the case of Prohibition, when society deemed that it was unsuccessful, law was changed via the legislative process. After the repeal of Prohibition, alcoholic beverages were again legal within society. During modern times, as society changes, its ethical attributes and preferences are reflected within the justice system. For instance, in several states, marijuana is now legal (though remains illegal federally). Thus, similar to Prohibition, the public drives legal change via the legislative process.

The leaders, managers, and administrators of organizations have a fiduciary interest and obligation to render decisions that are in the best interests of their respective stakeholders. This scenario is termed the principal-agency agreement, the principal-agency relationship, or the principal-agency conundrum. Despite the expectations that officers, administrators, leaders, and managers are of sound repute, reality often dictates painfully and different scenarios. Breaching of this responsibility poses ethical issues. For instance, Enron's leadership committed criminal acts in conjunction with egregious ethical violations.

UNETHICAL BEHAVIOR VERSUS ILLEGAL BEHAVIOR

The notable scandals of Enron, Worldcom, and HealthSouth represent examples wherein a breaching of ethics resulted in criminality. Thus, the unethical practices exhibited by Enron's leadership were also illegal. However, not all cases in which unethical practices exist are deemed illegal. For instance, in a work environment, firing a competent, high-performing employee in order to hire a relative or friend is not necessarily illegal, but it is unethical.

WHISTLEBLOWING

Within American society, employees may be faced with an ethical decisions regard whether to disclose certain information that may involve illegal or unethical practices that exist within the work setting. However, when someone initiates such disclosure, fears of reprisal and retaliation exist. However, some legal protections exist whereby whistleblowers may be safeguarded. Often, whistleblowing incites much public debate. For instance, the deeds of Edward Snowden remain debatable within American society.

Whistleblowers may be protected by a variety of laws and regulations. These safeguards vary with respect to the type and content of disclosures occurring during whistleblowing. Safeguards also vary according to the state where the incident occurs. Thus, no universal, solitary approach exists for protecting whistleblowers – each case is unique.

ETHICAL PRESENTATION AND IMAGERY

Both individuals and organizations may often have the need to present some type of image during their business endeavors. Presenting some type of image may necessitate the uses of marketing and advertising practices. Ethical considerations are engrained among such endeavors. For instance, marketing and advertising initiatives may involve ethical considerations of product transparency regarding product safety or dangerousness, product service and recalls, or any other types of risks. Other ethical dimensions may include pricing of services and products, consumer privacy, truthfulness of advertising and marketing, subliminal messages, and so forth.

ORGANIZATIONAL POLICY

Ethical principles may be expressed within organizational policies. Policy consists of both the actions and inactions of an organization with respect to its operations and governance. Although policy is not law, it does govern and influence the behaviors and conducts of organizational personnel. Policy may be unwritten or written. Policies may be crafted to govern a variety of organizational contexts – public affairs, technology, social behaviors, professional conduct, security, resource use, and so forth. Essentially, policy expresses what is allowable versus disallowable or acceptable versus unacceptable. Two obvious examples are foodstuffs and beverages. For instance, neither Kentucky Fried Chicken (KFC) nor Coca Cola reveals its secret ingredients or proprietary recipes publicly.

SOCIAL RESPONSIBILITY

Social responsibility represents the notion that organizations and individuals have an ethical obligation toward societal benefit. Before the existence of protective environmental legislation, various organizations disposed of harmful pollutants indiscriminately thereby causing harm to both people and the environment. During modern times, in conjunction with protective legislation, such practices are disallowed and deemed unethical. Essentially, these notions imply that organizations have a social responsibility to incite no harm against people, property, or land.

Social responsibility is not constrained with respect to considerations of organizational practices, nature, and people. For instance, corporations may give back to their respective communities through some form of benevolence. Examples include providing uniforms for little league teams, contributing foodstuffs to homeless shelters, or by donating monies to support local hospitals or schools. Such notions imply that organizations have a social responsibility toward positive welfare within their respective communities and locales.

ETHICAL CULTURE

Business organizations are not comprised randomly of individuals or groups. Instead, they represent some form of community wherein various cultures and sub-cultures may exist among the various organizational levels, components, and hierarchies. Participation in a business organization is volitional – one may be offered a job or may resign freely. Business organizations are both social and economic entities wherein exist various political structures.

Given these notions, organizations may seek to attain a culture of ethics throughout their respective enterprises. Emphasizing and practicing integrity may deter or abate instances of scandal, such as the incidents of Worldcom or HealthSouth. Organizational productivity may be enhanced when personnel are attentive to work tasks without negative distractions of politics or strained relationships within the work setting. Leadership consistency and transparency provide high-level examples of integrity whereby subordinates may be inspired to behave ethically. Essentially, ethics must permeate all facets of the organizational construct, ranging from the highest officers to the lowest workers.

Chapter 7
BUSINESS CRIME AND CYBERLAW

BUSINESS CRIME
What is a business crime? The following is a summary of business crimes:

- **Bank Fraud** involves engaging in an act or pattern of activity where the purpose is to defraud a bank of funds.
- **Blackmail** involves a demand for money or other consideration under threat to do bodily harm, to injure property, to accuse of a crime, or to expose secrets.
- **Bribery** When money, goods, services, information or anything else of value is offered with intent to influence the actions, opinions, or decisions of the taker. You may be charged with bribery whether you offer the bribe or accept it.
- **Computer fraud** occurs when computer hackers steal information sources contained on computers such as: bank information, credit cards, and proprietary information.
- **Counterfeiting** occurs when someone copies or imitates an item without having been authorized to do so and passes the copy off for the genuine or original item. Counterfeiting is most often associated with money however can also be associated with designer clothing, handbags and watches.
- **Credit Card Fraud** is the unauthorized use of a credit card to obtain goods of value.
- **Embezzlement occurs** when a person who has been entrusted with money or property appropriates it for his or her own use and benefit.
- **Extortion** occurs when one person illegally obtains property from another by actual or threatened force, fear, or violence, or under cover of official right.
- **Forgery** occurs when a person passes a false or worthless instrument such as a check or counterfeit security with the intent to defraud or injure the recipient.
- **Health Care Fraud** occurs when an unlicensed health care provider provides services under the guise of being licensed and obtains monetary benefit for the service.
- **Insider Trading** occurs when a person uses inside, confidential, or advance information to trade in shares of publicly held corporations.
- **Insurance Fraud** involves engaging in an act or pattern of activity wherein one obtains proceeds from an insurance company through deception.
- **Investment Schemes** occurs when an unsuspecting victim is contacted by a person who promises to provide a large return on a small investment.
- **Kickback** occurs when a person who sells an item pays back a portion of the purchase price to the buyer.
- **Larceny/Theft:** When a person wrongfully takes another person's money or property with the intent to appropriate, convert or steal it.
- **Money Laundering** is the investment or transfer of money from racketeering, drug transactions or other embezzlement schemes so that it appears that its original source either cannot be traced or is legitimate.
- **Racketeering** is the operation of an illegal business for personal profit.
- **Securities Fraud** is the act of artificially inflating the price of stocks by brokers so that buyers can purchase a stock on the rise.

- **Tax Evasion** occurs when a person commits fraud in filing or paying taxes.
- **Telemarketing Fraud** occurs when a person operates out of boiler rooms and place telephone calls to residences and corporations where the person requests a donation to an alleged charitable organization or where the person requests money up front or a credit card number up front, and does not use the donation for the stated purpose.
- **Welfare Fraud** is to engage in an act or acts where the purpose is to obtain benefits (i.e. Public Assistance, Food Stamps, or Medicaid) from the State or Federal Government.
- **Advanced Fee Schemes** occur when a person induces a victim to give him some type of advanced fee in return for a future benefit. The future benefit never occurs and the victim never receives the advanced fee back.
- **Check Kiting: a** bank account is opened with good funds and a rapport is developed with the bank. Actor then deposits a series of bad checks but prior to their discovery, withdraws funds from the bank.
- **Coupon Redemption:** Grocery stores amass large amounts of coupons and redeem them to manufacturers when in fact merchandise was never sold.
- **Directory Advertising:** Actor either impersonates sales person from a directory company like the yellow pages or fraudulently sells advertising which the victim never receives.
- **Fortune Telling:** Actor advises victim that victim is cursed. Actor advises victim that the curse must be removed. Actor advises that she must meditate to the spirits and will require payment. Over a period of time, victim pays fortune teller thousands of dollars to remove curse.
- **Gypsies:** Actor states that victim's money is cursed. In order to remove the curse, the money must be placed into a bag or box that the actor provides. The bag or box is switched. Actor advises victim to perform certain rituals over the money and the curse will be removed. The bag or box cannot be opened for a period of time when it is opened, the money is gone.
- **Home Improvement:** Actor approaches a home owner with a very low estimate for a repair or improvement. Inferior or incomplete work is performed. Once the repairs are completed, actor intimidates the victim to pay a price much greater than the original estimate.
- **Inferior Equipment:** Actors travel around selling inferior equipment such as tools at high prices.
- **Jamaican Switch:** Actor #1 approaches a victim looking for the address of a prostitute. Actor #1 shows a large sum of money to the victim. Actor #2 arrives and tells Actor #1 where he can find the prostitute but cautions on taking all the money as the prostitute might rob him. Actor #1 asks the victim to hold the money for him. Actor #1 puts his money into a handkerchief with the victim's money. Actor #1 shows the victim how to hide the money under his arm, inside his shirt while switching handkerchiefs. Victim takes the handkerchief and the parties split up, however, Actor #1 leaves with victim's money.
- **Land Fraud:** Actor induces victim to purchase tracks of land in some type of retirement development which does not exist.
- **Odometer Fraud:** Unscrupulous used car salesman purchased used cars and turn back the odometers. The used car is sold at a higher price due to its low mileage.

- **Pigeon Drop:** Actor #1 befriends the victim. Actor #2 shows both Actor #1 and victim a "found" package containing a large amount of cash. Actor #1 insists that the found money be divided equally but only after each person puts up his own money to demonstrate good faith. All the money is put in one package and the package is later switched.
- **Police Impersonation:** Actor tells victim that his bank is being operated by fraudulent bank officers. Actor instructs victim to take money out of bank and place it into a good bank. After the money is withdrawn, the actor allegedly takes the money to the police station for safe-keeping. The victim never sees the money again.
- **Ponzi:** An investment scheme where the actor solicits investors in a business venture, promising extremely high financial returns or dividends in a very short period of time. The actor never invests the money, however, does pay dividends. The dividends consist of the newest investors funds. The first investors, pleased to receive dividends, encourage new investors to invest. This scheme falls apart when the actor no longer has sufficient new investors to distribute dividends to the old investors or the actor simply takes all the funds and leaves the area.
- **Pyramid:** An investment fraud in which an individual is offered a distributorship or franchise to market a particular product. The promoter of the pyramid represents that although marketing of the product will result in profits, larger profits will be earned by the sale of franchises. For example, if a franchise price is $10,000.00, the seller receives $3,500.00 for every franchise sold. Each new franchise purchaser is presented with the same proposal so that each franchise owner is attempting to sell franchises. Once the supply of potential investors is exhausted, the pyramid collapses. Many times, there are no products involved in the franchise, simply just the exchange of money.
- **Quick Change:** Victim is confused by actor's speedy series of money exchanges and, in the end, is short changed.
- **Shell Game:** Actor #1 manipulates a pea beneath three walnut shells or bottle caps. Actor #1 moves the caps around and shows victim the cap with the pea under it. With the encouragement of another player, also Actor #2, victim places larger and larger bets as to which cap contains the pea. The game is ended by Actor #1 when the take is large enough.
- **Utilities Impersonators:** Actor impersonates utilities employees by wearing jumpsuits with name tags. Actor approaches victim with story about a gas leak or electrical surge to gain entry to the home. Valuables are taken by actor.
- **VCR Scam:** Actor purports to sell new VCR's or televisions at an extremely low cost due to his connections. Victim pays for the VCR or television only to discover that the box has been filled with rocks.
- **West African Investment Scams** Actors target businesses and obtain business' bank account information from which all funds are later withdrawn.

LIABILITY

Who is Liable for Business Crime? Corporations were not initially held criminally responsible for corporate activities. A corporation was considered to be a legally fictitious entity, incapable of forming the Intent necessary to commit a criminal act. The Supreme Court ultimately rejected this notion in 1909 in **New York Central & Hudson River Railroad v. U.S.,** 29 S. Ct. 304 (1909). In this case, a railroad company employee paid rebates to shippers in violation of federal law. The court upheld the corporation's criminal conviction, finding no reason that corporations could not be held ***responsible for and charged with the knowledge and purposes of their agents, acting within the authority conferred upon them.*** The Supreme Court concluded that criminal liability could be imputed to the corporation based on the benefit it received as a result of the criminal acts of its agents. A corporation may be convicted for its agent's unlawful acts when the agent acted within the scope of his or her actual or apparent authority.

Another theory of corporate criminal liability is the ***collective knowledge doctrine.*** As knowledge of criminal activity is often the scienter[4] element of a particular crime, the requisite knowledge can be imputed to the corporation based on the collective knowledge[5] of the directors and officers.

It is now well settled that corporate directors, officers, and employees can be held criminally liable for any criminal acts that they personally commit regardless of whether they were acting in furtherance of the corporation's interests. A corporate director, officer, or agent must answer for any personal wrongdoing and cannot be shielded by the corporate entity. An officer and a director can also be held criminally responsible for criminal acts committed by their agents under the *respondeat superior* tort theory mentioned above. Directors, officers, and employees may also be criminally responsible for any crime that they aid and abet.

Directors and officers may also be subject to criminal liability for any crime under the theory that they failed to prevent the crime ***by neglecting to control the misconduct of those subject to their control.*** Under this theory of liability, a person is criminally liable based on his responsible relation to the criminal violation regardless of whether he has any knowledge of the criminal activity.

United States v. Park, 421 U.S. 658 (1975), John R. Park was president of Acme Markets, Inc., a national food chain headquartered in Philadelphia with 36,000 employees and 16 warehouses. In 1970, the FDA found problems with rodent infestation at Acme's Philadelphia warehouse facility. In 1971, the FDA found the same conditions in Acme's Baltimore warehouse. In 1972, the FDA's chief of compliance wrote to Park and asked that he direct his attention to the prolonged problems of warehouse infestation. The FDA inspected the Baltimore warehouse two months after Park was sent the letter and found the same problems. Acme and Park were both charged with violations of the Pure Food and Drug Act. Park was convicted and fined $500. The Court of Appeals reversed. The issue on appeal was whether or not Park liable for the warehouse problems when subordinates had been ordered to remedy the situation. The U.S. Supreme said yes. He was aware of the deficiencies in his subordinates' system and still took no action.

The most frightening part of being a defendant in a white collar criminal case – or any criminal case – is the potential penalties if convicted. Most white collar defendants have no prior experience with the criminal justice system, and the uncertainty of their future looms understandably large in their minds. In addition to criminal penalties, many white collar offenses may give rise to civil lawsuits, brought either by the federal or state government, or by the

[4] Intent or knowledge of wrongdoing.

[5] This doctrine aids the prosecution by imputing the knowledge of all employees to the corporation.

victims of the offense. Any civil liability imposed as a result of these suits is in addition to, and not a substitute for, the penalties imposed in the criminal case.

The criminal penalties for white collar crimes vary. Most of the laws authorize a monetary fine, a prison sentence or a combination of the two. The criminal laws authorize maximum penalties, which are often quite severe. Most defendants, however, receive less than the maximum sentence. Courts often follow **sentencing guidelines**, which may vary depending on the jurisdiction. These guidelines are meant to ensure that criminal sentences are uniform, so the sentencing judge is often given very little discretion on the sentence imposed. The guidelines take into account the crime for which the defendant has been convicted, and any prior criminal record of the defendant. In some cases, the court may consider factors that will allow it to depart, or impose a sentence different from the sentence required by the guidelines.

Defendants without a significant criminal record may be sentenced to probation, a suspended jail sentence or a jail sentence far shorter than the maximum. They may have fines levied against them, and may be required to forfeit any profits or pay restitution to their victims.

CYBERCRIME

Computer crime has been referred to as **cybercrime**, **e-crime**, **electronic crime**, **virtual crime**, or **hi-tech crime.** It is an act performed by a knowledgeable computer user, sometimes referred to as a hacker that illegally browses or steals a company's or individual's private information. In some cases, this person or group of individuals may be malicious and destroy or otherwise corrupt the computer or data files.

Below is a listing of the different types of computer crimes today.

- **Child pornography**– Making or distributing child pornography.
- **Cyber terrorism**– Hacking, threats, and blackmailing towards a business or person.
- **Cyberbully or Cyberstalking**– Harassing others online.
- **Creating Malware**– Writing, creating, or distributing malware (e.g. viruses and spyware.)
- **Denial of Service attack**– Overloading a system with so many requests it cannot serve normal requests.
- **Fraud**– Manipulating data, e.g. changing banking records to transfer money to an account.
- **Harvesting**– Collect account or other account related information on other people.
- **Identity theft**– Pretending to be someone you are not.
- **Intellectual property theft**– Stealing another persons or companies intellectual property.
- **Phishing**– Deceiving individuals to gain private or personal information about that person.
- **Salami slicing**– Stealing tiny amounts of money from each transaction.
- **Spamming**– Distributed unsolicited e-mail to dozens or hundreds of different addresses.
- **Spoofing**– Deceiving a system into thinking you are someone you really are not.
- **Unauthorized access**– Gaining access to systems you have no permission to access.
- **Wiretapping**– Connecting a device to a phone line to listen to conversations.

ECONOMIC ESPIONAGE
In general terms, economic espionage is the unlawful or clandestine targeting or acquisition of sensitive financial, trade or economic policy information; proprietary economic information; or technological information.

The Economic Espionage Act of 1996 (EEA), 18 U.S.C. §§ 1831-1839, defines the term ***economic espionage*** as the theft or misappropriation of a trade secret with the intent or knowledge that the offense will benefit any foreign government, foreign instrumentality, or foreign agent. The act of receiving, purchasing, or possessing a trade secret known to have been stolen or misappropriated, as well as any attempt or conspiracy to commit economic espionage are punishable as a federal crime under the EEA.

The **Electronic Fund Transfer Act** (EFTA) is a federal law enacted in 1978 to protect consumers when they use **electronic** means to manage their finances. **Electronic fund transfers** (**EFT**) are commonly used and initiated through **electronic** technology, replacing the use checks, deposit slips and other paper transactions. This law was passed in 1978 as a result of the growth of electronic ATM machines and electronic banking. The use of paper checks has steadily declined since then, but the check served as hard evidence of payment. The explosion of electronic financial transactions created a need for new rules that would give consumers the same level of confidence that they had in the checking system. This includes the ability to challenge errors and correct them within a 60-day window, and to limit liability on a lost card to $50 if the card is reported as lost within two business days.

The Digital Millennium Copyright Act (DMCA) was signed into law by President Clinton on October 28, 1998. The legislation implements two 1996 World Intellectual Property Organization (WIPO) treaties: the WIPO Copyright Treaty and the WIPO Performances and Phonograms Treaty. The DMCA also addresses a number of other significant copyright-related issues. The DMCA is divided into five titles:

- Title I, **the WIPO Copyright and Performances and Phonograms Treaties Implementation Act of 1998**, implements the WIPO treaties.
- Title II, the **Online Copyright Infringement Liability Limitation Act**, creates limitations on the liability of online service providers for copyright infringement when engaging in certain types of activities.
- Title III, the **Computer Maintenance Competition Assurance Act**, creates an exemption for making a copy of a computer program by activating a computer for purposes of maintenance or repair.
- Title IV contains six miscellaneous provisions, relating to the functions of the Copyright Office, distance education, the exceptions in the Copyright Act for libraries and for making ephemeral recordings, "webcasting" of sound recordings on the Internet, and the applicability of collective bargaining agreement obligations in the case of transfers of rights in motion pictures.
- Title V, the **Vessel Hull Design Protection Act**, creates a new form of protection for the design of vessel hulls.

Chapter 8

TORT AND CYBER TORTS

WHAT IS A TORT?

Conduct that harms other people or their property is generally called a *tort.* It is a private wrong against a person for which the person may recover damages. The injured party may sue the wrongdoer to recover damages to compensate him for the harm or loss caused. The conduct that is a tort may also be a crime.

Some torts require *intent* before there will be liability and some torts require no intent. In other words, in some cases there is liability for a tort even though the person committing the tort did not have any intent to do wrong. For example, a person going on private property without the consent of the landowner is liable for the tort of trespass even though the person may have not known he was on someone else's property (*e.g.,* he made an honest mistake as to the location of the boundary line).

In other torts, there must be intent. For example, in the case of slander, it is necessary to show that the defendant intended to cause harm, or, at least had the intent to do an act that a reasonable person would know would likely cause harm. As a general rule, motive is irrelevant except as evidence to show the existence of intent.

DIFFERENCE BETWEEN A TORT AND A CRIME

A *crime* is a wrong arising from a violation of a *public duty.* A *tort* is a wrong arising from the violation of a *private duty.* Again, however, a crime can also constitute a tort. For example, assault is a tort, but it is also a crime. A person who is assaulted may bring criminal charges against the assailant and may also sue the assailant for damages under tort law. An employee's theft of his employer's property that was entrusted to the employee constitutes the crime of embezzlement as well as the tort of conversion.

TYPES OF TORTS

There are basically three types of torts:

- intentional torts;
- negligence; and
- strict liability.

An **intentional tort** is a civil wrong that occurs when the wrongdoer engages in intentional conduct that results in damages to another. Striking another person in a fight is an intentional act that would be the tort of battery. Striking a person accidentally would not be an intentional tort since there was not intent to strike the person. This may, however, be a negligent act. Careless conduct that results in damage to another is **negligence.**

Generally, liability because of a tort only arises where the defendant either intended to cause harm to the plaintiff or in situations where the defendant is negligent. However, in some areas, liability can arise even when there is no intention to cause harm or negligence. For example, in most states, when a contractor uses dynamite which causes debris to be thrown onto the land of another and damages the landowner's house, the landowner may recover damages from the contractor even if the contractor was not negligent and did not intend to cause any harm. This is called **strict liability** or absolute liability. Basically, society is saying that the activity is so dangerous to the public that there must be liability. However, society is not going so far as to outlaw the activity.

Acme Construction Company was constructing a highway. It was necessary to blast rock with dynamite. The corporation's employees did this with the greatest of care. In spite of their precautions, some flying fragments of rock damaged a neighboring house. The owner of the house sued the corporation for the damages. The corporation raised the defense that the owner was suing for tort damages and that such damages could not be imposed because the corporation had been free from fault. Was this defense valid? No. While ordinarily fault is the basis of tort liability, there are cases in which absolute liability is imposed on the actor. This means that when harm is caused, it is no defense that none was intended or that due care had been exercised to prevent the harm.

Other examples of absolute liability situations would be harm caused by storage of flammable gas and explosives, crop dusting when the chemical that is used is dangerous, factories which produce dangerous fumes, smoke or soot in populated areas, and the production of nuclear material.

INTENTIONAL TORTS

TRESPASS

A trespass is an *unauthorized action* with respect to a person or property. A *trespass to the person* consists of any contact with someone's person for which consent was not given. This is technically described as a *battery*. An *assault* would be a situation where a plaintiff reasonably believed a battery upon his person was about to be committed. An example of an assault would be where one person swings his fist at another person. If the person made contact, this would be an assault and a battery. A defense to assault and battery would be in cases of self defense.

A *trespass to land* involves going on or above the property of another without permission. A trespass can also involve the unpermitted use of the airspace of another's property as well as actually going on the actual property. However, this rule has been modified to allow the flight of aircraft above the land as long as it does not interfere with the proper use of the land.

A *trespass to personal property* is the use of someone's property without person. A *conversion* occurs when personal property is taken by a defendant and kept from its true owner without permission of the owner. Conversion is the civil side of the crime of theft.

DEFAMATION

A form of publication which tends to cause one to lose the esteem of the community is defamation. This is injury to reputation. A person is liable for the defamation of another. In order to prove defamation, the plaintiff must prove:

- that a statement was made about the plaintiff's reputation, honesty or integrity that is not true;
- publication to a third party (i.e., another person hears or reads the statement); and
- the plaintiff suffers damages as a result of the statement.

Slander is a form of defamation that consists of making false oral statements about a person which would damage that person's reputation. If I spread a rumor that my neighbor has been in jail and this is not true, I could be held liable for slander. Defamation which occurs by written statements is known as *libel.* Libel may also result from a picture or visual representation. Truth is an absolute defense to slander or libel.

Some statements, while libelous or slanderous, are *absolutely privileged* in the sense that the statements can be made without fear of a lawsuit for slander. The best example is a statement made in a court of law. An untrue statement made by a witness about a person in court which damages that person's reputation will generally not cause liability to the witness as far as slander is concerned. However, if the statement is untrue, and the person knows the statement is untrue, the crime of perjury may have been committed.

If a communication is made in good faith on a subject that the communicating party has a legitimate right or interest in making the communication, such a communication could be exempt from slander liability due to a *qualified privileged.*

Smith, a district manager of Acme Recording Company, was investigating complaints of mismanagement of the a city office of the company. As part of his investigation he called at the home of Ann, the secretary of that office. She expressed the opinion that part of the trouble was caused by stealing of parts and equipment by Jones, another employee. Jones was later discharged and sued Ann for slander. Was she liable? No. The circumstances of the investigation, the relevance of the matter to the employer's business, and the fact that the statement was privately told to a superior, led to the conclusion that Ann did not make the statement with malice. Because the statement was not made maliciously and was made to a representative of the employer regarding a matter within the range of corporate business, Ann was protected by a qualified privilege from liability for slander.

The media also enjoys a qualified privilege for stories that turn out to be false as long as the information was released without malice (*i.e.,* without intent to harm) and a retraction or correction is made when the matter is brought to the attention of the publishing party.

INTENTIONAL INFLICTION OF EMOTIONAL DISTRESS

At one time, a person could not recover mental distress unless there was a tort associated with the mental distress. However, there is now a separate tort for intentionally causing mental distress. This tort arises when a defendant purposely subjects a plaintiff to unnecessary emotional distress. Outrageous conduct must generally be present. For example, if a person bawls someone out in public with the intent to humiliate the person, this could possibly be the tort of intentional infliction of mental distress. Damages must be proven, however. A collection agency that uses harassing techniques to collect a debt could possibly be held liable for committing this tort.

INVASION OF PRIVACY

Invasion of privacy is the intrusion into the personal life of another, without just cause, which can give the person whose privacy has been invaded a right to bring a lawsuit for damages against the person or entity that intruded. Celebrities are not protected in many situations, since they have voluntarily placed themselves already within the public eye, and their activities are considered newsworthy. However, an otherwise non-public individual has a right to privacy from:

- intrusion on one's solitude or into one's private affairs;
- public disclosure of embarrassing private information;
- publicity which puts him/her in a false light to the public; and
- appropriation of one's name or picture for personal or commercial advantage. Celebrities generally can recovery for this type of breach of privacy

A defense to a charge of invasion of privacy is that the person making the disclosure had a legitimate reason for doing so. For example, investigation of a person's credit when the person has applied for a loan is a legitimate reason. Investigations of insurance claims are privileged.

NEGLIGENCE

Negligence is the failure to follow the degree of care that would be followed by a reasonably prudent person in order to avoid foreseeable harm. A person can be negligent if he or she acts with less care than a reasonable person would use under similar circumstances.

Bob drove a car on a country road at 35 miles an hour. The maximum speed limit was 45 miles an hour. He struck and killed a cow that was crossing the road. The owner of the cow sued Bill for the value of the cow. Bill raised the defense that since he was not driving above the speed limit, there could be no liability for negligence. Was this defense valid? No. A person must at all times act in the manner in which a reasonable person would act under the circumstances. The fact that Bill was driving within the speed limit was only one of the circumstances to consider. The weather or the condition of the road may have made it unreasonable to drive at 35 miles an hour. Driving slower than the speed limit does not in and of itself prove that the driver was acting reasonably.

The reasonable person standard varies in accordance with the situation. The degree of care required of a person is that which an ordinarily prudent person would exercise under *similar circumstances*. This does not necessarily mean a degree of care that would have prevented the harm from occurring. This degree of care varies. For example, if one is engaged in a service involving skill (such as a medical doctor) the care exercised by the doctor must be measured in light of what king of care an ordinarily prudent skilled person *(i.e.,* a doctor) would exercise. The question the jury seeks to determine is what care and skill would reasonably be expected under the circumstances involved in the case.

The elements required to establish negligence are:

- the presence of duty;
- a voluntary act or failure to act that breaches the duty;
- proximate causation of harm; and
- damages (*i.e.,* the breach of duty causes harm to the plaintiff).

Torts involve duties created by law. Just because someone is hurt does not mean that someone else must pay for the harm. There must have been a duty which has been broken. A plaintiff will not be allowed to recover from a defendant if the defendant did not break a duty that was owed to the plaintiff. For example, if a burglar breaks into my house and trips over an item of furniture, I am not liable to the burglar because I had no duty to him. However, if a guest in my house trips over a piece of furniture, I may have a duty to that guest.
The breach of duty must result from a voluntary act or failure to act.

Black was a voluntary psychiatric outpatient treated by Dr. Smith. Dr. Smith became aware that Black was prone to violence. Black told Dr. Smith that he intended to do serious harm to Jones. Shortly thereafter, Black killed Jones. The parents of Jones sued Dr. Smith on the theory that he was liable for the death of their son because he failed to give a warning to Jones or notify the police of Black's threat and violent nature. The court would hold that there was no liability because there was no *duty* to communicate any warning. The court would reach this result on the ground that psychiatry is not such a precise science that the doctor would know that a real danger existed, and it would tend to undermine the confidentiality of the psychiatrist-patient relationship if the psychiatrist were required to give such warnings.

In order for someone to be legally responsible for damages, it is necessary to show that the wrongful act was the *proximate cause* of the harm.

The injury must be shown to be the natural and probable result or consequence of the act of negligence alleged to have been committed. The plaintiff must prove that any negligence of which the defendant is accused proximately caused the Plaintiff's injury. There may be more than one proximate cause of an accident. Multiple acts of negligence by different people may cause the same accident, yet each may be deemed to be a proximate cause of the accident. Sometimes there is an intervening cause which comes after the original negligence of the defendant which may reduce the amount of the defendant's liability. If this intervening cause is the substantial reason for the injury, then the defendant will not be liable at all.

The final element of negligence is *damages.* A plaintiff may recover monetary damages to compensate the plaintiff for economic losses such as lost wages and medical expenses. A plaintiff may also recover noneconomic losses such as for pain and suffering. Punitive damages may also be appropriate. Punitive damages are designed to punish the defendant for his wrongdoing and are generally only appropriate if the plaintiff can prove gross negligence or willful misconduct by the defendant.

DEFENSES TO NEGLIGENCE

If the negligence of the plaintiff is partially responsible for his harm, his recovery from the defendant may be reduced or barred. This is called *contributory* or *comparative* negligence. In a small minority of states, the common law contributory negligence rule is followed which states that if the plaintiff contributes to his harm, he cannot recover from the defendant. In most states, this rule has been rejected because it has been regarded as unjust in situations where the plaintiff's negligence was slight in comparison to the defendant's negligence.

Comparative negligence provides that there should be a comparing of the negligence of the plaintiff and the defendant. This is the rule followed in most states. The negligence of the plaintiff would not bar recovery in these states, but would only reduce the plaintiff's recovery to the extent that the harm was caused by his own negligence. For example, if the jury decides that the plaintiff has sustained damages of $100,000.00, but that his own negligence was one-fourth the cause of the damage, the plaintiff would only be allowed to recover $75,000.00. Some states combine the contributory and comparative negligence rules and refuse to allow the plaintiff to recover anything if his negligence is more than 50% of the cause of the harm.

Assumption of risk is a defense which a defendant can raise which basically states that the plaintiff has knowingly assumed the risk of the harm that was caused. A fan hit by a basketball at a basketball game has assumed the risk of getting hit because it is a known danger that basketballs are thrown into the stands by players (when another player fails to make the catch) from time to time. However, the doctrine of assumption of risk has been watered down by the doctrine of comparative negligence. For example, if a plaintiff drives an automobile knowing his brakes are defective and he fails to stop at a railroad crossing and is therefore hit by a train, comparative or contributory negligence would be more appropriate than assumption of risk, although the plaintiff could arguably be deemed to have assumed the risk of an accident by driving with defective brakes that he knew to be defective.

Kendra took part in a friendly game of touch football. She had played before and was familiar with football. Michael was on her team. In the course of play, Michael bumped into Kendra and knocked her to the ground. He stepped on her hand, causing injury to a little finger that later required its amputation. She sued Michael for damages. He defended on the ground that she had assumed the risk. Kendra claimed that assumption of risk could not be raised as a defense because the state legislature had adopted the standard of comparative negligence and she was not negligent in taking part in the game. There was nothing in the fact of participation in the game that would have alerted a reasonable person to the fact that such an injury was foreseeable. However, having taken part in the game, she voluntarily assumed risks of normal harm that could reasonably be associated with the game. Her experience with the game showed that she knew what could be expected, and there was no proof that the defendant acted recklessly or caused harm intentionally. That is, nothing went beyond the reasonable expectations of a reasonable person. Thus, the comparative negligence statute did not apply, and Kendra claim was barred by her assumption of risk.

IMMUNITY FROM NEGLIGENCE

Certain persons and entities are not subject to tort liability. This is called *immunity* from liability. Governments are generally immune from tort liability. Both states and the federal government have abolished governmental immunity by statute in some situations. For example, under the Federal Tort Claims Act, damages may be recovered from the United States for the negligence of any employee of the United States under circumstances that the United States, if a private person, would have been liable. Very young children are immune from tort liability.

RES IPSA LOQUITUR

The plaintiff ordinarily has the burden of proving that the defendant did not exercise reasonable care and was therefore negligent. The doctrine of *res ipsa loquitur* (the occurrence or thing speaks for itself) permits an inference of negligence when:

- the event is of a kind which ordinarily does not occur in the absence of someone's negligence;
- it is caused by something within the exclusive control of the defendant;
- it is not due to any voluntary action or contribution on the part of the plaintiff; and
- the defendant has superior knowledge as to the cause of the event.

Examples of this doctrine would be its application in the case of objects such as bricks or window panes falling from the defendant's premises, falling elevators, the collapse of structures, and the escape of gas or water from the gas or water main.

Collette worked in a building owned by Acme Company. As part of her job, she was going from one floor to another when the elevator stopped moving. She was alone in the elevator for about an hour before she was rescued. The emergency phone in the elevator was dead. She sued the Acme Company for the mental distress to which she was subjected. Acme Company claimed that it was not liable because there was no proof that it had been negligent. Collette claimed Acme had the burden of proving that it was not negligent. Was she correct? Yes. The concept of res ipsa loquitur justified the conclusion that Acme was negligent, and Acme had the burden of disproving that inference. Res ipsa loquitur has frequently been applied in elevator cases because it applies when (a) the occurrence resulting in injury is such as does not ordinarily happen if those in charge use due care; (b) the instrumentalities involved are under the management and control of the defendant; and (c) the defendant possesses superior knowledge or means of information as to the cause of the occurrence.

NEGLIGENCE PER SE

Negligence per se is negligence due to the violation of a public duty under a law that defines the failure of care required to constitute negligence. For example, driving laws may specify that exceeding a certain rate of speed is legally negligent. Negligence per se may also be declared when a person does or omits to do something which is so beyond reasonable behavior standards that it is negligent on its face. For instance, when a doctor leaves a sponge inside a patient, his actions are inherently negligent.

DIVISION OF LIABILITY

In situations where two or more defendants have caused harm to the plaintiff as a result of the defendants' negligence, they may be held *jointly and severally* (*i.e.,* collectively and individually) liable. Except in partnership situations joint and several liability generally only arises when it is not possible to determine how much harm was caused by each person involved.

FRAUD

Fraud is generally defined in the law as an intentional misrepresentation of material existing fact made by one person to another with knowledge of its falsity and for the purpose of inducing the other person to act, and upon which the other person relies with resulting injury or damage. Fraud may also be made by an omission or purposeful failure to state material facts, which nondisclosure makes other statements misleading.

To constitute fraud, a misrepresentation or omission must also relate to an existing fact', not a promise to do something in the future, unless the person who made the promise did so without any present intent to perform it or with a positive intent not to perform it. Promises to do something in the future or a mere expression of opinion cannot be the basis of a claim of fraud unless the person stating the opinion has exclusive or superior knowledge of existing facts which are inconsistent with such opinion. The false statement or omission must be material, meaning that it was significant to the decision to be made. Sometimes, it must be shown that the plaintiff's reliance was justifiable, and that upon reasonable inquiry would not have discovered the truth of the matter. For injury or damage to be the result of fraud, it must be shown that, except for the fraud, the injury or damage would not have occurred.

To constitute fraud the misrepresentation or omission must be made knowingly and intentionally, not as a result of mistake or accident, or in negligent disregard of its truth or falsity. Also, the plaintiff must prove that the defendant intended for the plaintiff to rely upon the misrepresentation and/or omission; that the plaintiff did in fact rely upon the misrepresentation and/or omission] and that the plaintiff suffered injury or damage as a result of the fraud. Damages may include punitive damages as a punishment or public example due to the malicious nature of the fraud.

There are many state and federal laws to regulate fraud in numerous areas. Some of the areas most heavily litigated include consumer fraud, corporate fraud, and insurance fraud.

LIABILITY OF PARENTS

A parent is not ordinarily liable for a tort committed by a child. However, there are exceptions. If the parent knows that the child has a dangerous tendency, such as the tendency to set things on fire, the parent could be liable if the parent did not take reasonable steps to prevent such an occurrence. Such steps could be getting psychological counseling for the child or watching the child very thoroughly.

If a child is a reckless driver and the parent knows that the child is a reckless driver, the parent might be liable if the child uses the parent's car with the parent's permission and causes an accident. This is called *negligent entrustment.*

In about half of the states of the U.S., a parent supplying a family car to a family member (child) is liable for any harm negligently caused by the family member (child). This assumption of liability is normally agreed to by the parent when he/she signs the minor child’s driver’s license application.

BUSINESS TORTS
In general, the term "business torts" refers to the intentional and improper interference with the business interests of another.

UNFAIR COMPETITION
Unfair competition is very similar to trademark and service mark infringement. It is unfair competition to imitate signs, store fronts, advertisements, and the packaging of goods of a competitor. The essence of an unfair competition claim is that one business has done something that confuses the public about another business's product in a way that is so improper that a court needs to stop it or award damages to protect the commercial market.

The actor, director, and writer Woody Allen was involved in an interesting unfair competition case in the U. S. District Court for the Southern District of New York in 1985[6]. Mr. Allen sued a look-alike and others because of an advertisement for video-rental stores using an actor that looked like him who was filmed renting videos from one of the defendants. The court found in favor of Mr. Allen on the theory that the public might well think that the picture was of Woody Allen, or that Woody Allen was in some way endorsing the product.

PRODUCT DISPARAGEMENT
Damages may also result from the tort of disparagement of goods or slander of title. This would occur when a person makes a false statement about one businessman's title to goods or the quality of goods, and the result of the statement causes another person or persons to refrain from dealing with the plaintiff.

WRONGFUL INTERFERENCE WITH CONTRACTS
Wrongful interference with a person's contract or with his right to earn a living can be a tort. This tort has been called contract interference or tortuous interference with contracts. The interference must generally be intentional and without legal justification. Of course, the right to make a living or to conduct one's business is subject to the rights of others, and legitimate competition between businesses in seeking to gain customers would not give rise to this tort. This tort can be difficult to prove because of the right of competition. Generally, it is necessary to prove that the defendant intentionally persuaded another to *breach a contract* with the plaintiff.

In a 1988 Texas case, a city hired a consulting engineer who recommended that the city terminate the contract of a person because of the person's defective work. The employee sued the engineer. The consulting engineer was held not liable for intentional interference with the terminated employee's contract because the consulting engineer was under a duty to keep the city properly informed of the quality of the employee's work when it was defective. However, if the consulting engineer had advised the city to fire a clerical worker just because the consulting engineer did not like the clerical worker, this could give rise to the tort of intentional interference with the contract of another.

---

[6] **610 F. Supp. 612 (S.D.N.Y. 1985)**

COMPUTER TORTS

Both federally and among the states, law involving technology, especially virtual environments and resources, is an emerging domain. Damage to the hardware of a computer will impose tort liability under the same principles of law as would apply if it were a typewriter or a car or any other tangible piece of property. Intentionally damaging software can also give rise to civil liability. Theft of computer hardware or software constitutes the tort of conversion.

Negligent use of a computer is a tort. If someone knows that a computer is not operating properly, but continues to use it and causes damages to a third person due to computer errors, the computer user can be liable for negligence. A company may be liable to persons who are harmed because the company's management:

- Negligently failed to maintain its computers, resulting in computer error; or
- Negligently hiring, or failing to supervise, its computer operators.

The law regarding protection of privacy applies whether a computer is involved or not. However, computers have resulted in a greater awareness of possible invasions of privacy. This is because so much information can be stored in computers very quickly and easily. Therefore, computers can share information about you and can compile a great deal of data about you in one place very quickly. A person who wrongfully discloses personal, computerized, information regarding others can be liable for damages. A company may be liable if it negligently hires, or fails to supervise, an employee who releases private information regarding others. In some States, a firm may be liable if it maintains inadequate computer security, thus enabling an outsider to obtain private information.

A person's credit standing or reputation can be damaged if a computer contains false information, and this false information is supplied to a third person. In order to avoid liability, the person in control of the data must exercise reasonable care to prevent errors and to correct errors. Liability under this theory would be called defamation by computer.

Employers in a city formed an association to exchange information on job applicants. In a computer, the association stored information received from members about the grounds for discharging employees. Mary had been employed as a bank teller. She was later fired because she was arrested for embezzlement of bank funds. Mary was never able to obtain other work in the community because of the computer printout of the association showing her arrest. She sued the association for defamation. It raised the defense that she had been arrested for embezzlement. She replied that it was publicly known that shortly after she was arrested, she was released because it was established that the embezzlement had been committed by a cashier in the bank and that the cashier was arrested and convicted for the crime. Is the association protected by the fact that the computer was correct in what it stated? No. The association was clearly negligent in failing to update its records. It was obvious that Mary’s arrest would have a significant effect on her reputation. The association was therefore under the duty to take notice of the conviction of the cashier and to clear the record as to Mary. Having failed to do so, the association is not protected from defamation liability.

WRONGFUL DISCHARGE

Under the *employment at will* doctrine, the employer has historically been allowed to terminate the contract at any time for any reason or for no reason. Some State Courts and some State Legislatures have changed this rule by limiting the power of the employer to discharge the employee without cause. For example, Court decisions have carved out exceptions to this doctrine when the discharge violates an established public policy, such as discharging an employee in retaliation for insisting that the employer comply with the State's Food and Drug Act. Most states recognize two public policy exceptions to the employee-at-will doctrine:

- One is the whistle-blower defense that protects employees against discharge for reporting illegal conduct or conduct that violates public policy;

- Another protects employees who refuse to participate in illegal conduct.

Courts may sometimes construe an employer's statements concerning continued employment as a part of the employment contract, and therefore require good cause for the discharge of an at-will employee. Also, written personnel policies used as guidelines for the employer's supervisors have been interpreted as restricting the employer's right to discharge at-will employees without just cause. Employee handbooks or personnel manuals have been construed as part of the employee's contract. This is why all personnel manuals and employee handbooks should contain a disclaimer. A sample disclaimer would be: *This employee handbook is not intended to create any contractual rights in favor of you or the company. The company reserves the right to change the terms of this employee handbook at any time.*

Pursuant to federal law and some state statutes, employers cannot lawfully discriminate against employees on the basis of age, race, sex, national origin, disability, religion or color. *Anti-retaliation statutes* protect many employees of state and federal agencies. They generally prohibit the firing, demotion, reprimands, and pay cuts of employees who report the misconduct of their employees.

CONVERSION

Conversion is a civil claim that can be brought when a party wrongfully takes another's money or property. Conversion is any act of control wrongfully exerted over another's personal property. The control exerted must cause an actual interference with one's ownership or right of possession. Neither legal title nor absolute ownership of the property is necessary. A party need only prove that he was entitled to immediate possession at the time of conversion. The fact that plaintiff regained possession of the converted property does not prevent him from suing for damages for the conversion.

A manual taking of the property is not necessary; it is only necessary to show that someone assumed control or ownership over the property, or that the alleged converter has applied the property to his or her own use. A person who converts another's property to their own use must pay damages for the value of the past use of the property even if it is returned.

FALSE IMPRISONMENT
False imprisonment involves detaining a person without that person's consent. It can take the extreme form of kidnapping or the less extreme form of detaining a shopper for suspected shoplifting without reasonable grounds.

A defense to false imprisonment would be consent of the detainee, or if a store owner had reasonable grounds to believe that the detainee was guilty of shoplifting (shopkeeper's privilege). This privilege allows a store owner (or his employee) to detain a suspected shoplifter based on reasonable suspicion for a reasonable time. This privilege applies even if the store owner was wrong about the customer so long as the owner actions were based on reasonable suspicions and treated the customer in a reasonable manner. This privilege does not protect the owner from damages due to the use of unnecessary force in detaining the customer.

A customer was shopping at the handbag counter of the defendant's store. She did not make any purchase and left the store. When she was a few feet away from the store, an employee of the store tapped her lightly on the shoulder to attract her attention and asked her if she had made any purchase. When she inquired why, the employee asked, "What about that bag in your hand?" The customer said that it belonged to her and she opened it to show by its contents that it was not a new bag. The employee gave the customer a "real dirty look" and went back into the store without saying a word. The customer then sued the store for false imprisonment. Was the store liable? No. Judgment would be for the store. There was no false imprisonment because there was no actual detaining of the customer. The circumstances did not show the use of force or threat of force that stopped the customer from proceeding on her way. Her action of stopping and showing the contents of her handbag was voluntary.

MALPRACTICE
Malpractice is a failure by an physician or other professional to use the care and skill that other members of their profession would use under similar circumstances. When an accountant, doctor, attorney, or some other professional contracts to perform services, there is a duty to exercise skill and care as is common within the community for persons performing similar services. Failure to fulfill that duty is malpractice.

Chapter 9

INTELLECTUAL PROPERTY RIGHTS

In contrast to real estate and tangible personal property, Intellectual Property refers to what the minds of men and women have created.

TRADEMARKS AND SERVICE MARKS

A "trademark" is a word, design or combination used by an individual or a business to identify its goods or services. In some cases a trademark can also be a sensory mark–a sound, a color or a smell. While marks identifying services rather than goods are technically referred to a "service marks" we will use the term trademarks to include service marks. Trademarks protect names used to identify goods (or services) and their source of origin. The law protects trademarks in part because trademarked items tend to carry with them certain quality assurances - one would expect an automobile carrying the *Rolls Royce* trademark to be far superior to most other automobiles. You may use any kind of name or symbol as a trademark to identify your product.

A mark is any word, name, symbol, or design that identifies a product or service. A *trademark* identifies a product (for example, *Coca-Cola*). A *service mark* identifies a service (for example, *Holiday Inn*). A mark may be registered with the United States Patent and Trademark Office (USPTO) if the mark distinguishes a person's product or service from products or services of competitors. Registration of a mark on the *Principal Register* of the USPTO entitles a person the exclusive use of the mark. Registration can also be accomplished with a State (usually with the Secretary of State of a particular state). However, State registration does not provide as much protection as Federal registration. Before a mark can be registered, it must be used by the "owner," and it must distinguish goods or services from others. The owner of a mark cannot register it with the United States Patent and Trademark Office unless the mark is used in interstate commerce.

Generic terms that merely describe a class of products cannot be registered. For example, the term *motor oil* or the word *airline* would not be accepted for registration. Descriptive or geographical terms cannot be registered unless they have acquired a secondary meaning. A mark acquires a secondary meaning when, through long usage, the public identifies the mark with a particular product. For example, *Best Western* Motels involves a mark which has a secondary meaning.

One can be an owner of a trademark or service mark, whether or not it is registered. This is common law protection. Registration is proof of ownership and makes ownership rights easier to enforce. The basic question in lawsuits over marks is whether or not the general public is likely to be confused as to the origin of the service or product.

If the owner of a mark permits widespread use of the mark to describe a general class of products, the exclusive right to the mark may be lost. Two examples are *cellophane* and *aspirin.*

Trade dress is the total appearance of a product, including its packaging, label, shape, and size. Trade dress may also include physical structures associated with a particular product or service, such as the "golden arches" of McDonald's. Trade dress may qualify as a protected trademark or service mark if it is distinctive and identifies the source of a specific product or service.

COPYRIGHTS

A "copyright" offers protection for original works of authorship. Copyright protection affords the author of a copyrighted work with specific rights that the author can give or sell to others or keep for him/herself. The concept of copyright protection in the United States is set forth in the original U.S. Constitution which allows Congress to pass laws that promote and encourage the process of the useful arts.

The word *copyright* can be defined as a property right in an original work of authorship (such as a literary, musical, artistic, photographic, or film work) fixed in any tangible medium of expression, giving the holder the exclusive right to reproduce, adapt, distribute, perform, and display the work. Copyright protection may be received regarding a wide range of creative, intellectual, or artistic forms or *works*. These include poems, plays, and other literary works, movies, choreographic works (dances, ballets, etc.), musical compositions, audio recordings, paintings, drawings, sculptures, photographs, radio and television broadcasts. The creator of the work has a limited monopoly on the work and can, with some exceptions, prohibit others from copying or displaying the work. The United States copyright law is contained in Chapters 1 through 8 and 10 through 12 of Title 17 of the *United States Code.*

Works published after 1922, but before 1978 are protected for 95 years from the date of publication. If the work was created, but not published, before 1978, the copyright lasts for the life of the author plus 70 years. However, even if the author died over 70 years ago, the copyright in an unpublished work lasts until December 31, 2002. And if such a work is published before December 31, 2002, the copyright will last until December 31, 2047.

All works published in the United States before 1923 are in the *public domain.* The term public domain refers to creative materials that are not protected by intellectual property laws such as copyright, trademark or patent laws. The public owns these works, not an individual author or artist. Anyone can use a public domain work without obtaining permission, but no one can ever own it. Once a copyright expires, it is in the public domain and no longer has protection. Works created by the federal government are also in the public domain.

A copyright is obtained simply by creating the work. It comes into existence automatically on the date it is created. However, in order to get federal protection of a copyright, the creator of the work has to file two copies of the work with the Copyright Office in Washington, D.C.

Copyright law is designed to create an incentive for creativity by allowing the author to profit from his work. The Act tries to balance this need to protect the author with the public's need for free and open discussion. A copyright owner has the exclusive right to:

- reproduce the work;
- prepare derivative works, such as a script from the original work (*e.g.,* movie script for Book *The Rainmaker*);
- distribute copies or recordings of the work; and
- publicly display the work in the case of paintings, sculptures and photographs.

The Copyright Act contains several exemptions that allow a person or institution to use or copy a copyrighted work without the owner's permission. Three commonly used exemptions are:

- the fair use doctrine which allows copying for such purposes such as teaching;
- the right of libraries to make limited copies; and
- certain performances and displays for teaching or religious purposes.

The *fair use* doctrine allows reasonable use of copyrighted works (without requiring the author's permission) for teaching, research, and news reporting. The Federal Act states: "[T]he fair use of a copyrighted work, including such use by reproduction in copies . . . for purposes such as criticism, comment, news reporting, teaching (including multiple copies for classroom use), scholarship, or research, is not an infringement of copyright."

There are four important factors that must be looked at when determining whether or not the fair use doctrine applies:

- the purpose of the use, including whether such use is of a commercial nature or is for nonprofit educational purposes;
- the nature of the copyrighted work;
- the amount of the portion used in relation to the copyrighted work as a whole; and
- the effect of the use on the potential market for or value of the copyrighted work.

If a work is a "work made for hire," this means that a person was hired specifically to create the copyrighted work. The employer of the creator of the work can register the copyright and is entitled to protection.

PATENTS

A "patent" is a grant of a property right by the Government to an inventor. The United States Constitution gives Congress the right to provide for patent protection in legislation in order to encourage useful inventions. The patent itself provides a detailed description of the invention, and how it is used or how to make it. Thus, if you obtain a patent you cannot keep the matter secret, which is the province of Trade Secret Law. A patent enables the owner to exclude others from making, using or selling the invention for the life of the patent.

Federal statutes give an inventor the exclusive right to use, sell, and market his invention. The types of things that can be patented are things that are new, useful, and not obvious to those in the business to which the invention relates. An invention also may be a process, a new chemical or even a new type of plant.

Patents are granted by the U.S. Patent and Trademark Office in Washington, D.C. There are three types of patents:

- *Utility Patents:* These are granted for most new products or processes and are valid for 20 years;
- *Design Patents:* These are granted for new and original designs for manufactured goods and are good for 20 years;
  Plant Patents: These are granted for developing a new type of plant.

The difference between a design patent and a utility patent is that a design patent protects the ornamental design, configuration, improved decorative appearance, or shape of an invention. This patent is appropriate when the basic product already exists in the marketplace and is not being improved upon in function but only in style. For example, designer eyeglass frames, the original Coca-Cola bottles, and "Pet Rocks" would have all been protected with design patents. A U.S. design patent generally lasts for 14 years.

A utility patent protects any new invention or *functional* improvements on existing inventions. This can be to a product, machine, a process, or even composition of matter. Examples of a utility patent would include a better carburetor, a new type of self-fastening diaper or a new recipe. The life of a U.S. utility patent lasts 20 years from the date of filing assuming the patent is granted, but the owner of the patent must pay maintenance fees to the United States Patent and Trademark Office (USPTO) to keep a utility patent from expiring.

A plant patent may be issued for a new and distinct, invented or discovered asexually reproduced plant including cultivated mutants, hybrids, and newly found seedlings, other than a plant found in an uncultivated state. A plant patent permits its owner to exclude others from making, using, or selling the plant for a period of up to twenty years from the date of patent application filing. Plant patents are not subject to the payment of maintenance fees.

Before a patent is granted the applicant must submit his idea to a patent examiner in the patent office who will make a determination as the whether or not the invention is new and not obvious to a person of ordinary skill in the area in which the invention is related. The examiner's decision can be appealed to the Board of Patent Appeals or the Court of Appeals for D.C. circuit.

The owner of a patent is required to mark the word patent on the item patented and also put the patent number on the item. Failure to do this can prevent the patent holder from recovering damages is an infringement case.

Employers sometimes require employees to sign an agreement to assign any right to an invention of the employee to the employer. The invention must be related to the employer's business, or this assignment would possibly be void as a violation of public policy.

TRADE SECRETS

A formula, process, or information that is secret, and gives its owner a business advantage may be protected under State laws concerning trade secrets. Trade secrets, basically, are any formula, device, or information that is used in a business, and is of such a nature that it gives the owner an advantage over competitors who do not have the information. Customer lists may be protected unless they can be easily developed from public information. Trade secrets are protected under State law rather than Federal law. This protection may be by virtue of common law or statutory law, such as the Uniform Trade Secrets Act. When a trade secret is made public, it loses its protection as a trade secret unless it is disclosed in a restrictive manner to persons who know of its confidential nature.

Generally, computer programs may be copyrighted. The Computer Software Copyright Act protects copyrighted programs from infringement. In some cases, computer programs may be patented. However, since patents are public record, there is a danger that the program might be copied by someone. Trade secrets laws are sometimes used to protect computer programs.

Sometimes creators of software will require users to sign a licensing agreement which provides greater protection than the copyright laws. Sample restrictions include limited reverse engineering, which is a method of learning the structure of a program and limiting the renting of the program of third parties in order to prevent unauthorized copying.

REMEDIES FOR VIOLATION OF PROPERTY RIGHTS

When property is harmed, taken, or destroyed, the most common remedy is an action for monetary damages. The property itself may be recovered if unlawfully taken. Wrongful use of a copyright, trademark, service mark, or patent can result in injunctive action, as well as a suit for damages. If an infringement is intentional, profits resulting from the infringement may also be obtained.

Infringement of a trademark or service mark occurs when a person uses or copies the trademark or service mark of another person without the person's permission. (e.g., putting *Nike* label on shoes and selling them)

Chapter 10

CONTRACT LAW

A contract is a binding agreement between two or more parties. This agreement creates one or more obligations. Each party to a contract is legally bound to do, or to refrain from doing, certain acts. The essence of a contract is that by mutual agreement, parties create obligations that can be legally enforced.

The elements of a contract are: an agreement; between competent parties; based upon the genuine assent of the parties; supported by consideration; made for a lawful objective; and in the form required by law.

A contract may relate to virtually any type of transaction. Contracts may relate to performance of a service, sale, or transfer of ownership of property, or a combination of these types of transactions. Parties to a contract may be individuals, partnerships, corporations, or even governments. There may be more than two persons to a contract. With some exceptions, only the parties making a contract have rights or duties under the contract.

It is possible for other persons to have rights and duties with respect to a contract other than the original parties to the contract. For example, rights under a contract may be assigned to a third person. Also, a contract may be made for the benefit of a third person as in a life insurance contract. A life insurance contract involves the insurance company, the insured, and the beneficiary.

A valid contract is a legally-binding contract that is made in accordance with all legal requirements. A voidable contract is an agreement that would be binding and enforceable except the circumstances surrounding its execution, or the fact that one of the parties lacks "capacity," makes the contract voidable at the option of one of the parties. For example, a person who has been forced to sign an agreement may avoid being bound by the agreement. A void agreement is an agreement which is without legal effect. For example, an agreement which deals with the performance of an illegal act is void.

An executed contract is a contract that has been completely performed. Nothing remains to be done by either party. For example, if you go into a furniture store and agree with the salesman to pay $400.00 for a chair and then pay the salesman cash and take delivery of the furniture, the contract has been completely executed. In an executory contract, something remains to be done by one or both of the parties. If a contract is executed between a seller and a buyer regarding the purchase of land, and both parties agree that the sale will be consummated after the buyer obtains his loan and the seller gives a certificate of title (showing no defects), the contract is enforceable, but it is said to be executory.

An option contract is a contract that gives the right to one party to enter into a second contract with the other party at a later date. One of the most common forms of option contracts deals with the sale of real estate. In this type of contract, the prospective buyer will be granted an option to purchase the property within a specified period of time. The prospective buyer will pay the seller a sum of money since the seller is, in effect, taking the property off the market during the option period. If the prospective buyer exercises his option during that time, a second contract is entered into regarding the sale of the property. If the option period expires, then neither party has any obligation to the other. The money paid to the seller for the option is retained by the seller.

AGREEMENT

One of the essential elements of a contract is an agreement. An agreement shows that the parties have bound themselves to act or refrain from acting in a manner specified by the contract. It is essential to a contract that there be an offer and, while the offer is still in existence, it must be accepted without qualification. An offer expresses the willingness of the offeror to enter into a contract agreement regarding a particular subject. A contract is based upon an agreement. An agreement arises when one person, the offeror, makes an offer and the person to whom is made, the offeree, accepts. There must be both an offer and an acceptance. If either is not present, there is no contract. An offeror may make an offer to a particular person or it may be made to the public at large (for example, a reward offered to the public for return of lost property).

To constitute an offer, the offeror must intend to create a legal obligation, or he must appear to intend to create a legal obligation. This intent can be shown by conduct. For example, when one party signs a written contract and sends it to the other party, this action is obviously an offer to enter into a contract on the terms of the writing. Again, the offeror must intend to create a legal obligation. No contract comes into being when an offer is made jokingly, or under any other circumstances that would cause a reasonable person to believe there was no intent to enter into a binding agreement.

An invitation to negotiate is not an offer. An invitation to negotiate is merely a preliminary discussion or an invitation by one party to the other to negotiate or make an offer. For example, a school asking a teacher whether or not the teacher wishes to continue teaching at the school the following year is a preliminary discussion and not an offer that could be accepted. If the teacher indicated that he would like to continue teaching, then a formal offer could be made.

Generally, newspaper advertisements, price quotations, and catalog prices are just invitations to negotiate and cannot be accepted in a contractually-binding manner. No seller has an unlimited supply of any commodity and therefore cannot possibly be deemed to have intended to make a contract with everyone who sees the advertisement or seeks to accept the price offered.

Assuming that an offer is made with intent to be bound, it still is not a legal offer unless it is communicated to the offeree. This offer may be communicated by the offeror or at his direction. If the offeree hears about the offer indirectly, through the grapevine so to speak, he cannot accept the offer until it is communicated to him by the offeror or at the offeror's direction.

An offer can be withdrawn before acceptance and therefore prevent a contract from arising. If an offer is terminated, an attempted acceptance after the termination has no legal effect. Ordinarily, an offer may be revoked at any time by the offeror. All that is required is the showing by the offeror of his intent to revoke the offer and communication of this intent to the offeree.

Offers may be terminated in any one of the following ways: Revocation of the offer by the offeror; counteroffer by offeree; rejection of offer by offeree; lapse of time; death or disability of either party; or performance of the contract becomes illegal after the offer is made.

The general rule is that the revocation is effective only when it is made known to the offeree. Until it is communicated to the offeree, directly or indirectly, the offeree has reason to believe that there still is an offer that may be accepted. The offeree may rely on this belief. If the offeror seeks to revoke the offer, but the offeree accepts the offer before notice of the revocation, a valid contract is created.

A conditional acceptance is a counteroffer. For example, if Jones accepts the $10,000.00 price, but adds a term by stating that new tires must be put on the car, this is a conditional acceptance and therefore a counteroffer.

A rejection terminates an offer. A rejection is an offeree's communication that an offer is unacceptable.

When an offer states that it will be open until a particular date, the offer terminates on that date if it has not yet been accepted. This is particularly clear when the offeror declares that the offer shall be void after the expiration of a specific time. If the time passes, and the offeree attempts to accept the offer, this is in effect a counteroffer from the offeree and can be accepted or rejected by the offeror.

If the offer does not specify a time, it will terminate after a reasonable period of time has passed. What constitutes a reasonable time depends on the circumstances of each case. For example, if the commodity to be sold or purchased is a perishable commodity, such as food, the reasonable time would be shorter than if the matter to be sold is machinery.

If either the offeror or the offeree dies or becomes mentally incompetent before the offer is accepted, the offer is automatically deemed to be terminated.

If the performance of the contract becomes illegal after the offer is made, the offer is deemed to be terminated. For example, if there is an offer made to sell alcoholic beverages to a store, but a city ordinance is passed prohibiting the sale of alcoholic beverages before the offer is accepted, the offer is terminated.

If the offeror does not otherwise specify, a mailed acceptance takes effect when the acceptance is properly mailed. This is known as the "Mailbox Rule." If the offeror specifies that an acceptance shall not be effective until received, there is no acceptance until acceptance is received. The Mailbox Rule also would not apply in a situation where the offeror requires receipt of a payment to accompany an acceptance. Improper mailing of an acceptance can cause the acceptance to take effect only when received.

Smith owned land. Jones mailed an offer to Smith to buy his land. Smith agreed to this offer and mailed back a contract signed by him. While this letter was in transit, Smith orally notified

Jones that his acceptance was revoked. Was Smith bound by a contract? Yes, since the acceptance was effective when mailed. Subsequent revocation had no effect.

COMPETENT PARTIES

The law generally presumes that everyone has the capacity to contract. But if a party does lack capacity, then the contract is usually voidable and the party without capacity may avoid the contract.

Parties to an agreement must have contractual capacity before the agreement will be binding on both parties. Contractual capacity is the ability to understand that a contract is being made and to understand its general nature. The fact that a person does not fully understand the full meaning and all ramifications of a contract does not mean that the person lacks contractual capacity.

Some classes of persons such as people under the age of 21, or in most states, under the age of 18, are deemed by law to lack contractual capacity. The common law rule was, and is, that anyone under the age of 21 years is a minor. However, many states have reduced the age limit from 21 to 18 years. Some states have the age of majority as 19.

With some exceptions, a contract made by a minor is voidable. The minor, in other words, may avoid the legal liability under a contract. Upon reaching the age of majority, a minor may affirm or ratify the contract and therefore make it contractually binding on him. Any expression of the minor's intention to avoid the contract will accomplish avoidance.

A minor can only avoid a contract during his minority status and only for a reasonable time after he reaches the age of majority. After a reasonable period of time, the contract is deemed to be ratified and cannot be avoided.

When a minor avoids a contract, there are certain rules of law regarding the effect on any property received by the minor under the contract. If the minor still has what he received from the other party, he must return it to the other party upon seeking to avoid the contract. If he does not return the property in such a situation, he cannot avoid the contract. If the minor cannot return what he has received pursuant to the contract because it has been spent, damaged or destroyed, he still can avoid the contract. He can avoid the contract and is only required to return that part of the consideration he still has. Even if he has nothing left, or what he has is damaged property, he still can avoid the contract.

Helen, age 17, wanted to buy a motorcycle. She did not have the money to pay cash but persuaded the dealer to sell a cycle to her on credit. The dealer did so partly because Helen said that she was 22 and showed the dealer an identification card that falsely stated her age as 22. Helen drove the motorcycle away. A few days later, she damaged it and then returned it to the dealer and stated that she avoided the contract because she was a minor. The dealer said that she could not do so because (a) she had misrepresented her age and (b) the motorcycle was damaged. Can she avoid the contract? Yes. In a state that follows the common law rule, neither the damage to the property nor Helen's misrepresentation of her age will prevent her from avoiding the contract. Some states would hold that because of the misrepresentation of age, Helen must pay for the damage that she has done, but she can avoid the contract. A few states would hold that Helen cannot avoid the contract because she misrepresented her age.

After a minor reaches the age of majority, he can ratify the contract. Once the contract has been ratified, the ex-minor cannot change his mind and avoid the contract. Ratification consists of any words or conduct of the minor which shows an intent to be bound by the contract. For example, Smith buys a car from Jones Ford Company for $10,000.00 when Smith is 17 years of age. Smith finances the car with Jones for 5 years making installment payments each month. Smith reaches his 18th birthday and continues to make payments for two months to Jones and then has a wreck. Smith decides that he is going to avoid the contract and get his $10,000.00 back. However, the fact that Smith reached the age of 18 and continued to make payments on the car and use the car would keep him from being able to avoid the contract. Smith's conduct constituted a ratification of the contract. However, many Courts refuse to recognize payment as ratification unless further evidence is given of an intent to ratify a contract or an understanding by a minor that payment might constitute a ratification. In the situation with Smith and Jones, Jones would argue that Smith continued to use the car after he reached 18 as well as made payments on the car.

Parents of a minor are not liable regarding the contracts made by the minor merely because they are the parents of the minor. However, if a minor makes a contract and a parent or any other adult signs along with the minor as a co-signer, the parent or other adult can be held liable. For example, if Smith, who is a minor, buys a car from Jones Auto and Smith's father co-signs the loan documents with Smith, Smith's father can be held liable on the loan even if Smith seeks to avoid the contract.

A person who is mentally incompetent (non compos mentis) lacks the capacity to make a contract. The cause of the mental incompetency is immaterial. It can be the result of a mental illness, excessive use of drugs or alcohol, a stroke, etc. If the person does not have the mental capacity to understand that a contract is being made or the general nature of the contract, the person lacks contractual capacity. A person who is mentally incompetent may ordinarily avoid a contract in the same manner as a minor. If the person later becomes competent, he can ratify or avoid the contract at that time.

CONSENT

The third element of contract deals with the consent or understanding of the parties regarding the proposed contract. The consent or assent of a party to an agreement must be genuine and voluntary. This assent will not be genuine or voluntary in certain cases of mistake, deception or undue pressure

The agreement of parties may be affected by the fact that one or both of them made a mistake. A unilateral mistake is a mistake made by one party to the agreement. A mistake that is unknown to the other party usually does not affect the enforceability of the agreement. A unilateral mistake regarding a fact does not affect the contract. For example, if a customer orders a water-resistant coat thinking that this means waterproof, the customer cannot get out of the contract unless the sale was made with some sort of misrepresentation as to the meaning of those words.

An exception to this would be if the seller knew that the buyer misunderstood those terms, but went ahead and sold the coat anyway.

Adam claimed that Bill owed him money. Adam was under the impression that Bill did not have much money. On the basis of this impression, Adam made a settlement agreement with Bill for a nominal amount. When Adam later learned that Bill was in fact reasonably wealthy, Adam sought to set the agreement aside. Was Adam entitled to do so? No. A unilateral mistake of fact does not affect the binding character of an agreement. Bill made no misrepresentation and therefore was not guilty of fraud. There was no obligation on Bill to volunteer any information as to his financial condition.

Failure to read a document before signing it can cause the signer to be liable under the terms of the document. For example, suppose the president of ABC Corporation signs a promissory note in two places without reading it. In one place he was signing as president of the corporation. However, in the other place, he signed under a statement that said that if the corporation defaulted on the loan, the president would personally pay for the debt. In such a situation, unless there was misrepresentation involved, the president could be held personally liable due to his negligence in not carefully reading the document.

A person who has the ability and the opportunity to read a document before signing it is contractually bound by the terms of the document even if the person signed it without reading it. The signer cannot avoid liability based on the argument that no explanation was given to him as to the terms of the contract.

Even if a person is unable to read or understand the terms of the agreement, he is still bound by the terms of the agreement since he should have tried to obtain an explanation of the agreement. The exception to this rule is that if the other party knows, or has reason to know, that the signer cannot read nor has a limited education, some courts would hold that the contracting party should have read the document to the other party or explained the terms.

If a party relies on the explanation of another party as to the contents of the agreement, the contract may be avoided under two circumstances:

- The party was justified in relying on the explanation of the other party; and
- The explanation was fraudulent.

The party making the explanatory statements does not have to be a lawyer, but can be any person who handles this type agreement on a regular basis and therefore has a greater knowledge of the content than the other person. This rule would not apply if the agreement was negotiated between the two parties and therefore both parties had an understanding of the terms as evidenced by the negotiation.

If both parties to an agreement make the same mistake regarding a key factual matter, the agreement is void. For example, a contract is void if both parties mistakenly believe that the contract can be performed when, in fact, it is impossible to perform it. For example, suppose Smith promises over lunch to sell Jones an antique car in Smith's garage. Assume both parties believe the automobile is in Smith's garage. However, the car had been destroyed by fire an hour before the agreement and Smith had not learned of this. Since this fact was unknown to both parties, there is a mutual mistake as to the possibility of performing the contract. The agreement is therefore void.

When parties to an agreement make a mistake as to the legal effect of the contract, the contract is still binding. For example, suppose Smith sold Jones a vacant lot and Jones planned to build an office on the lot. Both Smith and Jones assume that this would be a lawful use of the property. However, if after purchasing the property and applying for a building permit, Jones is told that the property is zoned for residential use, the contract is still binding. However, if the contract had represented that the property could be used for the building of an office, it could be rescinded by Jones.

Rescission of a contract means to put the parties back in the same circumstances they were in before making the agreement. If the agreement involved the sale of goods, the goods would be returned to the seller and the money for the goods would be returned to the buyer.

When one party to a contract knows of a fact that has a bearing on the transaction, the failure to disclose this information to the other party is called nondisclosure. Generally, the law does not attach any significance to nondisclosure. The theory is that it is preferable that the party lacking the knowledge ask questions of the party with the knowledge rather than imposing some sort of duty on the party with the knowledge to volunteer the information. Thus, generally, an agreement of the parties is not affected by the fact that one party did not disclose material information to the other party.

Ordinarily there is no duty on a party to a contract to volunteer information to the other party. The nondisclosure of information that is not asked for by a party does not hurt the validity of the contract. For example, Jones wants to buy Smith's house. Jones, prior to signing the contract, makes an inspection of the house and sees several cracks in the roof and walls. He assumes that these cracks are just the result of the house settling. Smith makes no disclosure one way or another about the cracks. Jones buys the house and later discovers that the house has severe foundation problems. He sues Smith for the damages incurred in repairing the foundation problems. Under the general rule, Smith would have been under no duty to disclose the foundation problems to Jones

There are some exceptions to this general rule regarding nondisclosure. In some instances, the failure to disclose information that was not requested can be regarded as fraudulent, giving the party harmed by the nondisclosure the same remedies as if a statement were fraudulently made. These exceptions fall generally into one of four categories:

- Unknown defect or condition;
- Confidential relationship;
- Fine print; and
- Active concealment.

Many courts would hold that there is a duty for one party, who knows of a defect or a harmful condition, to disclose this information to the other party if:

- the defect or harmful condition is obviously unknown to the other party and
- is of a nature that the other party would be unlikely to discover or inquire about the defect or condition.

Going back to the other hypothetical about Jones buying Smith's house, assume that Smith, while not a professional engineer or building contractor, did have some knowledge about foundations. Smith also knew that several of his neighbors had foundation trouble due to the type of soil in their neighborhood. He therefore had reason to know that the cracks in his wall and roof were the result of foundation problems and not the result of the house simply settling. Assume that Jones did not know that the neighbors of Smith had foundation problems. In this situation, Jones would have a strong argument that the contract should be rescinded or that Smith should pay Jones damages for the cost of repairs to the foundation.

If two parties have a confidential relationship, such as that of attorney and client, the attorney has a duty to reveal anything that is material to his client when dealing with this client in a business matter. The attorney's silence has the same legal consequences as knowingly making a false statement of a material fact to his client.

Courts may find an intent to conceal when a printed contract contains clauses in such fine print that it is reasonable to believe that the other party will not take the time to read the provisions. Of course, no relief will be granted if the fine print is not material. In other words, if the provisions in fine print are such that the party reading the contract would have entered into the contract in any event, the provisions in the fine print would not cause the contract to be invalid.

Active concealment can cause a contract to be invalid or result in liability to the concealing party. This is more than a failure to volunteer information. Active concealment consists of hiding information from the other party by concealment. For example, using the Smith and Jones house transaction as an example, suppose that Smith had painted over the cracks in the wall and the ceiling in order to hide the foundation problem. He would be guilty of active concealment and the contract could be rescinded, or Jones could recover damages from Smith in the amount of the foundation repair costs.

Fraud consists of five elements:

- The making of a false statement;
- With knowledge that the statement is false or with reckless disregard as to whether or not the statement is false or true;
- With the intent that the listener rely on the statement;
- With the result that the listener relies on the statement;
- With the consequence that the listener is harmed.

Smith was thinking of buying the house of Jones. Smith noticed watermarks on the ceiling, but Jones stated that the roof had been repaired and was in good condition. Smith was not told that the roof still leaked and that the repairs had not been able to stop the leaking. Smith bought the house. Sometime later, heavy rains caused water to leak into the house. Smith claimed that Jones was guilty of fraud. Was he correct? Yes. The statement that the roof had been repaired would suggest to the ordinary person that the repairs had been successful. This conclusion was reinforced by the statement that the roof was "in good condition." The net result was that what was said and what was not said had the effect of representing an untrue condition of the roof and therefore misled Smith and caused him to be harmed. Because this was done with knowledge of the true facts, Jones had committed fraud.

An essential element in proving fraud is to prove that one relied on the statement which is alleged to be fraudulent. If the alleged victim had the same knowledge of the true facts as the alleged wrongdoer, no fraud is present. If the victim should have known the facts or if a reasonable person would have known that the statement was not true, there is no fraud. If false statements are made after a contract has been signed, it is obvious that there was no reliance on the false statements and therefore there is no fraud.

Smith offers to sell Jones a car and represents that the car has never been in a wreck. Jones, who has worked on cars for many years, notices some dents underneath the car that could only have been made by a wreck. Jones buys the car anyway. Even if Smith knew this statement was false and was trying to deceive Jones, there is no fraud since Jones did not rely on Smith's representation.

Ordinarily, a statement of opinion cannot be the basis for fraud liability. The theory is that a person hearing the statement should recognize it as merely the speaker's personal viewpoint.

A statement of law of Les by stating: "No, it has never been in a wreck." In fact, the auto had been seriously damaged in a wreck and, although repaired, was worth much less than it would have had it not been in a wreck. When Les learned the truth, he sued Acme and the salesperson for damages on the basis of fraud. They raised the defense that the salesperson did not know that the statement was false and had not intended to deceive Les. Did the conduct of the salesperson constitute fraud? Yes. The salesperson making the statement did not know whether the car had been in a wreck or not. Nevertheless, the salesperson made the statement as though it was true and as though he knew that the statement was true. This constituted reckless indifference as to whether or not the statement was true. The reckless indifference as to the truth of a statement satisfies the mental state element of fraud. The salesperson was therefore guilty of fraud.

An agreement may be set aside if it was not in fact entered into voluntarily by both of the parties. If either party entered into the agreement because of undue influence or physical or emotional duress, it may be set aside.

Undue influence arises in a situation where a confidential relationship exists and one party has such influence over the other party that the other party's free will is dominated to the benefit of the influencing party. Confidential relationships which may result in undue influence can be such things as the relationship of an elderly parent and an adult child, a physician and patient, an attorney and client, or any other relationship of trust and confidence in which one party exercises a significant amount of control or influence over another. Because of the possibility that a person in such a confidential relationship may dominate the will of another and take unfair advantage of that person, the law presumes that undue influence has occurred if the dominating party obtains any benefit from a contract made with the person alleged to have been unduly influenced. The contract is then voidable and may be set aside unless it can be proven that no such undue influence took place.

Smith, upon reaching the age of 75 and being in ill health, decided to move in with his oldest adult son. He lived with his oldest adult son for several years prior to his death. Upon his death, it was discovered that he deeded all of his property to his oldest son. The younger son contested the deed, stating that his older brother exercised undue influence over their father in getting him to give all of his property to the oldest son. A presumption of undue influence would arise which would have to be overcome by the oldest son. One way to overcome this presumption would be to show that the father consulted a disinterested third party, preferably an attorney, without the older son being present, and was counseled by the third party. This is not absolute proof of the lack of undue influence, but it is a very important element of proof.

Persuasion and argument are not in themselves undue influence. An essential element of undue influence is that the person making the contract does not exercise his free will. Unless there is a confidential relationship, such as that between a parent and child, Courts are most likely to take the attitude that the person who claims to have been dominated was merely persuaded.

An agreement made under duress may be set aside if the duress took the free will of the person seeking to avoid the contract away. In a duress situation, a party enters a contract to avoid a threatened danger. This threat may be a threat of physical harm to person or to the property of someone.

A person makes a contract under duress when there is violence or the threat of violence to the extent that the person is deprived of his free will and makes the contract to avoid harm. The threatened harm may be directed at a relative of the contracting party as well as against the contracting party. If a contract is made under duress, the agreement is voidable.

CONSIDERATION

Another of the elements needed to make an agreement binding is consideration. Even though there has been an offer and an acceptance, an agreement may not be enforceable if there is no consideration. Consideration is what the promisor demands and receives as the price for the promise. The promisor is the person making the promise, and the promisee is the person to whom the promise is made. Consideration consists of something that the promisor is not otherwise entitled to. It is not necessary to use the word consideration in a contract.

Consideration is the price paid for the promise. When thinking of consideration, think in terms of legal value as opposed to economic value. While economic value (e.g., money) is the most common form of consideration, consideration does not have to involve money. In order for a contract to be enforceable, each party to the contract must change his or her legal position in some way.

If an agreement lacks consideration, it is generally not a binding and enforceable contract. There are a few exceptions to this rule. A person sued for breaking a promise generally will not be held liable when no consideration was received for the promise. Smith signs an agreement with his employer, Acme, stating that he will not compete with Acme should he leave the employ of Acme. This promise by Smith is not binding unless it is supported by consideration. If Acme tells Smith that he will be fired unless he signs this agreement, that is adequate consideration; or, if at the time Acme is considering hiring Smith, Acme states that it will not hire Smith unless he agrees to enter a covenant not to compete, this covenant would then be binding. The consideration would be the hiring of Smith.

A promise to do something that is illegal is not consideration. Neither is a promise not to do something that is already prohibited by law. These types of promises will not form a valid contract.

Ordinarily, Courts do not consider the adequacy of the consideration given for a promise. Smith agreed to provide janitorial service to Acme for six months at $400.00 per month. After three months, Smith decided that $400.00 was not enough money, and he sought to get out of his contract, stating that the consideration for the services was inadequate. Is there a binding contract? The contract is binding since, again, the law is not normally concerned with the value or quantity of consideration that the promisor demands and receives for the promise. The employment contract was binding even if the compensation to be paid was in fact low.

LAWFUL OBJECTIVE

The fourth element of a contract is that it must be made for a lawful objective. Courts will not enforce contracts that are illegal or violate public policy. Such contracts are considered void. For example, a gambling contract would be illegal in many states.

If the illegal agreement has not been performed, neither party has the right to sue the other for damages or to require performance of the agreement. If the agreement has been performed, neither party can sue the other for damages nor did to have the agreement set aside.

Jones was asked by Smith to find a buyer for his restaurant in exchange for a payment of 15% of the sales price if Jones found a buyer. Jones did not have a real estate license nor did he claim to have one. Jones obtained a buyer and was paid one-half of the commission. Smith refused to pay any more commission saying that he did not have to since Jones did not have a realtor's license as required by state law. Is Smith correct? Smith also said that Jones had to return the part of the commission that he had already paid to Jones. Is this correct?

Smith is correct about not having to pay Jones the rest of the commission since the state licensing statute was violated by Jones acting as a realtor without a license. Smith's agreement to pay Jones a commission was void and cannot be enforced. However, Smith is incorrect regarding his contention that Jones has to pay back the part of the commission Smith paid to Jones. A court will not help either party enforce an illegal contract. In most cases, parties to an illegal agreement are denied remedies of any nature. A Court will not require parties to perform an illegal agreement, and a Court will not award damages because a party fails to perform.

An agreement may involve the performance of several promises, some of which are legal and some illegal. The legal parts of the agreement may be enforced if they can be separated from the parts that are illegal. However, if the illegal parts would be such as to affect the whole agreement, the legal parts of the agreement will not be enforced. When possible, an agreement will be interpreted as being lawful. In other words, if an agreement is susceptible to two interpretations, one legal and the illegal, the Court will generally use the legal interpretation unless it is clear that the interpretation as to illegality is very clearly indicated.

An agreement which calls for the commission of a crime is illegal and therefore void. For example, a person could not enforce an agreement with another party to burn a house down. Also, an agreement that calls for the commission of a civil wrong (such as a tort) is illegal and void. For example, an agreement to slander a third party is void.

Ordinarily, a Court will not consider whether a contract is fair or unfair, wise or foolish. However, in some instances, Courts will hold that a contract will not be enforced because it is too harsh or oppressive to one of the parties. For example, a clause in a contract which provides that a party will pay a large penalty if he breaks the contract may be unenforceable, depending upon the circumstances. Another example would be a situation where one party agreed that the other party would not be liable for the consequences of gross negligence. This type of agreement would usually be void as against public policy.

Agreements that may harm the public welfare are contrary to public policy and are not binding. An agreement may not violate a statute, but it still may be so offensive to society that courts will rule that to enforce it would be contrary to public policy. Whether or not a contract is contrary to public policy is difficult to determine because the term "public policy" is difficult to define. The concept of public policy has to do with protecting the public from something that tends to be injurious to the public, or contrary to the public good, or which violates an established interest of society. Contracts which violate public policy frequently relate to the protection of the public welfare, health or safety; to the protection of the person; or the protection of recognized social institutions. For example, a contract that would prohibit someone from marrying would be unenforceable as violating public policy.

An agreement which would require a person to lose some sort of statutory protection would be in violation of public policy. For example, state insurance statutes frequently provide that policies of a certain type (e.g., medical) must contain certain benefits. An insurance policy which fails to supply such benefits would violate public policy as declared in the statute.

An agreement which interferes with the proper performance of a duty of a public officer is contrary to public policy and void. An example would be an agreement between a mayor and a private citizen where the private citizen agreed to pay the mayor $10,000.00 if the mayor would hire the citizen's son as his executive assistant.

Agreements involving conflicts of interest can be void as violating public policy such as when a purchasing officer of a government buys from a company that the officer privately owns.

Any agreement intended to obstruct the process of law is void as being contrary to public policy. Suppose for example, in a medical malpractice case, an attorney offered to pay his expert witness, a physician, and $10,000.00 for testifying and an additional $15,000.00 if the attorney's client wins the case. This agreement would be void. The danger is that a witness might lie in order to help win the case.

Most states provide that gambling contracts are illegal. Lotteries which involve the element of a prize, chance, and consideration are also held to be held illegal. Of course, a state may allow a lottery run by the state or may legalize gambling in general, such as in Nevada. In some states, bingo games, lotteries, and raffles are legal if the proceeds go to charity. Giveaway plans and games are lawful as long as it is not necessary to buy anything or give anything of value in order to participate. If participation is free, the element of consideration is not present and therefore there is no lottery.

Statutes frequently require that a person obtain a license or certificate before practicing certain professions such as law or medicine, or before carrying on a particular business such as that of a real estate broker or stock broker. If the license is required to protect the public from unqualified persons, such as an unlicensed physician, any contract made by the unlicensed person in the course of his medical practice would be void. In a North Carolina case, a statute required that contractors be licensed. An unlicensed contractor entered into a contract to make repairs. The Court held that the contractor could not recover from the owner either the price agreed to in their contract or the reasonable value of the services actually performed since the contractor was unlicensed.

If a license is strictly a revenue raiser, such as a privilege license to conduct a store at a particular location, it would be rare for an agreement made in violation of the licensing statute to be held invalid. Someone operating a store without a permit would not have its entire sales declared void, but it might be fined for failure to obtain the appropriate license.

When a businessman sells his business, he may compete with the buyer of his business unless there is a valid restrictive covenant or covenant not to compete. The same is true when an employee leaves the employ of a company and begins soliciting customers of his former employer.

When an ongoing business is sold, it is commonly stated in the sales contract that the seller shall not go into the same area or a similar business again within a certain geographical area or for a certain period of time or both. Such an agreement is valid and enforceable.

Restrictions to prevent competition by a former employee are held valid when they are reasonable and necessary to protect the interests of the employer. For example, a provision in an employment contract which prohibited an employee for two years from calling on any customer of the employer called on by the employee during the last six months of employment would generally be valid. Courts will closely examine covenants not to compete signed by individuals in order to make sure that they are not unreasonable as to time or geographical area. For example, suppose a company only operated within a certain city and the covenant not to compete provided that an employee of the company could not solicit business in the city or within 100 miles of the city if he ever left the employ of the company. Such an agreement would be unreasonable as to its geographical area. The company had no need to be protected regarding such a large geographical area.

An agreement between a doctor and a clinic that if the doctor leaves the employ of the clinic, he will not practice within the city in which the clinic is located for the remainder of the doctor's life would be unreasonable as to time. Courts may also look to public welfare. If the city needed more than one doctor (assuming there was just one), the Court might declare the restriction as contrary to public policy.

When a restriction of competition is invalid because it is too long or covers too great a geographical area, Courts will generally do one of two things. Some Courts will trim the restrictive covenant down to a period of time or geographical area that the Court deems reasonable. Other Courts refuse to enforce the restrictive covenant at all and declare it void.

PROPER FORM

The fifth element of a contract is that it must be in the form required by law. Do all contracts have to be in writing? No - oral contracts can be just as valid and enforceable as written contracts. However, state statutes require that certain contracts must be in writing in order to be enforceable by a court. These statutes are called statutes of fraud. Statutes of fraud require that either the contract itself be in writing and signed by the parties or there must be a sufficient memorandum of the agreement signed by the party being sued for breach of contract.

The statute of frauds normally does not apply if it is possible under the terms of the agreement to perform the contract within one year. If no time for performance is specified in the oral agreement and the performance will not necessarily take more than one year, the statute of frauds would not apply.

Smith claimed that he and Jones had made an oral contract (i) to start a business under the name of Acme Textile Mill, Inc., (ii) to incorporate the business, and (iii) to divide the stock equally. The alleged contract was not performed. Smith sued Jones for breach of contract. Jones raised the defense of the statute of frauds, asserting that it was not specified that the contract should be performed within one year. Was this defense valid? No. The contract could have been performed within one year. Writing was therefore not required. The statute does not apply if the contract contemplated performance within one year or if in fact it could be performed within one year.

Contracts involving the sale of land must be evidenced by writing. This would include deeds and mortgages, as well as the contract between the buyer and the seller setting forth the terms of the sale. This statute applies only to the agreement between the owner and purchaser of the real property. It does not apply to collateral agreements such as between a real estate agent and one of the parties to the sales contract regarding the real estate agent's commission.

Another type of contract that must be in writing is the promise to answer for the debt of another person. For example, an oral promise by the president of Acme Company to pay the debt owed by Acme to Tenth National Bank would not be enforceable.

A promise by the executor or administrator of an estate to use personal funds to pay a debt of the estate must be in writing. An executor of a deceased person's estate has a duty to pay the debts of the person from the person's estate. If the executor promises to pay a debt of the decedent from his personal funds, this must be in writing. However, if the executor makes a contract on behalf of the estate, like hiring an attorney to represent the estate, this type of agreement could be enforceable even if it is not in writing.

A promise made in consideration of marriage must be in writing. An example of this would be a prenuptial agreement. If a contract provides for the sale of goods with a price of $500.00 or more, this type of contract must ordinarily be in writing.

The statute of frauds requires a writing to evidence the contracts which it states must be in writing. This does not necessarily have to be a formal contract signed by both parties. It can be a letter signed by only one party setting forth the terms of the oral agreement. However, the writing, whether it be a letter or memorandum, must be signed by the person "to be charged." This means it must be signed by the person against whom you are seeking to enforce the contract. The writing must contain all of the material terms of the contract so that a Court can determine what has been agreed to. A letter from the seller of real estate to a potential buyer which did not adequately describe the property involved in the sale would not be enforceable. The description of the land must be adequate in order to allow the Court to know exactly what land is being referred to.

In a telephone conversation, Smith agreed to buy Jack's house. All the details of the transaction were agreed to in the conversation. The next day Jack wrote Smith a letter stating: "This confirms the agreement we made last night that I should sell you my home." Later, Jack refused to go through with the transaction. Smith sued Jack. Will Smith recover? No. Because the subject matter of the contract was the sale of an interest in land, the statute of frauds required that the contract be evidenced by a writing. The letter written by Jack did not satisfy the statute of frauds, since such a letter must set forth all the material terms of the contract so that there is no need to resort to outside evidence to establish any of the terms of the contract.

The letter, memorandum, or other writing may consist of more than one writing if there is a sufficient link between them. For example, two or three letters from a seller of land to the potential buyer describing the terms would satisfy the statute of frauds even if one of the letters alone would not be sufficient. It is not necessary that the writing be made with the intent to create a writing to satisfy the statute of frauds. A letter or memorandum signed by a seller of land to the potential buyer could satisfy the statute of frauds even if the seller did not intend for this letter to be used against him should he renege on his agreement.

In dealing with the statute of frauds, the first question is whether the contract is one that has to be in writing. The second question is whether or not there is a sufficient writing that can be enforced. With the parol evidence rule, there is already a written contract, and the question is whether evidence outside of the written contract is admissible in court. If a contract is in dispute, often a question arises as to whether or not the writing evidencing the contract represents all that the parties agreed to. The general rule is that spoken words (i.e., parol evidence) will not be allowed to modify or contradict the terms of the written contract that is complete on its face. Exceptions to this rule are made in cases of fraud, accident, or mistake, or it can be shown that the writing is not the complete or true contract.

The parol evidence rule prevents a party from avoiding liability on a written contract by presenting evidence that the writing does not mean what it says. The reason for the rule is to give stability to written contracts and to prevent someone claiming that there were oral terms that never found their way into the written agreement. Parol evidence will be allowed when:

- the writing is incomplete;
- the writing is ambiguous;
- the writing is not a true statement of the agreement of the parties because of fraud,
- accident or mistake; or
- the existence, subsequent modification, or illegality of a contract is in question.

If the written contract is obviously incomplete or if the parties admit that it is incomplete, Courts will allow evidence as to what was orally agreed to, in addition to what was agreed upon in writing. If the terms of the contract are ambiguous, parol evidence will be allowed to explain the contract so as to make it not ambiguous. For example, if a written contract might have two different meanings, parol evidence may be admitted to clarify what the contract really means. However, the fact that the parties disagree as to the meaning of the contract does not mean that it is ambiguous.

A contract which looks complete on its face may have omitted a provision that should have been included. Parol evidence may be admitted to show that this provision was omitted due to a mistake or because of fraud of the party drawing up the contract. Parol evidence is, of course, admissible to prove fraud. For example, if the seller of property orally represented that the land was zoned to permit commercial use, and the land in fact was not zoned for commercial use, this evidence can be admitted in seeking to avoid the contract.

INTERPRETATION OF CONTRACTS

If there is a dispute as to the interpretation of a contract, Courts seek to enforce the intent of the parties to the contract. The intent which will be enforced is what a reasonable person would believe that the parties intended. The intent that will be enforced is the intent as it reasonably appears to a third person (e.g., the judge or jury).

In interpreting contracts, ordinary words are to be interpreted according to their ordinary meaning. Trade terms and technical terms are to be interpreted according to their trade or technical meaning. Software, when referring to a computer, does not mean something that is soft, but it means the actual program.

The way parties have used terms in their prior relationships can also be used to determine what the parties meant by the words they used in a contract.

Sometimes a written contract is sent with additional printed material. The question arises whether the additional material is part of the contract. For example, when goods are purchased, the buyer often receives a manufacturer's manual or various pamphlets. When a worker gets a new job, the worker oftentimes gets an employee handbook. Sometimes the original written document provides the answer as to whether or not the printed material is part of the contract. Sometimes the contract will expressly refer to and incorporate into the contract the terms of the other written material. For example, a contract for the sale of the inventory of a business may state that the seller does hereby sell to the buyer the goods described in Exhibit "A" attached hereto. Exhibit "A" will then list specifically the items of inventory. In that case, Exhibit "A" would be a part of the contract.

The provisions of a contract must be construed as a whole. Provisions are not to be read out of context and interpreted out of context.

If an occurrence or a nonoccurrence of an event has an effect on the existence of a contract, the event is called a condition. A condition precedent is the occurrence of an event that precedes the existence of an obligation to perform or the existence of a contract. For example, in a fire insurance policy, there is no obligation on the insurance company to make a payment until there is a fire loss. The occurrence of such a loss is therefore a condition precedent to the duty of the insurer to make payment.

The parties may agree that the contract will terminate if a particular event occurs or does not occur. Such a provision is called a condition subsequent. For example, in a contract for the purchase of land, the contract may contain a condition subsequent that cancels the contract if the zoning board turns down a buyer's application to obtain a zoning permit to use a building for a particular purpose. The contract may state something to the effect that this contract will be void if the buyer is unable to have the property rezoned from residential to commercial within 90 days from the date of the agreement.

In some cases, a conflict can be solved by considering the form of the conflicting terms. If a contract is partly printed or typewritten and partly handwritten, the handwritten part would prevail if it conflicted with the typewritten or printed part. If there is a conflict between the printed part and a typewritten part, the typewritten part would prevail. If there is a conflict between an amount or quantity expressed both in words and figures, as on a check, the amount or quantity expressed in words prevails.

A contract is ambiguous when it is uncertain what the intent of the parties was and the contract is capable of more than one reasonable interpretation. Sometimes ambiguous terms can be explained by the admission of parol evidence. Also, Courts abide by the rule that an ambiguous contract is interpreted against the party who drafted it. In other words, the party who did not draft the contract will be given the benefit of the doubt so to speak. Also, sometimes the background or circumstances surrounding the contract can eliminate ambiguity. For example, in a Minnesota case, suit was brought in Minnesota on a Canadian policy of insurance. The question arose as to whether the dollar limit of the policy referred to Canadian dollars or American dollars. The Court concluded that Canadian dollars were intended since the insurer and the insured were both Canadian corporations, the policy was entered into in Canada, and over the years premiums had been paid in Canadian dollars, and a prior claim on the policy had been settled by using Canadian dollars.

Again, if two interpretations are reasonably possible, the contract will be interpreted in favor of the person who did not draft the contract and against the person who did draft it. An example of this would be preprinted insurance policies. Any clause which is capable of two interpretations will usually be interpreted against the insurer and in favor of the insured.

Sometimes a Court may imply a term to cover a situation where the parties fail to provide the term. The Court may also imply a term if it's necessary to give a contract a construction or meaning that is reasonable. For example, if a contract does not state its duration, the Court may imply that the contract is to be performed or continue for a reasonable time – reasonable in relation to the type of contract that it is. However, a term will not be implied in a contract when the Court concludes that the parties intended for the contract to be silent on a particular point.

In every contract there exists an implied covenant of good faith and fair dealing. For example, when a contract to purchase a house is made subject to the condition that the buyer can obtain financing, the buyer must make a reasonable good faith effort to obtain the financing or be held in breach of the contract. The implied duty to act in good faith means an honest, good faith effort to satisfy the condition of the contract.

As a general rule, a party is bound by a contract even if it proves to be a bad bargain. However, if a court is called upon to interpret a contract, if possible, the court will interpret it in such a way as to avoid hardship, particularly when the hardship would hurt the party who had the weaker bargaining position.

When a contract has contacts with more than one state, it is a contract in interstate commerce, and it is necessary to determine which state's law governs the contract. The rules that govern that decision are called the law of conflicts of law. The parties may specify the jurisdiction whose law is to govern. If that jurisdiction bears a reasonable relationship to the contract, the choice will be given effect by the Court.

Assuming there is no choice of law in the contract, the law of the state where the contract is made determines whether or not the contract is valid. Matters regarding the performance of the contract, for example, damages for nonperformance or defenses for nonperformance, are generally governed by the law of the state where the contract is to be performed. An example of performance would be where a contract was made in Mississippi to sell cotton to a Tennessee merchant. If the contract provided that delivery was to be made in Tennessee with payment made in Tennessee, the contract would be performed in Tennessee.

The state in which the contract is made is determined by finding the state in which the last act essential to the formation of the contract was performed. For example, if I send a contract signed by me to someone in Tennessee with the request that they sign the contract if the terms are acceptable, the signing of the contract in Tennessee would be the last act necessary for the formation of the contract and would therefore be considered a Tennessee contract.

The modern trend, when no provision is stated in the contract as to which state's law will apply, is to apply the center of gravity rule. Under this rule, the court will choose to follow the law of the state which has the most significant relationship to the parties, the contract, and its performance. The courts consider the place where the contract was made, where the negotiations occurred, where the performance was made, the location of the subject matter of the contract (e.g., land location), the residence of the parties, and the states of incorporation and principal place of business if a corporation is involved.

THIRD PARTIES AND ASSIGNMENTS

Ordinarily, only the parties to contracts have rights and duties with respect to the contracts. However, exceptions are made in the case of third-party beneficiary contracts and assignments.

When a contract is intended to benefit a third person, this person is a third-party beneficiary and may enforce the contract. A life insurance contract is a third-party beneficiary contract. The insurance company promises the insured person to make payment to the beneficiary. Suppose you have a life insurance policy with Metropolitan Life Insurance Company and your wife is the beneficiary. If you die, Metropolitan Life will pay the insurance proceeds to your wife. If the Company refuses to pay in accordance with the terms of the policy, your wife has the right to bring a lawsuit against the Company in her name. She may do this even though she was not a party to the contract.

The beneficiary does not have to be specifically named, but may be described as a class of people. For example, a union contract is between the union and the employer. However, an employee, one of the class of individuals covered by the union contract, can bring suit on the contract even though he is not specifically named in the contract.

Not everyone who benefits from the performance of a contract between other persons is entitled to sue as a third-party beneficiary. In order to be a third-party beneficiary, the contract must clearly show an intent to give direct benefits to the third person. Anyone else who might benefit by the contract is called an incidental beneficiary and has no rights under the contract. An incidental beneficiary may not sue to enforce the contract. A Court would hold that such a beneficiary did not have "standing" to sue for breach of the contract. For example, if a private employer makes a contract with the U. S. Government to employ and train disadvantaged unemployed persons, these unemployed persons are merely incidental beneficiaries of the contract. They cannot sue for damages if the contract with the government is broken by the employer.

An assignment is a transfer of rights that a party has under a contract to another person, called an assignee. The assigning party is called the assignor. An assignee of a contract may generally sue directly on the contract rather than suing in the name of the assignor. The other party to the original contract is called the obligor. For example, suppose I sell my car to Larry for $10,000.00. He does not have $10,000.00 in cash, but executes an agreement stating that he agrees to pay me $500.00 a month for 20 months. I then assign this contract to Peggy. Larry is the obligor, I am the assignor, and Peggy is the assignee.

Unless there is a statute that requires that certain language be used in an assignment or that the assignment be in writing, there are really no formal requirements for an assignment. Any words which show the intent to transfer rights under a contract are sufficient to constitute an assignment.

If there is no consideration for the assignment, this does not affect the validity of an assignment. This is so because an assignment is not a contract, but is the transfer of a property right. An assignment may therefore be made as a gift, although it is usually part of a business transaction and does involve consideration.

Any right to money may be assigned. This is true in cases where the assignor is entitled to the money at the time of the assignment or will be entitled to the money at some point in the future. My assigning my contract with Larry to Peggy is an example of an assignment of future rights to money. Any contract may be assigned with permission of the obligor. Personal service contracts cannot be assigned without the permission of the parties, such as a contract between an employee and an employer.

A contract may prohibit the assignment of any rights arising under the contract. Some Courts hold that this type of prohibition is binding, and any assignment in violation of the prohibition has no effect. However, as far as an assignment of a right to money is concerned, any contract which would prohibit the assignment of a right to money is invalid and would not prevent the making of such an assignment. This is the general rule.

A right to a performance may be assigned with certain exceptions. For example, suppose I have my car repaired and the repairman guarantees the repairs for 30 days. Unless the guarantee states that it will not apply to a purchaser of the car, if I do sell the car, the purchaser could also receive the guarantee.

If the assigning of a right would increase the burden of the obligor in performing the contract, an assignment is ordinarily not permitted. Lee contracts to paint Sally's two-story house for $1,000. Sally realizes that she will not have sufficient money, so she transfers her rights under this agreement to her neighbor Karen, who has a three-story house. Karen notifies Lee that Sally's contract has been assigned to her and demands that Lee paint Karen's house for $1,000. Is Lee required to do so? No. The right called for the performance of personal services. Such a right cannot be assigned without the consent of the person who is to render the personal services. This is particularly true in this case, because this type of assignment, if allowed, would increase the burden of performance; it is a greater burden to paint a three-story house than a two-story house.

Contracts involving personal satisfaction cannot be assigned without the permission of the obligor. For example, if a contract involves goods to be furnished that must be satisfactory to the buyer, this type of contract could not be assigned since the buyer's judgment may be different than the assignee's.

If a party to a contract has certain duties to perform under that contract and then transfers these duties to another person who is to perform them, there is a delegation of duties. In such a case, the original person who is to perform the duties remains liable if the person to whom he transfers the duties fails to adequately perform the duties. In other words, the party to the contract who delegated the duties remains liable in case of default of the person doing the work just as if no delegation had been made.

In some instances, a delegation of duties cannot be made unless consented to by the party entitled to the performance. An example of this would be when a personal element of skill or judgment of the original contracting party is involved. If I contract with a particular mechanic to repair my car because this mechanic is known for his expertise regarding the particular problem I am having, the mechanic would breach his contract with me if he delegated these duties to another mechanic without my permission.

An assignment does not relieve the assignor of any obligation under the contract. An assignor continues to be bound by the obligations of the original contract unless the other party to the contract releases him. For example, the fact that a buyer assigns the right to goods under a contract does not terminate the buyer's liability to make payment to the seller.

An obligee is someone owed an act or deed, such as paying money on a promissory note or contract. Ordinarily, the assignee is not subject to a suit by the obligee by virtue of the fact that an assignment has been made. For example, if someone assumes a loan in purchasing a house, the lender ordinarily cannot sue the assignee (i.e., purchaser and assumer of the loan) unless the assignee/assumer agreed, not only with the seller, but with the lender, to pay the loan.

The rights of the assignee regarding the assigned contract are no greater than those of the assignor. If the other party to the contract could have successfully defended against a suit brought by the assignor, that party (the obligor) will also prevail against the assignee.

Mack did plastering work in Nick's home. He did not have a license to do the plastering work, and by statute, he was barred from suing for the contract price for this work. Mack assigned his claim against Nick to Will, who then sued Nick for the amount due for Mack's work. The Court would hold in favor of Nick. The Court would rule that by virtue of the statute, Mack's lack of a license was a defense to the recovery on the contract from Nick. Will, as assignee of Mack, had no greater right than Mack to sue.

A valid assignment takes effect the moment it is made regardless of whether notice of the assignment is given to the other party to the contract. If the obligor is notified that there has been an assignment and that any money due must be paid to the assignee, the obligor's obligation can only be discharged by making payment to the assignee. In other words, payment to the assignor would not satisfy the contract after notice. If the obligor does not know of the assignment and makes payments to the assignor who does not turn the money over to the assignee, the assignee cannot sue the obligor, but does have a remedy against the assignor. However, if the obligor both knows of the assignment and has been notified to make future payments to the assignee, any payments made by the obligor to the assignor have no effect and do not reduce the debt of the obligor. If Acme Furniture sells furniture to Smith on a retail installment contract, and Acme then assigns this contract to Tenth Bank, Acme is the assignor, the buyer is the obligor, and Tenth Bank is the assignee. When Tenth Bank and Acme notify the buyer that future payments are to be made to Tenth Bank, the buyer must make these payments to Tenth Bank. If he makes payments to Acme, the payments will not reduce the debt unless Acme forwards the money on to

Tenth Bank. If the buyer did not know of the assignment and continued to make payments to Acme, and Acme pocketed the money and did not turn it over to Tenth Bank, Tenth Bank could not recover from the buyer, but could sue Acme to recover the payments.

When an assignment is made for consideration, the assignor warrants:

- That the right assigned is valid;
- That the assignor owns the claim assigned; and
- That the assignor will not interfere with the assignee's enforcement of the obligation.

The assignor does not warrant that the other party will pay or perform as required by the contract. In other words, this is not impliedly warranted. However, it can be warranted by contract. In other words, the assignor can agree to pay the assignee if the obligor does not pay.

DISCHARGE – PERFORMANCE

A contract is discharged by performance of the terms of the agreement.
An offer to perform is a tender. If a person offers to perform the contract pursuant to its terms and the other party refuses to allow performance, the contract is discharged. A tender of payment is an offer to pay the amount due when it is due–for example, on a note. The tender must be legal tender–for example, by cash, a check (if allowed), or a bank wire.

Payments must be applied in the manner stated by a debtor. If a debtor does not specify how payments are to be applied, the creditor can apply payments to any legal debt that is owed. State law may require application of payments to the oldest debt. If no time is specified, payment must be in a reasonable time.

A payment by a check is a conditional payment. The debt is revived if the check bounces. The payee can sue on the check or on the debt.

The phrase time is of the essence is a phrase sometimes used in a contract. This phrase in effect means, "the specified time and dates in this agreement are vital and thus, mandatory." Therefore, any delay, reasonable or not, slight or not, will be grounds for cancelling the agreement. An example of this would be in the case of the sale or purchase of perishable property or property that fluctuates rapidly in value. If a contract states that time is of the essence, but it obviously is not, courts will ignore this clause. When time is not of the essence, courts generally permit parties to perform their obligations within a reasonable time.

If a party acts in good faith, and substantially performs a contract, he will be allowed to recover to the extent he has performed. He may have to pay any damages the other party has suffered. Good faith is important. For example, if a contractor does not follow building specs on purpose (e.g., trying to cut costs), he will not recover anything.

Greg contracted to build a house and garage for Bill for $50,000.00. The job was completed according to the specifications in all respects except that Greg forgot to put a tool shed next to the garage as was required by the contract specifications. Bill refused to pay Greg. Greg sued Bill. Bill raised the defense that Greg was not entitled to any money until the contract was completely performed and that the performance was incomplete because the tool shed had not been constructed. Was Bill correct? No. Under the doctrine of substantial performance, Greg can recover $50,000.00 less such amount as would be required to complete the performance, that is to build the tool shed. The court reached this conclusion to avoid the hardship that would be imposed on Greg if he should lose everything because of a relatively minor breach of the contract.

The doctrine of substantial performance will not be applied when the contract makes it clear that a literal and exact compliance is required. The doctrine of substantial performance does not apply to a condition precedent. Example: Say a lender is obligated to lend money if a specific number of leases are signed (like on a loan to build a building). The Bank will have no obligation if the specific number of leases is not signed.

Dick contracted to build a house for Mike. When it was approximately 25 to 40 percent completed, Mike would not let Dick work any further because he was not following the building plans and specifications, and there were many defects. Mike hired another contractor to correct the defects and finish the building. Dick sued Mike for breach of contract, claiming that he had substantially performed the contract up to the point when he had been discharged. Was Dick correct? No. There was no substantial performance because the substantial performance of a building contract implies that the building be usable for the purpose for which it was intended. Because a performance that is only 25% to 40% complete would not produce a usable building, the substantial performance doctrine could not be applied.

With regard to a contract requiring performance to the satisfaction of the other party, the courts are divided as to:

- Whether the promisor must perform the contract to the satisfaction of the promisee; or
- Whether it is sufficient that the performance would satisfy a reasonable person under the circumstances.

When personal taste is an important element, the courts generally hold that the performance is not sufficient unless the promise is actually satisfied. Personal satisfaction is generally required when a person promises to make clothes or paint a portrait to the satisfaction of the other party. With respect to things mechanical, courts are more likely to hold that the performing party has performed satisfactorily if a reasonable person should be satisfied with what was done. In most instances, the courts require that the dissatisfaction be shown to be in good faith rather than the "dissatisfied" customer just trying to avoid paying for the work that has been done.

It is common for a person to guarantee the performance of a contract. For example, a builder may guarantee for one year that certain work will be satisfactory. Such a guarantee may also be made by a third person. For example, a surety company may guarantee to the owner that a contractor will perform a contract. In such a case, the obligation of the surety is in addition to the liability of the contractor, but the contractor is also still liable. However, a plaintiff cannot recover twice. He can recover only the amount of the liability. For example, a plaintiff can recover part from contractor and part from surety, or all from surety. However, the plaintiff cannot recover all from surety and all (again) from contractor.

A contract may be discharged pursuant to a provision in the contract or by a subsequent agreement. For example, there may be a discharge by the terms of the original contract when it says it will end on a certain date. There may be a mutual cancellation when both parties agree to end their contract. There may be a mutual rescission when both parties agree to annul the contract and return to their original positions as if the contract had never been made. This would require returning any consideration (for example, money) that had changed hands.

Sometimes parties may decide that their contract is not the one they want. They may want to replace it with another contract. If they do, the original contract is discharged by substitution. It is not necessary for the parties to state that they are making a substitution. If they make a new contract that is clearly inconsistent with a former contract, a court will hold that the earlier contract has been superseded by the later contract. It is preferable, however, to expressly state in the later contract that the earlier one has been superseded.

The fact that a second contract has been made does not always mean that the original contract has been canceled. The second contract may merely supplement or modify the original contract. In order for the later contract to take the place of the first, the parties should put language similar to the following in the second agreement: "This contract completely supersedes and replaces that certain contract entered into by the undersigned on March 5, 1989, dealing with the sale of the materials referred to in Exhibit "A."

The parties may agree to a different performance. This is called an accord. When the accord is performed, this is called an accord and satisfaction. The original obligation is discharged.

In order for there to be an accord and satisfaction, there must be a bona fide dispute; an agreement to settle the dispute; and the performance of the agreement. An example would be settlement of a lawsuit for breach of contract. The parties might settle for less than the amount called for under the contract.

Circumstances beyond the control of the contracting parties may discharge the contract. Impossibility of performance refers to external conditions as opposed to someone's personal inability to perform the contract. For example, the fact that a debtor does not have the money to pay a debt, and therefore cannot pay the debt, does not discharge the debt. This is not a case of impossibility. Even riots and shortages of raw materials, even though external factors, do not necessarily excuse the failure to perform a contract.

What if a seller cannot obtain the goods he needs from any supplier to meet his contractual obligation to sell the goods to a buyer? This will not discharge the seller's obligation unless the inability to obtain the goods was a condition subsequent to the contract. What if a road contractor is unable to obtain gravel from his usual source and would have to get it from a supplier at a much higher price? The contractor would not be discharged. If there is nothing in the contract requiring that the gravel be obtained from the usual source, there is no "impossibility of performance." Just because performance would be more costly or burdensome than originally planned, this does not mean that the obligation is discharged.

When the parties expressly refer to particular subject matter in a contract, the contract is discharged if the subject matter is destroyed through no fault of either party (assuming there is no insurance on the subject matter). When a contract calls for the sale of a wheat crop growing on a specific parcel of land, the contract is discharged if the crop is destroyed.

A farmer made a contract to sell and deliver 10,000 bushels of soybeans. A flood destroyed his entire crop. He claimed that he was discharged from his obligation under the contract. Was he correct? No. The contract obligated the farmer to deliver a stated quantity of soybeans. It did not require the delivery of the soybeans that were grown on the farmer's land. Therefore, the fact that the beans on his land were destroyed did not discharge the contract. The fact that the farmer probably intended to fill the contract by using the crop grown on his land had no significance because that intent was not made a term of the contract.

A contract is discharged when its performance is made illegal by a subsequent change in the law. For example, suppose there is a contract to construct a three-story building at a particular place. Prior to beginning construction, a zoning law is passed which prohibits such a building in this area. The contract would be discharged.

However, a change of law that merely increases the cost of one of the parties is not a "change of law" that discharges the contract. For example, Mack made a contract with Richard to build an apartment house for a specific price. A number of serious apartment house fires later occurred in the city, and an ordinance was adopted by the city council increasing the fire precautions that had to be taken in the construction of a new building. Compliance with these new requirements would make the construction of the apartment house for Richard more expensive than Mack had originally contemplated. Is Mack discharged from the contract to build the apartment house? No. Mack must perform the contract even though it has been made more expensive to do so because of the change of law. Mack is not discharged from the contract, because the change of law did not prohibit the construction of the building but merely made it more expensive to build.

If a contract obligates a party to perform an act that requires personal skill of a particular person, the death or disability of that person would discharge the contact. For example, if an all pro NFL quarterback was killed in a car accident, the contract would be discharged. However, if the act called for by the contract could be performed by others, or by the estate of the decedent (e.g., executor hiring someone), this rule does not apply.

In every contract, there is an implied covenant of good faith and fair dealing. One party to a contact is under an obligation to do nothing that would interfere with the performance of the other party. If one party makes the other party's performance impossible, the obligation to perform is discharged. For example, if a contractor refuses to allow his subcontractor access to the property where the subcontractor is to do the work, the contract is discharged as to the subcontractor. The subcontractor would have a cause of action against the contractor, but the contractor would not have a cause of action against the subcontractor.

If the conduct of the other contracting party does not make performance impossible, but only more difficult or expensive, or causes a delay, the contract may not be discharged, but the injured party will be entitled to damages for any loss he incurred. In our example, if the contractor eventually allowed the subcontractor on the work site, the contract would not necessarily be discharged, but the subcontractor could get damages for any loss he incurred.

Acts of God, such as tornadoes, lightning, and floods, usually do not terminate a contract, even though they make performance more difficult and delays in performance occur. Weather conditions constitute a risk that is assumed by a contracting party in the absence of a contrary agreement. Construction contracts commonly contain a weather clause, which either expressly grants an extension for delays caused by weather conditions or expressly denies the right to any extension of time or additional compensation because of weather condition difficulties.

Most insolvent debtors may voluntarily file for bankruptcy or be compelled to do so by creditors. The trustee in bankruptcy then takes possession of the debtor's property and distributes it as far as it will go among the creditors. After this is done, the bankruptcy court grants the debtor a discharge if it concludes that the debtor has acted honestly and has not attempted to defraud creditors. Even though all creditors have not been paid in full, the discharge by a bankruptcy court discharges ordinary contract claims against the debtor.

Statutes provide that after a certain number of years have passed a contract claim is barred. The time limitations provided by state statutes of limitations vary widely. Three years is a commonly use time in statute of limitations for breach of a contract.

A contract may also require that notice of any claim be given within a specified time. A party who fails to give notice within the time specified by the contract may be barred from bringing a suit against the other party.

BREACH AND REMEDIES

A breach of contract is a failure to perform the contract in the manner called for by the contract. A party is entitled to contractual remedies if the other party breaches a contract. A breach does not always result in a lawsuit or mean the end of a contract. One party may be willing to waive or ignore the breach. A waiver can be made by words or by conduct. Accepting a late payment on a note would be an example of a waiver by conduct. It is possible to make a waiver by silence. For example, failure to object to the manner of performance in a timely manner would be a waiver by silence.

A party who waives a breach gives up the right to damages or remedies regarding such breach, and cannot use the breach as an excuse to keep from performing the contract.

A waiver may be express or implied. An example of an implied waiver would be accepting a defective performance without objection. A waiver only applies to the specific matter waived. A party is entitled to require the other party to strictly perform all other contractual obligations set forth in the contract.

A party may retain the right to recover damages caused by another party's breach if the party expressly reserves the right to damages at the time the party accepts a defective performance. This reservation of rights should be, but does not have to be, in writing.

A contracting party is entitled to damages if the other party breaches a contract. Generally, damages are the sum of money necessary to put a party in the same or equivalent financial position as the party would have been had the contract been performed. A party may recover compensatory damages for any actual loss that the party can prove with reasonable certainty.

Compensatory damages include direct damages and consequential damages. An example of direct damages would be in a situation where the plaintiff has paid $10,000.00 for a truck, but the defendant refuses to deliver the truck. The direct damages would be $10,000.00. Consequential damages would arise in a situation where the failure to deliver the truck harmed the business of the plaintiff (e.g., the plaintiff lost a delivery contract). In this situation, the plaintiff could possibly get consequential damages for loss of the delivery contract.

Punitive damages are designed to punish. A Court uses punitive damages to make an example of a defendant in order to keep others from committing a similar wrongful act. Punitive damages are rare in a breach of contract case except bad faith insurance claims (e.g., when an insurance denies a claim for an invalid reason).

A non-breaching party has a duty to mitigate damages. In other words, a non-breaching party has the duty to take reasonable steps to minimize damages. The failure to mitigate damages may cause the victim to only be allowed to recover damages that would have resulted if mitigated. In our truck example, say the truck was purchased and was to be delivered on January 5, to allow the buyer to perform a delivery job for $500.00. Delivery was late. The delivery contract was lost. However, suppose the buyer could have rented a truck for $150.00. However, he failed to do this. His damages would therefore only be $150.00.

An appropriate remedy for a breach may be rescission of the contract. This places the parties in the position they would have been had the contract never been entered into. For example, money is returned to the buyer and the buyer returns the merchandise to the seller. If performance has been involved, the performing party may get the reasonable value of his performance under an unjust enrichment theory. Suppose that pursuant to a contract for the sale of land, a buyer has taken possession and made substantial improvements. If the contract is rescinded, the buyer will return the land and the seller will return the money. However, the seller may have to pay the buyer the reasonable value of the improvements.

Specific performance is an action to compel a party who breached a contract to perform the contract as promised. The subject matter of the contract must be unique, or an action for damages would be the proper remedy. Actions for specific performance are usually allowed with regard to a contract involving the sale of particular real estate; and a contract for sale of a particular business. Specific performance is not allowed regarding a contract for the sale of personal property unless the property is unique in some way like an antique, coin collection, or art objects.

Generally, a party cannot obtain specific performance of personal service contracts or employment contracts. This is because of the Thirteenth Amendment barring involuntary servitude. However, breach of a service or employment contract can subject the breaching party to a suit for damages.

In general, a contract may limit the remedies that a non-breaching party may obtain. For example, Johnston purchases a new truck from Acme Truck Sales. The contract may limit Johnston's remedies to having Acme repair the truck or replace the truck if it is defective.

A contract may state the amount of liquidated damages to be paid if the contract is breached. Upon a party's breach, the other party will recover this amount of damages whether actual damages are more or less than the liquidated amount. For example, the parties to a construction contract may stipulate that damages are to be paid of $1,000.00 for each day that the construction exceeds its contracted completion date. Another example would be with regard to a contract for the sale of land where the contract provides that the earnest money paid will be the sole remedy upon breach of contract by the buyer.

Courts will honor liquidated damage provisions if:

- Actual damages are hard to determine (e.g., breach of a restrictive covenant).
- The amount is not excessive when compared with probable damages.

If the agreed-upon liquidated damage amount is unreasonable, the Court will hold the liquidated damage clause to be void as a penalty. In such situations, the plaintiff would have to prove the actual damages.

In general, an exculpatory clause (i.e., a limitation of liability clause) that eliminates a party's liability for damages caused by a breach of contract is valid and enforceable. For example, in a construction contract, it may be provided that the contractor will not be liable for damage caused by delays of third parties (subcontractors, for example).

There is a trend in the law to invalidate an exculpatory clause if:

- The parties have unequal bargaining power and the clause is unfair;
- The clause eliminates liability for negligence, particularly if a negligent party is a public utility or the contract involves a fundamental good or service; or
- The exculpatory clause was obtained by fraud or other wrongful conduct.

Exculpatory clauses are typically upheld if agreed to by businesses with equal bargaining power.

A common type of exculpatory clause involves limiting liability on a loan to the collateral. In other words, if there is a default, the contract says that the damages will be limited to execution on the collateral (i.e., foreclosure on the property covered by the mortgage or deed of trust).

What happens if a limitation of remedies clause or a limitation of liability clause is not valid? In this situation, the plaintiff may sue pursuant to any other valid remedy, such as actual damages.

Chapter 11

PERSONAL PROPERTY AND BAILMENTS

PERSONAL PROPERTY AND BAILMENTS

Personal property includes rights that are intangible, such as accounts receivable or intellectual property such as a patent or trademark. It also includes movable property. Movable property includes things you can touch, such as furniture, car, and a computer. Personal property does not include rights in real property (i.e., land, things embedded in land, such as gasoline tanks, and things attached to the land, such as buildings).

Title can be acquired in different ways:

- Acquiring by purchase is probably the most common way we think of acquiring title.
- Gift.
- Finding lost property.
- Transfer by a nonowner.
- Occupation (i.e., taking and retaining property).
- Escheat.

GIFTS

A gift involves transferring title by voluntary action of the owner without receiving anything in exchange. A gift of property is a:

- passing of title;
- made with the intent to pass title;
- without receiving money or value in consideration for the passing of title.

Gifts can be classified as:

- Inter vivos gifts;
- Gifts causa mortis.
- Gifts and transfers to minors.
- Conditional gifts.
- Anatomical gifts

The ***donor*** is the person making the gift, and the *donee* is the person receiving the gift. A gift may be made as a result of something the donee has done, but this is not consideration unless receiving the "gift" is a condition of doing something - then it is not a gift.

An ***inter vivos gift*** is what we think of as an ordinary gift between two persons. An inter vivos gift is made if a donor intends to convey all rights to the property at the present time and delivers the property to the donee. The gift takes effect upon the donor's intent to transfer ownership and making delivery. The donee can refuse the gift. If there is no acceptance, the gift is not complete. Delivery ordinarily involves handing the gift over to the donee. This can be accomplished by physically delivering the gift or by ***symbolic delivery.*** An example of symbolic delivery would be delivery of keys to a car (the means of control) - symbolic of giving the car to someone. Giving a deed to a house to someone can be symbolic delivery of the real property. An inter vivos gift must be made before the death of the donor or it will fail

A **gift causa mortis** is a conditional gift made by a donor who believes that he or she will soon die, and it is made with the intent that a donee will own the property if the donor dies. This gift is conditional, and the donee must give it back if the donor does not die; the donee dies first; or the donor takes back the gift before death.

The **Uniform Gift to Minors Act** and the **Uniform Transfer to Minors Act** (UTMA) allow property to be given or transferred to a minor by delivering the property to a custodian. The custodian may use the property for the minor's benefit, education, and support. Under these Acts, a minor is usually entitled to possession of the property at age 21. A gift cannot be revoked once it is made in accordance with these Acts.

A ***conditional gift*** transfers rights only when certain stated conditions are met. A gift may be subject to a condition precedent or a condition subsequent. For example, "This car is yours when you graduate." Marriage and engagement gifts are generally conditional gifts. Most States allow recovery of an engagement gift only if the person seeking to recover the gift did not unreasonably terminate the engagement.

Anatomical gifts are gifts of organs or body parts. The Uniform Anatomical Gift Act allows anatomical gifts to be made by persons who are 18 or older, or by certain members of a decedent's family.

FINDING OF LOST PROPERTY

Property is lost when the owner does not know where property is located, but intends to find it. Another definition is, Lost property is property that an owner has misplaced without intending to give up ownership. A person who finds lost property does not acquire title to the property. At most, a finder of lost property is entitled to possession of the property until it is claimed by the owner.

Some States have statutes that permit the finder of lost property to sell or keep it after a certain period of time. Usually, these statutes require some sort of publication of notice.

TRANSFER BY NONOWNER

The general rule is that only an owner of property can transfer title. A person who does not own property cannot pass title to the property. If property is stolen, and the thief sells the property, the buyer gets possession, not title.

An exception to the above rule is that an agent of an owner can transfer title if authorized. For example, transferring property by means of a power of attorney is appropriate and will pass title to the property if the power of attorney authorizes such transfer.

OCCUPATION OF PERSONAL PROPERTY

Sometimes title may be acquired by taking and keeping possession of the property. A**bandoned personal property** is an example. This property is deemed abandoned when the owner gives up possession with the intent to give up ownership. For example, throwing something in the trash would be abandoned personal property.

ESCHEAT

Escheat statutes typically provide that a State owns personal property that is not claimed by anyone. These types of statutes are used in unclaimed property situations like corporate dividends, bank deposits, insurance payments, and refunds. Title passes to the government under certain conditions. Many States have the *Uniform Disposition of Unclaimed Property Act.*

TYPES OF OWNERSHIP

When two or more persons have rights to an item of personal property, this is a ***co-tenancy***. When two or more people own rights to the whole property, this is ***tenancy in common***. Tenants in common own an undivided fractional interest in the same property. For example, my wife and I may own 100 shares of General Motors as tenants in common (and this may be designated as such on the stock). We each own 50% of the whole certificate. If I die, the remaining stock does not automatically go to her. My Will, or statutory law if I have no Will, will control who gets the 50% that I own.

It is possible for property that is owned in tenancy in common to be ***partited.*** The subject of the partition action is divided, for example, in our stock example, each party would take 50 shares.

Joint tenancy ownership means that two or more persons jointly own property. This is a similar concept to tenancy in common. The main difference is that on the death of one, the survivor automatically takes the property. For example, in our stock example, if I died, the stock automatically would go to my wife outside of the Will.

State statutes usually require the words ***with right of survivorship*** or the ownership will be deemed to be tenancy in common. If a joint tenant transfers his or her interest in property to a third party, the owners become tenants in common. In many states, the deposit of money in a joint account raises a "presumption" of joint tenancy with right of survivorship. This presumption can be overcome by satisfactory evidence.

In certain States, most property acquired by either spouse during marriage is ***community property.*** For example, in California, property acquired by a husband or wife during the marriage is community property. Some statutes provide for the right of survivorship; others provide that half of the property of a deceased spouse shall go to the heirs of that spouse or permit the half to be disposed of by Will.

Bailments

A Bailment is the temporary placement of control over, or possession of, personal property by one person, the bailor, into the hands of another, the bailee, for a designated purpose upon which the parties have agreed.

The term ***bailment*** is derived from the French ***bailler,*** "to deliver." It is generally considered to be a contractual relationship since the bailor and bailee, either expressly or impliedly, bind themselves to act according to particular terms. The bailee receives only control or possession of the property while the bailor retains the ownership interests in it. During the specific period a bailment exists, the bailee's interest in the property is superior to that of all others, including the bailor, unless the bailee violates some term of the agreement. Once the purpose for which the property has been delivered has been accomplished, the property will be returned to the bailor or otherwise disposed of pursuant to the bailor's directions.

A bailment is not the same as a sale, which is an intentional transfer of ownership of personal property in exchange for something of value. A bailment involves only a transfer of possession or custody, not of ownership. A rental or lease of personal property might be a bailment, depending upon the agreement of the parties. A bailment is created when a parking garage attendant, the bailee, is given the keys to a motor vehicle by its owner, the bailor. The owner, in addition to renting the space, has transferred possession and control of the vehicle by relinquishing its keys to the attendant. If the keys were not made available and the vehicle was locked, the arrangement would be strictly a rental or lease, since there was no transfer of possession. A gratuitous loan and the delivery of property for repair or safekeeping are also typical situations in which a bailment is created.

Categories: There are three types of bailments: (1) for the benefit of the bailor and bailee; (2) for the sole benefit of the bailor; and (3) for the sole benefit of the bailee.

A bailment for the mutual benefit of the parties is created when there is an exchange of performances between the parties. A bailment for the repair of an item is a bailment for mutual benefit when the bailee receives a fee in exchange for his or her work.

A bailor receives the sole benefit from a bailment when a bailee acts gratuitously — for example, if a restaurant, a bailee, provides an attended coatroom free of charge to its customers, the bailors. By virtue of the terms of the bailment, the bailee agrees to act without any expectation of compensation.

A bailment is created for the sole benefit of the bailee when both parties agree the property temporarily in the bailee's custody is to be used to his or her own advantage without giving anything to the bailor in return. The loan of a book from a library is a bailment for the sole benefit of the bailee.

Elements: Three elements are generally necessary for the existence of a bailment: delivery, acceptance, and consideration.

Actual possession of or control over property must be delivered to a bailee in order to create a bailment. The delivery of actual possession of an item allows the bailee to accomplish his or her duties toward the property without the interference of others. Control over property is not necessarily the same as physical custody of it but, rather, is a type of constructive delivery. The bailor gives the bailee the means of access to taking custody of it, without its actual delivery. The law construes such action as the equivalent of the physical transfer of the item. The delivery of the keys to a safe-deposit box is constructive delivery of its contents.

A requisite to the creation of a bailment is the express or implied acceptance of possession of or control over the property by the bailee. A person cannot unwittingly become a bailee. Because a bailment is a contract, knowledge and acceptance of its terms are essential to its enforcement.

Consideration, the exchange of something of value, must be present for a bailment to exist. Unlike the consideration required for most contracts, as long as one party gives up something of value, such action is regarded as good consideration. It is sufficient that the bailor suffer loss of use of the property by relinquishing its control to the bailee; the bailor has given up something of value — the immediate right to control the property.

Rights and Liabilities: The bailment contract embodying general principles of the law of bailments governs the rights and duties of the bailor and bailee. The duty of care that must be exercised by a bailee varies, depending on the type of bailment.

In a **bailment for mutual benefit,** the bailee must take reasonable care of the bailed property. A bailee who fails to do so may be held liable for any damages incurred from his or her negligence. When a bailor receives the **sole benefit from the bailment**, the bailee has a lesser duty to care for the property and is financially responsible only if he or she has been grossly negligent or has acted in bad faith in taking care of the property. In contrast, a bailee for whose sole benefit property has been bailed must exercise extraordinary care for the property. The bailee can use the property only in the manner authorized by the terms of the bailment. The bailee is liable for any injuries to the property from failure to properly care for or use it.

Once the purpose of the bailment has been completed, the bailee usually must return the property to the bailor, or account for it, depending upon the terms of the contract. If, through no fault of his or her own, the return of the property is delayed or becomes impossible — for example, when it is lost during the course of the bailment — the bailee will not be held liable for nondelivery on demand. In all other situations, however, the bailee will be responsible for the tort of conversion for unjustifiable failure to redeliver the property as well as its unauthorized use.

The provisions of the bailment contract may restrict the liability of a bailee for negligent care or unauthorized use of the property. Such terms may not, however, absolve the bailee from all liability for the consequences of his or her own fraud or negligence. The bailor must have notice of all such limitations on liability. The restrictions will be enforced in any action brought for damages as long as the contract does not violate the law or public policy. Similarly, a bailee may extend his or her liability to the bailor by contract provision.

Termination: A bailment is ended when its purpose has been achieved, when the parties agree that it is terminated, or when the bailed property is destroyed. A bailment created for an indefinite period is terminable at will by either party, as long as the other party receives due notice of the intended termination. Once a bailment ends, the bailee must return the property to the bailor or possibly be liable for conversion.

Common Carriers

Common carrier refers to a person or entity in the business of transporting goods or people for hire, as a public service. A private carrier, in contrast, is employed to transport good for people for specific needs on an individual case basis. For example, city buses are a common carrier, as opposed to a private carrier such as a moving company which is hired on a one-time basis. A common carrier runs according to a regular schedule on a designated route.

Under common law rules, a common carrier is generally liable for all losses which may occur to property entrusted to his charge in the course of business, unless he can prove the loss happened in consequence of the act of God, or of the enemies of the United States, or by the act of the owner of the property. Common carriers are publicly licensed to provide transportation services to the general public.

Strict Liability: Common carriers are absolutely liable, regardless of negligence, for all loss or damage to goods in their possession, except if it is caused by an act of God, an act of a public enemy, an order of a public authority, an act of the shipper, or the nature of the goods.

Limits to Liability: Common carriers can limit their liability to an amount stated on the shipment contract. The shipper bears any loss occurring through its own fault or improper crating or packaging procedures.

Connecting Carriers: When connecting carriers are involved under a through bill of lading, the shipper can recover from the original carrier or any connecting carrier. Normally, the last carrier is presumed to have received the goods in good condition.

Warehouse Companies

Warehouse companies are liable for loss or damage to property resulting from negligence [UCC 7–204(1)]. A warehouse company can limit the dollar amount of liability, but the bailor must be given the option of paying an increased storage rate for an increase in the liability limit [UCC 7–204(2)].

Innkeepers

Those who provide lodging to the public for compensation as a regular business are strictly liable for injuries to guests (not permanent residents).

Hotel Safes: In many states, innkeepers can avoid strict liability for loss of guests' valuables by providing a safe. Statutes often limit the liability of innkeepers for articles that are not kept in the safe.

Parking Facilities: If an innkeeper provides parking facilities, and the guest's car is entrusted to the innkeeper, the innkeeper will be liable under the rules that pertain to parking lot bailees (ordinary bailments).

Chapter 12

SALES AND LEASES OF PERSONAL PROPERTY

A sale of *goods* is a present transfer of title to movable property for a price. This price may be a payment of money, an exchange of other property, or the performance of services. The parties to a sale are the person who owns the goods and the person to whom the title is transferred. The *transferor* is the *seller* or *vendor*, and the *transferee* is the *buyer* or *vendee.* The sale of goods is governed by Article 2 of the Uniform Commercial Code (UCC), a form of which has been adopted by every state. ***Goods,* which is the subject matter of a sale, mean anything movable at the time it is identified as the subject of the transaction.** The subject matter may ***not*** be:

- investment securities, such as stocks and bonds, the sale of which is regulated by Article 8 of the UCC;
- choses in action, such as insurance policies and promissory notes, because they are assigned or negotiated rather than sold, or which, because of their personal nature, are not transferable in any case; or
- real estate, such as a house, land, factory, or farm.

Most goods are tangible and solid, such as an automobile or a chair. But goods may also be fluid, such as oil or gasoline. Goods may also be intangible, such as natural gas and electricity. The UCC is applicable to both new and used goods. **Goods that are physically existing and owned by the seller at the time of the transaction are called *existing goods.*** All other goods are called future goods. *Future goods* include both goods that are physically existing but not owned by the seller and goods that have not yet been produced

A person can make a contract to sell goods at a future date. However, no sale can be made of future goods. Because the "seller" does not have any title to future goods, there can be no transfer of that title now, and therefore no sale. For example, suppose a farmer tried to transfer the title today to a future crop. He would have a contractual duty to transfer the crop when it came into existence. However, the contract itself would not pass the title to the crop.

A contract for services is an ordinary contract and is not a sale of goods. Therefore, such a contract would be covered by general contract law. However, what if the contract involved both goods and services? If a contract calls for both the rendering of services and the supplying of materials (goods) to be used in performing the services, the contract is classified according to its *dominant* element. If the sale of goods is dominant, it is a sales contract covered by Article 2 of the UCC. If the service element is dominant, it is a service contract and not covered by the UCC but is covered by general contract law. For example, a contract with someone who repaired bicycles is a contract for services, even if parts are supplied to perform the repairs. The supplying of the parts is not regarded as a sale but is merely incidental to the primary contract of making repairs. In contrast, the purchase of a television set, with the incidental service of installation, is a sale of goods because the purchase of the set is the dominant element.

GENERAL CONTRACT LAW VERSUS THE LAW OF UCC SALES
To make the law harmonize with general business practices, a sales contract is not required to meet all of the same standards as ordinary contracts. For a sales contract, it is sufficient that the parties by their conduct recognize the existence of a contract, even though it cannot be determined when the contract was made, and (generally) even though one or more terms are left open.

Merchants: In most instances, the UCC treats all buyers and sellers alike. In some cases, it treats *merchants* differently than it does the occasional or casual buyer or seller. The UCC recognizes that the merchant is experienced and has a special knowledge of the relevant commercial practices.

Firm Offer: Contract law as to *offers* is applicable to a sales contract, with the following exception. A *firm offer* by a *merchant* cannot be revoked if the offer:

- expresses an intention that it will not be revoked,
- is in a writing, and
- is signed by the merchant.

For example, on May 15, Smith, a dealer, offered in a signed instrument to sell a stereo set to Bill for $500. By the terms of the offer, Bill was given until June 25 to accept the offer. On June 15, Bill received a writing from Smith revoking the offer. On June 20, Bill wrote Smith, "I hereby accept your offer of May 15." Since Smith's offer was a firm offer, which could not be revoked before June 25, there was an enforceable contract. An express period of irrevocability in the offer cannot exceed three months. If nothing is said as to the duration of the offer, the offer can be revoked after a *reasonable time.* A firm offer is effective regardless of whether the merchant received any consideration to keep the offer open.

Acceptance: An offer to buy or sell goods may be accepted in any manner and by any medium that is reasonable under the circumstances. However, if a specific manner or medium is clearly required by the terms of the offer or the circumstances of the case, the offer can only be accepted in that manner.

Additional Term in Offer– Unless it is expressly specified that an offer to buy or sell goods must be accepted just as made, the offeree may accept an offer and at the same time propose an additional term. This is contrary to general contract law. Under general contract law, the proposed additional term would be considered a counteroffer and the original offered would be rejected. Under Article 2 of the UCC, the new term does not reject the original offer. A contract arises on the terms of the original offer, and the new term is a counteroffer. The new term does not become binding until accepted by the original offeror. If, however, the offer states that it must be accepted exactly as made, the ordinary contract law rules apply.

In a transaction between *merchants,* the additional term becomes part of the contract if that term does not materially alter the offer and no objection is made to it. However, if such an additional term from the seller operates solely to the seller's advantage, it is a material term and must be accepted by the buyer to be effective. A buyer may expressly or by conduct agree to a term added by the seller to the acceptance of the buyer 's offer. The buyer may agree orally or in writing to the additional term. There is an acceptance by conduct if the buyer accepts the goods with knowledge that the term has been added by the seller.

Conflicting Term in Offer- When a term of an acceptance conflicts with a term of an offer, ***but*** it is clear that the parties intended to be bound by a contract, the UCC recognizes the formation of a contract. The terms that are conflicting cancel each other out and are ignored. The contract then consists of the terms of the offer and acceptance that agree, together with those terms that the UCC or contract law implies into a contract.

Determination of Price – The price for goods may be expressly fixed by the contract. If not fixed by the contract, the price may be an open term, whereby the parties merely indicate how the price should be determined at a later time or make no provision whatever as to the price. When persons experienced in a particular industry make a contract for goods without specifying the price to be paid, the price will be determined by the manner that is customary in the industry. Ordinarily, if nothing is said as to price, the buyer is required to pay the reasonable value of the goods, which is generally the market price. In recent years, there has been an increase in the use of the *cost plus* formula for determining price. Under this formula, the buyer pays the seller a sum equal to the cost to the seller of obtaining the goods plus a specified percentage of that cost. The percentage represents the seller's profit.

The contract may expressly provide that one of the parties may determine the price. In such a case, that party must act in good faith. The contract may specify that the price shall be determined by some standard or by a third person. For example, Lee agreed to sell Glen 1,000 yards of cotton fabric at a price to be fixed by White, a cotton fabric expert. If White fixes the price at $7 a yard, that price is as binding on the buyer and the seller as though it had been fixed by agreement between them. If White refuses to fix a price through no fault of the parties, the price will be a reasonable price, probably the current market price.

Output and Requirement Contracts – Somewhat related to the open-term rule concerning price is the rule involved in output and requirement contracts that the quantity to be sold or purchased is not a specific quantity. Instead, it is the amount that the seller should produce or the buyer should require. Although this introduces an element of uncertainty, such sales contracts are valid. To prevent oppression, these contracts are subject to two limitations: (1) the parties must act in good faith, and (2) the quantity offered or demanded must not be unreasonably disproportionate to prior output or requirements or to a stated estimate.

Indefinite Duration Contract

When the sales contract is a continuing contract, such as one calling for periodic delivery of gas, but no time is set for the life of the contract, the contract runs for a reasonable time. It may be terminated on notice by either party.

Modification of Contract

An agreement to modify a contract for the sale of goods is binding even though the modification is not supported by consideration.

Parol Evidence Rule
The parol evidence rule applies to the sale of goods, with the slight modification that a writing is not presumed to represent the entire contract of the parties unless the court specifically decides that it does. If the court so decides, parol evidence is not admissible to add to or contradict the terms of the writing. If the court decides that the writing was not intended to represent the entire contract, the writing may be supplemented by proof of additional terms, as long as these terms are not inconsistent with the written terms.

Usage of Trade and Course of Dealing
The patterns of doing business as shown by the prior dealings of the parties may form part of their contract. These patterns may be looked to in order to find what was intended by the express provisions of the agreement and to supply otherwise missing terms.

Fraud and Other Defenses
The defenses that may be raised in a suit on a sales contract are, in general, the same as those that may be raised in a suit on any other contract. A defrauded party may cancel the transaction and recover what was paid or the goods that were delivered, together with damages for any loss sustained. If the buyer obtained title by means of fraud, the title is voidable by an innocent seller.

Bulk Sale
A bulk sale is a sale of goods by a business which engages in selling items out of inventory (as opposed to manufacturing or service industries), often in liquidating or selling a business. This type of sale is governed by the bulk sales law which is Article 6 of the UCC. When merchants are about to transfer a major part of their materials, supplies, merchandise, or other inventory (not in the ordinary course of business), advance notice of the transfer should be given to creditors. This notice should be given by the transferee. If the notice required by Article 6 is not given, the creditors of the seller may enforce their claims on property in the hands of the buyer. Creditors may also reach the property in the hands of any subsequent transferee who knew that there had not been compliance with the UCC or who did not pay a reasonable value for the goods. This provision is designed to protect the creditors of a merchant from the merchant's selling all the inventory, pocketing the money, and then disappearing, leaving the creditors unpaid.

Ordinarily, the bulk purchaser who receives the goods does not become liable for the debts of the bulk seller merely because the requirements of Article 6 have not been satisfied. However, if the buyer mixes the transferred goods with other goods so that it is not possible for the creditor to identify the transferred goods that are subject to the creditor's claim, the bulk buyer is personally liable for the debts of the bulk seller, up to the value of the transferred goods.

REVIEW CONCEPTS

What is the Uniform Commercial Code?
The Uniform Commercial Code (UCC) is a model statute covering things such as the sale of goods, credit, bank transactions, conduct of business, warranties, negotiable instruments, loans secured by personal property and other commercial matters. All states have adopted and adapted

the entire UCC, with the exception of Louisiana, which only adopted parts of it. Article 2 of the UCC deals with sales.

How does the UCC define a "sale"?
A sale of goods is a present transfer of title to movable property for a price. This price may be a payment of money, an exchange of other property, or the performance of services.

What are goods?
Goods are anything movable at the time it is identified as the subject of the transaction. Most goods are tangible and solid, such as an automobile or a chair. But goods may also be fluid, such as oil or gasoline. Goods may also be intangible, such as natural gas and electricity. The UCC is applicable to both new and used goods. It does not apply to real estate.

What about a contract for services – like a contract with an electrician to wire a new house?
A contract for services is an ordinary contract and is not a sale of goods. Therefore, such a contract would be covered by general contract law.

What about a contract that deals with both goods and services?
If a contract calls for both the rendering of services and the supplying of materials (goods) to be used in performing the services, the contract is classified according to its dominant element. If the sale of goods is dominant, it is a sales contract covered by Article 2 of the UCC. If the service element is dominant, it is a service contract and not covered by the UCC but is covered by general contract law. For example, a contract with someone who repaired bicycles is a contract for services, even if parts are supplied to perform the repairs. The supplying of the parts is not regarded as a sale but is merely incidental to the primary contract of making repairs. In contrast, the purchase of a television set, with the incidental service of installation, is a sale of goods because the purchase of the set is the dominant element.

Are there any major differences between the law of sales as set forth in Article 2 of the UCC and general contract law? Yes, the following is a brief overview of the differences:

- **Merchants.** In most instances, the UCC treats all buyers and sellers alike. In some cases, it treats *merchants* differently than it does the occasional or casual buyer or seller. The UCC recognizes that the merchant is experienced and has a special knowledge of the relevant commercial practices.
- **Firm Offer.** Contract law as to *offers* is applicable to a sales contract, with the following exception. A *firm offer* by a *merchant* cannot be revoked if the offer:
    - expresses an intention that it will not be revoked,
    - is in a writing, and
    - is signed by the merchant.
- **Acceptance.** An offer to buy or sell goods may be accepted in any manner and by any medium that is reasonable under the circumstances. However, if a specific manner or medium is clearly required by the terms of the offer or the circumstances of the case, the offer can only be accepted in that manner.

- **Additional Term in Offer.** Unless it is expressly specified that an offer to buy or sell goods must be accepted just as made, the offeree may accept an offer and at the same time propose an additional term. The new term does not reject the original offer. A contract arises on the terms of the original offer, and the new term is a counteroffer. The new term does not become binding until accepted by the original offeror. If, however, the offer states that it must be accepted exactly as made, the ordinary contract law rules apply. In a transaction between *merchants,* the additional term becomes part of the contract if that term does not materially alter the offer and no objection is made to it. However, if such an additional term from the seller operates solely to the seller's advantage, it is a material term and must be accepted by the buyer to be effective.
- **Conflicting Term in Offer.** When a term of an acceptance conflicts with a term of an offer, ***but*** it is clear that the parties intended to be bound by a contract, the UCC recognizes the formation of a contract. The terms that are conflicting cancel each other out and are ignored. The contract then consists of the terms of the offer and acceptance that agree, together with those terms that the UCC or contract law implies into a contract.
- **Determination of Price.** The price for goods may be expressly fixed by the contract. If not fixed by the contract, the price may be an open term, whereby the parties merely indicate how the price should be determined at a later time or make no provision whatever as to the price. When persons experienced in a particular industry make a contract for goods without specifying the price to be paid, the price will be determined by the manner that is customary in the industry. Ordinarily, if nothing is said as to price, the buyer is required to pay the reasonable value of the goods, which is generally the market price.
- **Output and Requirement Contracts.** Somewhat related to the open-term rule concerning price is the rule involved in output and requirement contracts that the quantity to be sold or purchased is not a specific quantity. Instead, it is the amount that the seller should produce or the buyer should require. Although this introduces an element of uncertainty, such sales contracts are valid. To prevent oppression, these contracts are subject to two limitations: (1) the parties must act in good faith, and (2) the quantity offered or demanded must not be unreasonably disproportionate to prior output or requirements or to a stated estimate.
- **Indefinite Duration Contract.** When the sales contract is a continuing contract, such as one calling for periodic delivery of gas, but no time is set for the life of the contract, the contract runs for a reasonable time. It may be terminated on notice by either party.
- **Modification of Contract.** An agreement to modify a contract for the sale of goods is binding even though the modification is not supported by consideration.
- **Parol Evidence Rule.** The parol evidence rule applies to the sale of goods, with the slight modification that a writing is not presumed to represent the entire contract of the parties unless the court specifically decides that it does.
- **Usage of Trade and Course of Dealing.** The patterns of doing business as shown by the prior dealings of the parties may form part of their contract. These patterns may be looked to in order to find what was intended by the express provisions of the agreement and to supply otherwise missing terms.

What is a merchant?
The word "Merchant" is defined by § **2-104** of the UCC as a person that deals in goods of the kind or otherwise holds itself out by occupation as having knowledge or skill peculiar to the practices or goods involved in the transaction.

Why are merchants treated differently by the UCC? The UCC recognizes that the merchant is experienced and has a special knowledge of the relevant commercial practices.

What is a *bulk sale*?
A bulk sale is a sale of goods by a business which engages in selling items out of inventory (as opposed to manufacturing or service industries), often in liquidating or selling a business. This type of sale is governed by the bulk sales law which is Article 6 of the UCC. When merchants are about to transfer a major part of their materials, supplies, merchandise, or other inventory (not in the ordinary course of business), advance notice of the transfer should be given to creditors. This notice should be given by the transferee. If the notice required by Article 6 is not given, the creditors of the seller may enforce their claims on property in the hands of the buyer. Creditors may also reach the property in the hands of any subsequent transferee who knew that there had not been compliance with the UCC or who did not pay a reasonable value for the goods. This provision is designed to protect the creditors of a merchant from the merchant's selling all the inventory, pocketing the money, and then disappearing, leaving the creditors unpaid.

Statute of Frauds
A contract for the sale of goods may be oral or written. In some cases, it must be evidenced by a writing or it cannot be enforced in court. Whenever the sales price of goods is $500 or more, the sales contract must be evidenced by a writing to be enforceable. The writing evidencing the sales contract may be either a complete written contract signed by both parties or (b) a memorandum signed by the defendant. The writing must indicate that there has been a completed transaction as to certain goods. It needs to indicate that a sale has been made and the quantity of goods involved. Any other missing terms may be shown by parol evidence. The writing must be signed by the person who is being sued or by the authorized agent of that person. The signature must be placed on the paper with the intention of authenticating the writing. The signature may consist of initials or may be printed, stamped, or typewritten, as long as it is made with the necessary intent.

When the transaction is between merchants, an exception is made to the requirement of signing. The failure of a merchant to repudiate a confirming letter sent by another merchant within ten days of receiving such a letter binds the merchant who did not sign just as he had signed the letter. This makes it necessary for a merchant seller to watch the mail and to act within ten days of receiving a mailed confirmation. For example, Adam and Sam both merchants, entered into an oral agreement for the sale of mattresses to Adam for $1,000. Adam immediately sent Sam a letter confirming the agreement. Sam did not make a written objection to the contents of Adam's letter within ten days, but Sam refuses to deliver the mattresses. Sam is bound by the agreement.

A writing can satisfy a statute of frauds, even though it was not made for that purpose. When the buyer writes to the seller 30 days after delivery and merely criticizes the quality of the goods, the letter may satisfy the statute since it indicates that there was a sale of those goods. Formal contracts, bills of sale, and letters are common forms of writings that satisfy the requirement. Purchase orders, cash register receipts, sales tickets, invoices, and similar papers generally do not satisfy the requirement as to a signature, and sometimes they do not specify any quantity or commodity.

A sales agreement that does not satisfy the statute of frauds cannot be enforced. However, the oral contract itself is not unlawful and may be voluntarily performed by the parties.

Exceptions to Requirement of a Writing
The absence of a writing does not always bar proof of a sales contract.

- **Nonresellable Goods**. No writing is required when the goods are specially made for the buyer and are of such an unusual nature that they are not suitable for sale in the ordinary course of the seller's business. For example, four reinforced steel doors were custom made by the seller for the buyer's building. The doors were not suitable for sale to anyone else in the ordinary course of the seller's business, and they could only be sold as scrap. In this case, an oral contract of sale could be enforced. In order for the nonresellable goods exception to apply, the seller must have made a substantial beginning in manufacturing the goods or, if a distributor, in procuring them, before notice of repudiation by the buyer is received.
- **Receipt and Acceptance.** An oral sales contract may be enforced if it can be shown that the goods were delivered by the seller and were both received and accepted by the buyer. Therefore, if the buyer receives and accepts goods on credit, the seller may sue for the purchase price, even if it is over $500 and there is no writing. The receipt and acceptance of the goods by the buyer took the contract out of the statute of frauds. Both a receipt and an acceptance by the buyer must be shown.
- **Payment.** An oral contract may be enforced if the buyer has made full payment. In the case of part payment for divisible units of goods, a contract may be enforced only with respect to the goods for which payment has been made and accepted. If part payment is made for indivisible goods, such as an automobile, a part payment avoids the statute of frauds and permits proof of the entire oral contract.
- **Admission**. An oral contract may be enforced if the party against whom enforcement is sought admits in pleadings, testimony, or otherwise in court that a contract for sale was made. The contract, however, is not enforceable beyond the quantity of goods admitted.

REVIEW

Does the UCC require that all contracts regarding the sale of goods be in writing? A contract for the sale of goods may be oral or written. In some cases, it must be evidenced by a writing or it cannot be enforced in court. Whenever the sales price of goods is $500 or more, the sales contract must be evidenced by a writing to be enforceable. The writing evidencing the sales contract may be either a complete written contract signed by both parties or (b) a memorandum signed by the defendant. The writing must indicate that there has been a completed transaction as to certain goods. It needs to indicate that a sale has been made and the quantity of goods involved. Any other missing terms may be shown by parol evidence.

When the transaction is between merchants, an exception is made to the requirement of signing. The failure of a merchant to repudiate a confirming letter sent by another merchant within ten days of receiving such a letter binds the merchant who did not sign just as he had signed the letter. This makes it necessary for a merchant seller to watch the mail and to act within ten days of receiving a mailed confirmation.

Bill of Sale

A bill of sale is a document that transfers ownership of personal property from a seller to the buyer. It acts as a basic agreement for sale of goods, and a sales receipt. .A Bill of Sale also constitutes a record of the transaction for both the seller and buyer. It can provide the seller with a record of what has been sold, to whom, when, and for what price.

Most bill of sale forms should contain the following information:

- Amount of consideration paid for the transfer of title and date of purchase.
- Name and address of Seller
- Name and address of Buyer
- Specific information about the asset being transferred from the seller to the buyer.
- Guarantee from the seller that the item is free from all claims and offsets.
- Any representations or warranties
- Signature of the seller(s)
- Signature of a notary public.

FREQUENTLY ASKED QUESTIONS – BILL OF SALE

Does a bill of sale have to be recorded?

Generally, a bill of sale does not have to be recorded but may be required as proof of ownership.

Who must sign a bill of sale?

The owners of the property being sold must sign. If the property is owned jointly, both owners must generally sign.

May I use a bill of sale for the sale of a dog?

Yes. A pet is considered personal property and may be transferred by personal property bill of sale.

What does with or without warranties mean?

A bill of sale with warranties means that you assure the buyer that the property is yours and that you have the right to transfer the property and will defend the buyer from other persons who may claim the property. A bill of sale without warranties means that you quitclaim the property and do not warrant title. A quitclaim is used in several situations, such as where the seller cannot prove ownership in the seller, or where the seller just does not want to warrant title to the property. This is similar to a quitclaim deed as compared to a warranty deed.

What are the execution and witness requirements?
The requirements of how the bill of sale must be signed is governed by State law and varies from State to State. Some States require that a bill of sale be witnessed, others require that it be notarized and some do not require witnessing or a notary.

What does "as-is" mean?
This means that the seller you do not guarantee the condition of the property or that the property is free from defect. The transfer is generally without warranties and is used to protect the seller.

Chapter 13
PRODUCTS LIABILITY AND WARRANTIES

EXPRESS WARRANTIES
An express warranty is a statement by the seller relating to the goods, which statement is part of the basis of the bargain. This means that the buyer has purchased the goods on the reasonable assumption that they were as stated by the seller. Thus, a statement by the seller with respect to the quality, capacity, or other characteristic of the goods is an express warranty. For example, "This shirt is 100% cotton."

No particular form of words is necessary to constitute an express warranty. A sale does not need to state that a warranty is being made or that one is intended. It is sufficient that the seller assert a fact that becomes a part or term of the bargain or transaction between the parties. An express warranty may even be demonstrated by conduct. If the buyer asks to purchase a light blue shirt that is 100% cotton, and the seller hands over a light blue shirt, the seller's conduct expresses a warranty that the shirt is 100% cotton. The words on the label of a can for Florida orange juice is an express warranty that the orange juice comes from Florida.

"Sales talk" or "puffery" by a seller such as "this is the best used car money can buy" cannot ordinarily treat as a warranty. However, if the buyer has reason to believe that the seller has expert knowledge of the conditions of the market and the buyer requests the seller's opinion as an expert, the buyer would be entitled to accept as a fact the seller's statement as to whether a given article was the best obtainable, The statement could be reasonably regarded as forming part of the basis of the bargain.

When the contract is based in part on the understanding that the seller will supply goods according to a particular description or that the goods will be the same as the sample or a model, the seller is bound by an express warranty that the goods shall conform to the description, sample, or model.

If the express warranty is false, there is a breach of the warranty. The warrantor is then liable just as though the truth of the warranty had been guaranteed. It is no defense that the defendant honestly believed that the warranty was true, had exercised due care in manufacturing or handling the product, or had no reason to believe that the warranty was false.

IMPLIED WARRANTIES
An implied warranty is one that was not made by the seller but is implied by law. In certain instances, the law implies or reads a warranty into a sale, although the seller did not make it. That is, the implied warranty arises automatically from the fact that a sale has been made.

Express warranties arise because they form part of the basis on which the sale has been made. The fact that express warranties are made does not exclude implied warranties. When both express and implied warranties exist, they should be construed as being consistent with each other and cumulative if such a construction is reasonable. In case it is unreasonable to construe them as consistent and cumulative, an express warranty prevails over an implied warranty as to the subject matter of the sale, except in the case of an implied warranty of fitness for a particular purpose. A distinction is made between a merchant seller and the casual seller with regard to implied warranties.

WARRANTY OF TITLE

Every seller, by the mere act of selling, makes a warranty that the seller's title is good and that the transfer is lawful as to passage of title. A warranty of title may be specifically excluded, or the circumstances may be such as to prevent the warranty from arising. The latter situation is found when the buyer has reason to know that the seller does not claim to hold the title or that the seller is purporting to sell only such right or title as the seller or a third person may have. For example, no warranty of title arises when the seller makes the sale in a representative capacity, such as a sheriff, an auctioneer, or an administrator of a decedent's estate.

WARRANTY AGAINST ENCUMBRANCES

Every seller, by the mere act of selling, makes a warranty that the goods shall be delivered free from any lien of which the buyer at the time of the sales transaction had no knowledge.

WARRANTY OF FITNESS FOR A PARTICULAR PURPOSE.

A buyer may intend to use the goods for a particular or unusual purpose, compared to the ordinary use for which the goods are customarily sold. If so, the seller makes an implied warranty that the goods will be fit for that purpose when:

- the buyer relies on the seller 's skill or judgment to select or furnish suitable goods, and
- when the seller at the time of contracting knows or has reason to know the
- buyer's particular purpose and of the buyer's reliance on the seller's judgment.

When the buyer makes the purchase without relying on the seller's skill and judgment, no warranty of fitness for a particular purpose arises.

ADDITIONAL IMPLIED WARRANTIES OF MERCHANT SELLER

- **Warranty against infringement.** Unless otherwise agreed, every merchant seller warrants that the goods will be delivered free of the rightful claim of any third person by way of patent infringement, trademark infringement, or any other intellectual property law infringement.

- **Warranty of fitness for normal use.** A merchant seller makes an implied warranty of the **merchantability** of the goods sold. This warranty is in fact a group of warranties, the most important of which is that the goods are fit for the ordinary purposes for which they are sold.

WARRANTIES IN PARTICULAR SALES

- **Sale on Buyer's Specifications.** When the buyer furnishes the seller with exact specifications for the preparation or manufacture of goods, the same warranties arise as in the case of any other sale of such goods by the particular seller. However, no warranty of fitness for a particular purpose can arise since it s clear that the buyer is purchasing on the basis of the buyer's own decision and is not relying on the seller's skill and judgment.

- **Sale of Secondhand or Used Goods**. As far as the UCC is concerned, there is no difference between the warranties arising in the sale of used goods and those arising in the sale of new goods. With respect to used goods, what is "fit for normal use" will be a lower standard for used than for new goods.
- **Sale of Food or Drink.** The sale of food or drink, whether to be consumed or off the seller's premises, is a sale. When made by a merchant, a sale of food or drink carries the implied warranty that the food is fit for its ordinary purpose, *i.e.,* human consumption.

NECESSITY OF DEFECT

To impose liability for breach of the implied warranty of merchantability, it is ordinarily necessary to show that there was a defect in the product and that this defect made the product not fit for its normal use and that this caused the plaintiff's harm. A product may be defective because there is:

- a manufacturing defect,
- a design defect,
- inadequate instruction on how to use the product, or
- inadequate warning against dangers involved in using the product.

If the manufacturer's blueprint shows that there should be two bolts at a particular place on the property and the factory puts in only one bolt, there is a manufacturing defect. If the two bolts are put in but the product breaks because four bolts are required to provide sufficient strength, there is no manufacturing defect, but there is a design defect. A product that is properly designed and properly manufactured may be dangerous because the user is not given sufficient instructions on how to use the product. Also, a product is defective if there is a danger that is not obvious and there is no warning at all or a warning that does not describe the full danger.

FREQUENTLY ASKED QUESTIONS

Is there any basic warranty coverage that automatically comes with a consumer product?
Customers will almost always receive the basic protection of the implied warranty of merchantability and the implied warranty of fitness for a particular purpose. Most states prohibit anyone who offers a written warranty from disclaiming or modifying implied warranties.

What is a full warranty?
A warranty is a "full" warranty when:

- There is not a limit the duration of implied warranties
- Coverage is not limit to first purchasers
- Warranty service is free of charge, including such costs as returning the product or removing and reinstalling the product when necessary
- At the consumer's choice, either a replacement or a full refund if, after a reasonable number of tries, the product can't be repaired

- Consumers aren't required to perform any duty as a precondition for receiving service, except notice that service is needed

Is a warranty a contract the manufacturer must honor? Yes, a warranty is a contract that commits the manufacturer to stand behind the product.

If a product doesn't perform as anticipated, is it covered by any type of warranty?
A merchant seller makes an implied warranty of the *merchantability* of the goods he sells. This warranty is in fact a group of warranties, the most important of which is that the goods are fit for the ordinary purposes for which they are sold. The law says that merchants make this promise automatically every time they sell a product they are in business to sell.

I bought a washer because of what the salesperson said it would do. It does not do what he said. Do I have any legal recourse?
A buyer may intend to use the goods for a particular or unusual purpose, compared to the ordinary use for which the goods are customarily sold. If so, the seller makes an implied warranty that the goods will be fit for that purpose when:

- the buyer relies on the seller 's skill or judgment to select or furnish suitable goods, and
- when the seller at the time of contracting knows or has reason to know the buyer's particular purpose and of the buyer's reliance on the seller's judgment.

When the buyer makes the purchase without relying on the seller's skill and judgment, no warranty of fitness for a particular purpose arises.

I feel the product I purchased is wearing out prematurely. Isn't this covered under my warranty?
Implied warranties are promises about the condition of products at the time they are sold, but they do not assure that a product will last for any specific length of time. Everything that can possibly go wrong with a product does not fall within the scope of implied warranties. For example, implied warranties do not cover problems such as those caused by:

- Abuse;
- Misuse;
- Ordinary wear;
- Failure to follow directions; and
- Improper maintenance.

What is the statue of limitations claim for breach of warranty issue?
State statutes of limitation for breach of either an express or an implied warranty are *generally* four years from date of purchase. This means that buyers have four years in which to discover and seek a remedy for problems that were present in the product at the time it was sold. This does not mean that the product must last for four years. It means only that the product must be of normal durability, considering its nature and price.

Is there any type of warranty for a product I bought from a second-hand store?
As far as the UCC is concerned, there is no difference between the warranties arising in the sale of used goods and those arising in the sale of new goods. With respect to used goods, what is "fit for normal use" will be a lower standard for used than for new goods.

What is an express warranty?
Express warranties, unlike implied warranties, are not "read into" a sales contract by state law. An express warranty is a statement by the seller relating to the goods, which statement is part of the basis of the bargain. This means that the buyer has purchased the goods on the reasonable assumption that they were as stated by the seller. Thus, a statement by the seller with respect to the quality, capacity, or other characteristic of the goods is an express warranty. For example, "This shirt is 100% cotton."

Product Liability
Products liability refers to the liability of any or all parties along the chain of manufacture of any product for damage caused by that product. This includes the manufacturer of component parts, an assembling manufacturer, the wholesaler, and the retail store owner. Product liability suits may be brought by the consumer or someone to whom the product was loaned. While products are generally thought of as tangible personal property, products liability law has stretched that definition to include intangibles (gas), naturals (pets), real estate (house), and writings (navigational charts).

Products liability claims can be based *on negligence, strict liability,* or *breach of warranty of fitness* depending on the jurisdiction within which the claim is based. In a strict liability theory of liability, the degree of care exercised by the manufacturer is irrelevant. As long as the product is proven to be defective, the manufacturer will be held liable for the harm resulting from the defect.

Claims may be based on the common law of the states or on the Uniform Commercial Code (UCC). Article 2 of the UCC deals with the sales of goods and it has been adopted by most states. The most important products liability sections are the implied and express warranties of merchantability in the sales of goods.

In order to prevail on a product liability claim, the product complained of must be shown to be defective. There are three types of product defects that incur liability in manufacturers and suppliers*: design defects, manufacturing defects,* and *defects in marketing.* Design defects are inherent; they exist before the product is manufactured. While the item might serve its intended use, it can be unreasonably dangerous to use due to a design flaw. Manufacturing defects occur during the construction or production of the item. Only a few out of many products of the same type are flawed in this case. Defects in marketing deal with improper instructions and failures to warn consumers of latent or hidden dangers in the product.

Negligence – Due Care Must Be Exercised
Due care must be exercised in designing products, in selecting materials, in producing and testing products, and in placing warnings on labels informing users of dangers of which an ordinary

person might not be aware. The duty of care extends to inspecting and testing products that a manufacturer buys for use in the final product.

Privity of Contract Not Required – Can a manufacturer be held liable to any person who suffers an injury proximately caused by the manufacturer's negligently made product? The doctrine of privity in contract law provides that a contract cannot confer rights or impose obligations arising under it on any person or agent except the parties to it. The premise is that only parties to contracts should be able to sue to enforce their rights or claim damages as such.

A manufacturer who fails to use reasonable care in manufacturing its product may be liable for harm caused by the product to those whom the manufacturer should expect to be endangered by use of the product. *Privity of contract* is not required for recovery by an injured plaintiff on the ground of negligence in a product liability action. In other words, a manufacturer is liable for its failure to exercise due care to any person who sustains an injury proximately caused by a negligently made product, regardless of whether the injured person is in privity with the manufacturer.

Misrepresentation

When fraudulent misrepresentation to a user or consumer results in injury, it may serve as a basis of liability. A bad ad or label can show intent, but the injured party must have relied on it.

Strict Product Liability

The law has developed a doctrine known as "strict liability," that allows a person injured by a defective or unexpectedly dangerous product to recover compensation from the maker or seller of the product, without showing that the manufacturer or seller was actually negligent.

Unreasonably dangerous. Strict Liability rule applies only where the defective condition of the product makes it unreasonably dangerous to the user or consumer. Many products cannot possibly be made entirely safe for all consumption, and any food or drug necessarily involves some risk of harm, if only from over-consumption. Ordinary sugar is a deadly poison to diabetics, and castor oil found use under Mussolini as an instrument of torture. That is not what is meant by "unreasonably dangerous." The article sold must be dangerous to an extent beyond that which would be contemplated by the ordinary consumer who purchases it, with the ordinary knowledge common to the community as to its characteristics. Good whiskey is not unreasonably dangerous merely because it will make some people drunk, and is especially dangerous to alcoholics; but bad whiskey containing a dangerous amount of fuel oil, is unreasonably dangerous. Good butter is not unreasonably dangerous merely because, if such be the case, it deposits cholesterol in the arteries and leads to heart attacks; but bad butter, contaminated with poisonous fish oil, is unreasonably dangerous.

Requirements for Strict Product Liability

For a cause of action in strict product liability against a manufacturer:

- A product must be in a defective condition when the manufacturer sells it. The manufacturer must be normally engaged in the business of selling it.
- The product must be unreasonably dangerous to a user or consumer because of its defective condition (not required in all states).

- A plaintiff must incur physical harm to self or property by use or consumption of the product.
- The defective condition must proximately cause the injury or damage.
- The product must not have been substantially changed from the time it was sold to the time of the injury.

Under Section 402A of the Restatement (Second) of Torts, the elements of an action for strict product liability are:

- the product must be in a defective condition when the defendant sells it;
- the defendant must normally be engaged in the business of selling (or distributing) that product;
- the product must be unreasonably dangerous to the user or consumer because of its defective condition (in most states);
- the plaintiff must incur physical harm to self or property by use or consumption of the product;
- the defective condition must be the proximate cause of the injury or damage; and
- the goods must not have been substantially changed from the time the product was sold to the time the injury was sustained.

Proving a Defective Condition
It need not be shown why or how a product became defective, but it must be shown that at the time of the injury, the product's condition was essentially the same as it was in the hands of the manufacturer or seller.

Unreasonably Dangerous Products
A product is reasonably dangerous if:

- It is dangerous beyond the reasonable expectations of the ordinary consumer.
- A less dangerous alternative was economically feasible but the manufacturer failed to produce it.

PRODUCT DEFECTS

- **Manufacturing Defects** - A product "contains a manufacturing defect when the product departs from its intended design even though all possible care was exercised in the preparation and marketing of the product." This includes products that are physically flawed, damaged, or incorrectly assembled.
- **Design Defects -** A product "is defective in design when the foreseeable risks of harm posed by the product could have been reduced or avoided by the adoption of a reasonable alternative design by the seller or other distributor, or a predecessor in the commercial chain of distribution, and the omission of the alternative design renders the product not reasonably safe." To determine whether a product has a design defect, the focus is on its actual design and the reasonableness of that design. To succeed on this theory, a plaintiff has to show that there is a reasonable alternative design. A defendant is liable only when the harm was reasonably preventable.

Test for Design Defects
To determine whether a product has a design defect, the focus is on its actual design and the reasonableness of that design. To succeed on this theory, a plaintiff has to show that there is a reasonable alternative design. A defendant is liable only when the harm was reasonably preventable.

Bullock v. Philip Morris USA, Inc.[7]
Jodie Bullock smoked Philip Morris-branded cigarettes for forty-five years from 1956 until she was diagnosed with lung cancer in 2001. Despite proof as early as the 1950s that smoking caused cancer, Philip Morris contended in its ads, and its executives asserted in interviews, that there was no proof. Jodie Bullock sued Philip Morris on a product liability theory. At trial, the jury found that a defect in cigarettes' design, attributable to negligence, and awarded Bullock $850,000 in compensatory damages and $28 billion in punitive damages. Philip Morris appealed.

The California Court of Appeal for the Second District affirmed. Philip Morris failed to show any error with respect to its liability for products liability based on a design defect. "A product is defective in design for purposes of tort liability if the benefits of the design do not outweigh the risk of danger inherent in the design, or if the product, used in an intended or reasonably foreseeable manner, has failed to perform as safely as an ordinary consumer would expect."

Under what circumstances, if any, could Philip Morris have justified its continuing campaign to discredit the scientific arguments that linked smoking with lung cancer? If the science purporting to support a link between smoking and cancer were less solid, or if the accompanying statistics were less valid, Philip Morris might have been able to justify its claims to that effect. Also profiting from the sale of tobacco products was most likely the company's motivation for denying the asserted link between smoking and bad health (and any connection between smoking and other adverse consequences, such as addiction). That profit would very likely have been reduced if customers and potential customers came to believe that smoking and ill effects were inextricably linked. In support of this motive, the company might have argued that it gave jobs to many people in diverse occupations, from farming to factory work, advertising and distribution to wholesale and retail sales.

Inadequate Warnings
A product "is defective because of inadequate instructions or warnings when the foreseeable risks of harm posed by the product could have been reduced or avoided by the provision of reasonable instructions or warnings by the seller or other distributor, or a predecessor in the commercial chain of distribution, and the omission of the instructions or warnings renders the product not reasonably safe." There is no duty to warn about risks that are obvious or commonly known. There is a duty to warn of harm that can result from foreseeable misuse.

---

[7] 198 Cal.App.4th 543 (2011)

Defenses to Product Liability
One defense is that there is no basis for the claim because the plaintiff has not proved its elements.

Assumption of Risk
In some states, the following elements must be shown: (i) the plaintiff voluntarily engaged in the risk while realizing the potential danger, (ii) the plaintiff knew and appreciated the risk created by the defect, and (ii) the plaintiff's decision to undertake the known risk was unreasonable.

Product Misuse
If a party used a product for something for which it was not designed, the party may not be able to recover in strict liability (some courts hold, however, that if a misuse is reasonably foreseeable, a seller must take measures to guard against it).

Comparative Negligence (Fault)
Most courts consider a plaintiff's negligence in apportioning liability. Some courts will consider only a plaintiff's intentional conduct, however.

FREQUENTLY ASKED QUESTIONS

What is the difference between express warranties and puffing? A seller's statement about the value or worth of goods ("they're priceless") or a seller's statement of opinion ("this is the best used car to come along in years") is not an express warranty but puffing, which creates no warranty. A seller who is an expert can create a warranty by giving an opinion as an expert (an art dealer, for instance, who is an expert in twentieth-century paintings, who tells a buyer that a print is a Warhol warrants the accuracy of the opinion). What constitutes an express warranty and what constitutes puffing is often controlled by the reasonableness of a buyer's reliance (statements on which no reasonable person would rely are puffing). Whether a statement is made orally or in writing and its specificity can be relevant to reasonableness.

If warranties are inconsistent, what are the priorities? If express and implied warranties are inconsistent: (i) express warranties displace implied warranties except implied warranties of fitness for a particular purpose (an express warranty in a contract for a short-wave radio, for example, stating that the radio will receive signals from 4,000 miles away displaces an implied warranty of fitness that a short-wave radio will pick up signals from any distance, but telling a buyer that the radio will receive signals from 8,000 miles, for which reason the buyer buys the radio, may violate a warranty of fitness for a particular purpose, which prevails over express warranties); (ii) samples displace general descriptions; and (iii) technical specifications displace samples or general descriptions.

How can implied warranties of merchantability and fitness for a particular purpose be disclaimed? Unless circumstances indicate otherwise, implied warranties are generally disclaimed by expressions such as "as is," "with all faults," and other similar phrases that call buyers' attention to the fact that there are no implied warranties. To disclaim an implied warranty of fitness for a particular purpose, a disclaimer ("there are no warranties extending beyond the description on the face hereof") must be written and be conspicuous. A merchantability disclaimer must mention merchantability, but it need not be written; if it is in writing, the writing must be conspicuous (printed in larger or differently colored type or with a heading in capitals, for example).

What effect does a buyer's examination of the goods before contracting have on implied warranties? If a buyer examines goods or refuses to examine goods (or a sample or model) as much as he or she wants before contracting, there is no implied warranty with respect to defects that a reasonable examination will reveal (and the seller will not be liable for breach of warranty if the defects lead to an injury). A failure to examine goods available for inspection is not the same as a refusal to examine them; a refusal can occur only if a seller demands that a buyer examine the goods. A seller remains liable for latent (hidden) defects that a normal inspection would not reveal. What an examination should reveal depends on a buyer's skill and method of examination (for example, an auto mechanic buying a car should discover defects that a nonexpert would not be expected to find).

When does a cause of action accrue for breach of warranty? A cause of action accrues for breach of warranty when a seller tenders delivery, even if the nonbreaching party is unaware that a cause has accrued. If a warranty extends to future performance, however, discovery of its breach must await the time of performance, and the statute of limitations does not begin to run until that time (for example, the statute would not begin to run until winter on a furnace installed in summer).

To avoid liability on a negligence theory in a product liability suit, to what extent must a manufacturer exercise due care? A manufacturer must exercise due care to make a product safe for its intended use. Due care must be exercised in designing products, in selecting materials, in producing and testing products, and in placing warnings on labels informing users of dangers of which an ordinary person might not be aware. The duty extends to inspecting and testing products that a manufacturer buys for use in the final product.

Under the Restatement (Second) of Torts, Section 402A, what are the requirements for a cause of action in strict liability in a product liability suit? For a cause of action in strict liability in a product liability suit against a manufacturer, the requirements are: (1) the product must have been in a defective condition when the manufacturer sold it, (2) the manufacturer must be normally engaged in the business of selling the product, (3) the product must be unreasonably dangerous to a user or consumer because of its defective condition (not required in all states), (4) a plaintiff must suffer physical injury to self or property damage by use or consumption of the product, (5) the defective condition must proximately cause the injury or damage, and (6) the product must not have been substantially changed from the time it was sold to the time of the injury. It need not be shown why or how a product became defective, but it must be shown that at the time of the injury the product's condition was essentially the same as it was when it left the manufacturer or seller

Can an injured bystander recover from a manufacturer or seller on a strict liability theory? Yes - all courts extend the strict liability of manufacturers and other sellers to injured bystanders (when the explosion of an automobile motor in traffic released a cloud of steam that blocked the view of other drivers, for example, the automobile manufacturer was held liable for the resulting multiple collisions).

Other than immediate sellers and manufacturers, who may be subject to strict liability? The strict liability doctrine has been expanded to include suppliers of component parts. Strict liability for personal injuries caused by defective goods extends to lessors. (Some courts have held that a lease gives rise to a contractual implied warranty that the leased goods will be fit for the duration of the lease - for instance, if U-Haul leases a trailer that has been improperly maintained, which causes an accident in which the lessee is injured, the lessee can sue U-Haul).

Chapter 14

CONSUMER PROTECTION

Pursuant to the common law doctrine of *caveat emptor,* the buyer could not recover from the seller for defects on the property that rendered the property unfit for ordinary purposes. *Caveat emptor* is Latin for *let the buyer beware.* Both Congress and state legislatures have enacted consumer protection laws intended to limit abuses inherent in the common law approach that would have the *buyer beware.* A person violating the provisions of a consumer protection statute is generally liable even though there was no intention to violate the law. Liability also exists even though the breach was a single occurrence rather than a pattern of repeated conduct

PROOF OF CONSUMER STATUS

A consumer claiming that there has been a violation of the consumer protection statute has the burden of proving that the statutory definition of *consumer* has been satisfied. The word *consumer* refers to individuals or households that use goods and services generated within the economy.

ACTION BY CONSUMER

Some consumer protection statutes provide that a consumer who is harmed by a violation of the statutes may sue the business or organization that acted improperly. The consumer may sue to recover a specified penalty or may bring an action on behalf of consumers as a class. Consumer protection statutes are often designed to rely on private litigation as an aid to enforcement of the statutory provisions. In such an action, a consumer must show that the defendant engaged in misconduct of the kind prohibited by the applicable consumer protection statute.

ADVERTISING

Consumer protection statutes commonly prohibit fraudulent advertising. Most advertising regulations are entrusted to an administrative agency, such as the Federal Trade Commission (FTC). The FTC is authorized to issue orders to stop false or misleading advertising. Statutes prohibiting false advertising are liberally interpreted. A business is liable for false advertising when it advertises a reduced price sale of a particular item, but that item is out of stock at the time the sale begins. It is no defense to the store that the pre-sale demand was greater than usual.

Under consumer protection statutes, *deception* rather than *fraud,* is the significant element. There can be a breach of a consumer protection statute even though there is no proof that the wrongdoer intended to defraud or deceive anyone. Instead of basing the law in terms of fault of the actor, the law is concerned with the problem of the buyer who is likely to be misled. The good faith of an advertiser or the absence of intent to deceive is immaterial. The purpose of false advertising legislation is to protect the consumer rather than to examine the advertiser's motives.

The FTC requires that an advertiser maintain a file containing the data claimed to support an advertising statement as to safety, performance, efficacy, quality, or comparative price of an advertised product. The FTC can require the advertiser to produce this material, If it is in the interest of the consumer, the FTC can make this information public, except to the extent that it contains trade secrets or material that is privileged.

CORRECTIVE ADVERTISING
When an enterprise has made false and deceptive statements in advertising, the Federal Trade Commission may require that new advertising be made in which the former statements are contradicted and the truth stated. This *corrective advertising* required by the Federal Trade Commission is also called *retractive advertising.*

SEALS OF APPROVAL
Many commodities are sold or advertised with a sticker or tag stating that the article has been approved or is guaranteed by some association or organization. Ordinarily, when a product is sold in such a way, it will in fact have been approved by some testing laboratory and will probably have proven adequate to meet ordinary consumer needs. Selling with a seal of approval of a third person makes, in effect, a guarantee that the product has been so approved. A seller is liable if the product was, in fact, not approved.

LABELING
Closely related to the regulation of advertising is the regulation of labeling products. Various federal statutes are designed to give the consumer accurate information about the product, while others require warnings about dangers of use or misuse. Consumer protection regulations prohibit the use in the labeling of products with such terms as *jumbo* or *giant* which tend to exaggerate and mislead.

SELLING METHODS
Consumer protection statutes prohibit the use of improper and deceptive selling methods. These statutes are liberally construed to protect consumers from improper practices.

DECEPTIVE PRACTICES
Consumer protection statutes and deceptive trade practice acts are violated when the statements or the business methods of the defendant are deceptive. It is not necessary to prove that the defendant was guilty of fraud. It is immaterial that the defendant who misrepresented the facts did not intentionally do so.

DISCLOSURE OF TRANSACTION TERMS

CONTRACT ON TWO SIDES
To be sure that the consumer sees disclosures required by federal law, special provision is made for the case when the terms of the transaction are printed on both the front and back of a sheet or contract. In such a situation, both sides of the sheet must carry the warning: **NOTICE: see other side for important information.** Also, the page must be signed at the end of the second side.

PARTICULAR SALES AND LEASES
The Motor Vehicle Information and Cost Savings Act requires a dealer to disclose to the buyer various elements in the cost of an automobile. The act prohibits selling an automobile without informing the buyer that the odometer has been reset below the true mileage. A buyer who is caused actual loss by odometer fraud may recover from the seller three times the actual loss or $1,500, whichever is greater. There is a breach of this statute when the seller has knowledge that the odometer has turned at 100,000 miles but the seller then states that the

mileage is 20,000 miles instead of 120,000. *The Consumer Leasing Act of 1976* requires that persons leasing automobiles and other durable goods to consumers make a full disclosure to the consumer of the details of the transaction.

Although the statute imposes liability only when the seller *knowingly* violates the statute, it is not necessary to prove *actual* knowledge. For example, an experienced auto dealer cannot claim lack of knowledge that the odometer was false when that conclusion was reasonably apparent from the condition of the car.

REFERRAL SALES

The technique of giving the buyer a price reduction for customers referred to the seller is theoretically lawful. In effect, it is merely paying the buyer a commission for the promotion of other sales. In actual practice, however, the referral sales technique is often accompanied by fraud or by exorbitant pricing. Therefore, consumer protection laws condemn referral selling in various ways. As a result, the referral system of selling has been condemned as unconscionable under the Uniform Commercial Code (UCC), and is expressly prohibited by the Uniform Consumer Credit Code (UCCC) which has been adopted by a number of states.

CONTRACT WITH CONSUMERS

Contracts with consumers are affected by consumer protection legislation in various ways.

FORM OF CONTRACT

Consumer protection laws commonly regulate the form of the contract, requiring that payments under the contract to be itemized and allocation to such items as principal, interest, and insurance are to be clearly indicated; Generally, certain portions of the contract or all of the contract must be printed in type of a certain size, and a copy must be furnished to the buyer. Such statutory requirements are more demanding than the statute of frauds section of the UCC. It is frequently provided that the copy furnished the consumer must be completely filled in.

CONTRACT TERMS

Consumer protection legislation does not ordinarily affect the right of the parties to make a contract on whatever terms they choose. It is customary, however, to prohibit the use of certain clauses that are believed to unconscionable to the debtor or that have too great a potential for abuse by a creditor.

ACCELERATION CLAUSES

An acceleration clause is a contractual provision which allows the holder to declare the remaining balance due and payable immediately upon the occurrence of a default in the obligation. Parties to a credit transaction may agree that payment should be made in installments but that if there is a default with respect to any installment, the creditor may declare the entire balance due at once. This cancels or destroys the schedule for payments by making the entire balance immediately due. Such acceleration of the debt can cause the debtor great hardship. Because of this, some statutes limit or prohibit the use of acceleration clauses.

PRICE GOUGING

Some consumer protection statutes are aimed at preventing price gouging with respect to goods or services for which the demand is abnormally greater than the supply. A New York statute provides: "During any abnormal disruption of the market for consumer goods and services vital and necessary for the health, safety, and welfare of consumers, resulting from stress of weather, convulsion of nature, failure or short age of electric power or other source of energy . . . no merchant shall sell or offer to sell any such consumer goods or services for an amount which represents an unconscionably excessive price." Consumer goods and services are defined as "those used, bought, or rendered primarily for personal, family, or household purposes." Such a statute protects, for example, purchasers of electric generators for home use during a hurricane-caused blackout.

CREDIT CARDS
The credit card permits the cardholder to buy on the credit or reputation of the issuer of the card.

UNSOLICITED CREDIT CARDS
The unsolicited distribution of credit cards to persons who have not applied for them is prohibited.

SURCHARGE PROHIBITED
According to some consumer protection statutes, a seller cannot add any charge to the purchase price because the buyer uses a credit card instead of paying with cash or a check.

UNAUTHORIZED FEE
A card holder is normally not liable for more than $50 for the unauthorized use of a credit card.

PAYMENTS
Consumer legislation may provide that when a consumer makes a payment on an open charge account, the payment must be applied toward payment of the earliest charges. The result is that, should there be a default at a later date, any right of repossession of the creditor is limited to the later, unpaid items.

PRODUCT SAFETY
The health and well-being of consumers is protected by a variety of statutes and rules of laws. Most states have laws governing the manufacture of various products and establishing product safety standards. The federal *Consumer Product Safety Act* provides for research and the setting of uniform standards for products in order to reduce health hazards. This act also establishes civil and criminal penalties for the distribution of unsafe products. It also recognizes the right of a person to sue for money damages and to obtain an injunction against the distribution of unsafe products. The Act also creates a Consumer Product Safety Commission to administer it. The federal *Anti-Tampering Act* makes it a federal crime to tamper with consumer products.

CREDIT, COLLECTION AND BILLING METHODS
The *Equal Credit Opportunity Act (ECOA)* was passed in order to make sure that consumer credit was awarded based on an applicant's credit worthiness rather than the applicant's age, sex, color, religion, or national origin. For example, a lender cannot consider the following when making a loan: race; marital status; receipt of public assistance income; receipt of alimony or

child support; or future plans for children. Spouses have rights to individual credit application and consideration. The other spouse's income does not have to be disclosed unless the applicant is relying on that income to qualify for credit.

The penalties for violating the ECOA are the actual damages and the possibility of punitive damages of up to $10,000. If there is a pattern or practice of violations, a class action may be filed which can result in damages up to $500,000 or 1% of the net assets of the defendant, whichever is less.

The *Truth-in-Lending Act (TILA)* is part of the Federal Consumer Credit Protection Act. The purpose of the TILA is to make full disclosure to debtors of what they are being charged for the credit they are receiving. The Act merely asks lenders to be honest to the debtors and not cover up what they are paying for the credit. *Regulation Z* is a federal regulation prepared by the Federal Reserve Board to carry out the details of the Act.

TILA applies to *consumer credit* transactions. Consumer credit is credit for personal or household use and not commercial use. TILA applies to both *open end* and *closed end* transactions. Examples of open -end transactions are credit cards, lines of credit, and revolving charge accounts. Closed-end transactions involve a fixed amount to be paid back over a period of time such as a note or a retail installment contract. Open-end disclosure requirements include: finance charges (including interest), the dates that bills will be sent and what, if any, security interest is being taken. Bills must contain the following information:

- balance from last statement;
- payments and credits;
- new charges made since last statement;
- finance charges on unpaid balance;
- the billing period covered by the bill;
- the time period in which payment can be made in order to avoid a finance charge (e.g., 30 days); and
- information regarding billing errors -- what to do and where to inquire about billing errors.

When an organization solicits consumer to use its credit card, the solicitation must include the following disclosures:

- fees for issuing the card;
- APR for the card;
- minimum or fixed finance charges;
- any transaction charges;
- grace periods (if any);
- how the daily balance is computed;
- when payments will be due;

- what the late payment will be; and

- any charges that will be assessed for going over the credit limit.

Disclosures regarding closed-end credit must include:

- amount being financed;
- finance charges
- annual percentage rate;
- number of payments and when due;
- total cost of financing (price of goods plus all finance charges);
- any penalties for prepayment or late payment;
- any security interest or lien in the goods sold or used as collateral; and
- any credit insurance cost.

In advertisements that include part of the credit terms, all the credit terms must be disclosed. If payments are disclosed, the creditor must disclose the *annual percentage rate* (APR), the down payment, and the number of payments.

Regulation Z gives a *three-day cooling-off period* for certain credit contracts. This cooling-off period applies in a credit situation when the debtor's home is given as security for the loan or a home solicitation sale is involved. The *Home Equity Loan Consumer Protection Act of 1988* applies to home equity loans and provides for additional disclosures, e.g., that the debtor can lose his home in the event of a default.

The penalties for violation of the TILA include an amount equal to two times the amount of the finance charges with a minimum recovery of $100 and a maximum recovery of $1000 plus any punitive damages. In a class action law suit the maximum amount of damages is $500,000 or 1% of the creditor's net worth, whichever is less.

The *Fair Credit Billing Act* requires monthly statements on open-end credit transactions. The bill must contain an address for the debtor to write in order to report errors in the bill. Any such notification must be sent within 60 days of the bill's receipt. The creditor then has thirty days in which to acknowledge the notification and ninety days to take action. The debtor does not have to pay the protested amount during this period of time. Once the matter is resolved, the debtor must pay the correct amount owed. If the creditor does not comply with the time limits of the Act the debtor does not have to pay the disputed amount, even if it is correct.

The *Fair Credit Reporting Act* regulates the use of information on a consumer's personal and financial condition. The most typical transaction which this Act would cover would be where a person applies for a personal loan or other consumer credit. *Consumer credit* is credit for personal, family, or household use, and not for business or commercial transactions. Also, this Act can apply when a person applies for a job or even a policy of insurance when certain investigations are made of the applicant.

The purpose of the Act is to ensure that consumer information obtained and used is done in such a way as to insure its confidentiality, accuracy, relevancy and proper utilization. Under the Act, *consumer reports* are communications in any form by which furnishes information on consumers to potential creditors, insurers or employers.

Upon request, a credit bureau must tell a consumer the names and addresses of persons to whom it has made a credit report on that consumer during the previous six months. It also must tell, when requested, what employers were given such a report during the previous two years.

Some information obtained by credit reporting bureaus is based on statements made by persons, such as neighbors who were interviewed by the bureau's investigator. Needless to say, these statements are not always correct and are sometimes the result of gossip. In any event, such statements may go on the records of the bureau without further verification and may be furnished to a client of the bureau who will regard the statements as accurate. A person has the limited right to request an agency to disclose the nature and substance of the information possessed by the bureau to see if the information is accurate. If the person claims that the information of the bureau is erroneous, the bureau must take steps within a reasonable time to determine the accuracy of the disputed items. If no correction is made, the debtor can write a 100 word statement of clarification which will be included in future credit reports, even if the agency disagrees with clarification.

The FCRA requires that a credit reporting agency follow reasonable procedures to assure accuracy of the information it gathers. Adverse information obtained by investigation cannot be given to a client after three months unless it is verified to determine that it is still valid.

Credit reporting bureaus are not permitted to disclose information to persons not having a legitimate use for this information. It is a federal crime to obtain or to furnish a credit report for an improper purpose. Under the FCRA, agencies can only disclose information to the following:

- a debtor who asks for his own report;
- a creditor who has the debtor's signed application for credit;
- a potential employer; and
- a court pursuant to a subpoena.

The *Consumer Leasing Act* is an amendment to TILA and provides disclosure protection for consumers who lease goods. Basically, these disclosures fall into three categories:

- how much is paid by the consumer over the life of the lease;
- how much, if any, is owed by the consumer at the end of the lease; and
- whether or not the lease can be terminated.

The *Fair Debt Collection Practices Act (FDCPA)* prohibits harassment or abuse in collecting a debt such as threatening violence, use of obscene or profane language, publishing lists of debtors who refuse to pay debts, or even harassing a debtor by repeatedly calling the debtor on the phone. Also, certain false or misleading representations are forbidden, such as representing that the debt collector is associated with the state or federal government, or stating that the debtor will go to jail if he does not pay the debt. This Act also sets out strict rules regarding communicating with the debtor.

The FDCPA applies only to those who regularly engage in the business of collecting debts for others – primarily to collection agencies. The Act does not apply when a creditor attempts to collect debts owed to it by directly contacting the debtors. It applies only to the collection of consumer debts and does not apply to the collection of commercial debts. Consumer debts are debts for personal, home, or family purposes.

When a collector contacts a debtor, if the debtor asks for verification of the debt, the collector must provide this verification in writing. The debtor must include the amount of the debt, the name of the creditor, and the debtor's right to dispute the debt.

The collector is restricted in the type of contact he can make with the debtor. He can't contact the debtor before 8:00 a.m. or after 9:00 p.m. He can contact the debtor at home, but cannot contact the debtor at the debtor's club or church or at a school meeting of some sort. The debtor cannot be contacted at work if his employer objects. If the debtor tells the creditor the name of his attorney, any future contacts must be made with the attorney and not with the debtor. The debtor can call off the collection contacts at any time. The collector would then have to use other collection means like filing suit.

The Act prohibits contacting other people about the debtor's debts, with the exception of the debtor's spouse and parents. Another exception is that third parties can be contacted in order to get the debtor's address, phone number and place of employment. Contact with the debtor by postcard is prohibited because someone other than the debtor may see the contents of the postcard.

When a collection agency violates the Act, it is liable to the debtor for damages, and it is no defense that the debtor in fact owed the money that the agency was seeking to collect. Debtors can collect up to $1,000 in actual damages in addition to actual damages. Also the Federal Trade Commission can get a cease and desist order to stop any unlawful practices.

If a creditor files a civil suit for the debt and gets a judgment, he will have to execute on that judgment unless the defendant voluntarily pays the judgment. One way of execution is *garnishment* where a judgment creditor serves a writ of garnishment on the debtor's employer. The employer is then required to withhold part of the debtor's wages for payment to the creditor in satisfaction of the judgment. The Consumer Credit Protection Act limits the amount that can be garnished to 25% of the debtor's net wages. A judgment creditor can also garnish a debtor's bank account or an account receivable due to the debtor. Basically, any debt due to the debtor can be garnished.

PRIVACY AND INFORMATION LAW

OnGuardOnline.gov provides practical tips from the federal government and the technology industry to help you be on guard against Internet fraud, secure your computer, and protect your personal information. The Federal Trade Commission (FTC) maintains *OnGuardOnline.gov*. Much of the following information in this section came from the *OnGuardOnline.gov* website.

Protect your personal information.
To an identity thief, your personal information can provide instant access to your financial accounts, your credit record, and other assets. Anyone can be a victim of identity theft. There are almost 10 million victims every year. Some cases start when online data is stolen. You can go to *www.ftc.gov/idtheft* to learn what to do if your identity is stolen. When it comes to crimes like identity theft, you can't entirely control whether you will become a victim. But following these tips can help minimize your risk while you're online:

If you're asked for your personal information (*e.g.,* your name, email or home address, phone number, account numbers, or Social Security number) find out how it's going to be used and how it will be protected before you share it. If you have children, teach them to not give out your last name, your home address, or your phone number on the Internet.

If you get an email or pop-up message asking for personal information, do not reply or click on the link in the message. The safest course of action is not to respond to requests for your personal or financial information. If you believe there may be a need for such information by a company with whom you have an account or placed an order, contact that company directly in a way you know to be genuine. In any case, do not send your personal information via email because email is not a secure transmission method.

If you are shopping online, do not provide your personal or financial information through a company's website until you have checked for indicators that the site is secure, like a lock icon on the browser's status bar or a website URL that begins "https:" (the "s" stands for "secure"). Unfortunately, no indicator is foolproof; some scammers have forged security icons.

Read website privacy policies. They should explain what personal information the website collects, how the information is used, and whether it is provided to third parties. The privacy policy also should tell you whether you have the right to see what information the website has about you and what security measures the company takes to protect your information. If you do not see a privacy policy, or cannot understand it, consider doing business elsewhere.

Know with whom you're dealing.
It is remarkably simple for online scammers to impersonate a legitimate business, so you need to know whom you're dealing with. If you're shopping online, check out the seller before you buy. A legitimate business or individual seller should give you a physical address and a working telephone number at which they can be contacted in case you have problems.

Phishing is the act of sending an e-mail to a user falsely claiming to be an established legitimate enterprise in an attempt to scam the user into surrendering private information that will be used for identity theft. The e-mail directs the user to visit a Web site where they are asked to update personal information, such as passwords and credit card, social security, and bank account numbers, that the legitimate organization already has. The Web site, however, is bogus and set up only to steal the user's information.

For example, in 2003 there was a phishing scam in which users received e-mails supposedly from eBay claiming that the user's account was about to be suspended unless he clicked on the provided link and updated the credit card information that the genuine eBay already had.

Because it is relatively simple to make a Web site look like a legitimate organizations site by mimicking the HTML code, the scam counted on people being tricked into thinking they were actually being contacted by eBay and were subsequently going to eBay's site to update their account information. By spamming large groups of people, the "phisher" counted on the e-mail being read by a percentage of people who actually had listed credit card numbers with eBay legitimately.

Phishers send spam or pop-up messages claiming to be from a business or organization that you might deal with, for example, an Internet service provider (ISP), bank, online payment service, or even a government agency. Again, the message usually says that you need to "update" or "validate" your account information. It might threaten some dire consequence if you do not respond. The message directs you to a website that looks just like a legitimate organization's, but is not. The purpose of the bogus site is to trick you into divulging your personal information so the operators can steal your identity and run up bills or commit crimes in your name. Do not take the bait. Never reply to or click on links in email or pop-ups that ask for personal information. Legitimate companies do not ask for this information via email. If you are directed to a website to update your information, verify that the site is legitimate by calling the company directly, using contact information from your account statements.

Every day, millions of computer users share files online. File-sharing can give people access to a wealth of information, including music, games, and software. You download special software that connects your computer to an informal network of other computers running the same software. Millions of users could be connected to each other through this software at one time. Often the software is free and easily accessible. But file-sharing can have a number of risks. If you do not check the proper settings, you could allow access not just to the files you intend to share, but also to other information on your hard drive, like your tax returns, email messages, medical records, photos, or other personal documents. If you decide to use file-sharing software, set it up very carefully. Take the time to read the End User Licensing Agreement to be sure you understand and are willing to tolerate the side effects of any free downloads.

Many free downloads come with potentially undesirable side effects. *Spyware* is software installed without your knowledge or consent that adversely affects your ability to use your computer, sometimes by monitoring or controlling how you use it. To avoid spyware, resist the urge to install any software unless you know exactly what it is. Your anti-virus software may include anti-spyware capability that you can activate, but if it does not, you can install separate anti-spyware software, and then use it regularly to scan for and delete any spyware programs that may sneak onto your computer.

Use anti-spyware software, as well as a firewall, and update them all regularly. Firewalls help keep hackers from using your computer to send out your personal information without your permission. While anti-virus software scans incoming email and files, a firewall is like a guard, watching for outside attempts to access your system and blocking communications to and from sources you don't permit. Some operating systems and hardware devices come with a built-in firewall that may be shipped in the "off" mode. Make sure you turn it on. For your firewall to be effective, it needs to be set up properly and updated regularly.

If your operating system does not include a firewall, get a separate software firewall that runs in the background while you work, or install a hardware firewall — an external device that includes firewall software.

Be sure to set up your operating system and Web browser software properly, and update them regularly.
Hackers also take advantage of Web browsers (like Internet Explorer or Netscape) and operating system software (like Windows or Linux) that are unsecured. Lessen your risk by changing the settings in your browser or operating system and increasing your online security. Check the "Tools" or "Options" menus for built-in security features. If you need help understanding your choices, use your "Help" function.

Your operating system also may offer free software *patches* that close holes in the system that hackers could exploit. In fact, some common operating systems can be set to automatically retrieve and install patches for you. If your system does not do this, bookmark the website for your system's manufacturer so you can regularly visit and update your system with defenses against the latest attacks. Updating can be as simple as one click. Your email software may help you avoid viruses by giving you the ability to filter certain types of spam.
If you are not using your computer for an extended period, turn it off or unplug it from the phone or cable line. When it's off, the computer doesn't send or receive information from the Internet and isn't vulnerable to hackers.

Protect your passwords.
Keep your passwords in a secure place, and out of plain view. Don't share your passwords on the Internet, over email, or on the phone. Your Internet Service Provider (ISP) should never ask for your password. In addition, hackers may try to figure out your passwords to gain access to your computer. You can make it tougher for them by:

- Using passwords that have at least eight characters and include numbers or symbols.
- Avoiding common words: some hackers use programs that can try every word in the dictionary.
- Not using your personal information, your login name, or adjacent keys on the keyboard as passwords.
- Changing your passwords regularly (at a minimum, every 90 days).
- Not using the same password for each online account you access.

Internet fraud - If a scammer takes advantage of you through an Internet auction, when you're shopping online, or in any other way, report it to the Federal Trade Commission, at *ftc.gov.* The FTC enters Internet, identity theft, and other fraud-related complaints into Consumer Sentinel, a secure, online database available to hundreds of civil and criminal law enforcement agencies in the U.S. and abroad.

Deceptive Spam - If you get deceptive spam, including email phishing for your information, forward it to *spam@uce.gov.* Be sure to include the full header of the email, including all routing information. You also may report phishing email to *reportphishing@antiphishing.org.* The Anti-

Phishing Working Group, a consortium of ISPs, security vendors, financial institutions and law enforcement agencies, uses these reports to fight phishing.

Divulged Personal Information – if you believe you have mistakenly given your personal information to a fraudster, file a complaint at *ftc.gov*, and then visit the Federal Trade Commission's Identity Theft website at *www.ftc.gov/idtheft* to learn how to minimize your risk of damage from a potential theft of your identity.

Debtor Creditor Relations

Mechanic's liens are fairly simple to understand (and may even be within the experience of some students). Generally, a lienholder must file written notice of the lien within 60 to 120 days from the last date on which work was provided.

Artisan's Lien

An **artisan's lien,** too, is a fairly simple device. Normally, the lienholder must have retained possession of the property and have agreed to provide services on a cash, not a credit, basis. To protect a lien and surrender possession simultaneously, a lienholder must record notice of the lien under state lien law. Under an artisan's lien, a creditor can recover payment from a debtor for labor and materials furnished in the repair of personal property.

Judicial Liens

These liens help ensure that a judgment is collectible. Judicial lien is a lien obtained by judgment, levy, sequestration or other legal or equitable process or proceeding. If a court finds that a debtor owes money to a creditor and the judgment remains unsatisfied, the creditor can ask the court to impose a lien on specific property owned and possessed by the debtor. After imposing the lien, the court issues a writ directing the local sheriff to seize the property, sell it and turn over the proceeds to the creditor.

Under Bankruptcy proceedings, a creditor can obtain a judicial lien by filing a final judgment issued against a debtor through a lawsuit filed in state court. A certified copy of a final judgment may be filed in the county in which the debtor owns real property. A bankruptcy debtor can file a motion to avoid Judicial Lien. A Motion to avoid Judicial Lien can be filed by a debtor in either a chapter 7 or chapter 13 bankruptcy proceeding. In a Chapter 7 proceeding, an Order Avoiding Judicial Lien will remove the debt totally.

Writ of Attachment and Writ of Execution

Prejudgment attachment requires notice to the debtor and an opportunity to be heard (under the Fourteenth Amendment's due process clause). The creditor must have an enforceable right to payment, file an affidavit, and post a bond. The court issues a writ of attachment. The sheriff seizes the debtor's property, which can be sold to satisfy the judgment.

If a debtor does not or cannot pay an adverse judgment, the creditor can go back to court for a **writ of execution.** The sheriff seizes the debtor's property, which can be sold to satisfy the judgment. Before the property is sold, the debtor can pay the judgment and redeem the property.

Attachment is a court-ordered seizure and taking into custody of property prior to the securing of a judgment for a past-due debt. To use attachment as a remedy, a creditor (1) files with a court an affidavit, stating that a debtor is in default and the grounds on which attachment is sought, and (2) posts a bond to cover costs, the value of the loss of use of the good by the debtor, and the value of the property. The court directs the sheriff or other officer to seize nonexempt property, which can be sold to satisfy a judgment. A writ of execution is a court order directing a sheriff to seize and sell any of the debtor's nonexempt real or personal property within the court's jurisdiction. This is used when a debtor will not or cannot pay a judgment.

Writ of Execution. If a creditor is successful in a suit against a debtor, the court awards the creditor a judgment against the debtor (usually for the amount of the debt plus interest and costs incurred in obtaining the judgment). If the debtor does not pay the judgment, the creditor can go back to court and obtain a writ of execution under which some of the debtor's property can be seized and sold.

Garnishment. Garnishment is a collection remedy directed at a debtor's property or rights held by a third person (typically, an employer or a bank). Garnishment is a state law remedy and the procedures differ from state to state. In some states, a separate order may be required for, for example, each pay period to garnish wages.

Laws Limiting the Amount of Wages Subject to Garnishment

Federal and state laws limit the amount that can be garnished from wages. State laws often provide for larger exemptions, and state and federal statutes can be applied together to reduce the amount that may be garnished.

Garnishment occurs when a creditor obtains a court order to collect a debt by seizing property of the debtor held by a third party (such as a paycheck held by an employer or a checking account held by a bank). Garnishment is used in some cases in which debts are not paid.

A **Composition with Creditors** is an agreement among several creditors of a debtor, usually a business. Usually, the agreement involves paying a lessened amount over a period of time.

Foreclosure is the procedure by which a party who has loaned money secured by a mortgage or deed of trust on real property (or has an unpaid judgment), forces the sale of the real property to recover the money due, unpaid interest, plus the costs of foreclosure, after the debtor fails to make payment. The lender must serve a notice of default on the debtor after a certain time period from when the payment becomes past due, which varies by state. The notice will give the borrower a certain time period and amount necessary to be paid in order to "cure" the default and avoid foreclosure. If the delinquency and costs of foreclosure are not paid within this time, then the lender (or the trustee in states using deeds of trust) will set a foreclosure date for selling the property at public sale. The property may be redeemed by the borrower by paying all delinquencies and costs, up to the time of sale and in some state, for a period after sale.

There is also judicial foreclosure which is used in several states with the mortgage system or in deed of trust. This procedure is used when the amount due is greater than the equity value of the real property, and the lender wishes to get a deficiency judgment for the amount still due after sale. However, some states give deficiency judgments

Suretyship and Guaranty

The distinction between the two statuses has been abolished in some states.

Surety
A surety is primarily liable: the creditor can hold the surety responsible for payment of the debt when the debt is due, without first exhausting all remedies against the debtor. A surety agreement does not have to be in writing to be enforceable (but it usually is).

Guaranty
A guarantor is secondarily liable: the principal must first default. The contract between guarantor and creditor must be in writing to be enforceable unless the "main purpose" exception applies.

Defenses of the Surety and the Guarantor
Actions Releasing the Surety
Any material change in the contract between principal and creditor without prior consent of the surety (or guarantor) may discharge the surety, even if the change does not affect the risk. If the debt is paid, or tender of payment is made and rejected, the surety is discharged.

Defenses of the Principal Debtor
A surety can use any defenses available to the principal (except personal defenses). This is the most important concept in suretyship, because most defenses available to a surety are those of the principal.

Rights of the Surety and the Guarantor

Laws Assisting Debtors
Each state allows a homestead exemption, which permits a debtor to retain all or part of the family home free from the claims of unsecured creditors or trustees in bankruptcy. Personal property that is most often exempt (up to at least a specified dollar amount) includes:

- Household furniture.
- Clothing and certain personal possessions.
- A vehicle (or vehicles) for transportation.
- Certain animals.
- Equipment the debtor uses in a business or trade.

Chapter 15

BANKRUPTCY

The philosophy of the United States bankruptcy laws is to allow a debtor who has gotten hopelessly in debt an opportunity to start over and to provide for appropriate distribution of the debtor's estate to his creditors.

THE FEDERAL LAW

The Bankruptcy consists of federal laws which are enforced and interpreted by federal courts. The 2005 changes, which fall under the Bankruptcy Abuse Prevention and Consumer Protection Act (BAPCPA), introduced what many experts consider to be among the most sweeping changes to personal bankruptcy law, particularly for those who seek to liquidate their debts.

Jurisdiction over bankruptcy cases is in the United States district courts. These courts may refer all bankruptcy cases and related proceedings to bankruptcy courts which are adjunct courts to the federal district courts. As a practical matter, the United States district courts almost always refer bankruptcy proceedings to the adjunct bankruptcy courts.

KINDS OF BANKRUPTCY PROCEEDINGS

Three common bankruptcy proceedings available to individuals and businesses are:

- Liquidation, sometimes called a *Chapter 7* bankruptcy;
- Reorganization, sometimes called a *Chapter 11* bankruptcy; and
- Extended Time Payment, sometimes called a *Chapter 13* bankruptcy.

Chapter 7 bankruptcy is one in which all of the debtor's assets (with some exceptions) will be liquidated in order to pay debts. Debts that are not paid or which are only partially paid are discharged, with some exceptions.

Chapter 11 bankruptcy allows a debtor to reorganize and continue a business with protection from creditors and without liquidation. This proceeding normally applies to individuals and corporations with large and complex debts,

Chapter 13 bankruptcy provides a form of reorganization for individual consumers. A plan must be proposed by the debtor that provides for repayment of the debt with protection from court procedures of creditors.

The bankruptcy code has a special chapter for family farmers and family fishermen, Chapter 12, but they may opt to file under Chapters 11 or 13 instead. Municipalities seeking bankruptcy protection do so under Chapter 9, which mandates reorganization.

VOLUNTARY AND INVOLUNTARY BANKRUPTCY
The principal difference between a voluntary case and an involuntary case is the manner in which the proceedings are initiated. With a few exceptions, a *voluntary bankruptcy* case is commenced by the debtor filing a petition with the bankruptcy court. An *involuntary bankruptcy* case is commenced by creditors of the debtor filing a petition with the bankruptcy court. If there are 12 or more creditors, at least three whose unsecured claims total $12,300 or more must sign the involuntary petition. By unsecured claims, I mean claims which are not secured by a security interest, mortgage, deed of trust, or similar such security device. If there are fewer than 12 creditors, not including employees or insiders, any creditor whose unsecured claim is at least $12,300 may sign the petition. An insider would be someone like the debtor's relatives, partners, directors, or controlling shareholders. For purposes of the $12,300 figure, regarding creditors who hold security for a claim, only the amount of the claim which is in excess of the security is counted.

A debtor may contest an involuntary bankruptcy petition. If an involuntary petition is dismissed other than by consent of all petitioning creditors and the debtor, the court may award the debtor his expenses, such as attorneys' fees. Damages may be recovered against any creditor who files a petition in bad faith (i.e., without reasonable grounds).

AUTOMATIC STAY
After the filing of the bankruptcy petition, the debtor needs protection from the collection efforts of its creditors. Therefore, the bankruptcy law provides that the filing of either a voluntary or involuntary petition operates as an *automatic stay* which prevents most creditors from taking action against the debtor. This is similar to an injunction against the creditors of the debtor. The automatic stay ends when the bankruptcy case is closed or dismissed or when the debtor is granted a discharge.

LIST OF CREDITORS
It is the debtor's responsibility to furnish the bankruptcy court with a complete list of creditors. Failure to list a creditor will result in that creditor not being discharge by the court. In other words, the debt of any unlisted creditor is not affected by the bankruptcy.

TRUSTEE IN BANKRUPTCY
The *trustee* in bankruptcy can be elected by the creditors. A trustee will be appointed by the court if a trustee is not elected by the creditors. The trustee automatically "owns" all of the nonexempt property of the debtor and also property inherited by the debtor within six months after the filing of the petition. The trustee possesses the rights of a *most favored creditor* of the debtor (like he had a security interest in property). This means that the trustee can set aside certain transfers of property by the debtor.

THE BANKRUPT'S ESTATE
The debtor's estate, which is held by the trustee generally consists of:

- all property owned by the debtor at the time of the filing of the petition that is not exempt under the Bankruptcy Code;
- property inherited by the debtor within six months after filing for bankruptcy; and

- property recovered by the trustee by setting aside improper transfers (e.g., transfers to defraud creditors) and preferences (discussed below). An example of an improper transfer would be where a debtor had, a few months before declaring bankruptcy, conveyed land to his brother without consideration in order to keep the land out of the bankruptcy estate.

VOIDABLE TRANSFERS

The trustee can set aside transfers of property which were made to prevent creditors from satisfying their legal claims. These transactions can be set aside by the trustee if they were made by the debtor within one year of bankruptcy when the debtor's actual intent was to hinder, delay, or defraud creditors by making such a transfer. The trustee may also set aside certain transfers of property when the effect of the transfer was to make the debtor insolvent.

Preferential Transfers

A transfer of property by the debtor to a creditor may be set aside and the property recovered by the trustee if:

- The transfer was made to pay a debt incurred at some earlier time;
- The transfer was made when the debtor was insolvent and within 90 days before the filing of the bankruptcy petition; ***and***
- By virtue of the transfer the creditor received more than he would have received in a liquidation of the debtor's estate.

Transfers to insiders may also be set aside if made within 12 months prior to the date the petition was filed. Examples of insiders would be the debtor's relatives, partners, directors and controlling persons of a corporation.

Certain transfers by a debtor may not be set aside as preferences. For example, a transfer for a present consideration, such as a cash sale, may not be set aside. A payment by a debtor in the ordinary course of business, such as payment of a utility bill, may not be set aside. A payment by a debtor whose debts are primarily consumer debts may not be set aside if the value of the transfer is less than a certain specified amount. Child support and alimony payments are not subject to the preferential provisions.

PROOF OF CLAIM

Bankruptcy law regulates the manner in which creditors present their claims and how the assets of the debtor are to be distributed in payment of these claims. As mentioned earlier, the debtor must file a list of creditors. The creditors that wish to participate in distribution of the proceeds of the liquidation of the debtor's estate must file a *proof of claim.* A proof of claim is a written statement signed by the creditor which describes the claim against the debtor and the basis of the claim. Ordinarily it must be filed within 90 days after the first meeting of creditors. A creditor must file its proof of claim even if the trustee in fact knows of the existence of the claim. A claim is a right to payment, whether it is disputed or undisputed by the debtor.

PRIORITY OF CLAIMS

Creditors who hold a lien securing the indebtedness of the debtor do not lose their lien as a result of the bankruptcy. With the court's permission, they may enforce their debt by selling the security (whether it be land covered by a mortgage or a security interest on personal property). Creditors who are not secured share in the remaining assets of the debtor. Some have priority over others. Each claim must be paid in full before any lower claim is paid anything. If a class of claims cannot be paid in full, the claims in that case are paid on a pro rata basis.

A general summary of the order of priority is as follows:

- Secured debts;
- Administrative expenses;
- Claims arising in the ordinary course of the debtor's business;
- Certain wage claims;
- Claims for contributions to employee benefit plans (pensions);
- Claims by consumer creditors;
- Taxes; and
- General creditors.

DEBTOR'S DUTIES AND EXEMPTIONS

The Bankruptcy Code provides that the debtor has certain duties after filing his petition. The Code also provides for specific exemptions of some of the debtor's estate from the claims of creditors.

The debtor must file with the court a list of his creditors, a schedule of his assets and liabilities, and a statement regarding his financial affairs. He must also appear for examination under oath at the first meeting of creditors.

The *Code* allows the debtor to keep certain of his property and claim it as being exempt from the claims of creditors. This is known as *exempt property.* Generally, the debtor has a choice of exempt property as described under State law or exempt property as described under the Federal Bankruptcy law. The debtor will of course choose the law which is most favorable. Some general exemptions under federal law are:

- The debtor's aggregate interest, not to exceed $15,000 in value, in real property that the debtor or a dependent of the debtor uses as a residence;
- The debtor's interest, not to exceed $2,400 in value, in one motor vehicle;
- The debtor's interest, not to exceed $400 in value in any particular item or $8,000 in aggregate value, in household furnishings, household goods, wearing apparel, appliances, books, animals, crops, or musical instruments, that are held primarily for the personal, family, or household use of the debtor or a dependent of the debtor;
- The debtor's aggregate interest, not to exceed $1,000 in value, in jewelry held primarily for the personal, family, or household use of the debtor or a dependent of the debtor;
- The debtor's aggregate interest in any property, not to exceed in value $800 plus up to $7,500 of any unused amount of certain exemptions;
- The debtor's aggregate interest, not to exceed $1,500 in value, in any professional books, or tools of the trade of the debtor or the trade of a dependent of the debtor;
- Any unmatured life insurance contract owned by the debtor, other than a credit life insurance contract;

- Professionally prescribed health aids for the debtor or a dependent of the debtor;
- The debtor's right to receive a social security benefit, unemployment compensation, or a local public assistance benefit;
- Veterans' benefits; and
- Alimony, support, or separate maintenance, to the extent reasonably necessary for the support of the debtor and any dependent of the debtor.

DEBTOR'S PROTECTION AGAINST DISCRIMINATION

Federal, state, and local laws may not discriminate against anyone on the basis of a discharge in bankruptcy. Employees may not be discriminated against due to bankruptcy.

DISCHARGE IN BANKRUPTCY

The decree of the bankruptcy court which terminates the bankruptcy proceedings is generally a *discharge* that releases the debtor from most debts.

DENIAL OF DISCHARGE

The court may refuse to grant a discharge under certain conditions. Examples are:

- If within one year of filing the petition, the debtor has fraudulently transferred or concealed property with the intent to defraud creditors;
- The debtor has failed to keep proper financial records;
- The debtor has made a false oath or account in the bankruptcy proceeding;
- The debtor has failed to satisfactorily explain any loss of assets;
- The debtor has refused to obey a lawful order of the bankruptcy court;
- The debtor has obtained a discharge by a bankruptcy court within the last eight years.

REORGANIZATIONS AND PAYMENT PLANS UNDER CHAPTERS 11 and 13

As an alternative to liquidation, the Bankruptcy Code permits parties to restructure the organization and finances of a business so that it may continue to operate. A plan for reorganization of a business must be confirmed by the court. Generally, these plans must be acceptable to the majority of the creditors, and then the decision of the court is binding upon the minority creditors who do not accept the plan. Individuals, partnerships, and corporations in business may reorganize under the Bankruptcy Code. This is referred to as a Chapter 11 plan.

With regard to business reorganization, the first step is to file a plan for the reorganization of the debtor. This plan divides ownership interest and debts into those that will be affected by the adoption of the plan and those that will not. It will specify what will be done to those interests and claims that are affected by the plan. The plan must be confirmed by the court. Once the plan is confirmed, the owners and creditors of the business have only the rights that are specified in the plan and cannot change their positions.

The Code also allows individual debtors who meet certain financial criteria to adopt extended time payment plans for the payment of debts. An individual debtor on a regular income may submit a plan for installment payment of outstanding debts. This is called a Chapter 13 Plan. This plan must be confirmed by the court. Once it is confirmed, debts are paid in the manner specified in the plan. After all payments called for by the plan are made, the debtor is given a discharge. The plan is, in effect, a budget of the debtor's future income with respect to outstanding debts. The plan must provide for the eventual payment in full of *all claims entitled to priority* under the Bankruptcy Code. The plan will be confirmed if it is submitted in good faith and is in the best interest of the creditors.

Sweeping Changes in 2005

The Bankruptcy Abuse Prevention and Consumer Protection Act (BAPCPA) was signed into law in April 2005 and went into effect on October 17, 2005. This act, designed to curb instances of bankruptcy fraud, had a direct impact on chapter seven bankruptcies. The most significant change was a requirement for Chapter 7 filers to pass a ***means test*** to determine whether they might be able to file Chapter 13 and pay back their debts over a five-year period. Debtors whose income was above the state median (a variable based on the number of people in the debtor's household) would be required to file Chapter 13. Even those deemed eligible to file for Chapter 7 still face stricter requirements. Mandatory debt counseling must be completed within 180 days prior to filing for bankruptcy and the debtor must provide a certificate of counseling. The debtor must also supply additional proof of assets, including the most recent year's tax return, evidence of payment from employers made 60 days before filing, and other forms and documents (including a photo ID). The amount of time before a debtor can file again for Chapter 7 bankruptcy has risen from six years to eight years.

FREQUENTLY ASKED QUESTIONS

What are the most common reasons for filing chapter 7?

The most common reasons for filing a Chapter 7 bankruptcy include such things as:

- extended periods of unemployment, causing the debtor to be unable to pay his or her debts as they become due;
- large and often unanticipated medical expenses;
- seriously overextended credit beyond the debtor's ability to repay, often accompanied by unreasonably high interest rates;
- marital problems which lead to financial hardship, and
- other large unexpected expenses.

Must I employ an attorney?

It is not necessary to hire an attorney to file for bankruptcy. However, in most cases the benefits of hiring an attorney outweigh representing yourself. Keep in mind that the bankruptcy code is very complex and filing a bankruptcy petition requires a thorough knowledge of the bankruptcy code and other laws. An experienced attorney can help you correctly list all of your obligations and help you keep as much property as possible and eliminate as much debt as possible. If you do not file the paperwork correctly, the problems you may face could exceed the cost of an experienced attorney.

Can I keep my home and automobile?

In a Chapter 7 bankruptcy, the debtor in many cases will be able to retain their home and automobile. Generally, the only way a debtor could lose the home or automobile would be when the debtor is behind in his or her obligation and cannot reach a payment agreement with the creditor, or the home or automobile has equity in excess of the exempt amount. If either of these two conditions exist, the debtor should consider filing a Chapter 13 petition, which permits the development of a plan for repaying creditors without necessarily liquidating assets.

If I am married must both of us file?
It is not required that both spouses file bankruptcy if one spouse decides to file. However, the non-filling spouse will still be liable on joint debts of the parties. It follows then that if the majority of debts are in the spouses' names, both spouses should file bankruptcy or some of the benefits of bankruptcy will be lost.

What is the advantage to purchased forms over free forms?
The advantage to purchasing bankruptcy forms as opposed to utilizing free forms include the certainty of obtaining exactly the right forms needed for the debtor's particular situation. In addition, by purchasing bankruptcy forms, often the debtor will receive detailed instructions on the appropriate use of the forms. This will prevent unnecessary delay in filing the case and increases one's chances of having the bankruptcy approved by the trustee.

How creditors are notified that I have filed?
After a debtor has filed for bankruptcy protection, creditors are notified of the filing and the existence of the automatic stay by the bankruptcy court. Creditors will be given information regarding the first meeting of creditors, as well as deadlines for filing proofs of claim.

Will creditors stop calling after I file?
It is the debtor's responsibility to furnish the bankruptcy court with a complete list of creditors. Assuming a creditor has been listed by the debtor, the creditor should cease all collection efforts. The automatic stay acts as an injunction against the continuance of any action by any creditor against the debtor or the debtor's property. Anyone who willfully violates the stay in the case of an individual debtor can be liable for actual damages caused by the violation and sometimes liable for punitive damages.

Are there alternatives to bankruptcy?
Prior to making a decision to file bankruptcy, each individual should first attempt to contact his or her creditors and determine whether it is possible to obtain their cooperation in working out a different payment schedule. Most people would be surprised to learn that creditors often are willing to make reasonable modifications to assist the debtor in repayment. Communication and honesty are the key. The debtor should also take a close look at the value of his or her assets. If any have a resale value, consider whether a sale of those assets and the application of the proceeds of the sale to one's debt will reduce the debt to a more manageable level and make bankruptcy a less attractive option.

Another option that may be explored is a consolidation loan. It may be possible for some debtors to obtain a consolidation loan to repay one's debt, which very often will result in lower overall payments.

The Consumer Credit Counseling Service (CCC) is a nationwide nonprofit organization that attempts to work with both the debtor and his or her creditors to devise a more manageable repayment plan. This service very often results in revised payment plans which are acceptable to both the debtor and the creditor, thereby eliminating the need to file bankruptcy.

How do locate an attorney if I want one?
There are many ways of selecting an attorney. Perhaps the most familiar way is to ask friends or relatives who have hired attorneys in the past whether they would recommend that particular attorney. Another method is to contact the state bar association. Often state bar organizations have referral services. Also, organizations like the American Bankruptcy Institute and the Commercial Law League of America operate certification programs and can refer a debtor to a certified attorney in the debtor's geographical area.

Will I be allowed to keep my credit cards?
Federal Bankruptcy Law requires you to list all of your creditors, not just the creditors whose debt you would like to discharge. Some creditors may allow you to keep their credit cards, but it depends on the creditor. It also depends on what your credit card balance is at the time of the bankruptcy; what the credit card issuer is willing to do, and how well you convince them that you can, and will, pay the present and any future credit card debt.

Can I borrow money after bankruptcy?
After bankruptcy it is possible to borrow money for virtually any purpose. However, this does not mean that you will be able to borrow on the same terms that would be available to someone with good credit. Borrowing money after bankruptcy could involve higher interest rates, additional security (collateral), and/or a larger down payment.

Where do I file for bankruptcy?
The proper place to file for bankruptcy is the bankruptcy court in the federal court district and division where the debtor resides or owns property.

Will I be required to attend a court hearing?
A debtor must attend the first meeting of creditors. While not a formal court hearing, creditors may appear and ask questions regarding the debtor's financial affairs and property. The trustee is required to examine the debtor orally at the meeting of creditors to ensure that the debtor is aware of the potential consequences of seeking a discharge in bankruptcy, including the effect on credit history, the ability to file a petition under a different chapter, the effect of receiving a discharge, and the effect of reaffirming a debt.

What is the filing fee?
The filing fees for consumer bankruptcy cases, at this time (2008) range from $185.00 in a Chapter 13 case to $200.00 in a Chapter 7 case.

How long before the bankruptcy is complete?
The length of time needed to complete a bankruptcy depends upon the type of case filed. In a typical Chapter 7 bankruptcy case, a discharge will granted after the time period allowed for challenging the discharge has elapses, usually sixty days after the first meeting of creditors. This usually means a discharge is granted about four months after the petition for bankruptcy is filed.

In a Chapter 13 bankruptcy case, because the bankruptcy plan covers a period of time anywhere from three to five years, the discharge is granted after the plan has been completed.

If I am a co-signer for a debt, how does bankruptcy affect the obligation?
Should the principal borrower file for bankruptcy, the co-signer's obligation is not affected. He or she may still be held liable on the obligation even if the principal borrower obtains a discharge of the obligation.

What information is required for filing?
When filing for bankruptcy protection, the court will require that you provide the bankruptcy trustee with all information regarding all assets and debts. This means you should be prepared to provide the court with the following:

- The name and complete mailing address of those who you owe, complete with any account numbers, the total amounts due and the amount of monthly payments. If the debt is for a credit card, record the last date you charged on this credit card. If your last charge was less than 90 days ago, you need to write down the amount you charged and the reason for the purchase.
- Your current paycheck stubs; if you are unemployed, including copies of documents showing any other income you receive (*e.g.,* unemployment, worker's compensation, child support, supplement security income (SSI), social security, retirement, an estate, etc);
- Your mortgage and deed if you own or are purchasing a home or other real property;
- Copies of your car, boat, motorcycle, mobile home or other titles to motor vehicles; and
- Copies of your tax returns (for at least the past three years) and copies of any court proceedings filed against presently filed against you.

Are IRA accounts exempt?
Generally, such accounts are not exempt unless allowed by state law.

Are pension plans and 401(k) plans exempt?
Pension plans, 401(k) plans, and other ERISA-qualified plans are generally *excluded* from the bankruptcy estate. ERISA means the Federal Employee Retirement Income Security Act. Under this act, pension plans, 401(k) plans, and other ERISA-qualified plans are specifically prohibited from being assigned or alienated. What this means to the debtor is that the plan is excluded from the bankruptcy estate and remain the property of the debtor.

Can I be fired from my job for filing bankruptcy?
Employees may not be discriminated against due to a bankruptcy filing.

Can I go to jail if I do not pay my debts?
While the United States Constitution contains no express provision against imprisonment for debt, federal district courts follow the laws of the various states in which they sit wherein imprisonment for debt has been abolished.

Do I have to list all debts and assets?
If you knowingly and fraudulently conceal an asset from the court or fail to list all debts, you have committed a felony and can be fined up to $5,000, imprisoned for up to five years, or both. In addition, the court can deny you your discharge, or dismiss your bankruptcy proceeding.

How often may I file a Chapter 7?
The Bankruptcy Abuse Prevention and Consumer Protection Act (BAPCPA) was signed into law in April 2005 and went into effect on October 17, 2005. This act increased the amount of time before a debtor can file again for Chapter 7 bankruptcy from six years to eight years.

May I discharge alimony payments in bankruptcy?
Alimony payments are generally not dischargeable in bankruptcy proceedings. However, a question occasionally arises over the nature of a particular award - is it alimony, or is it a property settlement? The distinction is important, because a property settlement may be dischargeable in bankruptcy proceedings. The fundamental inquiry then becomes whether the intent of the divorce court and the ex-spouses was to provide support or divide marital property. In determining whether a debt is in the nature of support/maintenance or whether it is properly characterized as a division of property, courts consider a number of factors.

May I discharge student loans?
Student loans are not dischargeable, regardless of the age of the loan, unless the borrower can establish substantial hardship.

What is a Chapter 13 plan?
Under Chapter 13, all debts are combined and the debtor advises the court how much of the total debt he is able to pay. The court will accept repayment percentages as low as ten percent of the total debt, though plans that propose repaying at least seventy percent are recommended. The court discharges, or legally forgives, that portion which cannot be repaid, and the debtor begins making payments on the remainder. These payments must be finished at the end of three years, though extensions can be granted.

The debtor has flexibility in preparing his plan; the main criterion is its workability. The advantages to the debtor are many, and include the retention of unsecured property, the fact that the consent of the creditors is not necessary, and the fact that one hundred percent paybacks are not necessary. Secured creditors (those who have a lien on certain property), have limited remedies. If they do not accept the plan, they can only repossess a secured item for the present market value of the item. Any unpaid balance on the original contract or promissory note then becomes an unsecured debt. Another advantage is that the mere filing of the petition stops collection efforts by creditors.

Certain debts, however, are not dischargeable under Chapter 13 proceedings. For example, a Chapter 13 proceeding does not discharge alimony, child support, guaranteed student loans, and taxes.

How long before a bankruptcy can be removed from your credit report, and what is involved in having a bankruptcy removed?

After 10 years, the bankruptcy must be dropped from your credit report. The policy of most credit bureaus is to remove Chapter 11 and Chapter 13 cases from credit reports after 7 years to encourage debtors to file under these chapters. If your records are not updated by the credit reporting agencies automatically, you can send a letter of dispute to have the records updated.

What is a "motion to cram-down"?

For confirming a bankruptcy plan, creditors are divided into *classes* based on the nature of their claims against the debtor. Each class gets the opportunity to vote yes or no on the plan for reorganization, which can be confirmed only if at least one class votes yes. This means a yes vote from more than 50% of the number of creditors and 75% in the total value of claims. If one or more classes vote against the plan, but at least one class votes in favor, the debtor can still get the plan of reorganization approved through the process of cram down. Cram down requires a debtor to prove that the plan is fair and equitable to the non-consenting class and that the plan doesn't unfairly discriminate against them. If the debtor does so, the plan is crammed down the non-consenting class and approved.

Chapter 16

SECURED TRANSACTIONS IN PERSONAL PROPERTY

SECURED TRANSACTION

A secured transaction is created when a buyer or borrower (debtor) grants a seller or lender (creditor or secured party) a security interest in personal property (collateral). A security interest allows a creditor to repossess and sell the collateral if a debtor fails to pay a secured debt.

A secured transaction involves a sale on credit or lending money where a creditor is unwilling to accept the promise of a debtor to pay an obligation without some sort of collateral. The creditor (the secured party) requires the debtor to secure the obligation with collateral so that if the debtor does not pay as promised, the creditor can take the collateral, sell it, and apply the proceeds against the unpaid obligation of the debtor.

A security interest is an interest in personal property or fixtures that secures payment or performance of an obligation. Personal property is basically anything that is not real property. A fixture is personal property that has become so attached or adapted to real estate that it has lost its character as personal property and is deemed to be part of the real estate. An example would be a central air conditioning unit within a commercial building.

CREATION OF A SECURITY INTEREST

A security interest is said to attach at the time it becomes enforceable. There are three prerequisites to the attachment of a security interest:

- There must a security agreement;
- Value must be given; and
- The debtor must have rights in the collateral (for example, he must own it or be leasing the collateral).

A security interest is not enforceable unless the collateral is in the possession of the secured party; or the debtor has signed a security agreement that contains a description of the collateral, value has been given, and the debtor has rights in the collateral.

The agreement of the creditor and the debtor that the creditor shall have a security interest in the goods must be evidenced by a written security agreement unless the creditor retains what is known as a possessory security interest by taking possession of the collateral.

To be enforceable, a written security agreement must be signed by the debtor and reasonably describe the collateral. For example, a security agreement describing collateral as "Furniture as per attached listing," but with no listing attached fails to sufficiently describe the collateral and therefore is not an enforceable security agreement.

The first prerequisite to the attachment of a security interest is that there must be a security agreement. The next prerequisite is that there must be value given. The giving of value normally takes place when the secured party lends money to the debtor or the debtor agrees to repay the obligation. In order for a security interest to attach, the debtor must have rights in the collateral which generally means the debtor either owns the collateral or has rights to possess the collateral such as in a leasing arrangement.

PURCHASE MONEY SECURITY INTEREST
A purchase money security interest secures the unpaid price for collateral or a loan used to buy the collateral.

THE NATURE AND CLASSIFICATION OF COLLATERAL
The UCC divides personal property or goods into different classes: consumer goods, equipment, inventory, general intangibles, farm products and fixtures.

As far as tangible personal property is concerned, the goods are classified by the debtor's intended use. For example, a television set in the hands of a manufacturer or a retailer would be classified as inventory. However, if it were in a person's hands who intended to use it at home, it would be a consumer good.

Goods are consumer goods if they are used or bought primarily for personal, family, or household use. An example would be the family's television set.

Goods are classified as equipment if they are used or bought primarily for use in a business. For example, the computers at an office would be equipment.

Goods are classified as inventory if they are held by the debtor primarily for sale or lease to others. An example would be a television set bought by someone who sells televisions and appliances for a living. Also, raw materials used in manufacturing such as steel used to manufacture cars would be classified as inventory. Materials consumed in a business such as typing paper would be inventory.

General intangibles would be something like a promissory note which you held as collateral with regard to money you lent to another person.

Goods are farm products if they are crops or livestock or supplies used in farming operations.

A fixture is personal property that has become so attached or adapted to real estate that it has lost its character as personal property and is deemed to be part of the real estate (e.g., a central air conditioning unit within a commercial building).

A debtor may grant a security interest to secure future loans. This involves granting a security interest in property a debtor may acquire later. The security interest attaches when the future credit is given or when a debtor gets the property. Inventory of a dealer changes rapidly, and therefore any bank or finance company is going to expressly provide that the security interest will bind after acquired property. In other words, the security agreement will provide that the goods acquired after the initial loan will also be covered by the security interest. This is called a floating lien.

A secured transaction automatically covers proceeds from the collateral unless this is expressly excluded in the agreement. Proceeds include cash, checks, and accounts receivable arising from the sale of collateral. It would also include insurance proceeds in case the collateral was damaged such as in a fire. In such a situation, the financing company holding the security interest would have rights to the insurance proceeds.

PERFECTION OF SECURED TRANSACTIONS

When a security interest in property is superior to other interests and claims to the property, it is said to be perfected. In other words, to secure protection against third parties' claims to the collateral, the secured party must perfect the security interest. This is generally done by filing a financing statement in the proper governmental office. In many states, the proper governmental office in which to file UCC-1 Financing Statements (UCC-1) is the office of the state's secretary of state.

PERFECTION BY CREDITOR'S POSSESSION

Loans may be secured by a pledge where the creditor takes possession of the collateral like shares of stock. Perfection of the security interest takes place upon taking possession. If the collateral is tangible personal property, the creditor has the alternative of perfecting the security interest by taking possession of the collateral or filing a UCC-For example, Adam borrowed $500.00 from Betty. He orally agreed that Betty should have a security interest in certain equipment that was in his backyard. There was nothing in writing, and no filing of any UCC-1 was made. Nine days later, Adam agreed that Betty should take possession of the equipment until he repaid the loan. Betty took possession of the equipment. What kind of interest did Betty have in the equipment? When Betty took possession of the collateral, she acquired a perfected security interest. The perfection dated from the time she took possession. The fact that possession was taken eliminated the need for a written security agreement. The taking of possession also gave her perfection without the necessity of filing a UCC-1. Therefore, the security interest of Betty became perfected at the moment Betty took possession of the collateral.

PERFECTION FOR CONSUMER GOODS

If the collateral is consumer goods, the creditor does not have to file a UCC-1 or take possession of the goods in order to perfect a purchase money security interest in the goods because this type of an interest is perfected as soon as it attaches (automatic perfection). A creditor who sells goods to a consumer on credit and retains a security interest has a purchase money security interest.

Smith sells a refrigerator to Bob on credit and obtains a proper security agreement so that the refrigerator may serve as collateral for the payment of the amount due. Does Smith have a perfected purchase money security interest? Smith does have a perfected purchase money security interest since credit was advanced to enable Bob to purchase the consumer goods.

In an ordinary credit sale of consumer goods, no filing of a UCC-1 is required in order to perfect the secured party's interest. Consumer credit sales are treated differently from secured credit sales of inventory since, for most consumer transactions, the amount involved would not warrant the expense of preparing and filing a UCC-1. However, if no UCC-1 Financing Statement is filed, a resale by the consumer buyer to another consumer will destroy the seller's security interest if the second purchaser does not have knowledge of the security interest of the seller. For example, a consumer buys a refrigerator under an installment contract and the appliance store retains a security interest in the refrigerator. The appliance store does not file a financing statement. The consumer later on sells the refrigerator to a neighbor who is unaware of the prior security interest. The neighbor will take free of the security interest of the appliance store. However, if the seller of consumer goods does file a financing statement, he has priority over a subsequent purchaser even if the purchaser does not have actual knowledge of the seller's security interest.

PERFECTION FOR MOTOR VEHICLES In most States, a security interest in non-inventory collateral for which a certificate of title is issued (like a car) can be perfected only by having the lien stated on the certificate of title.

PERFECTION BY FILING A FINANCING STATEMENT
A financing statement is a different instrument from the security agreement. The financing statement must be signed by the debtor and give the address of the secured party. It also must give the address of the debtor and contain a statement indicating the kinds or describing the items of collateral. A security agreement may be filed as a financing statement if it contains the information necessary for a financing statement.

The financing statement does not set forth the terms of the agreement between the parties. This is done in the security agreement. The financing statement gives notice to the world that the secured creditor has a security interest in the collateral described in the statement.

Filing of the financing statement is usually required to perfect the creditor's interest in inventory or the proceeds. An exception is made when a statute requires the security interest to be designated on the title certificate issued for the property - e.g., title certificate of an automobile. A security interest in a car that is inventory (e.g., held for sale by Acme Chevrolet) is perfected by filing under the UCC. However, a privately-owned car is generally protected by a notation on the title certificate.

Place of Filing
The UCC gives each State the option to describe where financing statements will be filed. Local filing would be in the county of residence or place of business of the debtor. Central filing would be a principal office in the State Capitol. Dual filing would be a combination of both local and central filing. Dual filing would mean that the financing statement must be filed both at the secretary of state's office and at the office in the county where real property records are kept. The place of filing sometimes depends upon the type of collateral (equipment, inventory, farm products) and whether or not the debtor has more than one place of business in the State.

Defective Filing
If the filing of the UCC-1 is defective because the information in the statement is seriously misleading or filing is made in the wrong county or office, the filing fails to perfect the security interest. This means that other creditors who have liens on the collateral may have a right to the

collateral that is superior to that of the secured creditor. A Trustee in Bankruptcy also may have a right superior to the original secured creditor if the filing is defective.

LOSS OF PERFECTION

Perfection by possession is lost if a creditor returns the collateral to the debtor. Regarding consumer goods, perfection may be lost by resale of the goods by the consumer to another consumer if the buyer purchases the goods without knowledge of the perfection.

The filing of a financing statement is effective for five years. At the conclusion of five years, the perfection of the security interest terminates unless a continuation statement has been filed. The continuation statement is merely a statement by the secured party that identifies the original financing statement by its file number and declares that it is still effective. The state's secretary of state's office generally approves pre-printed forms.

In most cases, perfection is lost if collateral is removed to another state unless a creditor files a financing statement in the new state within four months after removal. Regarding motor vehicles, perfection is lost if a new title is issued and the lien is not stated on the title.

TERMINATION STATEMENT

Once the debt has been paid, the debtor has the right to require the creditor or the creditor's assignee to send the debtor a termination statement which states that the security interest is no longer claimed under a specified financing statement. The debtor then may present this statement to the filing officer who marks his record that the financing statement is terminated.

SECURED PARTY VS. UNSECURED PARTY

If there are two security interests, one perfected and one not perfected, the perfected security interests prevails, i.e., is able to seize the collateral subject to the security interest and sell it to recover the amount due on the secured loan or secured sale.

PERFECTED SECURED PARTY VS. PERFECTED SECURED PARTY

If you have two perfected security interests, the first to be perfected (e.g. filed) prevails. A perfected purchase money security interest in inventory prevails over other creditors (even prior perfected liens) if the purchase money security interest is perfected before a debtor receives the collateral and notice is given to prior secured parties before the debtor receives possession of the goods. For example, suppose a bank has a perfected lien on the inventory of a pet store. If a supplier sells reptiles to the store on credit, taking a security interest on the reptiles, the supplier's security interest would have priority if the supplier files his financing statement before the store gets the reptiles and notifies the bank of the security interest before the store receives the reptiles.

If the collateral is not inventory (such as equipment), the purchase money secured creditor will prevail if a financing statement is filed within ten days after the debtor takes possession of the collateral. For example, Tenth National Bank (TNB) makes a loan to Smith and files a financing statement covering all of Smith's copying equipment, including after-acquired equipment. Later, XYZ Copiers, Inc, sells a copier to Smith on a retail installment contract and takes a security interest in the copier. XYZ Copiers' security interest is superior to TNB's security interest as long as Copiers files its financing statement within ten days of Smith's receipt of the copier.

SECURED PARTY VS. BUYER OF COLLATERAL FROM DEBTOR

What if the debtor sells collateral which is subject to a security interest? If the security interest is not perfected and the buyer takes title without knowledge of the security interest, the buyer takes free of the security interest. If the security interest was perfected, the buyer takes title subject to the security interest unless the goods being sold is inventory. Purchase of inventory by a buyer in the ordinary course of business destroys the security interest, and the buyer takes free of any security interest.

RIGHTS OF PARTIES AFTER DEFAULT

When a debtor defaults on an obligation in a secured transaction, the secured party has certain rights under UCC with respect to enforcing his claim against the collateral. These rights can be specified by the security agreement itself. The UCC also provides for procedures that the secured party can follow in the event the security agreement does not itself provide for all necessary procedures.

In the event of default, the secured party is entitled to take the collateral from the debtor. Self-help repossession is when the secured party simply goes and takes the collateral himself. This is allowed if it can be done without causing a breach of the peace. In other words, if the debtor will allow the secured party to take the collateral without the debtor causing any trouble, self-help repossession is lawful. If taking the collateral cannot be done without causing a breach of the peace, the secured party must use court action. The secured party must go to court and get the court to order the collateral to be seized and sold pursuant to the security agreement and the UCC.

The secured party may sell the collateral at either a private sale or a public sale providing this is done in a commercially reasonable manner. Notice of the sale of the collateral has to be given, and the debtor has the right to redeem the collateral prior to its sale. Proceeds from the sale of collateral are applied first to the expenses incurred by the secured party in seizing the collateral and making the sale. Next, the proceeds are used to pay the outstanding indebtedness. Next, the proceeds are used to pay any indebtedness owed to any other secured party. Finally, if there is any money left, it is to be paid to the debtor.

Chapter 17
INSURANCE

RISK

Individuals and businesses establish plans to protect their personal and financial interests against events that threaten to undermine their security. This concept is risk management. The most common method of risk management is the transfer of risk from an individual or a business to an insurance company. As with other areas of law, the area of insurance has its own special concepts and terminology. It is also pointed out that when a broker deals with an applicant for insurance, the broker is, in effect, the applicant's agent, but that an insurance agent is an agent of the insurer, not an agent of the applicant.

Insurance Terminology – Insurable Interest

A person can insure anything in which he or she has an insurable interest. One must have a reasonable expectation of benefit from the continued life of another to have an insurable interest in that person's life. This interest must exist when the policy is obtained. In the case of property, an insurable interest exists when one would sustain a pecuniary loss from its destruction. This interest must exist when the loss occurs.

The Insurance Contract

Insurance policies generally are in standard form; and in some states, standardization of forms is required.

Application

The application is part of the insurance contract. Because an insurance company evaluates the risk based on the information in the application, misstatements or misrepresentations can void a policy.

Effective Date

An insurance applicant may be protected between the time an application is received and the time the insurance company either accepts or rejects it, or an applicant may not be protected until a formal written policy is issued.

Provisions and Clauses

The words used in an insurance contract have their ordinary meaning and are interpreted in light of the nature of the coverage. Ambiguity and uncertainty are interpreted against the insurance company. In some cases, the unambiguous language of a clause in an insurance policy would appear to provide so little coverage that courts have held that it would be unconscionable to allow the insurer to enforce it. Insurance policies are typically long and detailed, in language drafted by an insurance group. Consumers often do not read the policies and, even when they do, often do not understand the provisions. In those cases, the courts may determine that if the insured had read and understood the clause, he or she would have considered the coverage unacceptable.

CANCELLATION

Defenses against Payment
An insured can cancel a policy at any time; an insurer can cancel only on written notice. The reasons for cancellation depend somewhat on the type of insurance, but generally policies are canceled for nonpayment of premiums or anything that materially affects the risk insured against – fraud, misrepresentation, gross negligence, crimes by the insured, *etc.* Not all defenses are available to an insurer, however.

Coinsurance Clauses – These provide that if a property owner insures the property up to a specified percentage of its value, the owner will recover any loss up to the face amount of the policy. If the insurance is for less, the owner suffers a proportionate share of the loss.

Good Faith Obligations – Essentially, the parties to an insurance contract are responsible for the obligations the contract imposes. These include basic contract duties (act in good faith, disclose all material facts). An insurer must investigate and attempt to settle claims, and the insured must cooperate.

Bad Faith Actions – If an insurer's denial of a claim or refusal to settle a claim for a reasonable amount within a policy's limits is in bad faith, the insured may recover damages, including punitive damages, in tort.

Title insurance – Title insurance companies issue title insurance policies to insure title to real property against defects that might otherwise render title unmarketable. The amount of the policy is usually equal to the purchase price of the property being purchased. Typically, title insurance companies issue title insurance policies after a title search of the property has been conducted but before closing has occurred. A title insurance policy does not affect the quality of the title being purchased but simply provides a guarantee of accuracy regarding the quality of title to the land itself. A property owner could file an action against the title insurance company if some defect that was not disclosed in the title insurance policy rendered title unmarketable, but that very same property owner would have no right to proceed against the title insurance company simply because its investigation revealed that there are defects in the title.

Title policies exclude a number of items from coverage, such as defects in title, that are not evidenced by a recording in the public records but which are known to the purchaser of the property. Title policies may also exclude items that can only be ascertained by a physical inspection of the property such as the accuracy of the survey and the presence of any adverse possessors. Other common exceptions to title include government zoning regulations, tax assessment schemes affecting the property, and easements. In the event that a defect renders title to the property unmarketable, the title policy will usually provide the title insurance company with the option of paying the claim (up to the full amount of the policy – which is generally the purchase price of the property) or litigating the claim. The policy itself remains in force only for as long as the insured continues to own the particular property. Subsequent purchasers of the land must purchase their own policies.

Business Insurance – A business may be vulnerable to all sorts of risks. A key employee may die or become disabled; a customer may be injured when using a manufacturer's product; the patron of an establishment selling liquor may leave the premises and injure a third party in an automobile accident; or a professional may overlook some important detail, causing liability for malpractice. Should the first situation arise (for instance, if the company president dies), the business may have some protection under a key-person insurance policy. In the other circumstances, other types of insurance may apply.

- **General Liability.** Comprehensive general liability insurance can cover virtually as many risks as the insurer agrees to cover. Among the types of coverage that a business might wish to acquire, for example, is protection from liability for injuries arising from on-premises events not otherwise insured against, such as company social functions. Some specialized establishments may be subject to liability in individualized circumstances, and policies can be drafted to meet their needs. In many jurisdictions, for example, statutes impose liability on a seller of intoxicating liquor when a buyer of the liquor, intoxicated as a result of the sale, injures a third party. Legal protection may extend not only to immediately consequent injuries, such as quadriplegia in an automobile accident, but also to the loss of support suffered by a family because of the injuries. Insurance can provide coverage for these injuries and losses.
- **Product Liability.** Manufacturers may be subject to liability for injuries that their products cause, and product liability insurance can be written to match specific products' risks. Coverage can be procured under a comprehensive general liability policy or under a separate policy. The coverage may include expenses involved in recalling and replacing a product that has proved to be defective.
- **Professional Malpractice.** Attorneys, physicians, architects, and engineers, for example have increasingly become the targets of negligence suits. Professionals may purchase malpractice insurance to protect themselves against such claims. The large judgments in some malpractice suits have received considerable publicity and are sometimes cited in what has been termed "the insurance crisis," because they have contributed to a considerable increase in malpractice insurance premiums in recent years.
- **Workers' Compensation.** Workers' compensation insurance covers payments to employees who are injured in accidents arising out of and in the course of employment (that is, on the job). Workers' compensation is governed by state statutes which provide for fixed awards to employees or their dependents without considering issues of proof or negligence. Such statutes make the employer strictly liable for the injuries of his employees but workers' compensation is an exclusive remedy that bars any common-law remedies that might have otherwise been asserted by the employees.

AUTO INSURANCE

The cheapest form of auto insurance is **liability auto insurance.** This is because it only covers any damage you cause to a person, another vehicle or property in the process of an accident. It also only covers you when you are at fault for the accident and not when someone else is at fault. Anyone driving a car should carry at least a minimum level of liability auto insurance. Most, if not all, states require drivers to have liability insurance and usually set forth a minimum amount of coverage that each driver is required to have. Many insurance agents will tell individuals that they should get additional coverage rather than just the minimum coverage required by the state because you can become open to lawsuits if the medical bills of the individual become higher than your coverage amount.

Collision auto insurance will help cover your car for any damage that happens after an accident. Whether the accident is your fault or not, collision coverage will allow you to get the money needed to fix your car after an accident. This type of auto insurance generally covers all types of accidents whether it is from another car or an object. You can save money on collision auto insurance coverage by choosing a high deductible so that your premiums will be lower. Although since this form of auto insurance coverage is limited to the value of your car it may not be worth it to purchase this form of auto insurance if you have an older vehicle.

Comprehensive auto insurance will help cover your car against any damage or loss that results from fire, theft, vandalism, wind, hail, explosion or other natural events. This type of insurance can cover your vehicle against all natural events as well as losses from the theft of your vehicle. The insurance company will pay to fix your vehicle from any of these events less the amount of deductible that you choose when signing the insurance policy. However, you should always carefully read your policy since the type of coverage and conditions can vary depending on the policy you are signing.

LIFE INSURANCE

There are two basic types of life policies: **cash-value policies,** which cover you for your entire life and include an investment component; and **term policies,** which cover you for a specific period of time and provide a death benefit only.

Term life insurance covers you for a specified period of time (usually from 5 to 30 years) and usually has the lowest premium in the early years, making it the most affordable life insurance initially. Term life insurance does not build cash value. If you are still living at the end of the term, your insurance coverage ends unless you can renew the policy. When you renew (assuming your policy has that feature) it will renew at a higher price reflecting your now older age. Term insurance has no buildup of cash as with whole life (*e.g.*, cash-value insurance).

Listed below are various types of term insurance.

- ***Level Term*** - a fixed amount of coverage with premiums that are fixed over a certain period of time, usually in 10-year increments.
- ***Increasing/Decreasing Term*** - amount of coverage increases or decreases throughout the term, premiums typically remain level.
- ***Renewable Term*** - includes a renewal provision that gives the policy owner the right to renew the insurance coverage at the end of the specified term without submitting evidence of insurability.
- ***Convertible Term*** - gives the policyholder the right to convert the term policy to a permanent policy.
- ***Group Term*** - insurance purchased typically by an employer or professional association that is intended to cover several people, usually resulting in reduced premiums.

Whole life is a type of permanent life insurance. It's called permanent because a whole life policy provides life-long protection and is guaranteed to do so by the insurance company. With whole life, you pay a fixed premium for life, instead of the increasing premiums found on term life insurance policies.

The most important reason to own life insurance is to provide support for your dependents should you or your spouse die prematurely. The idea is to allow surviving family members to maintain something close to the standard of living they enjoyed prior to you or your spouse's death. The amount of insurance necessary to manage this depends, in part, on how much income you and your spouse currently earn. Generally, the lower your income, the less you have to replace and the less life insurance you need.

Guaranteed level term life insurance

Many insurance companies now also offer level term life insurance. This type of life insurance policy has premiums that are designed to remain level for a period of 5, 10, 15, 20, 25 or even 30 years. Level term life insurance policies have become extremely popular because they are very inexpensive and can provide relatively long term coverage. Most level term life insurance policies contain a guarantee of level premiums. However, some policies do not provide such guarantees. Without a guarantee, the life insurance company can surprise you by raising your life insurance rate, even during the time in which you expected your premiums to remain level. Needless to say, it is important to make sure that you understand the terms of any life insurance policy you are considering.

With a term policy, you get "pure" life insurance coverage. Term insurance provides a death benefit for only a specific period of time. If you die during the coverage period, your beneficiary (the person you named to collect the insurance proceeds) receives the death benefit (the face amount of the policy). If you live past the term period, your coverage ends, and you get nothing back.

Permanent Life Insurance Policies

How permanent insurance works. With a permanent policy, your premium payments for the first few (or more than a few) years cover more than the insurance company's cost of your risk of death. The excess money goes into a reserve account, which is invested by the insurance company. Unless the company is disastrously managed, these investments yield returns in the form of interest or dividends. A proportion of these are passed along to you. You can add these returns to your policy reserves or borrow against them, after a set time. And if you decide to end the policy, you can cash it in for the "surrender value."

Traditional Whole Life Insurance

Whole life insurance is a type of permanent insurance or cash value insurance. Unlike term insurance, which provides coverage for a particular period of time, permanent insurance provides coverage for your entire life. When you make premium payments, you pay more than is needed to pay for the current costs of insurance coverage and expenses. The excess payment is credited to a cash value account. This cash value account allows the insurance company to charge a level, guaranteed premium and to provide a death benefit and cash value throughout the life of the policy.

As you make payments, the cash value account grows. With traditional whole life insurance, the cash value account is guaranteed and held in the insurance company's general portfolio – you don't get to choose how the cash value account is invested. However, the cash value can potentially grow beyond its guaranteed amount through the payment of dividends (profits earned by a "mutual" insurer). The cash value grows tax deferred and can either be used as collateral to borrow from the insurance company or be directly accessed through a partial or complete surrender of the policy. It is important to note, however, that a policy loan or partial surrender will reduce the policy's death benefit, and a complete surrender will terminate coverage altogether.

Universal life insurance

Universal life insurance differs from whole life insurance in that this type of life insurance policy distinguishes and itemizes the protection element (death benefit), the expense element, and the cash value element. By separating the three elements, the insurance company can build more flexibility into the life insurance policy. This flexibility allows (within certain guidelines) the life insurance policy owner to modify the face amount or the premium in response to changing needs and circumstances.

Universal Life insurance is a variation of Whole Life insurance. The difference is that with Universal Life, the term life portion of the policy is separate from the investment or cash portion of the policy. Also, with Universal Life policies, the investment portion of the policy is invested in money market funds as opposed to stocks, bonds and mutual funds. The cash value portion of the policy is an accumulation fund that investment interest is credited to and death benefits are paid from. With Universal Life insurance, the insured can vary the amount of his/her annual death benefit and annual premium payments. Insured people may also make partial surrenders of the policy and/or take policy loans against the cash value of the policy. A partial surrender is when an insured withdraws some of the funds that have accumulated in the investment or cash portion of the policy.

There are basically two types of Universal Life insurance. Under Option A, there is a set death benefit for the insured regardless of premiums paid to keep the policy in force. Under Option B, the death benefit for insured is equal to a set amount plus the current cash value of the policy at the time of the insured's death. Option B usually pays out more than Option A following the death of an insured.

A universal life insurance policy will generally provide very broad premium guidelines (i.e., minimum and maximum premium payments), but within these guidelines you can choose how much and when you pay premiums. Reducing or increasing premiums will impact the growth of the cash value component and possibly the death benefit. You are also free to change the policy's death benefit directly (again, within the limits set out by the policy) as your financial circumstances change. Be aware, however, that if you want to raise the amount of coverage, you'll need to go through the insurability process again, probably including a new medical exam,

Variable Life insurance

Variable life insurance provides permanent protection for you and is the type of life insurance with account flexibility for the more risk-oriented policy holder. Variable Life insurance is also a form of Whole Life insurance. As with Whole Life and Universal Life insurance, part of the premium payment goes toward the term life portion of the policy, part to administrative expenses and part to the investment or cash value portion of the policy. There is a major difference between the investment portion of Variable Life and that of other forms of life insurance. With Variable Life, the insured person (you) is able to choose how to invest the funds in the investment portion of the policy.

The insured may select from an array of investments such as stocks, bonds and mutual funds as long as they are within the insurance companies portfolio. Usually, there are a few times during the year that the insured person may modify his/her investment selections. Variable Life insurance is generally more expensive than other forms of Life insurance. Death benefits may fluctuate up or down depending on investment performance however, there is usually a minimum level for benefits so they will not drop below a certain level.

Like other types of permanent life insurance, variable life insurance has a cash value account. A variable life insurance policy, however, allows you to choose how your cash value account is invested. A variable life policy generally contains several investment options, known as subaccounts, which are professionally managed to pursue a stated investment objective. Choices can range from a fixed interest subaccount to a highly volatile international growth subaccount. Variable life insurance policies require a fixed annual premium for the life of the policy and may provide a minimum guaranteed death benefit. If the cash value account exceeds a certain amount, the death benefit will increase.

Variable universal life combines all of the options and flexibility of universal life with the investment choices of a variable policy. It is a true hybrid product, and you make most of the policy decisions. You decide how often and how much your premium payments are to be, within guidelines. With most variable universal life policies, you get no guaranteed minimum cash value or death benefit. Your premium payments in excess of administrative costs and the cost of insurance are invested in the variable subaccounts that you choose.

With both variable and universal life insurance, your policy may lapse if the cash value account falls below a certain level. Low-interest loans can be taken against your cash value account, and cash withdrawals are available. However, keep in mind that your policy's face amount is reduced by the amount of a policy withdrawal, and withdrawals may be taxable. You have the option of choosing a fixed or enhanced death benefit. Today, most variable universal life policies offer a rider that guarantees the death benefit at a certain level regardless of the performance of the subaccounts, provided that a stated minimum premium is paid for a predetermined number of years.

Chapter 18
AGENCY

Agency is a relationship based on an agreement authorizing one person, the *agent,* to act for another, the *principal.* For example, an agent may negotiate and make contracts with third persons on behalf of the principal. Actions of an agent can obligate the principal to third persons. Actions of an agent may also give a principal rights against third persons.

The term agency is often used in other ways. For example, the term is used sometimes to show that a person has the right to sell certain products. A car dealer might be referred to as having an automobile agency. But the dealer is not an agent in the sense of representing the manufacturer.

Also, sometimes an agency relationship is created even if this term is not used. This question or situation has been the result of numerous Court actions. It is important to be able to distinguish agencies from other relationships that are similar. Control and authority are key factors in distinguishing ordinary employees and independent contractors from agents.

Employees: An ordinary employee is not an agent unless the employee was hired to represent the employer in dealings with third persons. It is possible, though, for the same person to be both an agent and an employee. It depends upon the authority given the employee. An example would be the authority to make contracts on behalf of the employer.

Independent Contractors: An agent or an employee is different from an independent contractor. A principal or employer has control over an agent or employee, but not over an independent contractor. A principal or employer does not have control over the work performance of an independent contractor. A principal or employer is not bound by the actions of an independent contractor.

The separate identity of an independent contractor may be concealed in such a way that the public believes that it is dealing with the principal. When this happens, the principal is liable for the negligence of the independent contractor. In the New Jersey case of *Hill v. Newman*[8], Hill purchased furniture from Grant Furniture. When Hill complained that the furniture was damaged, she was told by Grant's that they would send someone to repair the damage. Newman, an independent contractor, was sent to repair the furniture. He identified himself to Hill as "the man from Grant's." The lacquer Newman put on the furniture exploded and seriously injured Hill. She sued both Newman and Grant. Grant claimed that Newman was an independent contractor and that Grant's was not responsible for his conduct. The Court held for Hill stating that when the separate identity of an independent contractor is concealed by a business that makes it appear that the independent contractor is an employee of the business, the business is liable for the negligence of the contractor. Since Grant's made it appear that Newman was its

---

[8] Hill v. Newman, 316 A.2d 8 (N. J. 1973)

employee, Grant was liable to the same extent it would be liable if Newman had been Grant's employee.

PURPOSE OF AGENCY

An agency can be created for the purpose of doing almost any act the principal could do. However, there are some acts that must be done in person and cannot be done by an agent. Examples would be: testifying in court for another individual, making a will, and voting.

WHO MAY BE A PRINCIPAL

Any competent person can be a principal and act through an agent. However, a person appointing an agent must be mentally and legally competent to appoint an agent. Otherwise, the appointment is voidable. Someone who had been declared NCM (i.e., mentally incompetent) by a Court cannot appoint an agent. A minor child cannot legally act through an agent appointed by the minor.

WHO MAY BE AN AGENT

A contract made by an agent is legally the contract of the principal. Therefore, it is irrelevant whether or not the agent had legal capacity to make a contract. A minor technically could act as an agent without hurting the enforceability of the contract. I don't recommend this though.

CLASSIFICATION OF AGENTS

A *general agent* is authorized by the principal to transact all the affairs of a particular kind of business. For example, a person appointed as manager of a store is a general agent.
A *special agent* is authorized by the principal to handle a particular business transaction or perform a specific act. For example, a specific power of attorney appointing an agent (attorney-in-fact) to sell a particular piece of real estate or a certain car would be the appointment of a special agent.

A universal agent is authorized by the principal to do any act that can be delegated to a representative. An example would be giving a person a general power of attorney. A general power of attorney is often given to a family member by someone in the military who is going overseas. This would give the family member authority to handle any business until the person in the military returned home.

AGENCY COUPLED WITH AN INTEREST

An agent has an *interest in the authority* when consideration has been given or paid for the right to exercise the authority. For example, when a lender in making a loan is given, as security, authority to collect rents due to the borrower and to apply those rents to the payment of the debt, the lender becomes the borrower's agent with an interest in the authority given to collect the rents.

An agent has *interest in the subject matter* when, for a consideration, the agent is given an interest in the property with which the agent is dealing. For example, when the agent is authored to sell property of the principal and is given a lien on the property as security for a debt owed to the agent by the principal, the agent has an interest in the subject matter.

CREATING THE AGENCY

An agency can come into being by appointment, conduct, ratification, or operation of law.

AUTHORIZATION BY APPOINTMENT

The usual method of creating an agency is by expressly appointing one person to act for another. This appointment may be oral; you can verbally appoint an agent. Some agency appointments have to be in writing. Most states require that agency appointments be in writing when the agent will be authorized to buy or sell land.

A written authorization of agency is called a *power of attorney.* The agent is referred to as an *attorney-in-fact.*

AUTHORIZATION BY CONDUCT

If the owner of a store places another person in charge, third parties (e.g., customers) may assume that the person in charge is the agent of the owner. In this case, person appears to outsiders to be authorized as an agent. The agent has *apparent authority.* The term apparent authority is used when:

- There is only the appearance of authority, but no actual authority; and
- The appearance of authority was created by the principal.

The test for the existence of apparent authority is whether or not the principal's words or conduct would lead a third person to reasonably believe that the "agent" has authority. If the principal has restricted the "agent's" authority, but a third person does not know of the restrictions, the principal can still be bound by the apparent agent's actions toward the third person. The third person must reasonably believe that the agent has authority, or there is no apparent authority. If the basis for the third person's belief in the authority is not reasonable, there is no apparent authority.

Edwards came to Sue's house and showed her order blanks with the name Elco Corporation. Edwards told Sue that he was the agent for the Elco Corporation, and he then solicited orders from Sue for merchandise manufactured by Elco. He also accepted a cash deposit from Sue for her order. Edwards was not an agent of Elco, and the forms he had shown Sue were counterfeit. Sue sued Elco on the grounds that Edwards appeared to be the agent of Elco and therefore had apparent authority to bind Elco. Was Sue correct? No. Apparent authority arises only when the conduct of the alleged principal is responsible for causing the appearance of authority. Elco did not cause the appearance of authority in this instance.[9]

In a Washington case, Walker v. Pacific Mobile Homes[10] Walker owned a trailer that he wanted to sell. He took it to Pacific Mobile Homes. A fellow named Stewart introduced himself as a salesman for Pacific. Stewart was the only person on the premises, and this had been the case several other times Walker had been at Pacific. Stewart said that he would take possession of Walker's trailer and try to sell it. Stewart filled out some forms of Pacific and later wrote Walker some letters that were on Pacific stationery. Stewart sold the trailer and skipped with the

---

[9] ***Elco* Shoe Mfgrs. v. *Sisk*,** 260 N.Y. 100, 183 N.E. 191 1932)

[10] Walker v. Pacific Mobile Homes, 413 P.2d 3 (WN 1966)

money. Walker sued Pacific. Pacific argued that Stewart had no authority to enter into a sales contract on behalf of Pacific. Also, Pacific argued that its salesmen were forbidden to sell used trailers for their owners. *The Court held against Pacific* and in favor of Walker. The fact that Stewart was apparently in charge whenever Walker went to Pacific gave Stewart the appearance of being able to sell trailers. Pacific should have watched over its sales lot more closely and kicked any trespassers like Stewart off. It was reasonable for Walker to believe that Stewart was not a trespasser. It was also reasonable for Walker to believe that Stewart had authority to sell trailers for Pacific.

AGENCY BY RATIFICATION

Suppose an agent tries to do an act for his principal that he is not authorized so to do; or suppose a person who is not the agent of another attempts to act as an agent anyway. Generally, the principal has the choice of ignoring the transaction or *ratifying* it. Generally, any unauthorized act may be ratified.

Intention to Ratify: Initially, ratification is a question of intention. It is a question of whether or not the principal intended to approve or ratify the action of the unauthorized agent. This intention may be expressed verbally or it may be demonstrated by the conduct of the principal. Examples of ratification:

- Paying for goods ordered by the agent.
- Performing the contract the agent made and accepting payment for performance of the contract.

A transaction by an agent may be ratified by the principal when the principal accepts the benefits of the unauthorized transaction. However, the principal must know what has happened. Conditions for Ratification: The principal must have full knowledge of all material facts. If the agent conceals a material fact, any alleged ratification by the principal is not valid unless the principal knows of these facts. There can be no ratification when the principal does not know that his agent has made a contract. For example, a building owner's agent and a contractor make unauthorized changes to an installation contract. If this is done without the owner's knowledge, there is no ratification by the owner. (There might be an apparent agency problem though). However, it is not always necessary to show that the principal had *actual* knowledge. Knowledge will be *imputed* if a principal knows of facts which would cause a prudent person to inquire as to what is going on. The court may rule that the principal should have known what was going on and therefore will be held to have sufficient knowledge to ratify the agent's acts. Form of Ratification: A ratification may be oral. However, if a contract cannot be enforced unless it is in writing, it is generally held that the ratification of the contract must also be in writing. For example, if an agent makes a contract for the sale of land without authority, ratification must be in writing because of the statute of frauds.

Effect of Ratification: When an unauthorized action is ratified, the effect is the same as though the act had been originally authorized. The principal and the person the agent dealt with are bound by the contract made by the agent.

PROVING THE AGENCY RELATIONSHIP

The burden of proving the existence of an agency relationship is on the person trying to benefit from the possible agency. The person who is trying to bind the principal because of the actions of an alleged agent has to prove:

- The alleged agent was in fact the authorized agent of the principal; and
- The agent had authority to do the act in question.

For example, a buyer of a computer alleges that a seller's agent breached an express warranty regarding the computer. The buyer must prove that the agent had actual or apparent authority to make the warranty. If the buyer can't prove this, the jury must find that there was no agency.

AGENT'S AUTHORITY

A very important aspect of the law of agency deals with determining the scope of the agent's authority.

SCOPE OF AGENT'S AUTHORITY

The scope of an agent's authority may be determined from the verbal authorization of the principal to the agent, or it may be implied from things the principal says or does in relation to the agent, or from the customs of the trade or business in which the principal and agent are involved.

Express Authority: If the principal tells the agent to perform a certain act, the agent has express authority to do this act. Express authority can be indicated verbally or in writing. Example: I tell my office manager to purchase a new desk for me.

Incidental Authority: An agent has implied incidental authority to perform any act which is reasonably necessary to carry out the express authority given to the agent. For example, if the principal authorizes the agent to purchase goods and does not furnish the funds for the agent to pay for the goods, the agent has implied incidental authority to purchase the goods on credit. Our office manager has incidental authority to purchase office supplies like typing paper.

Customary Authority: An agent has implied customary authority to do any act that is customary in the business in which the principal and agent operate. For example, an agent who has express authority to receive payments from third persons has the implied authority to issue receipts. A general manager of a business has the power to make any contract that is necessary for the usual and ordinary conduct of the business.

Apparent Authority: A person has apparent authority as an agent when the principal, by his words or conduct, leads a third person to reasonably believe that the person/agent has the authority that the agent appears to have, and the third person relies on this appearance of authority. The question of apparent authority is probably the most litigated question in agency law.

EFFECT OF PROPER EXERCISE OF AUTHORITY

When a duly-authorized agent makes a contract with a third person on behalf of the principal, there is a binding contract between the principal and the third person. The agent is not a party to this contract. In a situation where the owner of goods being sold is the principal, the owner's agent is not liable to the buyer for a breach of warranty claim with respect to the goods sold by the agent. This is because the owner, and not the agent, was technically the seller in the sales transaction.

Smith was agent for the Acme Sportswear. He contracted on behalf of Acme to provide the City High School football team with 60 "game "jerseys. The jerseys delivered to the school were of such poor quality that they were clearly not fit for the purpose of serving as "game" jerseys. The School Department sued Smith, the person who sold them the jerseys, for breach of warranty. *Judgment for Smith.* The contract for the jerseys was between Acme and the high school. Even though Marks called on the school and sold the jerseys to school personnel, he was authorized to do so as an agent for Acme. As an agent he is not a party to the contract and is not liable for breach of warranty. The principal, Acme, is liable for breach of warranty since it was the seller in the transaction.

DUTY TO ASCERTAIN EXTENT OF AGENT'S AUTHORITY

A third person who deals with a person claiming to be an agent cannot rely solely upon the statements made by the agent concerning the extent of the agent's authority. If the agent is not authorized to perform the act in question, or is not even the agent of the principal, the transaction between the alleged agent and the third person will have no legal effect between 0the principal and the third person.

Third persons are under a legal obligation to find out the extent of the agent's authority. For example, the third person could call the principal to verify the extent of the agent's authority and then confirm this authority in a letter to the principal. The letter could be later used in evidence if a dispute arises with regard to the agent's authority.

Agent's Acts Adverse to Principal: The third person is under an obligation to take notice of any acts that are clearly adverse to the interests of the principal. For example, if the agent is obviously making use of funds of the principal for the agent's personal benefit, people dealing with the agent should recognize that the agent may be acting without authority.

LIMITATIONS OF AGENT'S AUTHORITY

A person who has knowledge of a limitation of an agent's authority cannot disregard this limitation.

Obvious Limitations: In some situations, it will be apparent to third persons that they are dealing with an agent whose authority is limited. When third persons know that they are dealing with an officer of a private corporation or a representative of a governmental agency, they should recognize that such a person will ordinarily not have unlimited authority.
The agent owes certain duties to the principal.

Loyalty: An agent must be loyal or faithful to the principal and must not obtain any secret profit or benefit from the agency.

In the Pennsylvania case of Kribbs v. Jackson,[11] Kribbs owned real estate that had been leased through his agent, Jackson, at a monthly rental of $275.00. When this lease terminated, Jackson and a third person, Solomon, made an agreement that if Solomon obtained a new tenant for a rental of $500.00 a month, Jackson would pay Solomon $100.00 a month. Solomon did obtain a new tenant who paid a monthly rental of $550.00. Jackson continued to send Kribbs $275.00 a month, less his usual commission and janitor and utility costs. He paid Solomon $100.00 a month, and then kept the balance of the rental for himself. When Kribbs learned about this arrangement three years later, he sued Jackson for the money Jackson had kept for himself and for the money which Jackson had paid Solomon. Jackson argued that Kribbs accepted the $275.00 per month and had been satisfied. Jackson argued that the additional funds were the sole result of Jackson's "entrepreneurship." *The Court held in favor of Kribbs.* The Court stated that an agent must account to the principal for all profits secretly made in an agency transaction and for all sums of money the agent improperly permitted third persons to receive in connection with such transactions.

In the Illinois case of Allen Industries v. Sheldon Company[12] Joan Kulwin owned Allen Industries. Allen Industries owned a commercial building in Evanston, Illinois. Kulwin granted to the Sheldon Company the exclusive right to sell the building and agreed to pay a commission to Sheldon upon the sale. This commission was to be divided in half between Sheldon and a cooperating broker, should the cooperating broker secure a purchaser. On August 21, 1985, Sheldon Company presented Kulwin with a written offer in final contract form from J. W. Collier. Kulwin rejected this offer of $335,000.00 and made a counteroffer of $350,000.00. On August 22, Collier accepted the counteroffer. The contract called for the seller to finance part of the transaction by taking back a mortgage for $249,000.00 from Collier. Kulwin later found out that Maurice Leviton, the president of TLC Company, on August 16, 1985, advised Sheldon that he was preparing an all-cash offer on the property. He made this offer to Sheldon on August 22, and it was rejected by Sheldon since Kulwin had accepted Collier's offer at this point. Kulwin sued Sheldon for breach of fiduciary duty since he failed to inform her of all facts material to the sale. Kulwin argued that Sheldon failed to inform her of TLC's communications because Sheldon did not want to share half the commission with the broker who showed TLC the property. *The Court held in favor of Kulwin.* The Court held that as of August 21, when Kulwin was presented with Collier's offer by Sheldon, Sheldon knew that TLC's president had inspected the premises and was preparing a cash offer. Since these facts might have influenced Kulwin in accepting or rejecting Collier's offer, these were material facts that the agent had a duty to disclose to Kulwin. An agent who breaches the fiduciary duty to the principal is barred from recovery for services. Thus, Sheldon lost his commission.
An agent cannot act as an agent for both parties to a transaction unless both parties know that the agent is acting in a dual capacity and agree to the agent acting in this manner. For example, it is common for one attorney to close residential real estate transactions. However, both parties have to agree to this, and usually do.

---

[11] 129 A. 2d 490 (PA 1957)

[12] 505 N.E.2d 1104

An agent is not to accept secret gifts or commissions from third persons in connection with the agency. If the agent does this, the principal may sue the agent for the gifts or commissions.

Obedience and Performance: An agent is under a duty to obey all lawful instructions. An agent, who does not, is liable to the principal for any harm caused. For example, if an agent is instructed to only accept cash payments, but the agent accepts a check for payment, the agent is liable for any loss caused to the principal if the check is not honored ("bounces").
Reasonable Care: An agent has the duty to act with care that a reasonable person would exercise under the circumstances. Also, if the agent possesses a special skill, such as an attorney or a broker, the agent must exercise this skill.

Accounting: An agent must account to the principal for all property or money belonging to the principal that comes into the agent's possession. The agency agreement may state, and should state, the intervals that these accountings should be made or the dates on which they should be made.

An agent should keep the principal's property and money separate from his own. For example, an attorney handling a real estate transaction should keep any funds of the buyer, seller, and lender in a separate trust account. If money of the principal and the agent become mixed, the agent is liable for any loss that occurs.

Information: It is the duty of an agent to keep the principal informed of all facts that are relevant as far as protecting the principal's interests. In other words, the agent has a fiduciary duty to his principal.

TERMINATION OF AGENCY
An agency may be terminated by either the principal or the agent. It also may be terminated by operation of law.

TERMINATION BY ACT OF PARTIES
Expiration of Agency Contract: The agency may expire in accordance with the terms of the contract that created the agency. The contract may provide that agency shall last for a certain period of time – five years for example. It may state that the agency will last until a particular event happens – such as sale of a certain piece of real estate.
In the above two examples the agency will expire when:

- the period of time passes (five years); or
- the event occurs (e.g., the real estate is sold).

If no period of time is stated in the agency agreement, it will expire after a reasonable period of time – it may be terminated by either party. A better way of stating this is that if no period of time is stated, the agency will continue for a reasonable period of time, but it may be terminated at the will of either party.

Revocation by Principal: Any revocation by the principal must be clearly expressed. The intent to revoke must be clearly expressed. In Kinmon v. King Auction Co.,[13] a 1973 Alabama case, Kinmon owned a summer home he wanted to sell at auction. He hired King Auction Co. to make the sale. Kinmon later complained about King's efforts. King sold the property to the highest bidder for $35,000.00. Kinmon had expected twice that much and refused to convey title or pay King's commission. King sued Kinmon. Kinmon claimed that he had revoked King's authority to sell the property. The Court held in favor of King Auction Co., stating that King's authority had not been revoked by Kinmon. No revocation was made by the expression of dissatisfaction made by Kinmon of King's work. The intent to revoke must "be clearly and unequivocally expressed."

When the agency is based on a contract with the agent for a specified time, the principal is liable to the agent for damages if he discharges the agent without just cause. However, even if the principal terminates the agency without just cause, the agency is still terminated. The principal has the power to terminate the agency by discharging him, but not the right to do so.
If the agency agreement states that it can be terminated by either party at any time with or without cause, it is an *agency at will.* In this type of agency relationship, the agent has the right as well as the power to terminate the agency at any time. In any event, the agent has the right to terminate the agency if the principal is guilty of misconduct. If the agency contract states that it is to last for a specified period of time, the agent has no right to terminate the agency if the principal is not guilty of misconduct. If the agent wrongfully terminates the agency, he can be liable to the principal for damages.

TERMINATION BY OPERATION OF LAW

Anything that makes one of the parties to the agency contract unable to perform his duties will cause the agency to be terminated by operation of law:

- **Death:** The death of either the principal or the agent will generally cause the agency to be automatically terminated.
- **Insanity:** The insanity of either the principal or the agent will ordinarily terminate the agent's authority.
- **Bankruptcy:** Bankruptcy of either the principal or the agent usually terminates the agency.
- Impossibility: An agent's authority is terminated if it becomes impossible for the agent to perform his duties. For example, if an agent is appointed to sell a house for his principal, and the house burns down, the agency is terminated.
- **War:** When the Country of the principal is at war with the Country of the agent, the authority of the agent is usually terminated, or at least suspended until hostilities end.

DISABILITY OF THE PRINCIPAL UNDER THE UDPAA

The *Uniform Durable Power of Attorney Act* permits a power of attorney to provide that it will not be affected by any disability or incapacity which occurs after the power of attorney is created. This can be either a physical or mental incapacity. The UDPAA changes the common law and the general rule that insanity of the principal terminates the agency.

[13] 276 So.2d 569 (1973)

TERMINATION OF AGENCY COUPLED WITH AN INTEREST

An agency coupled with an interest is an exception to the general rule as to the termination of an agency. Such an agency cannot be revoked by the principal before the expiration of the interest. It is not terminated by the death or insanity of either the principal or the agent.

EFFECT OF TERMINATION OF AUTHORITY

If the agency is revoked by the principal, the authority of the agent to act for the principal is not terminated until notice is received by the agent. The right of the agent to bind the principal to *third persons* generally ends immediately upon termination of the agent's authority. Notice to third persons is not necessary as far as termination of the *right* of the agent to bind the principal to *third persons*. However, if the agency is terminated by the principal, *notice should be given to third parties*. If notice is not given, the agent may have the power to make contracts that will bind the principal and third persons. The reason for this rule is that a known agent (i.e., known to third persons) can continue to have the *appearance* of being an agent until notice is given to third persons. In the New Hampshire case of Record v. Wagner[14], Record owned a farm which was operated by his agent, Berry. Berry also lived on the farm. Berry hired Wagner in 1953 to bale hay. Berry told Wagner to bill Record for this work, which he did. Record paid Wagner. By the summer of 1954, the agency relationship had been terminated by Record, but Berry continued to live on the farm. From all outward appearances, nothing had changed. Berry asked Wagner again to bale hay and charge Record. Wagner performed the work, but Record refused to pay on the grounds that Berry was not his agent anymore. Wagner sued Record, and *the Court held in favor of Wagner*. The court said that since Berry had been terminated by Record, it was necessary for Record to give notice of the termination to third persons who had dealt with Berry. Since no notice had been given to Wagner, it was reasonable for him to assume that Berry was still Record's agent. Berry continued to have *apparent authority* to bind Record. Record could have a cause of action against Berry though.

LIABILITY OF AGENT TO THIRD PERSON — ACTION OF AUTHORIZED AGENT OF DISCLOSED PRINCIPAL

If an agent makes a contract with a third person on behalf of a disclosed principal and the agent has proper authority to do this, and if the contract is executed properly, the agent has no personal liability on the contract. Even if the principal fails to perform the contract, the agent cannot be held liable by the third party.

UNAUTHORIZED ACTION

If a person makes a contract as agent for another, but does not have authority to make this contract, the contract does not bind the principal. When a person claims to act as an agent for a principal, an implied warranty legally arises that this person has authority to act in the manner claimed. If the agent does not indeed have this authority, there is a breach of this warranty. If this breach results in damages to the third person, the third person might generally hold the agent liable. However, the agent is not liable for actions in excess of his authority when the third person knows that the agent is acting beyond the authority given by the principal. In the Missouri case of *Husky Industries v. Craig,*[15] Craig Industries was in the business of manufacturing

---

[14] 128 A.2d 921, 922 (1957).

[15] 618 S.W.2d 458 (1981)

charcoal at its two plants. Craig, the corporation's president, made a contract in the name of the corporation to sell the two plants to Husky Industries. However, Craig did not have authority from the board of directors of his company to make this contract. And in fact, the board of directors later voted not to accept the contract. Husky Industries sued Craig personally on the theory that he, as agent for the corporation, exceeded his authority and should be held personally liable for damages. The Court held in favor of Husky Industries. The Court held that an agent who claims to be contracting in the name of his principal, but does not have authority or is acting in excess of his authority, will be personally liable to the other party for the agent's breach of implied warranty of authority. In this case, it was significant that Husky Industries was not aware that Craig was unauthorized to make the contract. Had Husky known this, the result would have been different.

DISCLOSURE OF PRINCIPAL

There are three degrees to which the existence and identity of the principal may be disclosed or not disclosed. An agent's liability to a third person is affected by the degree of disclosure.

Disclosed Principal: When the agent makes the identity of the principal known to the third person and the agent also discloses to the third person that the agent is acting on behalf of that principal, the principal is called a *disclosed principal.* The agent is not a party to, nor is the agent bound by, any contract made by the agent on behalf of the principal in such a situation.

Partially Disclosed Principal: When the agent discloses to the third person that there is a principal, but he does not give the principal's identity, the principal is a *partially disclosed principal.* In this situation, since the third party does not know the identity of the principal, the third person is making the contract with the agent, and the agent is therefore a party to the contract.

Undisclosed Principal: When the third person is not told and does not know that the agent is acting for a principal, the unknown principal is called an *undisclosed principal.* In this type of situation, the third person is making the contract with the agent, and the agent is a party to the contract.

ASSUMPTION OF LIABILITY

Agents may intentionally make themselves liable on contracts with third persons. For example, when the principal is located out of town and is not known locally, the agent may agree to potential liability in a situation if the agent is well known and the third person knows and trusts the agent, but does not know the principal.

EXECUTION OF CONTRACT

A simple contract that appears to be the contract of an agent can be shown by other evidence to have been intended as a contract between the principal and the third party. In the New York case of *Memorial Hospital v. Baumann*[16], Beverly Baumann went with her mother to Memorial Hospital, where her mother was placed in intensive care for heart problems. A nurse asked Beverly to sign various documents including one that authorized the hospital to release medical information and to receive the mother's insurance benefits direct. This form stated: "I

---

[16] 474 N.Y.S.2d 636

understand I am financially responsible to the hospital for charges not covered by this authorization." Beverly's mother died during her hospitalization, and the hospital sued Beverly to recover $19,013.42 in unpaid hospital charges, based on the form which Beverly signed. Beverly contended that she had signed the document as an agent for her mother, and therefore was not personally liable. The Court agreed with Beverly. The Court held that she acted as agent for a disclosed principal, her mother.

To avoid any question of interpretation, an agent should execute an instrument by signing the principal's name and either *by* or *per* and the agent's name. For example, Beverly should have signed this hospital form by printing her mother's name and underneath it, putting, *By: Beverly Baumann.*

TORTS AND CRIMES

Agents are liable for harm caused to third persons by the agents' fraudulent acts, intentional acts, or negligent acts. The fact that an agent was acting as an agent does not release him from liability if his conduct would have made him liable had he been acting for himself personally. Regarding liability for torts and crimes, there is no distinction made as to whether the person causing harm is an agent or an employee as far as the agent's liability is concerned. Jones was an employee of the State Highway Department. While repairing a state highway, Jones negligently backed a state truck onto the highway and caused a collision with Smith's car. Smith sued Jones, who argued that he was acting on behalf of the state, and therefore he should not be held liable for his negligence. Judgment for Smith. The fact that an employee or agent is acting on behalf of someone else does not excuse the agent or employee from liability for torts committed by the agent or employee. Jones was therefore liable for his negligence even though it occurred within the scope of his employment by the state.

If an agent commits a crime, such as stealing from a third person or shooting a third person, the agent is liable for the crime without regard to whether the agent acted in his own self-interest or in the interest of his principal. We will discuss the liability of the principal in such a situation later.

LIABILITY OF PRINCIPAL TO THIRD PERSONS – AGENT'S CONTRACTS

The liability of a principal to a third person on a contract made by an agent depends upon the extent of the disclosure of the principal.

Simple Contract With Principal Disclosed: When a disclosed principal authorizes an agent's transaction with a third person, and when the agent properly executes a contract with the third person, a binding contract exists between the principal and the third person. The principal and the third person may sue each other in the event of a breach of contract. The agent is not a party to the contract and is not liable for his performance, and therefore cannot be sued for any breach.

Simple Contract With Principal Partially Disclosed: A partially disclosed principal is liable for a simple contract made by an authorized agent. This is a situation where the third party knows that there is a principal, but does not know who it is. In such a situation, the third party may also sue the agent.

Simple Contract With Principal Undisclosed: What happens when a third person does not know there is a principal? An undisclosed principal is liable for a simple contract made by an authorized agent. Even though the third person initially contracted with the agent alone, the third person, upon learning of the principal, may sue the principal. He may also sue the agent.

PAYMENT TO AGENT
When the third person makes payment to an authorized agent, this payment is legally deemed to have been made to the principal. The principal must give the third person full credit for the payment even if the agent never delivers the payment to the principal. This is assuming that the third person made the payment in good faith and had no reason to know that the agent would be guilty of misconduct.

A payment made to a person with apparent authority to receive the payment is legally deemed to be a payment to the apparent principal. When payment by the debtor is made to a person who is not the actual or apparent agent of the creditor, this payment is not credited to the debt unless the person in fact pays the money over to the creditor. In the case of Liberty Mutual Insurance Co. v. Enjay Chemical Co.[17] DuPont licensed Exxon and Johnson & Johnson to use certain chemical processes in return for royalty payments to be made by check to DuPont. The parties agreed that these payments, which were to be made to DuPont, were to actually be made by check sent to a specified DuPont employee (CHD), in its control division. These checks were sent during the next nine years. CHD altered some of them so that he was named on the checks as the payee. He then cashed them and used the money for his own purposes. DuPont sued Exxon and Johnson & Johnson on the grounds that they still owed the money represented by the checks that CHD had forged. The Court held in favor of Exxon and Johnson & Johnson. The Court held that payment to an authorized agent has the legal effect of payment to the principal regardless of whether the agent later delivers the payment to the principal or embezzles it. CHD was the agent authorized to receive the royalty checks. Therefore, the defendants had effectively paid the royalties when they sent CHD the checks.

AGENT'S STATEMENTS
A principal is bound by a statement made by an agent while transacting business within the scope of his authority. This can be an important point if the agent is guilty of misrepresentation or fraud.

AGENT'S KNOWLEDGE
The principal is bound by the knowledge of any fact that is acquired by an agent while acting within the scope of actual or apparent authority. In the Louisiana case of Miguez Funeral Home v. First National Life Insurance Co[18], Trahan, who was in prison on a narcotics charge, wanted to apply for a funeral expense insurance policy. His father talked with an agent of First National Life Insurance Co. The father signed the application, and the agent falsely stated on the application that Trahan had signed it in his presence. Trahan was later killed in prison. When Miguez Funeral Home filed for payment on the policy, the insurance company refused to pay on the grounds that the application had not been signed by Trahan personally. (The insurance

---

[17] 316 A.2d 219 (Del. Super. Ct. 1974)
[18] 234 So.2d 496 (LA. APP. 1970)

company probably would not have issued the policy if it had known Trahan was in prison.) The Court held in favor of the funeral home. The Court held that the insurance agent was the agent of the insurance company, and since the agent knew the facts, the insurance company was deemed to have the same knowledge as its agent.

Exceptions: There are exceptions to this rule regarding a principal being deemed to have the same knowledge as his agent. For example, if the subject matter is outside the scope of the agent's authority, and the agent has no duty to inform the principal of this knowledge, the principal is not deemed to have this knowledge (unless he in fact has it). Other exceptions are when the agent is acting adversely to the principal's interest or when the third person acts in collusion with the agent for the purpose of cheating the principal. In these cases it is not likely that the agent would communicate knowledge to the principal, and the principal is therefore not bound by the knowledge of the agent.

Communication to Principal: When the law requires that a third person communicate with the principal, that duty may be satisfied by communicating with the agent. For example, an offeree effectively communicates the acceptance of an offer to the offeror when the offeree makes the communication to the offeror's agent. Also, an offeror effectively communicates the revocation of an offer to the offeree by communicating the revocation to the offeree's agent.

LIABILITY OF PRINCIPAL FOR TORTS AND CRIMES OF AGENT

Under certain circumstances the principal may be liable to the third person for the torts or crimes of the agent or employee. This is an extremely important area of principal and agency law.

VICARIOUS LIABILITY FOR TORTS AND CRIMES

Assume that an agent or an employee causes harm to a third person. Is the principal or employer liable for this conduct? If the conduct constitutes a crime, can the principal or employer be criminally prosecuted? The answer is that in many instances the principal or employer is liable civilly and may be prosecuted criminally. This concept of causing one person to be liable for the fault of another is known as *vicarious liability.* The rules of law governing vicarious liability of the principal and the employer are basically the same. Courts speak in terms of employees acting in the course of employment rather than agents acting within the scope of the agency.

The rule of law which makes an employer vicariously liable for the wrong of an employee is also known as the doctrine of *respondeat superior*.

Nature of Act: The wrongful act committed by the employee may be a negligent act, an intentional act, a fraudulent act, or a violation of a government regulation. This act may cause civil liability to the employer, or it may also subject the employer to criminal prosecution.
Negligent Act: An employer is generally liable under the doctrine of *respondeat superior* for a negligent act committed by his employee within the scope of employment.

Intentional Act: Under English Common Law, and later American Common Law, an employer was not liable for an intentional tort committed by an employee. However, the modern rule holds that an employer is liable for an intentional tort committed by an employee for the purpose of furthering the employer's business. An employer would not be liable for an intentional and unprovoked assault committed by an employee on a third person or customer of the employer because of a personal grudge or for no reason. However, an employer would be liable by the modern view when the employee's assault was committed in the belief that the employee was somehow advancing the employer's interests. For example, when an employee is hired to repossess property, such as in the case of an employee of a finance company hired to repossess automobiles, the employee is generally liable for any unlawful force used by the employee in retaking the property, such as an assault on the debtor.

Fraud: The Court decisions in recent years hold that an employer is liable for fraudulent acts or misrepresentations of his employee. However, in states that follow the common law rule of no liability for intentional torts, the employer is not liable for the employee's fraud when the employer did not authorize or know about the fraud.

Governmental Regulation: The principal may be liable because of the agent's violation of a governmental regulation. These regulations are most common in the area of business and of protection of the environment (for example, the Exxon Valdez incident in Alaska).

Course of Employment: The fact that a tort or crime is committed by an employee does not necessarily cause vicarious liability on the employer. It must also be shown that the employee was acting within the scope of his employment.

*Employee of the United State*s: The Federal Tort Claims Act states that the U. S. shall be vicariously liable whenever a federal employee driving a motor vehicle in the course of employment causes harm if the circumstances are such that a private employer would be liable. However, the statute also states that the employee shall be exempt from liability.

NEGLIGENT HIRING AND RETENTION OF EMPLOYEES

An employer is liable for an employee's tort according to the theory of negligent hiring or retention of an employee if the employer knew or should have known the employee posed an undue risk to others and harm is caused to a third party as a result of the employee's actions.

AGENT'S CRIMES

The principal is liable for the crimes of the agent committed at the principal's direction. However, a principal is not ordinarily held liable for a crime of an agent merely because it was committed while otherwise acting within the scope of the agent's authority or employment. This is assuming that the crime was not authorized by the principal. There are exceptions. Some states will impose liability on the principal when the agent has, in the course of employment, violated liquor sales laws or pure food laws. Some Courts hold that a principal may be criminally responsible for an agent's sale of liquor to a minor in violation of a liquor law, even though the sale was not known to the principal and violated specific instructions given to the agent.

OWNER'S LIABILITY FOR ACTS OF AN INDEPENDENT CONTRACTOR

If the work is done by an independent contractor rather than by an employee, the owner is not liable for harm caused by the contractor to third persons on their property. Also, the owner is not bound by the contracts made by the independent contractor. In the case of *Guillory v. Conoco*[19] (a Louisiana case), Conoco contracted with Daniel Construction Company to build an oil refinery. Daniel Company was to award and manage all subcontracts, enforce safety rules on its employees and subcontractors, and control and manage the entire project. Daniel subcontracted the roofing work to Morgan Roofing Company. Guillory, a Morgan employee, was working on the roof of a 48-foot-high tank without fall protection when he fell from the roof and was seriously injured. Two weeks earlier, a Conoco supervisor visiting the work site saw that Morgan Roofing employees were working without fall protection in violation of safety rules. The supervisor immediately notified Daniel Company. Guillory brought suit against Conoco, claiming it violated its duty to him by knowingly allowing the subcontractor to work employees without fall protection. Conoco argued that it was not liable for the harm caused by an independent contractor a subcontractor working under the control of the independent contractor. The Court held in favor of Conoco. The Court held that Conoco was not liable to Guillory for the torts of the independent contractor Daniel Company and the subcontractor Morgan Roofing Company since the right to control the work of the subcontractor was exclusively reserved to Daniel Company. This right to control is an extremely important element in determining whether or not a person is an agent or an independent contractor.

Exceptions to Owner's Immunity: There is a trend toward imposing liability on an owner when the work undertaken by the independent contractor is inherently dangerous. The law is beginning to take the position that if the owner wishes to engage in a particular activity, the owner must be responsible for the harm it causes and cannot be insulated from liability by hiring an independent contractor to do the work. The Courts in such cases regard the activity as having such a high potential of harm that the owner is not permitted to delegate to another the duty to protect the public from harm. For example, hiring someone to dynamite for you when you are constructing a road will not insulate you from any damages caused by the independent contractor while doing the dynamiting if the independent contractor is negligent. Regardless of the nature of the activity, the owner may be liable for torts in contracts of an independent contractor when the owner controls the conduct of the independent contractor. For example, if a franchisor, such as McDonald's, exercises a high degree of control over the franchisee, such as a local owner of a McDonald's franchise, the relationship will be recognized as an agency relationship, and the franchisor can be held bound by the actions of the franchisee. An example may be McDonald's control over the play land of each specific franchisee. If McDonald's has very specific rules and designs for the play equipment and these designs and rules are found to be negligent or defective, the franchisor, McDonald's, could be liable for injury to children that occur on the play land.

When the shield from liability based on the use of an independent contractor would make it possible for an enterprise using the contractor to avoid liability under copyright laws or to defraud others, the shield will be ignored.

Undisclosed Independent Contractor: In some situations, the owner appears to be doing the act in question because the existence of the independent contractor is not disclosed or apparent. This situation occurs most frequently when a franchisee does business under the name of a franchisor. Another example of this might be a restaurant in a hotel which appears to be the hotel restaurant, although it is operated by an independent business. In cases of an undisclosed

---

[19] 526 So.2d 801 (1988)

independent contractor, it is generally held that the franchisor is liable for the torts and contracts of the undisclosed independent contractor.

ENFORCEMENT OF CLAIM BY THIRD PERSON

A lawsuit may be brought against both the principal and agent if both are liable to a third person. However, the third person can only recover only once. He can recover part of his damages from the principal and part from the agent, or all from one of them.

TRANSACTIONS WITH SALES PERSONNEL

Many transactions with sales personnel do not result in a contract with the third person that the sales person is dealing with.

SOLICITING AND AGENTS

Giving an order to a salesman ordinarily does not cause a contract to be created because ordinarily the salesman is an agent whose authority is limited to soliciting offers from customers and then communicating these offers to the principal for acceptance or rejection. A *soliciting agent* does not have authority to make a contract that will bind the principal. The employer of the salesman is not bound by a contract until the employer accepts the order. To make this clear to buyers, an order form signed by the customer, who is given a copy, should state that the salesman's authority is limited, and no contract with the employer comes into existence until the order is approved by the home office. The customer also is not bound by any contract until the employer approves the order. If the customer withdraws his offer under these circumstances, there is no breach of contract since there is no contract to be broken.

If the person with whom the buyer deals has authority to make contracts, there is, by definition, a binding contract between the principal and customer from the moment the agent agrees with the customer. In other words, when the agent accepts the customer's order, a contract is formed. If the customer attempts to withdraw his order under such circumstances, this can constitute a breach of contract, making the customer liable for any damages to the seller.

Chapter 19

THE REGULATION OF EMPLOYMENT

The law relating to the employment relationship is based on the law of agency. *Agency* is a relationship based on an agreement authorizing one person, the *agent,* to act for another, the *principal.* For example, an agent may negotiate and make contracts with third persons on behalf of the principal. Actions of an agent can obligate the principal to third persons. Actions of an agent may also give a principal rights against third persons.

Employees

Technically, an ordinary employee is not an agent unless the employee was hired to represent the employer in dealings with third persons. It is possible, though, for the same person to be both an agent and an employee. It depends upon the authority given the employee. An example would be the authority to make contracts on behalf of the employer.

If an employee acts in a way that exceeds his authority, the employer may still be liable to a third party. In an employment/agency relationship, the employee/agent is under specific duty to the principal to act as authorized. As a rule, if an agent exceeds his authority or places the property of the principal at risk without authority, the principal is now responsible for all loss or damage naturally resulting from the agents unauthorized acts.

Throughout the entire relationship, the principal has the obligation toward the agent to exercise good faith in their relationship, and the principal has to use care to prevent the agent from coming to any harm in the during the agency relationship. This requirement is similar to the employer's responsibility to provide a safe and healthy working environment for the workers.

Independent Contractors

An independent contractor is a person or business who performs services for another person under an express or implied agreement and who is not subject to the other's control, or right to control, the manner and means of performing the services. The person who hires an independent contractor is not liable to others for the acts or omissions of the independent contractor. An independent contractor is distinguished from an employee, who works regularly for an employer. The exact nature of the independent contractor's relationship with the hiring party is important since an independent contractor pays their own Social Security, income taxes without payroll deduction, has no retirement or health plan rights, and often is not entitled to worker's compensation coverage.

There are a number of factors which to consider in making the decision whether people are employees or independent contractors. No one factor is controlling, and the characterization of the relationship by the parties is also not controlling.

One of the most important considerations is the degree of control exercised by the company over the work of the workers. An employer has the right to control an employee. It is important to determine whether the company had the right to direct and control the workers not only as to the results desired, but also as to the details, manner and means by which the results were accomplished. If the company had the right to supervise and control such details of the work performed, and the manner and means by which the results were to be accomplished, an employer-employee relationship would be indicated. On the other hand, the absence of supervision and control by the company would support a finding that the workers were independent contractors and not employees. Whether or not such control was exercised is not the determining factor, it is the right to control which is key.

Another factor to be considered is the connection and regularity of business between the independent contractor and the hiring party. Important factors to be considered are separate advertising, procurement of licensing, maintenance of a place of business, and supplying of tools and equipment by the independent contractor. If the service rendered is to be completed by a certain time, as opposed to an indefinite time period, a finding of an independent contractor status is more likely.

An agent or an employee is different from an independent contractor. A principal or employer has control over an agent or employee, but not over an independent contractor. A principal or employer does not have control over the work performance of an independent contractor. A principal or employer is not bound by the actions of an independent contractor.

Why is it Important to Determine Whether A Worker is an Employee?
There is no constant definition of who constitutes an employee. The answer will vary depending the issue and the statute to be applied. The issue, however, must be determined because of the following concerns.

Employee Payroll Deductions.
An employer paying an employee is subject to different payroll requirements than when paying an independent contractor. It is the employer's duty to pay Social Security (FICA), federal unemployment compensation (FUTA), IRS federal income tax withholdings, Medicare and state taxes for each of its employees. In addition, it is the employer's responsibility to withhold a certain percentage of the employee's wages for Federal income tax purposes.

An independent contractor is responsible for the payment of such taxes on his or her own. The principal merely pays the fee to the contractor and the contractor then pays the taxes at a later date, usually through four estimated payments per year. Thus, the principal is able to avoid the bookkeeping costs associated with such withholdings.

Employee Benefits.
In an effort to attract and retain superior personnel, employers offer employees a range of benefits which generally are not required to be offered, such as dental, medical, pension, and profit-sharing plans. Independent contractors have no access to these benefits. Where a worker is considered an employee, the worker is protected by the provisions of The Employee Retirement Income Security Act of 1974 (ERISA), which was enacted to protect employee benefit plan participants from retirement plan abuses, and the Fair Labor Standards Act of 1938 (FLSA) was enacted to establish standards for minimum wages, overtime pay, employer record-keeping and child labor.

Discrimination and Affirmative Action.
Title VII of the Civil Rights Act of 1964, as amended, and other related anti-discrimination statutes only protect employees from discrimination by employers. Additionally, the National Labor Relations Act protects only employees and not independent contractors from unfair labor practices.

Cost
Employees are more expensive to employ due to the above regulations which require greater expenditures on behalf of employees, as well as the fact that others must be hired to maintain records of the employees. In addition, by hiring independent contractors, the cost of overtime is eliminated (the federal wage and hour laws do not apply to independent contractors) and the employer is able avoid any work related expenses such as tools, training or traveling.

The employee may actually cause the employer to have greater liability exposure. An employer is "vicariously liable" if the employee causes harm to a third party while the employee is in the course of employment. While the employee may be required to indemnify or reimburse the employer for any liability incurred as a result of the negligence, generally the third party goes after the employer because the employee does not have the funds to pay the liability. The employer could sue the employee for this reimbursement, but will more likely write it off as an expense of doing business.

The cost of mistakes
If a worker is found to be classified as an independent contractor, but later found to constitute an employee, the punishment by the IRS is harsh. The employer is not only liable for the its share of FICA and FUTA, but also subject to an additional penalty equal to 20% of the FICA that should have been withheld. In addition, the employer is liable for 1.5% of the wages received by the employee. Where the IRS determines that the worker was deliberately classified as an independent contractor in order to avoid paying taxes, the fines and penalties can easily run into six figures for even the smallest business.

The employer may also be liable under the Fair Labor Standards Act of 1938 (FLSA) for amounts of unpaid wages or overtime compensation, attorneys' fees and costs. Any person who willfully violates the FLSA is subject to a fine of $10,000 and six months imprisonment.

Under the Employee Retirement Income Security Act of 1974 (ERISA), an employer may be liable for accrued but unpaid benefits. The tax advantages of a qualified retirement or fringe benefit plan to employers or employees may be lost as a result of misclassification. There is possible liability under the Social Security Act of 1935, state worker's compensation and unemployment compensation laws.

How Do You Determine Whether a Worker is An Employee?
The means by which this decision is reached usually depends on the factual circumstances and issues in the case. Most statutes do not define the term. Several tests have developed and are commonly used by courts to classify employees and independent contractors. These tests included the common law test of agency, which focuses on the right of control, the Internal

Revenue Service (IRS) 20 factor analysis (see below), and the economic reality analysis. Several courts also use a hybrid approach, using one test but combining factors from other tests.

Under the common law agency test, a persuasive indicator of independent contractor status is the ability to control the manner in which the work is performed. Under the common law agency approach, the employer need not actually control the work, but must merely have the right or ability to control the work for a worker to be classified an employee. Although this is a strong indication that the worker is an employee, other factors usually are considered. For example, it has been held that an employee is one who works for wages or salary and is under direct supervision. An independent contractor has been defined as one who does a job for a price, decides who the work will be done, usually hires others to do the work, and depend for their income not upon wages, but upon the difference between what they pay for goods, materials and labor and what they receive for the end result, that is upon profits. The common law test is specifically and consistently used to determine employee status in connection with FUTA and FICA taxes, in determining whether an employee is a statutory employee, as well as in federal income tax withholding.

The IRS 20-factor analysis is more an analytical tool and not a legal test used for determining worker status. The legal test is whether there is a right to direct and control the means and details of the work. However, the following 20 factors have been consistently and continually articulated by courts, regulatory agencies, commentators, and scholars as critical to the determination of the status of an individual worker. When these factors are satisfied, courts are more likely to find "employee" status. In addition, the IRS stated that these 20 factors are not inclusive but that "every piece of information that helps determine the extent to which the business retains the right to control the worker is important." The following is a summary of the 20 factor test. A "yes" answer to any of these questions would be evidence of an employer-employee relationship.

- Does the principal provide instructions to the worker about when, where, and how he or she is to perform the work?
- Does the principal provide training to the worker?
- Are the services provided by the worker integrated into the principal's business operations?
- Must the services be rendered personally by the worker?
- Does the principal hire, supervise and pay assistants to the worker?
- Is there a continuing relationship between the principal and the worker?
- Does the principal set the work hours and schedule?
- Does the worker devote substantially full time to the business of the principal?
- Is the work performed on the principal's premises?
- Is the worker required to perform the services in an order or sequence set by the principal?
- Is the worker required to submit oral or written reports to the principal?
- Is the worker paid by the hour, week, or month?
- Does the principal have the right to discharge the worker at will?

- Can the worker terminate his or her relationship with the principal any time he or she wishes without incurring liability to the principal?
- Does the principal pay the business or traveling expenses of the worker?

A "yes" answer to any of these questions would be evidence of an independent contractor relationship.

- Does the worker furnish significant tools, materials and equipment?
- Does the worker have a significant investment in facilities?
- Can the worker realize a profit or loss as a result of his or her services?
- Does the worker provide services for more than one firm at a time?
- Does the worker make his or her services available to the general public?

Contingent or Temporary Workers
A contingent worker is one whose job is temporary, sporadic, or differs in any way from the norm of full-time employment. When utilizing contingent and temporary workers, the advantages and disadvantages must be considered. Although contingency or temporary workers provide a cost savings as a short-term benefit, depending on their classification, they could be entitled to protection under the employment laws. Also, the IRS is really looking at the way employers classify its employees. It's important to be sure the classification given is the true classification. Whether a contingent worker who is placed by a staffing firm with its client is an employee depends on a number of factors, including whether the staffing firm or the client retained the right to control when, where, and how the worker performs the job, whether there is a continuing relationship with the worker, among other factors. What is unique about the worker placed by a staffing firm is the potential for joint liability between the staffing firm and the client.

Staffing firms may qualify as the employer of the placed worker, as well. For example, if the staffing firm pays the worker, provides training and workers' compensation coverage, it may create an employment relationship with the worker. The staffing firm and its client may share liability as employers of the worker. If a client of a staffing firm supervises, trains, and otherwise directs the worker with whom it has a continuing relationship, then perhaps the client will become an employer of the worker.

In a case that sought to determine liability for wage and hour violations, the Second Circuit Court of Appeals held that all relevant factors should be considered including (but not limited to):

- whether the manufacturer/contractor employer's premises and equipment were used for the subcontractor's work;
- whether the subcontractor had a business that could or did shift as a unit from one putative joint employer to another;
- the extent to which subcontractor performed a discrete line-job that was integral to the contractor's process of production;
- whether responsibility under the contracts could pass from one subcontractor to another without material changes;

- the degree to which the contractors or their agents supervised the subcontractor's work; and
- whether the subcontractors worked exclusively or predominantly for the contractors.

Who Constitutes an Employer?
Depending on the applicable statute or provision, an employer is one who employs or uses others to do his work, or to work on her behalf.

Title VII of The Civil Rights Act of 1964 applies to all firms or their agents engaged in an industry affecting commerce which employs 15 or more employees for each working day in each of 20 or more weeks in the current or preceding calendar year. *Commerce,* in this context, is defined as trade, traffic, transportation, transmission, or communication among the states, between a state and any other place, within the District of Columbia or within a possession of the United States. *Industry affecting commerce* means any activity, business, or industry in commerce or in which a labor dispute would hinder or obstruct commerce or the free flow of commerce. Lack of intent to affect commerce is no defense to coverage.

How are employees counted where the statute applies only to employers with a minimum number of employees? For example, Title VII provides that an employer is covered by the proscriptions of the statute if it employs 15 or more employees for each working day in each of 20 or more calendar weeks in the current or preceding calendar year. But what is a *working day*? It is generally computed by counting the number of employees maintained on the payroll in a given week, as opposed to the number of employees who work on any one day. However, this form of calculation is merely the majority approach; other courts have found that part-time employees who work for any part of each day of the work week should be counted, while part-time employees who work full days for only a portion of the work week should not be counted.

OTHER EMPLOYMENT ACTS AND LAWS

The **National Labor Relations Act** (NLRA) guarantees employees the right to form a labor union and requires employers to deal with a duly-elected union as the bargaining agent for the employees. The NLRA prohibits employers from interfering with employees and from discriminating against an employee as a result of the employee's union activity.

The **Family and Medical Leave Act** (FMLA) is a federal act that entitles employees of an employer with 50 or more employees to up to 12 weeks of unpaid leave during any 12 month period for the following reasons:

- birth or adoption of a child;
- to care for a spouse, child or parent with a serious health problem; or
- a serious health problem of the employee that makes the employee unable to do his or her job.

To be eligible for this leave, an employee must be employed by an employer for 12 months or more and have worked at least 1250 hours during the 12 months prior to the leave.

The Occupational Safety and Health Act of 1970 (OSHA) was passed in order to insure as much as possible safe and healthy working conditions for employees. OSHA provides for establishing safety and health standards and for enforcement of these standards. The Secretary of Labor has been granted broad authority under OSHA to write occupational safety and health standards. Any person adversely affected by these regulations of the Secretary of Labor can challenge their validity in a U.S. Court of Appeals. The Secretary's standards will be upheld if they are reasonable and supported by substantial evidence. The Secretary must show a need for a new standard by showing that it is reasonably necessary to protect employees against a significant risk of material health impairment. The Secretary also must show that the standard is economically feasible.

For most kinds of employment, state **workers' compensation statutes** govern compensation for injuries. The statutes provide that the injured employee is entitled to compensation for accidents occurring in the course of employment. Every State has some form of workers' compensation legislation. The statutes vary widely from State to State. When an employee is covered by a workers' compensation statute, and when the injury is job connected, the employee's remedy is limited to what is provided in the worker's compensation statute. In other words, the employee cannot sue his employer for negligence. Generally, no compensation is allowed for a willful, self-inflicted, injury, or one sustained while the employee is intoxicated.

The **Federal Wiretapping Act** provides that it is unlawful to intercept oral or electronic communications. Both criminal and civil penalties are provided for by this Act. There are two exceptions: 1) An employer can monitor his/her/its telephones in the *ordinary course of business* through the use of extension telephone; and 2) An employer can monitor employee communications with the employee’s consent. Consent may be established by prior written notice to employees of the employer’s monitoring policy. Consent signed by the employee is preferable. Personal calls can be monitored only to the extent necessary to determine whether the call is a personal or business call. As soon as it is determined that the call is a personal call, the employer must quit listening. The Electronic Communications Privacy Act (ECPA) amended the federal wiretap statute to make it apply to e-mail communications. However, the same two exceptions exist (i.e., ordinary course of business and consent).

Title VII of the Civil Rights Act of 1964 (which was substantially amended in 1972 and 1991) prohibits terminating an employee or refusing to hire an applicant for a reason which amounts to discrimination because of race, color, sex, religion or national origin. The Act prohibits *disparate treatment* which is treating one employee less favorably than another because of race, sex, etc. The Act also prohibits *disparate impact* situations. This would be an employment practice which was neutral on its face (e.g., height requirement), but had a disparate impact on a protected class (e.g., women). Such policies must be justified by a *bona fide job necessity.* Certain tests which an employer might give to a job applicant might be found to be culturally biased and therefore have a disparate impact against a minority. This is not to say that all tests will be declared illegal by a Court. However, a test must have a reasonable relation to the job for which it is to be used. *Word of Mouth* hiring can also cause disparate impact.

The **Pregnancy Discrimination Act** requires that an employer treat pregnancy in the same manner that other disabilities are treated. Women that are temporarily disabled by pregnancy or childbirth must be provided with the same benefits as other disabled workers. This includes sick leave, insurance, and similar benefits. However, employers who do not provide sick leave or short term disability benefits to workers are not required to provide them to pregnant workers.

Quid pro quo sexual harassment involves supervisory personnel seeking sexual favors from employees under them in return for job benefits such as continued employment, promotions, raises, or a favorable performance evaluation. In such a case, when a supervisor's actions affect job benefits, Title VII's prohibition against sex discrimination comes into play, and the employer is liable under this Act.

A second form of sexual harassment is the so-called *hostile working environment harassment.* This a situation where a supervisor's conduct has sexual connotations and has caused anxiety or *poisoned the work environment.* This type of conduct may include such things as unwelcome flirtations, propositions, or any other abuse of a sexual nature. If this type of conduct causes an employee to quit his or her job, the employer may be liable for any damage caused to the employee.

The **Age Discrimination in Employment Act (ADEA)** prohibits discrimination against men and women over 40 and also prohibits mandatory retirement because of age. There are some exceptions to this mandatory retirement aspect. This Act only covers employers with 20 or more employees. The **Older Workers Benefit Protection Act of 1990 (**OWBPA) prohibits age discrimination in connection with employee benefits unless the employer can prove that the cost of benefits for older workers is more than for younger workers. Employers commonly require that employees taking *early retirement packages* waive all claims against their employers, including, any claim they have under ADEA. The OWBPA requires that employees be given a specific period of time to evaluate the package, and also requires employers to pay for eight hours of an attorney's time to aid each employee in this evaluation.

The **Americans with Disabilities Act** (ADA) makes it unlawful for an employer to discriminate against any qualified individual with a disability because of the disability. A qualified individual with a disability is any person who, with or without reasonable accommodation, can perform the essential functions of the job. The ADA applies to virtually every employment practice, from the application procedures for hiring to compensation, training, other terms and conditions of employment, and discharge. The statute defines *reasonable accommodation* to include physical alteration of existing facilities to make them accessible to people with disabilities, restructuring jobs, allowing part-time or modified working schedules, acquiring or modifying equipment, and hiring qualified readers for the blind or interpreters for the deaf. The ADA defines disability very broadly and includes any person with: (1) a physical or mental impairment which substantially limits one or more of the individual's major life activities; (2) a record of such an impairment; or (3) an individual who is regarded by the employer as having such an impairment. The test is a two-pronged test. First, you must decide whether or not there is a physical or mental impairment. If so, you must decide whether or not it substantially limits a major life function.

WARN Act

The Worker Adjustment and Retraining Notification (WARN) Act generally requires that 60 days advance notice of a "plant closing" (defined as employment loss for 50 or more workers during a 30-day period) or "mass layoff" (defined as employment losses at one location of 500 or more workers during a 30-day period, or 50-499 workers if they comprise at least 1/3 of the active workforce) be given to affected employees.

If an employer does not comply with the requirements of the WARN Act notices, employees can recover pay and benefits for the period for which notice was not given, up to a maximum of 60 days. All but small employers and public employers are required to provide written notice of a "plant closing" or "mass layoff" no less than 60 days in advance.

The number of employees is a key factor in determining whether the WARN Act is applicable. Only an employer that has 100 or more full-time employees or has 100 or more employees who in the aggregate work at least 4,000 hours per week are covered by the WARN Act. In counting the number of employees, consideration of U.S. workers at foreign sites, temporary employees, and employees working for a subsidiary as part of the parent company must be considered in the calculation.

There are three exceptions to the 60 day notice requirements. The first involves an employer who was actively seeking capital who in good faith believed that giving notice to the employees would have precluded from obtaining the need capital, referred to as the "faltering company" exception. The second exception occurs when a "sudden, dramatic, and unexpected" business circumstance not reasonably foreseen and outside the employer's control. The last exception includes a "natural disaster" exception such as a flood, earthquake or drought.

Constitutional Protections

An employer may not take an adverse employment action against a worker for exercising constitutional rights. However, this applies only where the employer is a public entity since constitutional rights exist against state action rather than action by private employers.

Military Leave

Under the Uniformed Services Employment and Reemployment Rights Act (USERRA), workers who enter military service and receive an honorable discharge are guaranteed reemployment, protected against discrimination and retaliation on the basis of their service or time in service. Though the Act specifically does not apply to temporary workers, it does apply to anyone with a realistic expectation of ongoing employment such as a seasonal worker who returns on a recurring basis or part-time workers who work on a continued basis. To take advantage of USERRA, an employee:

- must provide advance written or verbal notice to the employer (unless is unreasonable or unable to do so by military necessity),
- must take a leave from this particular employer of no more than a cumulative of five years, and
- must submit an application for reemployment within the required time period (which depends on the length of the individual's service).

If these requisites are satisfied, the employee must be allowed to return to the position in which she or he would have found themselves if they had remained with the employer, or a position of equivalent rank, pay and seniority. However, an employer is relieved of the obligation to reemploy under USERRA if its circumstances have changed so reemployment is impossible, or if it would impose an undue burden on the employer.

An employer is not required to pay the worker during the leave unless, of course, the worker chooses to use accrued allowable paid leave (though they are not required to use that leave). The act also contains provisions for the continuation of medical coverage and pension benefits (for which military leave constitutes standard work time with the employer).

Employment at-will

In most instances, the employment contract will not state its expiration date. In such a case, the contract may be terminated at any time by either party. However, the contract may expressly state that it will last for a specified period of time such as a contract to work as a general manager for five years.

Ordinarily a contract of employment may be terminated in the same manner as any other contract. If it is to run for a definite period of time, the employer cannot terminate the contract at an earlier date without justification. If the employment contract does not have a definite duration, it is terminable at will. This is called *employment at will.* Under the employment at will doctrine, the employer has historically been allowed to terminate the contract at any time for any reason or for no reason. Some State Courts and some State Legislatures have changed this rule by limiting the power of the employer to discharge the employee without cause. For example, Court decisions have carved out exceptions to this doctrine when the discharge violates an established public policy, such as discharging an employee in retaliation for insisting that the employer comply with the State's Food and Drug Act.

Courts may sometimes construe an employer's statements concerning continued employment as a part of the employment contract, and therefore require good cause for the discharge of an at-will employee. Also, written personnel policies used as guidelines for the employer's supervisors have been interpreted as restricting the employer's right to discharge at-will employees without just cause. Employee handbooks or personnel manuals have been construed as part of the employee's contract. This is why all personnel manuals and employee handbooks should contain a disclaimer. A sample disclaimer would be: *This employee handbook is not intended to create any contractual rights in favor of you or the company. The company reserves the right to change the terms of this employee handbook at any time.*

As mentioned earlier, many state courts will recognize limited public policy exceptions to the employment-at-will doctrine. For example, there is a limited public policy exception where an employee can prove that his discharge was motivated by refusal to engage in illegal acts for his employer.

Most states recognize two public policy exceptions to the employee-at-will doctrine:

- One is the whistle-blower defense that protects employees against discharge for reporting illegal conduct or conduct that violates public policy;
- Another protects employees who refuse to participate in illegal conduct.

Chapter 20

LAWS GOVERNING LABOR-MANAGEMENT RELATIONS

There are four main federal laws that form the basis of labor law and unionization:

- the Norris-LaGuardia Act of 1932,
- the Wagner Act of 1935 (also known as the National Labor Relations Act);
- the Wagner Act amendment,
- the Taft-Hartley Act of 1947 (also known as the Labor Management Relations Act); and
- the Landrum-Griffin Act of 1959.

Until these laws were passed, employers held virtually all of the power over the workplace.

The Norris La-Guardia Act

The Norris-LaGuardia Act was the first major law labor statute in the U.S. The opening section of the Act endorsed collective bargaining as a matter of public policy and established that government recognized that the job to a worker is more important than a worker is to a corporation and the only real power workers have is in impacting employers through concerted activity. This law sharply curbed the power of courts to intervene in labor disputes, including the use of injunctions.

This Law gave no new rights, but rather, unions were allowed to operate free from court control and interference, thus greatly facilitating collective bargaining. For example, this law did not directly outlaw yellow dog contracts[20], but declared them inconsistent with public policy and not enforceable in courts. Such agreements were later deemed to be unfair labor practices by NLRB.

Section 4 of the law declared federal courts could not issue injunctive relief in a labor dispute if it would prohibit any one participating in such a dispute from doing certain acts, judges could not restrain strikes, regardless of the objective, and could not restrain picketing activities, labor unions could urge other employees to join the concerted activity and could provide relief funds to strikers and publicize labor disputes.

The Wagner/National Labor Relations Act

The National Labor Relations Act established the right of employees to form unions, bargain collectively and to strike, and is the mainstay of union activity. At one time it had been illegal – in fact, criminal – for employees to join together in an effort to collectively bargain with employers.

[20] A yellow-dog contract or a yellow-dog clause of a contract is an agreement between an employer and an employee in which the employee agrees, as a condition of employment, not to be a member of a labor union.

The National Labor Relations Act
Congress placed administration of the Act in the hands of the National Labor Relations Board (NLRB) as an independent federal administrative agency, rather than in the hands of an industrial group. It also:

- set up standards to govern the exercise of power delegated to the agency;
- provided for the judicial enforcement of the agency's orders;
- empowered the Board to issue remedial orders, enforceable in court, to prevent unfair labor practices;
- established that it is an unfair labor practice to:
    - interfere with, restrain, or coerce employees in the exercise of their rights;
    - interfere with the formation of a labor organization;
    - discriminate in the hiring or tenure of employment or discourage membership in a labor organization;
    - retaliate for filing charges or testifying under the act; and/or
    - refuse to bargain with the representatives of the employees.

Businesses did not like the new law and set up many challenges to it until the U.S. Supreme Court declared the law constitutional and judicially endorsed the law and NLRB's powers.

The National Labor Relations Board (NLRB)
The NLRB enforces labor laws in the private sector. In doing so, once sufficient interest has been indicated by the employees, the NLRB conducts elections among employees to determine what union is to represent the employees in collective bargaining. The NLRB also decertifies unions which the employees no longer wish to represent them, issues appropriate regulations, hears unfair labor practice cases at the agency level, and otherwise administers the NLRA.

In collective bargaining, employees with a community of interests, that is, similar workplace concerns and conditions come together as a bargaining unit which the union will represent. The community of interest is based on factors such as similarity of the jobs the employees perform, similar training or skills, etc. The general rule is that there must be at least two employees in a bargaining unit, but an employer may agree to a one-person unit such as for an on-site craft worker (e.g., a carpenter who belongs to a carpenter's union being employed at a work-site as the only carpenter).

Employees may unionize either by signing a sufficient number of authorization cards, voting a union in during a union representation election or, in some cases, the NLRB ordering the employer to bargain with a union. The NLRB supervises the union election and certifies the results. Employers cannot interfere in any way with the employees' efforts to form a union.

Concerted Activity
Section 7 of the NLRA guarantees employees the right to engage in concerted activities for mutual aid or protection. This usually includes union organizing, union discussions among employees, and attempts by employees to solicit union support from other employees. Concerted activity need not involve a union, as activities by groups of employees not affiliated with a union to improve their lot are deemed protected concerted activities, as are acts by a single employee

who is not joined by other employees. Acts of violence or threats are not given protection as concerted activity.

Unions

Unions are composed of non-supervisory or managerial employees, including part-time workers. Specifically excluded from the NLRA are agricultural and domestic workers, independent contractors and those employed by their spouse or parent.

The union's shop steward is elected by the members and is their intermediary between the employer and the union. The steward may collect dues, recruit new workers, and help to resolve disputes between labor and management.

Many unions are formed with employees of a particular plant who may be part of a larger union network. For instance, the employees who pack meat at a meat processing plant may organize and become the local branch or affiliate of an international meat packer's labor organization, an industrial union. Unions may also be organized by a particular craft, totally detached from a particular workplace. In such cases, the business agent of the craft union (for instance, carpenters) represent the union craft worker's interest at a given job site. Employers will often contact the craft union when it needs the type of employees represented by that union.

Good Faith Bargaining

Under the NLRA an employer is required to bargain collectively, in good faith, with union representatives about wages, hours and terms and conditions of employment. These are mandatory subjects of bargaining. Employers may bargain about other matters (permissive subjects), but only a refusal to bargain about mandatory subjects of bargaining may form the basis of an unfair labor practice. If management and labor may differ as to whether or not a particular matter is a mandatory subject of bargaining and the disagreement is legitimate, it can form the basis of an unfair labor practice. For instance, a union may allege that management has committed an unfair labor practice by refusing to bargain over a mandatory subject of bargaining. If the matter proposed for negotiation is illegal, such as a proposal to have a closed shop, it is bad faith bargaining to even bring it up as a proposal and management's refusal to bargain cannot be the basis of an unfair labor practice.

The law requires only that management bargain in good faith about appropriate matters, not that one party necessarily agrees with the other's position and include it in the contract. The intent of collective bargaining between labor and management is to prevent management from unilaterally instituting workplace policies that closely affect workers. The fact that one side or the other does not receive what they want in the contract is not just cause for an unfair labor practice. As long as good faith bargaining is conducted, there has been compliance with the statute.

An example of bargaining in bad faith might occur when, for instance, management comes to the bargaining table and denies a raise to employees without offering any evidence whatever as to why and simply continues to say no to the union's proposal. It could also occur if one side rejects proposals out of hand without making counterproposals to the other side. Failing to show up for negotiations or refusing to sign the written agreement to which the parties orally agreed would also be bad faith bargaining.

Duty of Fair Representation
The statute imposes upon unions a duty of fair representation. This duty, not formally defined in the statute, and often used as a catch-all allegation, requires the union to represent all employees fairly and non-discriminatorily. If employees feel that one group has come out better than another in a contract, they will use the duty of fair representation as a basis for challenging the contract.

Collective Bargaining Agreements
If all goes well, bargaining between labor and management results in a collective bargaining agreement. This is the term for the contract that is reached between the employer and employees about workplace wages, hours and other terms and conditions of employment. There is no set form that this agreement must take, and it may be any length and contain any provisions which the parties decide.

Job and union security is the main issue for employees, while freedom from labor strife such as strikes, slowdowns and work stoppages is paramount for employers. Management will often wish to include a management security clause stating that they have the power to run their business and make business decisions as long as they are not in violation of the collective bargaining agreement or the law. Toward that end, in addition to wages and hours, collective bargaining agreements often also contain provisions regarding strikes, arbitration of labor disputes, seniority, benefits, employment classifications, etc.

The agreement will only be in effect for a certain specified period. Prior to that time, the parties will again have to come to the table and negotiate a new contract which takes place upon the expiration of the existing agreement.

The collective bargaining agreement may include a clause permitting mid-term negotiations. These are negotiations during the life of the contract rather than just prior to its expiration, about matters upon which the parties have agreed they will permit interim negotiations. The parties may not be able to agree on a particular provision, and rather than allow it to hold up the entire contract, will agree to come back together later and negotiate it. Alternatively, the parties may agree to mid-term negotiations because the contract may cover a fairly long period and the provision is one that may change quickly and need to be reviewed before the contract expiration date.

Unfair Labor Practices
Refusal to bargain in good faith is not the only unfair labor practice that an employer can commit. Others include engaging in activities that would tend to attempt to control or influence the union, or interfere with its affairs and discriminating against employees who join or assist unions. Actual interference by the employer need not be proved in order for it to be considered an unfair labor practice. Rather, the question is whether the activity tends to interfere with, restrain or coerce employees who are exercising rights protected under the law.

It is an unfair labor practice for employers to promise or give benefits, or in the alternative, for them to reduce them, in an effort to discourage unionizing efforts.

Strikes and Lockouts

The NLRA permits certain strikes by employees as a legitimate form of protest. When a union strikes, union members do not work, but instead, generally gather outside the employer's place of business and carry signs about the nature of the strike (picketing) and chant slogans. Engaging in such activity is for purposes of bringing attention to the strikers' demands, gathering support and discouraging others who may support the employer; for example, encouraging shoppers going into a grocery store not to patronize the store because the clerks are on strike.

Legitimate strikes may be called by the union either for economic reasons or because of unfair labor practices. For instance, the employees may strike when a collective bargaining agreement expires or if the employees are attempting to force economic concessions from the employer. If employees strike for legally recognized reasons, their actions are protected under the NLRA and they retain their status as employees.

Strikes which are not authorized by the union are called wildcat strikes and are illegal if they force the employer to deal with the employees rather than the union or impose the will of the minority rather than the majority.

If the employer replaces the strikers during the strike, once the strike is over, the strikers have a right to reinstatement if they offer an unconditional offer to return to work. If the striker's job is occupied, then only the unfair labor practice strikers are entitled to be reinstated. If a striker's job is filled during an economic strike, the striker is not entitled to reinstatement.

Just as the employees may stop working if they feel the need to strike, the employer may close the premises to employees and engage in a lockout. In a lockout, the employer curtails employment by either shutting down the plant or bringing in temporary nonunion employees after laying off striking workers. Under the NLRA the employer may not engage in lockouts as a way of avoiding bargaining or unionizing, but rather, as with strikes, to bring pressure to bear on the other side for legitimate purposes.

Many collective bargaining agreements contain no-strike, no lockout clauses which either prohibit or limit the availability of this action, and instead agree to use the grievance process to handle issues.

The Taft-Hartley Act

With the enactment of the NLRA and the subsequent gains made in unionism, the Taft-Hartley Act in 1947 was enacted as an amendment to the NLRA to curb excesses by unions, which had grown strong and powerful over the years. Unfair labor practices by unions include such activities as

- the union's refusing to bargain or refusing to do so in good faith as mentioned above
- coercing employees to join unions (or not join, as the case may be);
- charging members discriminatory dues and entrance fees;

- engaging in jurisdictional or secondary boycotts;[21]
- causing an employer to pay for goods or services that are not provided; or
- restraining or coercing employees in the exercise of his or her rights or employers in the selection of his or her representatives for collective bargaining.

The NLRA permits states to have *right-to-work laws,* which about half of them do. In a right-to-work state, employees of a unionized workplace who do not wish to join the union may not be required to do so. Despite their non-participation in the union, the union must still represent these employees as a part of the bargaining unit. If a state is not a right-to-work state, the union and employer may have as a part of their collective bargaining agreement as a union security device, a provision for a *union shop.* This provision, called a union shop clause, requires the employer to have all members or potential members of the bargaining unit agree that they will join the union within a certain amount of time after becoming employed.

It is also permissible for the collective bargaining agreement to contain an agency shop clause which requires non-union members to pay to the union the usual union dues and fees without joining the union and thereby becoming subjected to union rules. Some right-to-work laws do not allow this, and instead permit non-union employees of the bargaining unit to be *free riders,* that is, to receive union benefits without having to pay union dues or fees.

Closely related is the concept, now illegal, of *closed shops.* Closed shop provisions in collective bargaining agreements required employers to only hire union members.

Frequently union members disagree with the use to be made of union dues – particularly in an agency shop where employees who do not wish to belong to a union must still pay the union an amount equal to union dues (often called a service fee).

The Landrum-Griffin Act

This law is also known as the Labor Management Reporting and Disclosure Act. This legislation was enacted in response to congressional investigations into union corruption from 1957-59. After finding evidence of such corruption, the legislation was passed. Based upon the investigative findings, the purpose of the law is to establish basic ways of unions operating in order to ensure a democratic process, provide union members with a minimum bill of rights attached to union membership, and regulate the activities of union officials and use of union funds.

Under the Act, a bill of rights was provided for union members. Looking at some of the provisions of the Bill of Rights, one might think that they are so simplistic as to be taken as givens for an organization. The Landrum-Griffin Act also set forth specific procedures to be followed when unions hold elections, including:

---

[21] A secondary boycott is an attempt by labor to convince others to stop doing business with a particular firm because that firm does business with another firm that is the subject of a strike and/or a primary boycott.

- voting for officers by secret ballot;
- elections at least every three years (other times for different levels of the union, such as international officers), candidates being able to see lists of eligible voters; and
- provisions for members having an election declared improper.

Provisions were also enacted to safeguard union funds. Unions cannot use union funds for anything except benefiting the union or its members. Funds cannot be used to support union office candidates, and union officials, agents, employees, etc. cannot acquire financial interests which conflict with the union's. Stealing or embezzling union funds was made a federal crime by the law.

Labor Relations in the Public Sector

The NLRA applies only to the private sector. Historically, there has been little legislation affecting labor relations of public employees. The NLRA exempts these employees.
There is no uniform federal policy on public labor-management relations, though over half of the 50 states and the District of Columbia have collective bargaining statutes covering most, if not all, public employees.

Federal employees formed associations, but only postal workers had any power to influence the workplace. In 1962 President Kennedy established the right of federal employees to form and join unions. Federal employees are covered by the Civil Service Reform Act of 1978 which established the Federal Labor Relations Authority to administer federal sector labor law. This agency may be thought of as the federal employment counterpart to the private sector's National Labor Relations Board.

State, County, and Municipal Public Employees

Most public employee organizations at the state, county and municipal levels can be divided into three major categories – professional associations, craft unions and industrial-type unions. Professional associations are composed of a wide variety of professionals, such as the National Education Association (NEA) composed of over one million members, including school teachers, principals, administrators and other school specialists.

The Fraternal Order of Police does not consider itself a union, but many local lodges engage in traditional union activities such as collective bargaining, grievance handling, and representing the interest of its members to management.
Craft unions include the International Association of Firefighters (IAFF), which is an AFL-CIO affiliate, the United Mine Workers, the International Brotherhood of Electrical Workers, and the American Federation of Teachers (AFT), which limits its membership to classroom teachers only.

The dominant industrial-type union is the American Federation of State, County , and Municipal Employees (AFSCME), an AFL-CIO affiliate. AFSCME can represent an entire city or county or smaller units of government, such as a department or group of employees that cuts across many departments (e.g., agency clericals).

The AFL-CIO assists public worker' unions affiliated with it through its Public Employees Department formed in 1994, representing 4.5 million federal, state, and local government employees. The most important difference between public and private collective bargaining is the right to strike that is a mainstay of the private sector is prohibited in most government workplaces.

The striking prohibition is grounded in the need to protect public health and safety and prevent service personnel like police officers and firefighters from striking while crime rises and buildings burn, as well as the sovereignty doctrine deeming striking against a governmental employer as inconsistent with the government being the sovereign or highest authority.

State and federal employees have not always honored the prohibition on striking. While many have ignored the prohibition, probably the most famous example was when the federal air traffic controllers, represented by the Professional Air Traffic Controllers Organization (PATCO) went on strike in 1981. One of the reasons the strike was so memorable was undoubtedly because newly-elected President Ronald Reagan terminated 11,000 employees.

Chapter 21

EMPLOYMENT LAW

This section looks at some of the significant laws that regulate employment and the workplace. Unions and collective bargaining, the employment-at-will doctrine, employees' privacy rights, workers' compensation, workplace safety, and whistleblowing, are among the topics discussed. It also focuses on the kinds of discrimination prohibited by federal statutes. The most important is Title VII of the Civil Rights Act of 1964 and its amendments. Title VII prohibits employment discrimination on the basis of race, color, religion, national origin, or gender. Discrimination on the basis of age and disability are prohibited by the Age Discrimination in Employment Act of 1967 and the Americans with Disabilities Act of 1990, respectively. A class of persons defined by one or more of these criteria is known as a protected class. Discrimination against employees on these bases may also violate state laws prohibiting discrimination.

Application of the Employment-at-Will Doctrine: Under the at-will employment doctrine, employers can fire workers for good, bad, or no reason.

Exceptions to the Employment-at-Will Doctrine

- **Exceptions Based on Contract Theory:** Some courts have held that an implied employment contract exists between employer and employee under an employer's handbook, personnel bulletin, or the like that states that workers will be dismissed only for good cause. An employer who fires a worker contrary to this promise may be liable for breach of contract.
- **Exceptions Based on Tort Theory:** In a few cases, discharge may give rise to a tort cause of action (an abusive discharge may result in intentional infliction of emotional distress or defamation, for example).
- **Exceptions Based on Public Policy:** Under this exception (the most widespread common.
- **Law exception to the at-will doctrine**: an employer may not fire a worker in violation of a Fundamental public policy. The policy must be clearly expressed in statutory law. Firing workers who refuse to perform illegal acts violates public policy. Whistleblowers may be protected for public policy reasons.

Wage and Hour Laws

The Fair Labor Standards Act (FLSA) of 1938, which covers employers engaged in interstate commerce, regulates child labor, maximum hours, and minimum wages.

CHILD LABOR: Children under fourteen can work in only limited occupations, children under sixteen cannot work full-time except for a parent under certain circumstances, and children under eighteen cannot work in hazardous jobs or in jobs detrimental to their health and well-being.

Wages and Hours: The current federal minimum wage is **$7.25** per hour. Employees who agree to work more than forty hours per week must be paid no less than one and a half times their regular pay for all hours over forty.

Overtime Exemptions: Excepted from federal overtime regulations are employees who earn more than a specified amount per week and devote their efforts to certain duties.

The Occupational Safety and Health Act

The Occupational Safety and Health Act of 1970, provides for workplace safety standards. insure, as much as possible, safe and healthy working conditions for employees. OSHA provides for establishing safety and health standards and for enforcement of these standards. The Secretary of Labor has been granted broad authority under OSHA to write occupational safety and health standards. Any person adversely affected by these regulations of the Secretary of Labor can challenge their validity in a U.S. Court of Appeals. The Secretary's standards will be upheld if they are reasonable and supported by substantial evidence. The Secretary must show a need for a new standard by showing that it is reasonably necessary to protect employees against a significant risk of material health impairment. The Secretary also must show that the standard is economically feasible.

Procedures and Variation

Specific requirements of the act and penalties for its violation are also mentioned. Generally, an employer cannot discharge an employee who files a complaint with OSHA or who, in good faith, refuses to work in a high-risk area; an employer must keep records of work-related injuries and deaths and report every incident.

State Workers' Compensation Laws

These laws establish state procedures for compensating most workers injured on the job. A state agency or board administers the claims.

Requirements for Receiving Workers' Compensation: Recovery is predicated on an injury being accidental (not intentional) and occurring on the job or in the course of employment.

Family and Medical Leave

The Family and Medical Leave Act (FMLA) is a federal act that entitles employees of an employer with 50 or more employees to up to 12 weeks of unpaid leave during any twelve-month period for the following reasons:

- birth or adoption of a child;
- to care for a spouse, child or parent with a serious health problem; or
- a serious health problem of the employee that makes the employee unable to do his or her job.

FMLA eligibility requires the employee to have been employed with a company for 12 months. The **employee** must have worked at least 1,250 hours during the 12 months prior to the start of **FMLA** leave. The employer is one who employs 50 or more **employees** within a 75-mile radius of the worksite.

Violations of the FMLA: Remedies for violations include damages, job reinstatement, promotion, costs, and fees.

Employment Discrimination

Title VII of the Civil Rights Act of 1964 and its amendments prohibit job discrimination against employees, applicants, and union members on the basis of race, color, national origin, religion, and gender at any stage of employment. Nearly any employer with fifteen or more employees is covered.

The Equal Employment Opportunity Commission (EEOC) issues guidelines interpreting the law. Also, complaints about violations are registered first with the EEOC. If it is unable to resolve a situation and chooses not to sue to enforce the law, the victim may sue. The EEOC has established a priority as to which cases it will pursue.

Intentional Discrimination
In a disparate-treatment employment discrimination case, a plaintiff must initially show only that

- he or she is a member of a protected class,
- he or she applied and was qualified for the job in question,
- he or she was rejected by the employer, and
- the employer continued to seek applicants for the position or filled the position with a person not in a protected class.

Once this prima facie case is shown, an employer who cannot offer a legitimate defense loses. If the employer offers a legitimate defense, however, the plaintiff, to succeed, must show that the defense is a pretext and that discriminatory intent was the real motivation.

Unintentional Discrimination
If a plaintiff challenging an employment practice or procedure having a discriminatory impact on a protected class can show a connection between the practice and the impact, he or she makes out a prima facie case, and no evidence of discriminatory intent is necessary. The burden shifts to the employer to show that the practice or procedure is justified.

- A plaintiff can prove disparate impact by comparing the employer's work force to the pool of qualified members of a protected class available in the local labor market and relating any disparity to the employer's practice or procedure.
- A plaintiff can also prove disparate impact by comparing the employer's hiring rates for members of the majority class and members of a protected class. Disparate impact is shown if the rate for the latter is less than four-fifths of the rate for the former.

Discrimination Based on Race, Color, and National Origin

If a company's standards or policies for selecting or promoting employees have the effect of discriminating against employees or job applicants on the basis of race, color, or national origin and do not have a substantial, demonstrable relationship to realistic qualifications for the job in question, they are illegal. Discrimination against these protected classes in regard to employment conditions and benefits is also illegal. Discrimination on the basis of race in regard to employment conditions and benefits can also take the form of reverse discrimination against the members of a majority

Discrimination Based on Religion

Title VII prohibits government employers, private employers, and unions from discriminating against persons because of their religion. Employers must "reasonably accommodate" the religious practices of their employees.

Discrimination Based on Gender

Employers may not discriminate against employees on the basis of gender. In a gender discrimination suit, a plaintiff must show that gender was a determining factor in an employer's decision to hire, fire, or promote.

- **The Equal Pay Act of 1963** prohibits gender-based discrimination in wages paid for equal work when a job requires equal skill, effort, and responsibility under similar conditions.
- **The Pregnancy Discrimination Act of 1978** expanded Title VII to include discrimination based on pregnancy. An employer must treat an employee temporarily unable to perform her job due to a pregnancy-related condition the same as the employer would treat others similar in ability to work.

Constructive Discharge

Constructive discharge occurs when an employer causes working conditions to be so intolerable that a reasonable person in an employee's position would feel compelled to quit. An employee must show that the employer caused the intolerable conditions, and knew, or had reason to know, of the intolerable conditions and failed to correct them within a reasonable time. An employee can seek damages for loss of income, including back pay.

Sexual Harassment

Sexual harassment can take two forms: quid pro quo harassment and hostile-environment harassment. The former occurs when job opportunities, promotions, and the like are doled out on the basis of sexual favors. The latter occurs when an employee is subjected to sexual comments, jokes, or physical contact perceived to be offensive.

To be liable for sexual harassment, an employer must have taken a tangible employment action against an employee. Employers have an affirmative defense, however, if they took "reasonable care to prevent and correct promptly any sexually harassing behavior" (by establishing effective harassment policies and complaint procedures, for example), and the employee suing for harassment failed to follow these policies and procedures.

Plaintiffs in **retaliation cases** do not have to prove a challenged action adversely affected their workplace or employment. Instead, the challenged action must have been one that would likely have dissuaded a reasonable worker from making or supporting a charge of discrimination.

An employer is liable only if it knew, or should have known, about the harassment, and failed to act. In a case involving a nonemployee, an employer may be liable if it knew, or should have known, about the harassment, could exert control over the nonemployee, and failed to act.

Same gender harassment is covered by Title VII.

"Hostile or Offensive Environment"
In 1974, Mechelle Vinson began working at Meritor Savings Bank. Vinson later sued the bank, claiming that she had "constantly been subjected to sexual harassment." She claimed that Sidney Taylor, a vice president and branch manager, made sexual advances toward her, to which she acquiesced out of fear of losing her job. She testified that Taylor fondled her in front of other employees and forcibly raped her. Taylor denied the charges. The trial court concluded that any sexual relationship between Vinson and Taylor had no relationship to Vinson's continued employment and ruled in favor of the bank. Vinson appealed, and the appellate court ruled in her favor, finding that she had made out a case of harassing-environment discrimination. The bank appealed.

The Supreme Court rejected the bank's argument that in prohibiting discrimination under Title VII, Congress was concerned with "tangible loss" of "an economic character" and not "purely psychological aspects of the workplace environment." The Court pointed out that courts have uniformly held that "a plaintiff may establish a violation of Title VII by proving that discrimination based on sex has created a hostile or abusive work environment. . . . 'Sexual harassment which creates a hostile or offensive environment for members of one sex is every bit the arbitrary barrier to sexual equality at the workplace that racial harassment is to racial equality.'" Requiring an individual to "run a gauntlet of sexual abuse in return for the privilege of being allowed to work and make a living can be as demeaning and disconcerting as the harshest racial epithets." Holding that the bank's liability for the actions of its supervisory employees should be determined according to common law principles of agency, the Court remanded the case to the district court for further proceedings.[22]

"Equal Opportunity" Harassment
The prohibition against sexual harassment in the workplace is an extension of Title VII's prohibition against gender-based discrimination. This means that there can be no sexual harassment if no gender-based discrimination is involved. It also means, among other things, that Title VII does not protect employees from "equal opportunity" harassers—those who harass both sexes equally—because such persons are not discriminating on the basis of gender.

This point was made clear to Steven and Karen Holman, a married couple who worked for the Indiana Department of Transportation, when they sued their employer for sexual harassment. The Holmans alleged that their supervisor had sexually harassed each of them individually on separate occasions and that the supervisor retaliated against them—by denying them certain

[22] **Meritor Savings Bank, FSB v. Vinson, 477 U.S. 57, 106 S.Ct. 2399, 91 L.Ed.2d 49 (1986)**

privileges and pay—when they rejected his advances. In evaluating their claim, the court looked at the letter of Title VII, which states, "It shall be an unlawful employment practice for an employer to . . . discriminate against any individual with respect to compensation, terms, conditions, or privileges of employment, because of such individual's . . . sex." The court observed that in the Holmans' case, there was no discrimination "because of . . . sex" because the supervisor harassed both of them. Thus, concluded the court, the Holmans could not maintain a Title VII action against their employer. Holman v. Indiana, 211 F.3d 399 (7th Cir. 2000).

The Bottom Line
Harassment in the workplace takes many forms, including harassment based on gender, race, national origin, religion, age, and disability. In cases alleging sexual harassment, however, the harassment must be on the basis of sex (gender), or Title VII will not apply.

Remedies under Title VII
A plaintiff may obtain reinstatement, back pay, retroactive promotions, and damages. Compensatory damages are available only in cases of intentional discrimination. Punitive damages may be recovered in some cases, but the sum of compensatory and punitive damages is limited to specific amounts against specific employers.

E-Mail in the Workplace and "Universal Standards of Behavior"
Many employers today establish and implement policies that specify permissible and impermissible uses of the Internet in the workplace. Yet what if employees who violate such a policy claim that they did not "knowingly" do so? In this situation, if the employer discharges the employees for violating the policy, can the employees successfully claim that they were discharged without "just cause" and thus entitled to unemployment compensation? This question came before a Utah appellate court in Autoliv ASP, Inc. v. Department of Workforce Services. 29 P.3d 7 (Utah App. 2001).

Autoliv's Harassment and E-Mail Policies
Autoliv ASP, Inc., a supplier of auto-safety products, gives each of its more than six thousand employees an employee handbook. Among other things, the handbook states that Autoliv will not "tolerate or permit illegal harassment or retaliation of any nature within our workforce." The handbook also states that the use of e-mail "for reasons other than transmittal of business-related information" is prohibited and that violations of company policies can result in any of several disciplinary actions, including termination.

In 1999, Autoliv learned that an employee had received offensive and sexually harassing e-mail from other Autoliv employees. The company immediately investigated and learned that two employees had, on numerous occasions, sent messages containing jokes, photos, and short videos that were sexually explicit and clearly offensive in nature. Shortly thereafter, Autoliv terminated the two employees for "improper and unauthorized use of company e-mail." When the employees applied for unemployment benefits, a threshold question was whether they had been fired for just cause. If so, they would not be entitled to unemployment benefits. If not, they would be entitled to such benefits—and Autoliv would ultimately have to pay higher unemployment taxes as a result.

Were the Employees Fired for "Just Cause?"

Under the relevant state statute, to be fired for "just cause," employees had to have "knowledge of the conduct which the employer expected." The two employees testified that they had not "knowingly" engaged in misconduct. Further, if Autoliv concluded that they were engaging in misconduct, Autoliv should have warned them and allowed them to change their conduct. The agency agreed, noting that because abuse of the company's e-mail system was common among Autoliv employees, Autoliv should have notified the employees that their misconduct would not be tolerated before firing them. Because Autoliv had not done so, the termination was without "just cause."

Autoliv appealed the agency's decision to a state appellate court, asserting on appeal that it was "incomprehensible" for the agency to hold that a worker could be unaware of the dangers of sending sexually offensive materials to co-workers through a company's computer network. The court agreed with Autoliv, stating that "[s]uch materials in the workplace could have subjected the employer to sexual harassment and sex discrimination lawsuits." The court reversed the agency's decision, concluding that "in today's workplace, the e-mail transmission of sexually explicit and offensive jokes, pictures, and videos constitutes a flagrant violation of a universal standard of behavior."

Perceiving Conduct as Harassment

Sexual harassment is a major problem in the workplace. Over 40 percent of female federal employees, for example, reported incidents of sexual harassment in 1980 and roughly the same number reported incidents in 1987. Sexual harassment cost the federal government $267 million between May 1985 and May 1987 for losses in productivity, sick leave costs, and employee replacement costs. According to the United States Merit Systems Protection Board, victims of sexual harassment "pay all the intangible emotional costs inflicted by anger, humiliation, frustration, withdrawal, dysfunction in family life, as well as medical expenses, litigation expenses, job search expenses, and the loss of valuable sick leave and annual leave."

Sometimes, a person questions whether conduct he or she perceives as offensive should instead be viewed only as bad taste, poor manners, a lack of social grace, or an off-color sense of humor. It has been suggested that if a person feels belittled by an actor's conduct, it is harassment. If the person feels that the actor treated the person as an equal, it is not harassment.

Because women are disproportionately victims of rape and sexual assault, many women who are victims of mild forms of sexual harassment may worry whether a harasser's conduct is merely a prelude to violent sexual assault. Men, who are rarely victims of sexual assault, may view sexual conduct without a full appreciation of the social setting or the underlying threat of violence that a woman may perceive.

Paramour Liability

When, because of a romantic relationship, an employer hires, promotes, or otherwise favors someone (a "paramour"), an applicant or employee who is better qualified may believe that the employer should be held liable under Title VII on the ground of sex discrimination.

In King v. Palmer, 778 F.2d 878 (D.C. Cir. 1985), a nurse filed a discrimination claim against her employer because her supervisor had promoted another nurse allegedly on the basis of their romantic relationship. The plaintiff proved that kissing, embracing, and other "amorous behavior" played a part in the promotion decision. The court stated that Title VII is violated if a romantic relationship is a substantial factor in an employment decision. The court ordered the employer to promote the nurse who had been overlooked.

The Equal Employment Opportunity Commission (EEOC) has rejected claims of discrimination based on consensual romantic relationships. According to the EEOC, "[a]n isolated instance of favoritism toward a 'paramour' (or a spouse, or a friend)" may be unfair, but it does not constitute discrimination on the basis of sex. The reason is that when preferential treatment is based on a romantic relationship, other employees—both men and women—are equally disadvantaged for reasons other than their gender.

For example, Jane promotes Wallace, her fiancée, over Dora, who believes she is better qualified for the promotion. Dora was not denied the promotion because she is a woman, nor would she have received the promotion if she were a man. Thus, under the EEOC's guidelines, there would be no liability.

Most courts agree with the EEOC. For example, in DeCintio v. Westchester County Medical Center, 807 F.2d 304 (2d Cir. 1986), the court held that voluntary, romantic relationships cannot form the basis of a sex discrimination suit under Title VII. In that case, in April 1982, the Westchester County Medical Center (WCMC) opened a neonatal intensive care unit for the treatment of critically ill newborn children. The WCMC decided to add to the staff of the new unit a respiratory therapist with supervisory responsibilities at a salary higher than those of other staff respiratory therapists. One of the requirements for the position was certification by the National Board of Respiratory Therapists (NBRT). This had not previously been a requirement for members of the staff, none of whom had NBRT certification. On April 26, Jean Guagenti, a respiratory therapist with NBRT certification, was hired for the new position on the recommendation of James Ryan, the program administrator of the respiratory therapy department. In May, Anthony DeCintio, a staff respiratory therapist, filed a complaint with the Equal Employment Opportunity Commission (EEOC), charging the WCMC with sex discrimination in violation of Title VII arising from the hiring of Guagenti. He alleged that the certification requirement was created to exclude him from consideration for the new position and that the new position was created specifically for Guagenti. Six other male staff respiratory therapists also filed complaints. Eventually, the EEOC dismissed the complaints, and the therapists took their case to court. Finding, among other things, that Ryan and Guagenti had been in a consensual romantic relationship at the time Guagenti was hired and that the certification requirement was a pretext on Ryan's part to obtain the position for Guagenti, the court ruled in favor of DeCintio and the others. The WCMC appealed.

The U.S. Court of Appeals for the Second Circuit reversed. The court acknowledged that in the context of Title VII, "sex" refers to "membership in a [protected] class delineated by gender." The court could find no reason for extending Title VII's reference to "sex" "so broadly as to include an ongoing, voluntary, romantic engagement." Under the circumstances, "[a]ppellees were not prejudiced because of their status as males; rather, they were discriminated against because Ryan preferred his paramour. Appellees faced exactly the same predicament as that faced by any woman applicant for the promotion."

What remedies are available under Title VII of the Civil Rights Act of 1964, as amended?
Remedies under Title VII include job reinstatement, back pay, retroactive promotions, and damages. (Compensatory damages are available only in cases of intentional discrimination. Punitive damages may be recovered against a private employer only if the employer acted with malice or reckless indifference to an individual's rights. The sum of the amount of compensatory and punitive damages is limited by the statute to specific amounts against specific employers.)

State Employees Not Covered by the ADEA
In the late 1990s, suits against state agencies by state employees for age discrimination were dismissed because, under the Eleventh Amendment, a state is immune from a suit brought by a private individual in federal court unless the state consents to the suit.

Federal Employees Covered by the ADEA
The ADEA expressly covers federal employees.

Discrimination Based on Disability
The Americans with Disabilities Act (ADA) of 1990, which was designed to eliminate discriminatory hiring and firing practices that prevent otherwise qualified disabled workers from fully participating in the national labor force. Essentially, an employer must reasonably accommodate disabled persons unless to do so would constitute an undue hardship. States are immune from suits by state government employees.

Procedures under the ADA
The EEOC may bring a suit against an employer even if the employer has agreed with the employee to submit a claim to arbitration.

What Is a Disability?
ADA's definition of a disability is an impairment that "substantially limits" major life activities and outlines its boundaries (how a person functions on medication or with corrective devices). A plaintiff must prove that he or she has a disability. Some conditions are specifically excluded.

How to Interview Workers with Disabilities – Many employers have been held liable under the Americans with Disabilities Act (ADA) of 1990 simply because they asked the wrong questions when interviewing job applicants with disabilities. If you are an employer, you can do several things to avoid violating the ADA.

As a preliminary matter, you should become familiar with the guidelines on job interviews issued by the Equal Employment Opportunity Commission (EEOC). These guidelines indicate the kinds of questions that employers may—and may not—ask job applicants with disabilities. Often, the line between permissible and impermissible questions is a fine one. Consider these examples:

Ability to perform the job. As an employer, you may ask a job applicant, "Can you do the job?" You may also ask whether the applicant can perform specific tasks related to the job. You may not ask the candidate, "How would you do the job?"—unless the disability is obvious, the applicant brings up the subject during the interview, or you ask the question of all applicants.

Absenteeism. You may ask, "Can you meet our attendance requirements?" or "How many days were you absent last year?" You may not ask, "How many days were you sick last year?"

Drug use. Generally, employers may ask about the current or past use of illegal drugs but not about drug addiction. Therefore, as an employer, you may ask, "Have you ever used illegal drugs?" or "Have you done so in the last six months?" You may not ask, "How often did you use illegal drugs?" or "Have you been treated for drug abuse?"

Alcohol use. Generally, employers may ask about a candidate's drinking habits but not about alcoholism. Therefore, you may ask, "Do you drink alcohol?" or "Have you been arrested for driving while intoxicated?" but you may not ask, "How often do you drink?"

History of job-related injuries. Employers may not ask a job candidate with a disability any questions about the applicant's previous job-related injuries or about workers' compensation claims submitted in the past.

Once you have made a job offer, though, you may ask the applicant questions concerning his or her disability, including questions about previous workers' compensation claims or about the extent of a drinking problem. You may also ask for medical documents verifying the nature of the applicant's disability. Generally, though, you should ask such questions only if you ask them of all applicants or if they are follow-up questions concerning information about the applicant's disability that she or he already disclosed during a job interview.

Reasonable Accommodation

An employer cannot refuse to hire a disabled person who is otherwise qualified for a particular position. That the employer may have to make some reasonable accommodation for a disabled applicant, such as installing ramps for a wheelchair, will not cause the applicant to be considered unqualified.

- Employers who do not wish to make such accommodations must show that the accommodations will cause "undue hardship." This is subject to a case-by-case determination.
- The job application process, including questions and medical exams, must not be discriminatory. There must also be reasonable accommodation for disabled applicants.

Defenses to Employment Discrimination

Defenses to charges of employment discrimination include the following.

Business Necessity

An employer may defend against a claim of disparate-impact discrimination by asserting that a practice that has a discriminatory effect is a business necessity. If there is a definite connection between the practice and business, the practice may stand.

Bona Fide Occupational Qualification (BFOQ)

A trait must be essential to a job to qualify as a BFOQ if discriminating against those who do not have the trait amounts to otherwise illegal employment discrimination.

Seniority Systems
If no present intent to discriminate is shown, and promotions or other job benefits are distributed according to a fair seniority system, an employer has a good defense against some employment-discrimination suits, including those brought under the ADA.

After-Acquired Evidence of Employee Misconduct
After-acquired evidence of the plaintiff's wrongdoing cannot shield employers from liability for employment discrimination, though it may limit the amount of damages.

Affirmative Action
Affirmative action programs have caused much controversy.

QUOTA SYSTEMS
The United States Supreme Court applied a strict scrutiny analysis in an equal-protection challenge to an affirmative-action program in the granting of federal highway construction contracts. Such programs cannot make use of quotas or preferences for unqualified persons.

COURT DECISIONS ON RACE AND ETHNICITY
Among recent affirmative-action cases, most notably for employment the United States Supreme Court has held that once a program has succeeded, it must be changed or dropped. Some states have ended state-government -sponsored programs.

State Statutes
Generally, states prohibit the same kinds of discrimination prohibited under federal legislation. States also often provide protection for some individuals who are not protected under Title VII and may provide for additional damages. Some states have ended state-government -sponsored affirmative action programs.

Exceptions to the Employment-at-Will Doctrine

Contract Theory Exceptions. Some courts have held that an implied employment contract exists between employer and employee under an employer's handbook, personnel bulletin, or the like if the document states that workers will be dismissed only for good cause, and an employer who fires a worker contrary to this promise is liable for breach of contract. In a few states, all employment contracts are considered to contain an implied covenant of good faith, and an employee can claim breach of this covenant, if the employee is fired arbitrarily.

Public Policy Exceptions. An employer may not fire a worker in violation of a fundamental public policy (firing a worker for taking time to serve on a jury, for instance). In most states, firing workers who refuse to perform illegal acts violates public policy. Whistleblowers may be protected for public policy reasons.

Tort Theory Exceptions. In a few cases, discharge may give rise to a tort cause of action (for example, an abusive discharge may result in intentional infliction of emotional distress or defamation).

FREQUENTLY ASKED QUESTIONS

What are some important provisions of the Fair Labor Standards Act? The Fair Labor Standards Act (FLSA) of 1938, which covers employers engaged in interstate commerce, regulates child labor, maximum hours, and minimum wages. Children under sixteen years of age cannot work full-time except for a parent under certain circumstances. Children between sixteen and eighteen cannot work in hazardous jobs or in jobs detrimental to their health and wellbeing. Employees who agree to work more than forty hours a week must be paid no less than one and a half times their regular pay for hours over forty. Certain employees are exempt. A minimum wage must be paid to employees in certain industries. Effective July 24, 2009, the federal minimum wage increases to $7.25 per hour. This change reflects the third and final federal minimum wage increase as amended under the Fair Labor Standards Act (FLSA). Wage includes the reasonable cost to furnish employees with board, lodging, and other facilities if the employer customarily furnishes them.

Do federal labor laws cover all workers? No. Although coverage of the federal labor laws is broad and extends to all employers whose business activity either involves or affects interstate commerce. However, some workers are specifically excluded from these laws due to either the existence of industry-specific legislation. Other workers such as farm laborers and domestic servants are excluded from most federal labor laws but are not covered by other legislation.

What protection do employees have from the financial impact of retirement, disability, death, hospitalization, and unemployment? Federal and state governments participate in insurance programs designed to offer protection in this area. The Social Security Act of 1935 provides for old-age retirement, survivors, disability, and hospital insurance (OASDI). Employers and employees contribute under the Federal Insurance Contributions Act (FICA). Medicare is a federal health insurance program administered by the Social Security Administration for people sixty-five years of age and older and for some under sixty-five who are disabled. Under the Employee Retirement Income Security Act (ERISA) of 1974, the Labor Management Services Administration of the Department of Labor regulates operators of private pension funds (which employers are not required to establish). Employee contributions to pension plans vest immediately, and employee rights to employer contributions vest after five years of employment. Pension managers are required to invest cautiously and refrain from investing more than 10 percent of a fund in an employer's securities. Under the Federal Unemployment Tax Act of 1939, employers pay quarterly taxes to the states. The states deposit them with the federal government, which maintains an Unemployment Insurance Fund.

Why should immigration be permitted? Currently, immigrants revitalize nations and their economies, as well as enriching their cultures. In many countries, including the United States, the populations would grow increasingly older, resulting in, among other things, fewer workers to support those who are retired. Immigrants contribute to economies in other ways, too, often doing work that citizens reject, for example, and paying taxes without fully participating in the benefits that those taxes help to bestow. Immigrants are often responsible for a disproportionate number of the innovations, inventions, and other achievements that can improve a nation's life. Immigrants often follow different customs, or religions, or artistic traditions, which can enhance and diversify a culture. Why should immigration be restricted? Immigration should be restricted in some way because a nation might find itself otherwise overwhelmed. There could be too many persons seeking too few jobs, for example, or too many persons fleeing a temporarily discomfiting situation. There might be a movement of too many persons hostile to a nation, or its government, into its borders. There might be a large number of criminals who would seek refuge across international borders with too much ease.

Is penalizing employers the best approach to take in attempting to curb illegal immigration? Yes, because employment is the primary motivation for those who would immigrate illegally. (Why else would anyone voluntarily leave their home to live where they know nearly no one, likely do not speak the language or understand much of the culture, and would be unable to participate in the government?) Sanctioning those who would employ illegal immigrants would reduce the employers' willingness to hire the immigrants, thus eliminating the reason for the immigration. No, because penalizing employers puts the onus on those who are only taking economic advantage of a situation not of their making. In some cases, those employers might not be able to fill the jobs that they have available.

What is disparate-impact discrimination and how is it proved? Disparate-impact discrimination is caused by a practice or practices that have an unintended discriminatory impact on a protected class (that is, as a result of a practice, an employer's work force may not reflect the same percentage of members of protected classes that characterizes qualified individuals in the local labor market). A prima facie case is made out if a connection between the practice and the disparity is shown; proof of discriminatory intent is unnecessary.

What are some defenses available in employment discrimination cases? In a disparate-impact case, an employer may assert a business necessity defense (a business reason for a practice—against proof that requiring a high school diploma has a discriminatory effect, for instance, an employer might assert that doing a good job requires a high school education). Another defense is that a specific trait is a bona fide occupational qualification (BFOQ). Race cannot be a BFOQ; gender may be, but only if it is essential to a job. Another defense protects bona fide seniority systems (for example, in a suit seeking promotion of minorities ahead of others to compensate for past discrimination, an employer has a good defense if a present intent to discriminate is not shown, and promotions or other benefits are shown to be distributed according to a fair seniority system).

What is sexual harassment and under what circumstances might an employer be liable? Sexual harassment happens when promotions and so on are parceled out for sexual favors or when, in an employment environment, a worker must put up with comments or physical contact that is perceived as sexually offensive. An employer may be liable when an employee does the harassing, if the employer knew, or should have known, about the harassment and failed to take corrective action, or if the employee was in a supervisory position.

How is it possible for jurors and judges to overcome their own prejudices in deciding cases in which gender or another protected trait plays a key role? Bias can be subtle, unconsciously influencing the decisions of even the most professedly unbiased decision makers. It is the task that these individuals are given, after undergoing questioning to determine and challenge their biases and being reminded not to let prejudice sway their judgment. Jurors can be given instructions that set out considerations for them to evaluate the circumstances of a case and avoid undue prejudices. Is it possible to fully protect employees from discrimination in the workplace? No, because bias can be subtle, unconsciously influencing the actions of even the most avowedly unbiased individuals. Also, "fully protect" is a somewhat vague notion. Yes, if it remains a legal and moral goal, because over time, people are capable of overcoming even the most entrenched, rationalized prejudices.

Violence in the Workplace – Prevention Policy

Zero Tolerance. This Company has a policy of zero tolerance for violence. If you engage in any violence in the workplace, or threaten violence in the workplace, your employment will be terminated immediately for cause. No talk of violence or joking about violence will be tolerated.

"Violence" includes physically harming another, shoving, pushing, harassing, intimidating, coercing, brandishing weapons, and threatening or talking of engaging in those activities. It is the intent of this policy to ensure that everyone associated with this business, including employees and customers, never feels threatened by any employee's actions or conduct

Workplace Security Measures. In an effort to fulfill this commitment to a safe work environment for employees, customers, and visitors, a few simple rules have been created. They are as follows: Access to the Company's property is limited to those with a legitimate business interest

- All employees and employee vehicles entering the property must display Company identification.
- All visitors and visitor vehicles must register and display identification while on the property
- Access to the Company's property is limited to those with a legitimate business interest.
- All employees and employee vehicles entering the property must display Company identification. All visitors and visitor vehicles must register and display identification while on the property.
- All visitors and visitor vehicles must register and display identification while on the property.
- **All Weapons Banned.** The Company specifically prohibits the possession of weapons by any employee while on Company property. This ban includes keeping or transporting a weapon in a vehicle in a parking area, whether public or private. Employees are also prohibited from carrying a weapon while performing services off the Company's business premises. Weapons include guns, knives, explosives, and other items with the potential to inflict harm. Appropriate disciplinary action, up to and including termination, will be taken against any employee who violates this policy.
- Desks, telephones, and computers are the property of the Company. We reserve the right to enter or inspect your work area including, but not limited to, desks and computer storage disks, with or without notice.
- The fax, copier, and mail systems, including e-mail, are intended for business use. Personal business should not be conducted through these systems. Under conditions

approved by management, telephone conversations may be monitored and voice mail messages may be retrieved in the process of monitoring customer service.

- Any private conversations overheard during such monitoring, or private messages retrieved, that constitute threats against other individuals can and will be used as the basis for termination for cause.
- It is everyone's business to prevent violence in the workplace. You can help by reporting what you see in the workplace that could indicate that a co-worker is in trouble. You are in a better position than management to know what is happening with those you work with.
- You are encouraged to report any incident that may involve a violation of any of the Company's policies that are designed to provide a comfortable workplace environment. Concerns may be presented to your supervisor.
- All reports will be investigated and information will be kept confident.
- **Training Programs.** As part of its commitment to preventing workplace violence, the Company has established training programs for all employees. Training will be included as part of your orientation. Thereafter, you will be scheduled for annual refresher training during the month that you initially joined the business. "Please be advised that training is mandatory and attendance will be taken. If you fail to attend training or make-up sessions, you will be subject to suspension without pay until training is completed."
- **Education Offerings.** In order to promote a peaceful working environment, we encourage supervisors and employees to enroll in courses to learn more about working with each other. Courses covering communication, problem solving, building effective working relationships, stress management, and related or similar course topics are supported by tuition reimbursement, offered by our training department and, where appropriate, supported for attendance at outside seminars.
- **Employee Assistance Program.** The Company provides an employee assistance program **Employee Assistance Program**(EAP) for all full-time and part-time employees. This EAP offers services to these employees and their eligible dependents. While we receive periodic reports on the number and types of visits or calls made to the EAP, we do not receive information about individual contacts with the EAP. You are encouraged to use the EAP whenever you feel the need for guidance in coping with life's difficulties. If you have difficulty handling drugs or alcohol, the EAP can provide information on treatment. The EAP is a confidential service to be used when you need help.
- **Violence Prevention: Desks, telephones, and computers are the property of the Company.** We reserve the right to enter or inspect your work area including, but not limited to, desks and computer storage disks, with or without notice.
- We have created a violence prevention team to create and implement our workplace violence prevention program. The team will also handle the consequences of any incidents of violence that we experience, providing assistance to employees and information to the media. The team will take the steps necessary to continue or resume business. We believe that a multidisciplinary approach is best suited to handle workplace violence problems.
- If you have suggestions for ways to improve the safety and security at work, please pass them along to a team member or leave a suggestion in any one of their mail boxes. In the event of a major workplace incident that affects, or has the potential l to affect, the mental

health of our workforce, we will provide initial counseling and support services to you and your immediate family members.

- **Incident Management**
- As the crisis passes and support systems are put into place for individuals affected by the incident, the Company will make every effort to return to normal business operations. A reasonable effort will be made to notify employees, customers, stockholders, and others who need to know of the status of business operations directly whenever possible. In cases where direct contact is not possible or practical, an effort will be made to communicate through the news media and other available resources.

Chapter 19
Overview of Business Organizations

A corporation is an artificial person that is created by governmental action. The corporation exists in the eyes of the law as a person, separate and distinct from the persons who own the corporation (stockholders). This means that the property of the corporation is not owned by the stockholders, but by the corporation. Debts of the corporation are debts of this artificial person, and not of the persons running the corporation or owning shares of stock in it. The corporation can sue and be sued in it's own name. The shareholders cannot normally be sued as to corporate liabilities.

Model Corporation Acts

Most States have a general corporation code that lists certain requirements, and anyone who satisfies these requirements and files the necessary papers with the government may automatically become a corporation. In 1950, the American Bar Association published a *Model Business Corporation Act* (MBCA) to assist State Legislatures in modernizing State corporation laws. In 1984, a revision of this Model Act was published (RMBCA). All states have adopted various versions of the MBCA or the RMBCA with only slight variations.

Formation

A corporation is formed by obtaining approval of a Certificate of Incorporation, Articles of Incorporation, or a Charter from the State of incorporation. The Secretary of State is usually the official who approves or disapproves this certificate. *The Revised Model Business Corporation Act* (RMBCA) has done away with the Certificate of Incorporation in an attempt to simplify the paperwork handled by the Secretary of State. Under the RMBCA, a corporate existence begins when the Articles of Incorporation are filed with the Secretary of State.

One or more natural persons or corporations may act as *incorporators* of a corporation by signing and filing *Articles of Incorporation* with the designated state government official (usually the Secretary of State). These Articles are often filed in duplicate, and the Secretary of State, when satisfied that the Articles conform to the State's corporation statutes, stamps *filed* and the date on each copy. The Secretary of State then retains one copy and returns the other copy, along with a filing fee receipt, to the corporation.

The Articles of Incorporation must contain the following:

- The name of the corporation;
- The number of shares of stock the corporation is authorized to issue;
- The street address of the corporation's initial registered office and the name of its initial registered agent; and
- The name and address of each incorporator.

The Articles may contain optional provisions such as the purpose for which the corporation is organized. However, if the Articles contain no purpose clause, the corporation will automatically have the purpose of engaging in any lawful business. Also, if no reference is made to the duration of the corporation in the Articles, it will automatically have a perpetual duration. Under the RMBCA, corporate existence begins when the Articles are filed with the Secretary of State. Under the older practice still followed by many States, corporate existence begins upon the issuance of a Certificate of Incorporation by the Secretary of State.

Shareholders

The owners of a corporation are its shareholders. The shareholders elect a board of directors to oversee the major policies and decisions. The board of directors elects the officers and is responsible for the management and policy decisions of the corporation. The dealings of the corporation are carried out by the officers and employees of the corporation under the authority delegated by the directors of the corporation.

Shares must be issued to those individuals who will be owners of the corporation. This is also the case even if only one individual will own the corporation. Ownership of a corporation can be transferred by sale of all or a portion of the stock. Additional owners can be added either by selling stock directly from the corporation or by having the current owners sell some of their stock. Small businesses that are corporations are often owned by a small group of shareholders who all work in the business. Often these shareholders formally agree to certain restrictions on the sale of their shares, so they can control who owns the corporation.

Securities laws are meant to protect investors from unscrupulous business owners. These laws require corporations to follow certain procedures before accepting investments in exchange for shares of stock (the "securities"). Technically, a corporation is required to register the sale of shares with the federal Securities and Exchange Commission (SEC) and its state securities agency before granting stock to the initial corporate owners (shareholders). Many small corporations are exempted from the registration process under federal and state laws. For example, SEC rules don't require a corporation to register a "private offering," which is a non-advertised sale of stock to a limited number of people (generally 35 or fewer).

Directors

Each director must attend meetings of the board, which must be held no less than once a year. Each director on the board is given one vote. Usually the vote of a majority of the directors is sufficient to approve a decision of the board. Directors must make sure that major corporate actions are recorded (*e.g.,* minutes of meetings) and were taken behalf of the corporation.

Corporate Officers

Corporate officers are elected by the Board of Directors and are responsible for conducting the day-to-day operational activities of the corporation. Corporate officers usually consist of the following: a President, Vice-President, Secretary, and Treasurer, though one person may hold more than one office. Terms of directors often are for more than one year and are staggered to provide continuity. Shareholders can elect themselves to be on the board of directors.

Bylaws

The *bylaws* of a corporation are the internal rules and guidelines for the day-to-day operation of a corporation, such as when and where the corporation will hold directors' and shareholders' meetings and what the shareholders' and directors' voting requirements are. Typically, the bylaws are adopted by the corporation's directors at their first board meeting. They may specify the rights and duties of the officers, shareholders and directors, and may deal, for example, with how the company may enter into contracts, transfer shares, hold meetings, pay dividends and make amendments to corporate documents. They generally will identify a fiscal year for the corporation.

Classification of Corporations

A corporation is called a *domestic corporation* with respect to the State under whose law it has been incorporated. Any other corporation going into that State is called a *foreign corporation.* For example, a corporation holding a Texas Charter is a domestic corporation in Texas, but a foreign corporation in all other States. A foreign corporation must qualify to do business in a foreign State.

A corporation whose shares are held by a single shareholder or a closely-knit group of shareholders (such as a family) is known as a *close corporation.* The shares of stock are not traded publicly. Many of these types of corporations are small firms that in the past would have been operated as a sole proprietorship or partnership, but have been incorporated in order to obtain the advantages of limited liability or a tax benefit or both.

A corporation may be organized for the business of conducting a profession. These are known as *professional corporations.* Doctors, attorneys, engineers, and CPAs are the types of professionals who may form a professional corporation. Usually there is a designation *P.A.* or *P.C.* after the corporate name in order to show that this is a professional association or professional corporation.

A *nonprofit corporation* is one that is organized for charitable or benevolent purposes. These corporations include certain hospitals, universities, churches, and other religious organizations. A nonprofit entity does not have to be a nonprofit corporation, however. Nonprofit corporations do not have shareholders, but have members or a perpetual board of directors or board of trustees.

A *Subchapter S corporation* is a corporation in which the shareholders elect to be treated as partners for income tax purposes. Shareholders still have limited liability protection of a corporation, but income is treated like partnership income. *Subchapter S* refers to a particular subdivision of the Internal Revenue Code. The number of shareholders is limited and neither corporations nor partnerships can be shareholders in a Subchapter S corporation. Also, shareholders must be U.S. citizens or resident aliens.

"Citizenship" of Corporations

For certain purposes, such as determining the right to bring a lawsuit in Federal Court, a corporation today is deemed a citizen of any State in which it has been incorporated and also of the State where it has its principal place of business. Therefore, a corporation can be a citizen of more than one State. For example, a corporation incorporated in New York is a New York corporation even though its shareholders are citizens of many other States. A Delaware corporation having its principal place of business in New York is deemed to be a citizen of New York as well as of Delaware.

Before doing business in another State, a foreign corporation generally must register with the Secretary of State of that State, file copies of its Articles of Incorporation, pay certain taxes, and appoint a resident agent for service of process.

Piercing the Veil
Ordinarily, a corporation will be regarded and treated as a separate legal person, and the law will not look beyond a corporation to see who owns it. However, a court may disregard the corporate entity and pierce the corporate veil in exceptional circumstances. The decision whether to disregard the corporate entity and go directly against the shareholders is made on a case-by case basis, and courts generally will look to more than one factor. Factors that may lead to piercing the corporate veil are:

- Failure to maintain adequate corporate records and the commingling of corporate and personal funds;
- Grossly inadequate capitalization (debt/equity ratio too high);
- The formation of a corporation to evade an existing obligation;
- The formation of a corporation to perpetrate a fraud;
- Improper diversion of corporate assets; and
- Injustice and inequitable circumstances would result if the corporate entity were recognized.

A court will not go behind the corporate identity merely because a corporation has been formed to obtain tax savings or to obtain limited liability for its shareholders. One-person, family, and other closely-held corporations are permissible and fully entitled to all of the advantages of corporate existence. However, factors that lead to piercing the corporate veil more commonly exist in these kinds of corporations. It is extremely difficult to pierce a corporate veil in most situations. Some courts use different terminology when disregarding the corporate entity. The court may state that the corporation is the *alter ego* of the shareholders, and the shareholders should therefore be held liable.

A *holding company* is a company, usually a corporation, which is created to own the stock of other corporations, often using the stock holdings to control the management and policies of the corporations.

Promoters
Promoters are the people that bring the corporation into existence. They bring together other people interested in the company, solicit stock purchasers, and sometimes make contracts to be assigned later to the corporation. A corporation is not liable on a contract made by a promoter unless the corporation takes some sort of affirmative action to adopt the contract. The promoter still remains personally liable on the contract unless released by the other contracting party. The contract can provide that the promoter will be released from personal liability upon adoption of the contract by the corporation.

Corporate Powers
Corporations have some of the same powers as a natural person, such as the right to own property. If a corporation acts beyond the limits of its powers, the act is *ultra vires.* This is an act or contract that the corporation did not have authority to do or make. Modern corporation statutes give corporations broad powers, and the likelihood that a corporation will act beyond its powers is rare.

All corporations do not have the same powers. For example, corporations that operate banks, insurance companies, and railroads generally have special powers and are subject to special statutory restrictions.

As long as the Federal and State Constitutions are not violated, a State Legislature may give corporations any lawful powers. The RMBCA grants a corporation *the same powers as an individual to do all things necessary or convenient to carry out its business and affairs.*

Modern corporation statutes give corporations a wide range of powers. A corporation has perpetual succession or continuous life. In other words, it has the power to continue as a unit indefinitely or for a stated period of time regardless of any changes in the ownership of its stock. If no period of time is fixed for the duration of the corporation, the corporation will exist indefinitely until it is legally dissolved. If the period of existence is limited, the corporation can extend the period by meeting certain statutory requirements.

Samples of Corporate Powers

- Corporations have the power to enter into contracts just like an individual.
- Corporations have the power to borrow money in carrying out their business purposes.
- A corporation can borrow money by issuing *bonds.* The bonds issued by a corporation are subject to Article 8 of the UCC ("Investment Securities").
- A corporation may sell or lease its property. However, in most States a corporation may not sell or mortgage all or substantially all of its assets without the consent of the majority of the shareholders.
- Obviously a corporation has the power to incur debt and mortgage its property as security for debt.
- Corporations may acquire the stock of another corporation and be a stockholder of another corporation.
- Generally, a corporation may purchase its own stock if it is solvent, and this stock will be known as *treasury stock.* Treasury stock maintains the status of outstanding stock, but is regarded as inactive and cannot be taken into consideration regarding votes by the shareholders. Also, dividends cannot be declared regarding treasury stock. The RMBCA eliminates the concept of treasury stock and calls this type of stock authorized, but unissued, stock.
- A corporation has the power to do business in other States. However, by doing business in other States, the corporation may have to qualify as a foreign corporation to do business in that State which usually involves registering with the Secretary of State.
- A corporation may be a member of a partnership and may be a limited or general partner of a limited partnership.

- Corporations can pay pensions and establish pension plans for its employees.
- The RMBCA even authorizes a corporation to make charitable contributions.

Ultra Vires Acts

If a corporation acts beyond the scope of the powers granted by its charter and the statutes of the State under which it is governed, the corporation's act is declared as *ultra vires*. However, modern corporation statutes give such a broad scope of powers that it is difficult to find an action that is *ultra vires*. Say a mining corporation begins to manufacture television sets. In such a situation, there might be an *ultra vires* transaction if the corporate charter restricted the corporation's powers to mining and related-such activities. However, this type of situation is extremely rare.

Nonprofit corporations have a more restricted range of powers than business corporations, and it would be more likely to find an *ultra vires* act in a nonprofit corporation than a profit corporation.

Name of Corporation

A corporation must have a name to identify it. Most States require that the corporate name contain some indication that it is a corporation, such as *corporation, company, incorporated, limited,* or an abbreviation of these words.

Seal

A corporation may have a seal which can be used to show that a contract or a document is being executed pursuant to valid corporate authority.

Consolidations Mergers and Acquisitions

Mergers and acquisitions is a phrase used to describe certain types of financial activities in which corporations are bought and sold. A *merger* occurs when two corporations merge, in other words, one absorbs the other. One corporation preserves its original charter and identity and continues to exist. The other corporation disappears, and its corporate existence terminates. Generally, the corporate entity which continues the business after a merger will succeed to all of the rights and property of the other entity and will also be subject to all of its debts and liabilities.

A corporation may merely purchase or acquire the assets of another corporation. This would not be a merger. In an acquisition, the purchaser does not become liable for the obligations of the business whose assets are being purchased.

In a *consolidation* of two or more corporations, their separate existences cease, and a new corporation with the property and the assets of the old corporations comes into being.

A *merger* is different from a consolidation in that when two corporations merge, one absorbs the other. One corporation preserves its original charter and identity and continues to exist. The other corporation disappears, and its corporate existence terminates.

A *conglomerate* is the term describing the relationship of a parent corporation to subsidiary corporations engaged in diversified activities which are unrelated to the activity of the parent corporation. A subsidiary corporation is a corporation whose majority shareholder is another corporation *(parent corporation).* An example of a conglomerate could be a wire-manufacturing corporation that owns all of the stock of a newspaper corporation and of a drug-manufacturing corporation.

Antitrust
Consolidations, mergers, and asset acquisitions are sometimes prohibited by federal antitrust legislation on the grounds that the effect is to lessen competition in interstate commerce.

Liability of Successor Corporations
When corporations are combined in any way, the question arises as to who is liable for the debts and obligations of the predecessor corporations. Generally, the corporate entity which continues the business after a merger or a consolidation will succeed to all of the rights and property of the predecessors and will also be subject to all of the debts and liabilities of the predecessor corporations. For example, A merges into B. Suppose A had a contract with C. B did not. After the merger, B is liable to C on the contract.

FREQUENTLY ASKED QUESTIONS

- **How does an individual form a corporation?** One or more natural persons or corporations may act as *incorporators* of a corporation by signing and filing *Articles of Incorporation* with the designated state government official (usually the Secretary of State). These Articles are often filed in duplicate, and the Secretary of State, when satisfied that the Articles conform to the State's corporation statutes, stamps *filed* and the date on each copy. The Secretary of State then retains one copy and returns the other copy, along with a filing fee receipt, to the corporation.

What information must the Articles of Incorporation contain:

The articles of incorporation must contain:

- The name of the corporation;
- The number of shares of stock the corporation is authorized to issue;
- The street address of the corporation's initial registered office and the name of its initial registered agent; and
- The name and address of each incorporator.

The Articles may contain optional provisions such as the purpose for which the corporation is organized. However, if the Articles contain no purpose clause, the corporation will automatically have the purpose of engaging in any lawful business. Also, if no reference is made to the duration of the corporation in the Articles, it will automatically have a perpetual duration.

What are bylaws of a corporation?
The *bylaws* of a corporation are the internal rules and guidelines for the day-to-day operation of a corporation, such as when and where the corporation will hold directors' and shareholders' meetings and what the shareholders' and directors' voting requirements are. Typically, the

bylaws are adopted by the corporation's directors at their first board meeting. They may specify the rights and duties of the officers, shareholders and directors, and may deal, for example, with how the company may enter into contracts, transfer shares, hold meetings, pay dividends and make amendments to corporate documents. They generally will identify a fiscal year for the corporation.

What is a *close corporation*?
A corporation whose shares are held by a single shareholder or a closely-knit group of shareholders (such as a family) is known as a *close corporation.* The shares of stock are not traded publicly. Many of these types of corporations are small firms that in the past would have been operated as a sole proprietorship or partnership, but have been incorporated in order to obtain the advantages of limited liability or a tax benefit or both.

What is a *professional corporation*?
A corporation may be organized for the business of conducting a profession. These are known as *professional corporations* . Doctors, attorneys, engineers, and CPAs are the types of professionals who may form a professional corporation. Usually there is a designation *P.A.* or *P.C.* after the corporate name in order to show that this is a professional association or professional corporation.

What is a *non-profit* corporation?
A *nonprofit corporation* is one that is organized for charitable or benevolent purposes. These corporations include certain hospitals, universities, churches, and other religious organizations. A nonprofit entity does not have to be a nonprofit corporation, however. Nonprofit corporations do not have shareholders, but have members or a perpetual board of directors or board of trustees.

What is a *Subchapter S* corporation?
A *Subchapter S corporation* is a corporation in which the shareholders elect to be treated as partners for income tax purposes. Shareholders still have limited liability protection of a corporation, but income is treated like partnership income. *Subchapter S* refers to a particular subdivision of the Internal Revenue Code. The number of shareholders is limited and neither corporations nor partnerships can be shareholders in a Subchapter S corporation. Also, shareholders must be U.S. citizens or resident aliens.

What is the *registered agent* of a corporation?
The registered agent is the “mailbox” for the corporation. He or she is the person or entity designated by the corporation to receive any documents regarding a lawsuit against the corporation or other official communications. Many corporations use their attorney or a professional corporate service company for this service. The registered agent’s address must generally be a street address in the subject state and the agent must be located at that address. A post office box generally may not be used as the registered agent address.

When does a corporation's existence begin?
Under the corporate laws of some states, corporate existence begins when the Articles are filed with the secretary of state. Under an older practice still followed by many states, corporate existence begins upon the issuance of a Certificate of Incorporation by the secretary of state.

How is the business of a corporation carried out or managed?
The owners of a corporation are its shareholders. The shareholders elect a board of directors to oversee the major policies and decisions. The board of directors elects the officers and is responsible for the management and policy decisions of the corporation. The dealings of the corporation are carried out by the officers and employees of the corporation under the authority delegated by the directors of the corporation.

What are the general duties of directors?
Each director must attend meetings of the board, which must be held no less than once a year. Each director on the board is given one vote. Usually the vote of a majority of the directors is sufficient to approve a decision of the board. Directors must make sure that major corporate actions are recorded (*e.g.,* minutes of meetings) and were taken behalf of the corporation. Corporate officers are elected by the Board of Directors and are responsible for conducting the day-to-day operational activities of the corporation. Terms of directors often are for more than one year and are staggered to provide continuity. Shareholders can elect themselves to be on the board of directors.

What officers are elected by the directors?
Corporate officers usually consist of the following: a President, Vice-President, Secretary, and Treasurer, though one person may hold more than one office.

Who actually *owns* the property of a corporation?
A corporation is an artificial person that is created by governmental action. The corporation exists in the eyes of the law as a person, separate and distinct from the persons who own the corporation (stockholders). This means that the property of the corporation is not owned by the stockholders, but by the corporation. Debts of the corporation are debts of this artificial person, and not of the persons running the corporation or owning shares of stock in it.

How do the initial shareholders fit into the ownership of the corporation?
Shares must be issued to those individuals who will be owners of the corporation. This is also the case even if only one individual will own the corporation. Ownership of a corporation can be transferred by sale of all or a portion of the stock. Additional owners can be added either by selling stock directly from the corporation or by having the current owners sell some of their stock. Small businesses that are corporations are often owned by a small group of shareholders who all work in the business. Often these shareholders formally agree to certain restrictions on the sale of their shares, so they can control who owns the corporation.

What are security laws?
Securities laws are meant to protect investors from unscrupulous business owners. These laws require corporations to follow certain procedures before accepting investments in exchange for shares of stock (the "securities"). Technically, a corporation is required to register the sale of

shares with the federal Securities and Exchange Commission (SEC) and its state securities agency before granting stock to the initial corporate owners (shareholders). Many small corporations are exempted from the registration process under federal and state laws. For example, SEC rules don't require a corporation to register a "private offering," which is a non-advertised sale of stock to a limited number of people (generally 35 or fewer).

What do the designations *domestic corporation* and *foreign corporation* mean?
A corporation is called a *domestic corporation* with respect to the State under whose law it has been incorporated. Any other corporation going into that State is called a *foreign corporation.* For example, a corporation holding a Texas Charter is a domestic corporation in Texas, but a foreign corporation in all other States. A foreign corporation may have to qualify to do business in a foreign State.

How does a *foreign corporation* qualify to do business in another state?
Before doing business in another State, a foreign corporation generally must register with the Secretary of State of that State, file copies of its Articles of Incorporation, pay certain taxes, and appoint a resident agent for service of process.

What is meant by the phrases *doing* or *transacting* business in another state by a foreign corporation?
There are many factors used to determine whether a foreign corporation is transacting business in a state and therefore must qualify to do business in that state. Some criteria evaluated include:

- Whether the company has a physical presence in the state;
- Whether the company has employees in the state;
- Whether the company accepts orders in the state; and
- Whether the company has a bank account in the state

This is not a complete list and different states may have different criteria. However, these are some common factors to consider when trying to determine whether it is necessary for a foreign corporation to register or qualify in another state.

I have heard that a corporation can be a *citizen* of a state. What does this mean?
For certain purposes, such as determining the right to bring a lawsuit in Federal Court, a corporation today is deemed a citizen of any State in which it has been incorporated and also of the State where it has its principal place of business. Therefore, a corporation can be a citizen of more than one State. For example, a corporation incorporated in New York is a New York corporation even though its shareholders are citizens of many other States. A Delaware corporation having its principal place of business in New York is deemed to be a citizen of New York as well as of Delaware.

What does it mean to *pierce the corporate veil?*
Ordinarily, a corporation will be regarded and treated as a separate legal person, and the law will not look beyond a corporation to see who owns it. However, a court may disregard the corporate entity and *pierce the corporate veil* in exceptional circumstances. The decision whether to disregard the corporate entity and go directly against

the shareholders is made on a case-by case basis, and courts generally will look to more than one factor. Factors that may lead to piercing the corporate veil are:

- Failure to maintain adequate corporate records and the commingling of corporate and personal funds;
- Grossly inadequate capitalization (debt/equity ratio too high);
- The formation of a corporation to evade an existing obligation;
- The formation of a corporation to perpetrate a fraud;
- Improper diversion of corporate assets; and
- Injustice and inequitable circumstances would result if the corporate entity were recognized.

A court will not go behind the corporate identity merely because a corporation has been formed to obtain tax savings or to obtain limited liability for its shareholders. One-person, family, and other closely-held corporations are permissible and fully entitled to all of the advantages of corporate existence. However, factors that lead to piercing the corporate veil more commonly exist in these kinds of corporations. It is extremely difficult to pierce a corporate veil in most situations. Some courts use different terminology when disregarding the corporate entity. The court may state that the corporation is the *alter ego* of the shareholders, and the shareholders should therefore be held liable.

What are mergers and acquisitions?
Mergers and acquisitions is a phrase used to describe certain types of financial activities in which corporations are bought and sold. A *merger* occurs when two corporations merge, in other words, one absorbs the other. One corporation preserves its original charter and identity and continues to exist. The other corporation disappears, and its corporate existence terminates. Generally, the corporate entity which continues the business after a merger will succeed to all of the rights and property of the other entity and will also be subject to all of its debts and liabilities.

A corporation may merely purchase or acquire the assets of another corporation. This would not be a merger In an acquisition, the purchaser does not become liable for the obligations of the business whose assets are being purchased.

What is a holding company?
A *holding company* is a company, usually a corporation, which is created to own the stock of other corporations, often using the stock holdings to control the management and policies of the corporations.

What is an Annual Report?
A annual report is a report that must be filed with your state's secretary of state each year. This report generally must indicate:

- The corporation's name and its state or country of incorporation;
- The address of its registered office and the name of its registered agent at that office in this state;
- The address of its principal office;

- The names and business addresses of its directors and principal officers;
- A brief description of the nature of its business;
- The total number of authorized shares, itemized by class and series, if any, within each class; and
- The total number of issued and outstanding shares, itemized by class and series, if any, within each class

How do I determine if the corporate name I want to use is available?
Your state's secretary of state will make a determination of name availability for corporate entities in response to written requests. There is generally a small fee. If you wish to reserve a corporate name for a business entity, most states will allow you to after completion of and filing the appropriate form generally entitled "Application for Reservation of Name."

If I incorporate, will anyone else be able to use my name?
Issuance of a name by the secretary of state does not necessarily give a person the exclusive right to use of that name. Many businesses do not choose to incorporate. A secretary of state's office generally has no record of these and thus cannot search names of unincorporated businesses.

Is there a minimum age for officers of a corporation?
Most states do not have a minimum age requirement but do require that members of the board of directors must be at least 18 years old.

Sole Proprietorships

A *sole proprietorship* is a form of business ownership in which one individual owns a business. The owner may either be the only worker of the business or he may employ as many people as he needs to run the operation. He can use his own name or a trade name. If a trade name is used, oftentimes the business will be identified on official forms and in the case of a lawsuit by use of the designation "d/b/a" (doing business as). For example, "John Jones, d/b/a Multimedia Designs."

Advantages:
One advantage to a sole proprietorship is that the owner is not required to pay organizational fees, such as in a corporation. Also, he controls all of the decisions and receives all of the profits. The business's net earnings are not subject to corporate income tax, but are taxed as personal income.

Disadvantages:
One disadvantage of a sole proprietorship is that the owner is subject to unlimited personal liability for the debts of the business. This is not true in a corporate organization. Also, the investment capital is limited to the resources of the sole proprietor, and this may hurt the growth of the business. Corporations can issue stock and raise capital that way. Another disadvantage is that upon the death of the owner, his authority to make contracts terminates, and this, of course, will effectively kill the business. However, some courts can grant temporary authority for the executor of the owner's estate to continue the business while the estate is being administered.

Partnerships

A *partnership* involves combining the capital resources and the business or professional abilities of two or more people in a business. Law firms, medical associations, and architectural and engineering firms often operate under the partnership form.

Advantages:

One advantage is that a partnership allows more than one individual to pool financial resources without the requirement of a formal corporate structure and without the expense of organizational fees.

Disadvantages:

One disadvantage is that each partner has *unlimited personal liability* for the debts of the partnership. Also, the partnership is technically dissolved by the death of a partner, although there is some statutory relief with regard to winding up the affairs of the partnership after the death of one of the partners. A new partnership can then be formed.

Definition of Partnership

A partnership is defined by the UPA as a relationship created by the voluntary "association of two or more persons to carry on as co-owners of a business for profit." The people associated in this manner are called partners. A partner is the agent of the partnership. A partner is also the agent of each partner with respect to partnership matters. A partner is not an employee of the partnership. A partner is a co-owner of the business, including the assets of the business.

Rights of Partners

The partnership agreement is the heart of the partnership, and it must be enforced as written, with very few exceptions. Partners' rights are determined by the partnership agreement. If the agreement is silent regarding a matter, the parties' rights are typically determined by the UPA.

Name of Partnership

Unless a State statute requires a firm name, a partnership does not have to have one. However, it is customary to have a firm name, and a partnership will probably need one in order to get a tax identification number. A partnership may, as a general rule, adopt any firm name the partners' desire and may use a fictitious name. However, the name of the partnership cannot be the same as, or deceptively similar to, another partnership's name for the purpose of stealing business from the other partnership. Many States also require the registration of a fictitious name. For example, a husband and wife may transact business under a partnership name such as G & G Foods. This name does not reveal the names of the partners. Some States will require a certificate to be filed in a City Clerk's office which would state the names and addresses of the partners.

Who May be a Partner

Persons who are competent to enter into a contract may form a partnership. Generally, an insane person or a minor should not be a partner because they can declare the contract void. Even corporations can be partners in many States, such as Mississippi.

Creation of a Partnership
If parties operate a business for profit as co-owners, a partnership is deemed to be created even though the parties may not have labeled their relationship as a partnership. A partnership does not come into being if the partners do not agree to the elements of a partnership even though they may call it a partnership. The manner in which a business is described in a tax return or on an application for a license is significant in determining whether or not they intend to be operating as a partnership. Remember, a partnership is a voluntary association and exists because the parties agree to be in partnership. However, Courts are interested in substance rather than form. And even though people file an income tax return as a partnership, if they are in fact not partners, but merely have a relationship of, for example, an employer and employer, there is no partnership.

When the parties have not clearly indicated whether or not their business constitutes a partnership, the law has determined several guidelines to aid Courts in determining whether the parties have created a partnership.

- The fact that the parties share profits and losses is strong evidence of a partnership.
- An agreement that does not provide for sharing losses, but does provide for sharing profits, is still evidence of a partnership since it is assumed that the parties will also share losses.
- The sharing of gross revenue is itself very slight, if any, evidence of a partnership.
- Co-ownership of property does not necessarily create a partnership. Also, sharing profits or rents from property that two or more people own does not necessarily create a partnership.
- A partnership may be formed even if some of its members furnish only skill or labor rather than capital to the partnership.

The Partnership Agreement
As a general rule, partnership agreements do not have to be in writing. However, it is crazy to enter into an oral partnership agreement. A partnership agreement must be in writing if it is within the provisions of the statute of frauds, such as a contract that cannot be performed within one year. The formal document that is prepared to evidence the partnership agreement is termed as a partnership agreement or articles of partnership. If matters arise that are not covered by the agreement, the rights of the parties will be determined by statute (such as the UPA) or Court decisions.

Partners as to Third Persons
In some cases, persons who are in fact not partners may be held accountable to third persons as though they were partners. This liability arises when they conduct themselves in such a manner that others are reasonably led to believe that they are partners and to act in reliance on their belief. This is similar to the apparent agency doctrine. For example, suppose the partnership of Able and Baker, in registering its fictitious name, states that Able, Baker and Charlie are partners, and the registration certificate is signed by all three of them. If a creditor sees this registration statement and extends credit to the firm, relying on the fact that Charlie is apparently a partner, Charlie would have partnership liability insofar as that creditor was concerned, even if

he was not in fact a partner. However, liability would not arise if Charlie did not know of this registration certificate. However, if he signed the registration certificate, he had knowledge of it.

Partnership Property
In general, partnership property consists of all the property contributed by the partners or acquired for the partnership with its funds. A partnership may own real property as well as personal property.

Partners hold title to partnership property by "tenancy in partnership" or "tenants in common." This means that each partner has an equal right to use the partnership property for partnership purposes unless there is an agreement to the contrary. Also, a partner possesses no interest in any specific item of partnership property. (For example, a partner does not own 10% of the PC which his secretary uses.) A creditor of the partner cannot proceed against any specific items of partnership property. A creditor can only proceed against the partner's interest in the partnership.

Assignment of a Partner's Interest
A partner's interest in the partnership may be assigned by the partner. However, the assignee does not become a partner without the consent of the other partners. Without this consent, the assignee is only entitled to receive the assignor's share of the profits of the partnership and the assignor's interest when the partnership dissolves. The assignee has no right to participate in the management of the partnership or inspect the books of the partnership. A partnership agreement should prevent this type of assignment by giving the remaining partners the right of first refusal regarding any attempted assignment of a partner's interest.

Dissolution and Termination
Partnerships may be dissolved by acts of the partners, order of a Court, or by operation of law. From the moment of dissolution, the partners lose their authority to act for the firm except as necessary to wind up the partnership affairs or complete transactions which have begun, but not yet been finished.

A partner has the power to withdraw from the partnership at any time. However, if the withdrawal violates the partnership agreement, the withdrawing partner becomes liable to the co-partners for any damages for breach of contract. If the partnership relationship is for no definite time, a partner may withdraw without liability at any time.

A partnership may be dissolved by any of the following events:

- expiration of the time stated in the agreement;
- expulsion of a partner by the other partners;
- withdrawal of a partner.

If a partnership does not have a fixed duration, a partner may withdraw at any time and for any reason or no reason without liability to the partnership. If a partner wrongfully withdraws from a partnership, the partner is liable to the other partners for any damages caused by the withdrawal.

Dissolution by Operation of Law
A partnership is dissolved by operation of law in the following instances:

Death of any Partner
A partnership is automatically dissolved by the death of any partner. Even if the remaining parties continue the business after the death of a partner, a new relationship is created in the form of a partnership-at-will until a new formal agreement is executed. A similar result would occur in cases in which a partner withdraws or is expelled. If the other partners continue to operate the business, they are operating as a partnership-at-will until they form a more formal partnership by executing a partnership agreement.

Bankruptcy
Bankruptcy of the partnership or one of the partners causes the dissolution of the partnership.

illegality
A partnership is dissolved by an event which makes it unlawful for the business of the partnership to be continued. For example, if a State has a law that makes it unlawful for a judge to engage in the private practice of law, a law firm would be dissolved when one of its members becomes a judge.

Dissolution by Decree of Court
There are several situations in which one partner is permitted to obtain the dissolution of a partnership through a Court decree. A partner may judicially dissolve the partnership if one of the partners has been declared insane. Also, if one of the partners has become incapable of performing the terms of the partnership agreement, the partnership can be judicially dissolved. An example of this would be disbarment of an attorney in a law firm. The habitual drunkenness of a partner is a sufficient cause for judicial dissolution. Also, if dissensions in a partnership are so serious and persistent as to make the continuation of the partnership impractical, a judicial dissolution can be obtained. Finally, a partnership can be judicially dissolved if the partnership cannot continue in business except at a loss.

Notice of Dissolution
When the partnership is dissolved by an act of a partner, notice must be given to the other partners unless it is clear that the partner is withdrawing.

Notice of dissolution should also be given to third parties, and this notice should clearly state that the partnership has been dissolved. It is essential that actual notice of dissolution be given to persons who have dealt with the partnership. Failure to give proper notice continues the power of each partner to bind the others in respect to third persons on contracts within the scope of the partnership business.

Winding up Partnership Affairs
If a partner withdraws, is expelled, or dies, the survivor partners must wind up the business of the partnership unless there is an agreement to the contrary. In other words, they cannot continue the business of the partnership, other than winding up the partnership affairs, unless there is an express agreement that permits the continuance of the business by the remaining partners.

Although the partners have no authority after dissolution to create new obligations, they do have authority to do acts necessary to wind up the business.

All partnership agreements should have some sort of buy/sell formula in order to buy out the interest of a partner who wants to withdraw. This will allow the partnership business to continue without interruption.

Distribution of Assets
Creditors of the partnership have first claim on the assets of the partnership. Difficulties arise when there is a dispute between the creditors of the partnership and the creditors of the individual partners. The general rule is that the partnership creditors have first claim on the assets of the firm, and the individual creditors (creditors of the individual partners) share in the remaining assets, if any.

After the partnership's liabilities to non-partners have been paid, the assets of the partnership are distributed as follows:

- Each partner is entitled to a refund of advances made to, or for the benefit of, the partnership;
- Contributions to the capital of the partnership are then returned; and
- The remaining assets, if any, are divided equally as profits among the partners unless there is some agreement which would provide for unequal distribution.
- If the partnership has sustained a loss, the partners share it equally unless there is an agreement between them to the contrary.

Continuation of the Partnership Business
As a practical matter, the business of the partnership is commonly continued after dissolution and winding up. If the business continues, either with the surviving partners, or with them and additional partners, it is a new partnership. As a practical matter, the liquidation of the old partnership may, in effect, be merely a matter of bookkeeping entries.

Authority of Majority of Partners
The decision of the majority of partners will control as far as the day-to-day operations of the partnership. For example, a majority of the partners of a business can decide to increase the business's advertising and enter into a contract to increase the advertising. This contract will bind the partnership and all of the partners, individually.

When there is an even number of partners, there is a possibility of a partnership deadlock. If the decision is of a nature that it would be impossible to continue the business, and the partners continue to be deadlocked, any one of the partners may petition the Court to order the dissolution of the partnership.

Express Authority of Individual Partners
An individual partner can have express authority to perform certain acts. This authority either comes from the partnership agreement or because a sufficient number of partners have agreed to this authority. A partner has the authority to do the acts that are customary for a member of the

partnership who conducts the particular business of the partnership, whether it be a law partnership, medical partnership, accounting partnership, etc.

Customary Authority of Individual Partners
The customary or implied powers of individual partners to do business can be described as follows:

Contracts: A partner may make any contract necessary to the transaction of the partnership's business.

Sales: A partner may sell the partnership's goods in the regular course of business. However, this authority is limited to the goods held for sale by the partnership. Example: Mark, Sally and Lucy operate a car dealership as a partnership. Mark sells one of the cars of the partnership to Frank at a price below dealer cost. His motive was that the partnership could get its money back plus a profit in servicing the car. Sally and Lucy sue to avoid the sale to Frank on the grounds that Mark never was authorized to make such a sale to Frank. Is the sale binding on the partnership? The sale is binding since a partner in a *selling partnership* or trading partnership has authority to sell any of the partnership's inventory in the regular course of business. No express authorization is needed.

Purchases
A partner may purchase any kind of property within the scope of the partnership's business.

Loans
A trading partnership would be a partnership which is organized to buy and sell inventory like a grocery business or a car dealership. A partner in this type of partnership may borrow money for the partnership's business and may execute commercial paper (such as a note) or give security (such as a mortgage or a security interest in the personal property of the partnership). A partner in a nontrading partnership does not ordinarily possess the power to borrow in the name of the partnership. This type of partnership would be a partnership which does not buy and sell, such as a legal partnership, accounting partnership or medical partnership.

Insurance
A partner may insure the firm's property.

Employment
A partner may hire the employees that are necessary to carry out the purpose of the partnership.

Claims Against Firm
A partner may pay debts out of the partnership funds or by transferring partnership property.

Claims of Firm
A partner may receive payment of debts. Someone who makes a proper payment to a partner is protected even if the partner to whom the payment is made embezzles the money. The partnership debt would be deemed satisfied and canceled.

Limitations of Authority

The partners may agree to limit the normal powers of each partner. However, if a partner negotiates a contract for the partnership with a third person which exceeds the powers of the partner, the partnership is still bound if the third person was unaware of the agreement limiting the partner's powers. Of course the partner would be liable to the other partners for any loss caused by his breach of the agreement to limit his powers. If the third person knew of the agreement, the partnership would not be bound. A third person would be bound by any limitation on the partner's powers if there is any fact present that would put a reasonable person on notice that the partner's powers are limited.

Nature of Business

A third person must take notice of limitations which arise out of the nature of the partnership's business. The partnership may be organized for a particular kind of business or profession, and third persons are presumed to know the limitations that are commonly made on partners of such a business. For example, I would not have authority to sell computers from my firm's office without partnership approval since we practice law, not the business of selling computers.

Scope of Business

A partner cannot bind the partnership to a third person in a transaction which is not within the scope of the partnership's business unless the partner has express authority to bind the partnership.

Adverse Interest

A third person must take notice of an act of a partner which is obviously against the interests of the partnership. For example, using partnership funds to pay a personal debt would be against the interests of the partnership.

Prohibited Transactions

There are certain transactions a partner cannot enter into on behalf of the partnership unless he is expressly authorized. A third person who enters into such a transaction does so at the risk that the partner has not been authorized by the other partners to enter into such a transaction.

Cessation of Business

A partner cannot bind the partnership by a contract that would make it impossible for the partnership to conduct its usual business.

Suretyship

A partner has no implied authority to bind the partnership by contracts of surety, guaranty, or indemnity for purposes other than the partnership business.

Personal Obligations

A partner cannot satisfy personal obligations or claims of the partnership by interchanging them in any way. For example, a partner cannot satisfy a personal debt to a business by canceling a claim of the partnership against that business.

Duties of Partners

In many respects, the duties of a partner are the same as those of an agent.

Loyalty and Good Faith

Each partner must act in good faith toward the other partners and must not take any advantage over the other partners by misrepresentation or concealment. Each partner owes a duty of loyalty to the partnership, and this duty bars the making of any secret profit at the expense of the firm and bars the use of the firm's property for personal benefit. A partner cannot promote a competing business, and if he does so, he can be liable for any damages sustained by the partnership. For example, Bill and Steven are partners in a paint store. Steven opens another store in his own name. This second store competes with the partnership store. Bill objects to Steven's running his own store. Steven says he can do this because there is nothing in the partnership agreement that prohibits such competition. Is he entitled to run his own store in competition with the partnership store? *No.* Even though the partnership agreement is silent on this point, the duty of loyalty prohibits a partner from competing with the partnership. Therefore, Steven cannot run the competing store unless the partnership agreement, or a modification of the agreement, expressly gives him permission to do this.

Obedience

Partners must observe any limitations adopted by a majority of the partners with regard to the ordinary details of the partnership business. For example, if a majority of the partners operate a retail store and decide that no sales can be made on credit, a partner placed in charge of the store must obey this limitation. If a third person does not know of the limitation, the managing partner will have the power to make a binding sale on credit to such a person, but if the third person does not pay his bill, the partner who violated the limitation is liable for any loss caused by his disobedience to the limitation.

Reasonable Care

A partner must use reasonable care in transacting the partnership's business and is liable for any loss resulting from a failure to act with reasonable care.

Information

A partner has the duty to inform the partnership of all matters relevant to the partnership. For example, if one partner is going to buy out the interest of another partner, this must be revealed to the partnership.

Management

Each partner has the right to take an equal part in transacting the business of the partnership. It is irrelevant that one partner contributed more than another financially or that one contributed only services when the partnership was formed.

Inspection of Books

All partners are equally entitled to inspect the books of the partnership.

Share of Profits

Each partner is entitled to a share of the profits. The partners may provide that profits shall be shared in unequal proportions. However, in the absence of such an agreement, each partner is entitled to an equal share of the profits without regard to the amount of capital or services contributed to the partnership by each partner.

Compensation

In the absence of an agreement to the contrary, a partner is not entitled to compensation for services performed for the partnership. Partners may agree that one of the partners shall devote full time as manager of the business and may agree that a salary shall be paid to the partner in addition to the managing partner's share of the profits. This sometimes occurs in legal partnerships or accounting partnerships when one of the partners is appointed managing partner. In most cases, the managing partner practices his profession, but also handles the business affairs of the partnership and is paid or compensated in some way for this extra duty.

Repayment of Loans

A partner is entitled to reimbursement of money advanced to the partnership, such as travel expenses incurred on partnership business.

Contribution and Indemnity

If a partner pays more than his proportionate share of the debts of the partnership, he has a right to reimbursement from the other partners. If an employee of a partnership negligently injures a third person while acting within the scope of employment, and if the injured party collects damages from one partner, this partner is entitled to reimbursement from the other partners in order to divide the loss equally.

Distribution of Capital

If a partnership is dissolved, every partner is entitled to receive a share of the partnership property after due payment of all creditors and the repayment of loans made to the partnership by the partners. Unless otherwise stated in the partnership agreement, all partners are entitled to the return of their capital contributions to the partnership.

Liability of Partners and Partnership

Nature and Extent of Partner's Liability

Partners are jointly and severally liable for all torts committed by one of the partners in the scope of the partnership business. When partners are held to be liable for an injury caused to a third person, the third person may sue all or any of the members of the partnership.

Partners are also jointly and severally liable on all partnership contracts. Each member of a partnership has individual and unlimited liability for the debts of the partnership regardless of the member's investment or interest in the partnership. Even if a partner only owns 5% interest in the partnership, a judgment against the partnership in the amount of $100,000.00 can be collected from the 5% owner's personal assets, particularly if the partnership or the other partners did not have the money to pay this debt.

Liability for Breach of Duty

If a partner breaches a duty to the partnership, an injured partner may recover damages from the partner who breached the duty.

Liability of New Partners

A person admitted as a partner into an existing partnership has limited liability for all obligations of the partnership which arose before he was admitted as a partner. This type of claim could only be satisfied out of partnership property and would not extend to the individual property of a newly-admitted partner.

Effect of Dissolution on Partners' Liability

A partner will remain liable after dissolution of the partnership unless all claims against the partnership have been paid or the creditors of the partnership have released their claims. The dissolution of the partnership does not in and of itself discharge the existing liability of any partner.

Enforcement and Satisfaction of the Claims of Creditors

A partnership is sued by suing the partners doing business as the partnership – John Jones and Sally Jones d/b/a Jones Realty. Creditors of an individual partner must first seek payment from a partner's personal assets. If these assets are insufficient to satisfy the debt, then the creditor may seek a charging order against the partner's partnership interest. Pursuant to such an order, a court requires that the partner's share of the profits be paid to the creditor until the debt is discharged.

LIMITED PARTNERSHIPS

A *limited partnership* is a modified partnership. It is half corporation and half partnership. This kind of partnership is a creature of State statutes. Many States have either adopted the Uniform Limited Partnership Act (ULPA) or the Revised Uniform Limited Partnership Act (RULPA). In a limited partnership, certain members contribute capital, but do not have liability for the debts of the partnership beyond the amount of their investment. These members are known as limited partners. The partners who manage the business and who are personally liable for the debts of the business are the general partners. A limited partnership can have one or more general partners and one or more limited partners.

Under the ULPA, a limited partnership has to be created by executing a certificate which sets forth the name and business address of each partner, states which partners are general partners and which are limited partners, and states certain details about the partnership and the relative rights of the partners. This, of course, is not true in a general partnership. A general partnership is governed by a partnership agreement which is private and which may be oral or written.

The Revised Uniform Limited Partnership Act is somewhat less restrictive as to what needs to be disclosed in this certificate. For example, the names of the limited partners are not required.

The general partners manage the business of the partnership and are personally liable for its debts. Limited partners have the right to share in the profits of the business and, if the partnership is dissolved, will be entitled to a percentage of the assets of the partnership. A limited partner may lose his limited liability status if he participates in the control of the business.

Limited Liability Companies
A limited liability company (LLC) is a separate legal entity that can conduct business just like a corporation with many of the advantages of a partnership. It is taxed as a partnership. Its owners are called members and receive income from the LLC just as a partner would. There is no tax on the LLC entity itself. The members are not personally liable for the debts and obligations of the entity like partners would be. Basically, an LLC combines the tax advantages of a partnership with the limited liability feature of a corporation.

An LLC is formed by filing articles of organization with the secretary of state in the same type manner that articles of incorporation are filed. The articles must contain the name, purpose, duration, registered agent, and principle office of the LLC. The name of the LLC must contain the words limited liability company or LLC. An LLC is a separate legal entity like a corporation.

Management of an LLC is vested in its members. An operating agreement is executed by the members and operates much the same way a partnership agreement operates. Profits and losses are shared according to the terms of the operating agreement.

Limited Liability Partnerships
A *Limited Liability Partnership* (LLP) is essentially a general partnership with the limited liability of an LLC. It is owned by *partners* rather than *members*. It is may be easier in some respects to convert a general partnership into an LLP as opposed to an LLC. The partnership agreement would only have to be amended for an LLP, but redrafted as an operating agreement for an LLC.

Joint Ventures
A *joint venture* is a relationship between two or more people who combine their labor or property for a single business undertaking. They share profits and losses equally, or as otherwise provided in the joint venture agreement. The single business undertaking aspect is a key to determining whether or not a business entity is a joint venture as opposed to a partnership.

Elizabeth, Josephine, and Mark entered into an agreement to purchase a tract of land, build houses on it, sell the houses, and then divide the net profit. What kind of business organization was this? This would be a joint venture because resources were pooled, and the profit-sharing operation was limited to one particular operation. The fact that a long period of time might pass before the venture ended would not cause this organization to lose its status as a joint venture.

A joint venture is very similar to a partnership. In fact, some States treat joint ventures the same as partnerships with regard to partnership statutes such as the Uniform Partnership Act. The main difference between a partnership and a joint venture is that a joint venture usually relates to the pursuit of a single transaction or enterprise even though this may require several years to accomplish. A partnership is generally a continuing or ongoing business or activity. While a partnership may be expressly created for a single transaction, this is very unusual. Most Courts hold that joint ventures are subject to the same principles of law as partnerships. The duties owed by joint venturers to each are the same as those that partners owe to each other. For example, partners have a duty of loyalty to one another, and joint venturers would also have the same duty. If a joint venture is entered into to acquire and develop a certain tract of land, but some of the venturers secretly purchase and develop land in their own names to compete with the joint venture, the other joint venturers may be liable for damages for the breach of this duty of loyalty.

A joint venture will last generally as long as stated in the joint venture agreement. If the joint venture agreement is silent on this, it can be terminated by any participant unless it clearly relates to a particular transaction. For example, if a joint venture is created to construct a particular bridge, it will last until the project is completed or becomes impossible to complete because of bankruptcy or some other type situation.

With regard to liability to third persons, generally, joint venturers have the same liability as partners in a general partnership.

County Clerk's office. It must be recorded in the County in which the principal place of business of the partnership is located.

The Revised Uniform Limited Partnership Act is somewhat less restrictive as to what needs to be disclosed in this certificate. For example, the names of the limited partners are not required. Also, a certificate must only be filed with the office of the Secretary of State as opposed to County filing.

If there is no filing of a limited partnership certificate, both the limited and general partners will have the status and liability of general partners.

The general rule is that the limited partner's name cannot appear in the firm name. If the limited partner's name is used, and this gives the public the impression that the limited partner is an active partner, the limited partner can lose his protection of limited liability and will become liable as a general partner.

The general partners manage the business of the partnership and are personally liable for its debts. Limited partners have the right to share in the profits of the business and, if the partnership is dissolved, will be entitled to a percentage of the assets of the partnership. A limited partner may lose his limited liability status if he participates in the control of the business. The Revised Uniform Limited Partnership Act lists some activities known as *safe harbor* activities in which limited partners may participate without losing their limited liability.

Chapter 22
THE SALE OF A BUSINESS

Business Sales

The sale of any ongoing business, even a sole proprietorship, can be a complicated transaction. The buyer and seller (and their attorneys) must consider the law of contracts, taxation, real estate, corporations, securities, and antitrust in many situations. Depending on the nature of the business sold, statutes and regulations concerning the issuance and transfer of permits, licenses, and/or franchises should be consulted. If a license or franchise is important to the business, the buyer generally would want to make the sales agreement contingent on such approval. Sometimes, the buyer will assume certain debts, liabilities, or obligations of the seller. In such a sale, it is vital that the buyer know exactly what debts he/she is assuming.

In any sale of a business, the buyer and the seller should make sure that the sale complies with the Bulk Sales Law of the state whose laws govern the transaction. A bulk sale is a sale of goods by a business which engages in selling items out of inventory (as opposed to manufacturing or service industries). Article 6 of the Uniform Commercial Code, which has been adopted at least in part by all states, governs bulk sales. If the sale involves a business covered by Article 6 and the parties do not follow the statutory requirements, the sale can be void as against the seller's creditors, and the buyer may be personally liable to them. Sometimes, rather than follow all of the requirements of the bulk sales law, a seller will specifically agree to indemnify the buyer for any liabilities that result to the buyer for failure to comply with the bulk sales law.

Of course the seller's financial statements should be studied by the buyer and/or the buyer's accountants. The balance sheet and other financial reports reflect the financial condition of the business. The seller should be required to represent that it has no material obligations or liabilities that were not reflected in the balance sheet and that it will not incur any obligations or liabilities in the period from the date of the balance sheet to the date of closing, except those incurred in the regular course of business.

A sale of a business is considered for tax purposes to be a sale of the various assets involved. Therefore it is important that the contract allocate parts of the total payment among the items being sold. For example, the sale may require the transfer of the place of business, including the real property on which the building(s) of the business are located. The sale might involve the assignment of a lease, the transfer of good will, equipment, furniture, fixtures, merchandise, and inventory. The sale may also include the transfer of the business name, patents, trademarks, copyrights, licenses, permits, insurance policies, notes, accounts receivables, contracts, cash on hand and on deposit, and other tangible or intangible properties. It is best to include a broad transfer provision to ensure that the entire business is being transferred to the buyer, with an itemization of at least the more important assets to be transferred.

In making this allocation, the buyer's interests will often conflict with the seller's. The seller will ordinarily seek to maximize its capital gain and ordinary loss by allocating the price to items producing such a result. The buyer will normally seek to have the price allocated to depreciable assets and to inventory in order to maximize ordinary deductions after the business is acquired.

In its simplest form, the sale of a sole proprietorship could have provisions similar to the following:

I. In consideration of the mutual promises and covenants of the parties, Seller sells, assigns, transfers, and conveys to Buyer all the stock of goods, furniture and fixtures, accounts, and office supplies, including also the lease of the building occupied by Seller at (street address, city, county, state, zip code).

II. The consideration for these assets is $____________, receipt of which is acknowledged by Seller. The proration of the consideration is as follows:

A. Furniture and fixtures: $__________________.

B. Stock of Goods: $______________________.

C. Office supplies: $ ______________________.

D. Accounts receivable: $ __________________.

E. Lease: $________________________.

Total: $_________________

III. Buyer, and its successors and assigns, shall have and hold the property forever. Seller covenants with purchaser that the property is free from all encumbrances; Seller has the legal right to transfer and sell the property; and Seller will defend the title to the property against all persons. It is further a part of the consideration of this transfer that the name of Seller or any part of it shall not be use by Buyer in the operation of the business subsequent to this transfer nor will the name be sold or transferred by Buyer to any other person or persons. This restriction shall not be construed to prohibit the designation by Buyer that it is the successor to Seller.

Often such an agreement will contain a covenant not to compete similar to the following:

Seller shall not, either directly or indirectly, alone or with others, enter into or engage in the (type of nature of business) business within (restricted area, such as city or certain number of miles from business being sold) for a period of ____ years from the date of execution of this agreement. Further, seller shall not, during that period divulge, communicate, use to the detriment of buyer or for the benefit of any other person or persons, or misuse in any way, any confidential information or trade secrets of the business sold under this agreement, including customer lists, personnel information, and secret processes or other technical data.

For such a covenant to be enforceable it must be: i) necessary to protect a business; ii) reasonable in time; and iii) reasonable in the geographic scope (i.e., the territory covered).

The same matters should be considered in the sale of a business owned by a partnership as in the sale of a sole proprietorship. The contract of sale should distinguish the transaction as a sale of assets rather than as a sale of partnership interests. However, the sale of a partnership interest can be accomplished with language similar to the following:

Assignor, by this instrument, assigns all of Assignor's right, title, and interests in the Partnership, being a _____% share of the business, to Assignee. Assignor shall be relieved of any future liability for Partnership debts and shall no longer be entitled to any share of the Partnership profits or assets. Assignee shall be entitled to all future shares of the Partnership profits or any distribution of assets, in accordance with said Partnership Agreement and shall assume liability for a proportionate share of all future partnership losses in accordance with said Partnership Agreement.

The same matters should be considered in the sale of a business of a corporation or a limited liability company as in the sale of a sole proprietorship. The contract of sale should distinguish the transaction as a sale of assets rather than as a sale of stock in the corporation or membership units in a limited liability company.

All states have adopted some form of the Model Business Corporation Act (MBCA) or the Revised Business Corporation Act (RMBCA). Both the MBCA and the RMBCA require that the sale of all or substantially all corporate assets be authorized by the shareholders and/or directors of the corporation.

Chapter 23

CORPORATION LAW

THE CORPORATION AS A PERSON

A corporation is an artificial person that is created by governmental action. The corporation exists in the eyes of the law as a person, separate and distinct from the persons who own the corporation (stockholders). This means that the property of the corporation is not owned by the stockholders, but by the corporation. Debts of the corporation are debts of this artificial person, and not of the persons running the corporation or owning shares of stock in it. The corporation can sue and be sued in it's own name. The shareholders cannot normally be sued as to corporate liabilities.

In a Delaware case, Branmar Theatre Co. v. Branmar, Inc.23, a family corporation, leased a theater from Branmar, Inc. The lease prohibited it from assigning the lease. The holders of the stock of Branmar Theatre Co. sold their stock to the Schwartzes. The lessor, Branmar, Inc., claimed that this sale of stock was a prohibited assignment and threatened to cancel the lease. Can Branmar, Inc. cancel the lease? *NO.* The corporation had not made a prohibited assignment of the lease. The fact that the shareholders of the corporation had transferred their shares did not constitute a transfer of the lease. It merely transferred the ownership and control of the lessee corporation, but that corporation was still the tenant.

A corporation is formed by obtaining approval of a Certificate of Incorporation, Articles of Incorporation, or a Charter from the State of incorporation. The Secretary of State is usually the official who approves or disapproves this certificate. *The Revised Model Business Corporation Act* (RMBCA) has done away with the Certificate of Incorporation in an attempt to simplify the paperwork handled by the Secretary of State. Under the RMBCA, a corporate existence begins when the Articles of Incorporation are filed with the Secretary of State.

CLASSIFICATION OF CORPORATIONS

A *public corporation* is one established for governmental purposes and for the administration of public affairs. A city is a public or a municipal corporation acting under authority granted to it by the State.

A *private corporation* is one organized by persons, either profit or nonprofit. Private corporations are often called "public" when the stock is sold to the public and traded on the stock exchanges.

A corporation is called a *domestic corporation* with respect to the State under whose law it has been incorporated. Any other corporation going into that State is called a *foreign corporation.* For example, a corporation holding a Texas Charter is a domestic corporation in Texas, but a foreign corporation in all other States. A foreign corporation must qualify to do business in a foreign State.

---

[23] 264 A.2d 526 (1970)

Special service corporations are corporations formed for transportation, banking, insurance, and similar specialized functions. These corporations are subject to separate codes or statutes with regard to their organization.

A corporation whose shares are held by a single shareholder or a closely-knit group of shareholders (such as a family) is known as a *close corporation.* The shares of stock are not traded publicly. Many of these types of corporations are small firms that in the past would have been operated as a sole proprietorship or partnership, but have been incorporated in order to obtain the advantages of limited liability or a tax benefit or both.

A corporation may be organized for the business of conducting a profession. These are known as *professional corporations.* Doctors, attorneys, engineers, and CPAs are the types of professionals who may form a professional corporation. Usually there is a designation *P.A.* or *P.C.* after the corporate name in order to show that this is a professional association or professional corporation.

A *nonprofit corporation* is one that is organized for charitable or benevolent purposes. These corporations include certain hospitals, universities, churches, and other religious organizations. A nonprofit entity does not have to be a nonprofit corporation, however. Nonprofit corporations do not have shareholders, but have members or a perpetual board of directors or board of trustees.

A *Subchapter S corporation* is a corporation in which the shareholders elect to be treated as partners for income tax purposes. Shareholders still have limited liability protection of a corporation, but income is treated like partnership income. *Subchapter S* refers to a particular subdivision of the Internal Revenue Code. The number of shareholders is limited to 75 shareholders and neither corporations nor partnerships can be shareholders in a Subchapter S corporation. Also, shareholders must be U.S. citizens or resident aliens.

CORPORATIONS AND GOVERNMENTS

Most States have a general corporation code that lists certain requirements, and anyone who satisfies these requirements and files the necessary papers with the government may automatically become a corporation. In 1950, the American Bar Association published a *Model Business Corporation Act* (MBCA) to assist State Legislatures in modernizing State corporation laws. In 1984, a revision of this Model Act was published (RMBCA). States have adopted various versions of the MBCA or the RMBCA with only slight variations.

For certain purposes, such as determining the right to bring a lawsuit in Federal Court, a corporation today is deemed a citizen of any State in which it has been incorporated and also of the State where it has its principal place of business. Therefore, a corporation can be a citizen of more than one State. For example, a corporation incorporated in New York is a New York corporation even though its shareholders are citizens of many other States. A Delaware corporation having its principal place of business in New York is deemed to be a citizen of New York as well as of Delaware.

Before doing business in another state, a foreign corporation generally must register with the Secretary of State of that State, file copies of its Articles of Incorporation, pay certain taxes, and appoint a resident agent for service of process.

IGNORING THE CORPORATE ENTITY

Ordinarily, a corporation will be regarded and treated as a separate legal person, and the law will not look beyond a corporation to see who owns it.

Piercing the Corporate Veil

A Court may disregard the corporate entity and *pierce the corporate veil* in exceptional circumstances. The decision whether to disregard the corporate entity and go directly against the shareholders is made on a case-by-case basis. Factors that may lead to piercing the corporate veil are:

- Failure to maintain adequate corporate records and the commingling of corporate and personal funds;
- Grossly inadequate capitalization (debt/equity ratio too high);
- The formation of a corporation to evade an existing obligation;
- The formation of a corporation to perpetrate a fraud;
- Improper diversion of corporate assets; and
- Injustice and inequitable circumstances would result if the corporate entity were recognized.

Courts generally will look to more than one factor.

Susan sued the Mobile Construction Company. Philip was the only shareholder of the corporation. Susan obtained a judgment against the corporation. Philip then dissolved the corporation and took over all its assets. He agreed to pay all outstanding debts of the corporation except the judgment in favor of Susan. She sued Philip on the ground that he was liable for the judgment against the corporation. He claimed that the judgment was only the liability of the corporation and that he was not liable because he was merely a shareholder and had not assumed the liability for the judgment. Is Philip liable on the judgment? *YES.* If the corporation alone were liable to Susan, an injustice would be done because the corporation had been stripped of all its assets and therefore could not pay the judgment. The timing of the dissolution of the corporation and assumption of all of its debts but Susan's judgment showed that Philip maneuvered the corporate assets to his personal advantage. It would be unjust to allow him to keep the corporate assets after he had made it impossible for the corporation to pay the judgment to Susan. To prevent this injustice, the corporate entity would be ignored, and Philip would be liable on the judgment against the corporation.

It is extremely difficult to pierce a corporate veil in most situations. Some Courts use different terminology when disregarding the corporate entity. The Court may state that the corporation is the *alter ego* of the shareholders, and the shareholders should therefore be held liable.

The Court will not go behind the corporate identity merely because a corporation has been formed to obtain tax savings or to obtain limited liability for its shareholders. One-person, family, and other closely-held corporations are permissible and fully entitled to all of the advantages of corporate existence. However, factors that lead to piercing the corporate veil more commonly exist in these kinds of corporations.

PROMOTERS

Promoters are the people that bring the corporation into existence. They bring together other people interested in the company, solicit stock purchasers, and sometimes make contracts to be assigned later to the corporation. A corporation is not liable on a contract made by a promoter unless the corporation takes some sort of affirmative action to adopt the contract. The promoter still remains personally liable on the contract unless released by the other contracting party. The contract can provide that the promoter will be released from personal liability upon adoption of the contract by the corporation.

INCORPORATION

One or more natural persons or corporations may act as *incorporators* of a corporation by signing and filing *Articles of Incorporation* with the designated government official (usually the Secretary of State). These Articles are filed in duplicate, and the Secretary of State, when satisfied that the Articles conform to the State's corporation statutes, stamps *filed* and the date on each copy. The Secretary of State then retains one copy and returns the other copy, along with a filing fee receipt, to the corporation.

The Articles of Incorporation must contain the following:

- The name of the corporation;
- The number of shares of stock the corporation is authorized to issue;
- The street address of the corporation's initial registered office and the name of its initial registered agent; and
- The name and address of each incorporator.

The Articles may contain optional provisions such as the purpose for which the corporation is organized. However, if the Articles contain no purpose clause, the corporation will automatically have the purpose of engaging in any lawful business. Also, if no reference is made to the duration of the corporation in the Articles, it will automatically have a perpetual duration.

Under the RMBCA, corporate existence begins when the Articles are filed with the Secretary of State. Under the older practice still followed by many States, corporate existence begins upon the issuance of a Certificate of Incorporation by the Secretary of State.

FORFEITURE OF CHARTER

Under the RMBCA, the Secretary of State may administratively dissolve a corporation if:

- The corporation does not pay *franchise taxes* (these taxes are payable to the State, and the amount depends on the capital assets of the corporation);
- The corporation does not file its *annual report* within 60 days after it is due;
- the corporation is without a registered agent or a registered office for 60 days or more.

An annual report is a report filed with the Secretary of State which sets forth information such as the name of the corporation and the State where incorporated, the address of its registered office and name of its registered agent, the address of its principal office, the names and businesses addresses of its directors and principal officers, a brief description of the nature of the business, and information regarding the total number of authorized shares of stock.

Owners and officers of a dissolved corporation are not shielded from personal liability by using the corporate name in making contracts.

JUDICIAL DISSOLUTION
In some States, statutes provide that a judicial dissolution of a corporation may be implemented if the management of the corporation is deadlocked, and the deadlock cannot be broken by the shareholders.

CORPORATE POWERS
Corporations have some of the same powers as a natural person, such as the right to own property. If a corporation acts beyond the limits of its powers, the act is *ultra vires.* This is an act or contract that the corporation did not have authority to do or make. Modern corporation statutes give corporations broad powers, and the likelihood that a corporation will act beyond its powers is rare.

All corporations do not have the same powers. For example, corporations that operate banks, insurance companies, and railroads generally have special powers and are subject to special statutory restrictions.

As long as the Federal and State Constitutions are not violated, a State Legislature may give corporations any lawful powers. The RMBCA grants a corporation *the same powers as an individual to do all things necessary or convenient to carry out its business and affairs.*

PARTICULAR POWERS
Modern corporation statutes give corporations a wide range of powers. A corporation has perpetual succession or continuous life. In other words, it has the power to continue as a unit indefinitely or for a stated period of time regardless of any changes in the ownership of its stock. If no period of time is fixed for the duration of the corporation, the corporation will exist indefinitely until it is legally dissolved. If the period of existence is limited, the corporation can extend the period by meeting certain statutory requirements.

A corporation must have a name to identify it. Most States require that the corporate name contain some indication that it is a corporation, such as *corporation, company, incorporated, limited,* or an abbreviation of these words.

A corporation may have a seal which can be used to show that a contract or a document is being executed pursuant to valid corporate authority.

Bylaws are the rules and regulations of a corporation which govern its internal affairs. They are adopted by the shareholders, though in some States they may be adopted by the directors of the corporation. Of course the bylaws cannot conflict with the general corporate statutes of a State or the bylaws will be void.

A corporation may issue certificates representing corporate stock.

Corporations have the power to enter into contracts just like an individual.

Corporations have the power to borrow money in carrying out their business purposes.

A corporation can borrow money by issuing *bonds*. The bonds issued by a corporation are subject to Article 8 of the UCC ("Investment Securities").

A corporation may sell or lease its property. However, in most States a corporation may not sell or mortgage all or substantially all of its assets without the consent of the majority of the shareholders.

Obviously a corporation has the power to incur debt and mortgage its property as security for debt.

Corporations may acquire the stock of another corporation and be a stockholder of another corporation. A corporation owning stock in another corporation can own such a large percentage of the stock that it controls the operations of the corporation. In such a case, the corporation owning the stock is commonly called a *holding company*. Sometimes a holding company is organized solely for the purpose of controlling other companies. These other companies are called subsidiary companies. Courts normally recognize the holding company and its subsidiary company as separate and distinct legal entities. A corporation does not have to be a holding company to own a subsidiary.

Generally, a corporation may purchase its own stock if it is solvent, and this stock will be known as *treasury stock*. Treasury stock maintains the status of outstanding stock, but is regarded as inactive and cannot be taken into consideration regarding votes by the shareholders. Also, dividends cannot be declared regarding treasury stock. The RMBCA eliminates the concept of treasury stock and calls this type of stock authorized, but unissued, stock.

A corporation has the power to do business in other States. However, by doing business in other States, the corporation may have to qualify as a foreign corporation to do business in that State which usually involves registering with the Secretary of State.

A corporation may be a member of a partnership and may be a limited or general partner of a limited partnership.

Corporations can pay pensions and establish pension plans for its employees.

The RMBCA even authorizes a corporation to make charitable contributions.

ULTRA VIRES ACTS

If a corporation acts beyond the scope of the powers granted by its charter and the statutes of the State under which it is governed, the corporation's act is declared as *ultra vires*. However, modern corporation statutes give such a broad scope of powers that it is difficult to find an action that is *ultra vires*

Nonprofit corporations have a more restricted range of powers than business corporations, and it would be more likely to find an *ultra vires* act in a nonprofit corporation than a profit corporation.

CONSOLIDATIONS, MERGERS, AND CONGLOMERATES

DEFINITIONS

In a *consolidation* of two or more corporations, their separate existences cease, and a new corporation with the property and the assets of the old corporations comes into being.

A *merger* is different from a consolidation in that when two corporations merge, one absorbs the other. One corporation preserves its original charter and identity and continues to exist. The other corporation disappears, and its corporate existence terminates.

A *conglomerate* is the term describing the relationship of a parent corporation to subsidiary corporations engaged in diversified activities which are unrelated to the activity of the parent corporation. A subsidiary corporation is a corporation whose majority shareholder is another corporation *(parent corporation).* An example of a conglomerate could be a wire-manufacturing corporation that owns all of the stock of a newspaper corporation and of a drug-manufacturing corporation.

When the parent company is not engaged in production or rendering of services, it is customarily called a *holding company.* For example, Trustmark, Inc. is the holding company of Trustmark National Bank.

LEGALITY

Consolidations, mergers, and asset acquisitions are sometimes prohibited by federal antitrust legislation on the grounds that the effect is to lessen competition in interstate commerce.

LIABILITY OF SUCCESSOR CORPORATIONS

When corporations are combined in any way, the question arises as to who is liable for the debts and obligations of the predecessor corporations.

Generally, the corporate entity which continues the business after a merger or a consolidation will succeed to all of the rights and property of the predecessors and will also be subject to all of the debts and liabilities of the predecessor corporations. For example, A merges into B. Suppose A had a contract with C. B did not. After the merger, B is liable to C on the contract.

A corporation may merely purchase the assets of another business. This would not be a merger or consolidation. In an acquisition situation, the purchaser does not become liable for the obligations of the business whose assets are being purchased.

Chapter 24
CORPORATE STOCK AND BONDS

CORPORATION
A corporation is owned by its shareholders. An ownership interest in a corporation is represented by a share or stock certificate. Shareholders have certain rights, including the right to vote in the election of directors and the right to receive dividends as they are declared by the corporation. Shareholders are ordinarily exempt from liability for the acts of the corporation. The term "share" and the term "stock" are interchangeable.

NATURE OF STOCK
Each share represents a fractional interest in the total property owned by the corporation. The shareholder does not own an interest in any specific property of the corporation, and the corporation, as a separate legal entity, is the owner of all of its property.

"Capital" refers to the net assets of the corporation. Stock that has been issued to the shareholders of a corporation are said to be "outstanding." "Capital stock" refers to the value received by the corporation for its outstanding stock.

Corporate stock may have a specified par value. This means that a person acquiring the stock from the corporation must pay at least that particular amount. If stock is issued by a corporation for a price greater than its par value, some statutes provide that the par value is to be treated as stated capital, and the excess is capital surplus.

The RMBCA eliminates the concept of par value. Therefore, stock issued by corporations and States following the RMBCA will have "no par." This means that the subscriber pays the corporation an amount as determined by the board of directors.

"Book value" is the value which results by dividing the value of the corporate assets by the number of shares outstanding. The "market value" of a share of stock is the price at which the stock can be bought or sold on the open market.

CERTIFICATE OF STOCK
The corporation ordinarily issues a certificate of stock or share certificate to evidence the shareholder's ownership of stock.

KINDS OF STOCK
The stock of a corporation may be divided into two or more classes. Common stock is ordinary stock and is the most common type of stock issued. Each share usually entitles the holder to have one vote, to receive a share of the profits in the form of dividends, and to participate in the distribution of capital upon dissolution of the corporation. Preferred stock has priority over common stock. This priority may be with respect to dividends, and it may also be with respect to priority over common stock in the distribution of capital upon dissolution of the corporation. Preferred stock is ordinarily nonvoting.

ACQUISITION OF SHARES
Shares of stock may be acquired by (1) subscription, either before or after the corporation is organized, or (2) transfer of existing shares from a shareholder or from the corporation.

STATUTE OF FRAUDS
A contract for the sale of corporate shares must be evidenced by a writing or it cannot be enforced. However, no writing is required for a contract by which a broker agrees with a customer to buy or sell securities for the customer.

SUBSCRIPTION
A stock subscription is a contract or an agreement to buy a specific number of shares when they are issued. A pre-incorporation subscription of shares generally is regarded as an offer to the corporation. It is necessary for the corporation to accept the offer after formation. Some States hold the view that the subscriptions automatically become binding after the corporation is formed.

Stock subscriptions may be made after incorporation, in which event the transaction is like any other contract with the corporation. The offer of subscription may come from the shareholder or from the corporation.

TRANSFER OF SHARES
In the absence of a valid restriction, a shareholder may transfer shares to anyone. Restrictions on the transfer of stock are valid if they are not unreasonable. Small family corporations and other "close corporations" commonly have restrictions regarding the transfer of the corporate stock in order to keep the stock from falling in the hands of an outsider. Such a restriction may provide that other shareholders have the first right to purchase stock before a shareholder may sell it to an outsider. Also, there may be an agreement giving the corporation the right to purchase a shareholder's shares upon his death. The corporation can fund this transaction through a life insurance policy on the shareholder with the proceeds going to the corporation. The proceeds will then be used to buy the shareholder's stock.

A restriction on the right to transfer stock is not effective against a purchaser of the certificate unless the restriction is conspicuously noted on the certificate or unless the purchaser has actual knowledge of the restriction.

MECHANICS OF TRANSFER
The ownership of shares is transferred by delivery of the certificate of stock endorsed by its owner in blank or to a specified person. Ownership may also be transferred by the delivery of the certificate along with a separate assignment or a power of attorney executed by the owner.

EFFECT OF TRANSFER
Shares of stock are classified under Article 8 of the UCC as investment securities. Article 8 governs the rights of parties regarding transactions involving securities. Stock certificates are negotiable pursuant to Article 8, and just as various defenses cannot be asserted against the holder in due course of commercial paper, similar defenses cannot be raised against a person

acquiring a certificate of stock in good faith and for value. Defenses cannot be raised that the transferor did not own the shares, or did not have the authority to deliver the certificate, or that the transfer was made in violation of a restriction on transfer not known to the transferee and not noted conspicuously on the certificate.

Corporate stock is frequently delivered to a creditor as security for a debt owned by the shareholder. The delivery of the security to the creditor causes a perfected security interest to arise in favor of the creditor without the necessity of filing a UCC-1.

Until there is a transfer on its books, the corporation is entitled to treat the person whose name is on the books as the owner of the certificate as the true and lawful owner. The corporation can refuse to recognize a transferee when the corporation is given notice or has notice that the transfer is void. The corporation may also refuse to register the transfer of shares when the outstanding certificate is not surrendered to it unless there is satisfactory proof that it has been lost, destroyed or stolen.

RIGHTS OF SHAREHOLDERS

The control of the shareholders over the corporation is indirect. Ordinarily, once a year, the shareholders elect directors, and by this means they can control the corporation. At other times the shareholders have no power or right to control the corporate activity as long as it is conducted lawfully.

RIGHT TO VOTE

The right to vote means the right to vote at shareholders meetings for the election of directors and on other special matters that must be approved by the shareholders. A proposal to sell or mortgage all, or substantially all, of the assets of the corporation must be approved by the shareholders under most States' laws.

Generally, for each share owned, each shareholder is entitled to one vote on each matter on which there is a vote. This procedure is called straight voting, and it is the normal method for shareholder voting on corporate matters. However, in the case of voting to elect directors, cumulative voting is mandatory in many States. This is a form of voting that is designed to give proportional representation on the board of directors to minority shareholders. Under a cumulative voting plan, each shareholder has as many votes as the number of shares owned multiplied by the number of directors to be elected. Minority shareholders may then cast all of their votes for a candidate who will represent their interests on the board of directors. Under straight voting, minority shareholders would always be outvoted.

A shareholder has the right to authorize another to vote the shares owned by the shareholder. This is known as voting by proxy.

A voting trust exists when, by agreement, a group of shareholders transfers their shares in trust to one or more persons as trustees who are authorized to vote the stock while the agreement is in effect.

PREEMPTIVE OFFER OF SHARES
If the capital stock of a corporation is increased, shareholders can have the preemptive right to subscribe to a certain percentage of the new shares. This percentage is based upon the percentage of ownership they have of the outstanding stock in the corporation. The RMBCA provides that shareholders do not have preemptive rights unless the articles of incorporation give this right.

INSPECTION OF BOOKS
A shareholder has the right to inspect the books of the shareholder's corporation. A request for inspection must be made in good faith, for proper motives, and at a reasonable time and place. The purpose of the inspection must be reasonably related to the shareholder's interest as a shareholder. For example, a shareholder is entitled to inspect the records to determine the financial condition of the corporation or the quality of its management. A shareholder is entitled to inspect the books to obtain information needed for a lawsuit against the corporation or its directors or officers.

Sometimes inspection is denied. For example, a corporation has the right to deny the inspection by a shareholder under certain circumstances. For example, if the inspection was being made in order to aid competitors of the corporation, the corporation could deny the shareholder the right to inspect the books.

The RMBCA requires a corporation to furnish annual financial statements. These statements include a balance sheet as of the end of the fiscal year, an income statement for that year, and a statement of changes in shareholders' equity for that year. These statements are provided to the shareholders.

DIVIDENDS
A shareholder has the right to receive a proportion of dividends as they are declared, subject to the rights of preferred shareholders over common shareholders. There is no absolute right that dividends be declared, but only that dividends, when declared, must be paid in this manner.

State corporation laws commonly provide that no dividends may be declared unless there is a surplus for their payment. The surplus is generally calculated as the amount of corporate assets in excess of the outstanding liabilities and the paid-in capital of the corporation. In some States, statutes provide that dividends may be declared from current net profits.

Assuming that a fund is available for the declaration of dividends, it is then a matter primarily within the discretion of the board of directors as to whether or not a dividend will be declared. The fact that there is a surplus that could be used does not determine that there must be a dividend declared.

In general, a Court will refuse to substitute its judgment for the judgment of the directors of the corporation regarding dividends. However, the Courts will compel the declaration of a dividend when it is apparent that the directors have compiled a surplus beyond any practical business need.

Usually a dividend is paid in money. However, it may be paid in property, such as shares of stock of the corporation itself or shares of stock that the corporation owns in other corporations.

The shareholder who was the owner on the date the dividend was declared (the record date) is entitled to the dividend. This is important when stock is transferred and a cash dividend is declared prior to the transfer being made. Transferor gets dividend. The board of directors may state that the dividend will be payable to those who will be holders of record on a later date than the date the dividend was declared. This later date will then be the record date. The record date of stock dividends is the date of distribution. Whichever party is the owner of the shares when the stock dividend is distributed is entitled to the stock dividend.

CAPITAL DISTRIBUTION

Upon the dissolution of the corporation, the shareholders are entitled to receive any balance of the corporate assets that remain after the payment of all creditors.

SHAREHOLDERS' ACTIONS

When the corporation has the right to sue its directors or officers or third persons for damages caused by them to the corporation, one or more shareholders may bring such an action if the corporation refuses to bring the action. This is called a derivative action, i.e., a shareholder derivative action. Any money recovered is paid into the corporate treasury. Generally, a shareholder bringing this type of suit must show that a demand was made on the directors to enforce the right in question, and that the directors refused to enforce the right.

Minority shareholders may sue majority shareholders for oppressive conduct, such as causing a corporation to pay unreasonable compensation to majority shareholders who are corporate officers.

LIABILITY OF SHAREHOLDERS

The shareholder is ordinarily protected from liability for the acts of the corporation. The shareholder is not personally responsible for the debts and the liabilities of the corporation. The corporate capital may be exhausted by the claims of creditors, but there is no personal liability to the shareholders for any unpaid balance. However, liability may be imposed on a shareholder as though there were no corporation if the Court ignores the corporate entity because the corporation is so defectively organized, it is deemed not to exist. Also, whenever shares issued by a corporation are not fully paid for, the original subscriber receiving the shares may be liable for the unpaid balance if the corporation is insolvent and the money is required to pay the creditors.

If dividends are improperly paid out of capital, the shareholders generally are liable to creditors to the extent the capital is depleted. In some States, the liability depends upon whether the corporation was insolvent at the time and whether there were debts existing at that time. As a practical matter, these types of situations generally arise only in close corporations.

THE PROFESSIONAL CORPORATION

The liability of a shareholder in a professional corporation is limited to the same degree as that of a shareholder in an ordinary business corporation. The statutes that authorize the formation of professional corporations usually require that share ownership be limited to duly-licensed professionals. If a shareholder in a professional corporation, such as a corporation of physicians, is guilty of malpractice, and the shareholder is also the physician who committed the malpractice, the physician is usually liable personally for the tort. The corporation is also liable.

BONDS

A bond is an instrument promising to repay a loan to a corporation, which is secured by corporate assets. The relation between a bondholder and the corporation is that of a creditor-debtor. The principal on the debt is paid on the maturity date. The interest is paid periodically. Bondholders have no right to vote.

Chapter 25

LIMITED LIABILITY COMPANIES

Limited Liability Company

During the last 15 years or so, the limited liability partnership (LLP) and the limited liability company (LLC), have been added to the options for business entities. An initial consideration in choosing between these forms is the number of participants. An LLP must have two or more partners, but in many states, an LLC can have a single member (owner).

A limited liability company (LLC) is a separate legal entity that can conduct business just like a corporation with many of the advantages of a partnership. It is taxed as a partnership. Its owners are called members and receive income from the LLC just as a partner would. There is no tax on the LLC entity itself. The members are not personally liable for the debts and obligations of the entity like partners would be. Basically, an LLC combines the tax advantages of a partnership with the limited liability feature of a corporation.

A particularly attractive feature of the LLC entity is its flexibility of management. The statutes governing LLCs do not set out strict rules for the issuance of ownership interests, recreation of classes of interest or distributions to different classes. There are no requirements for complex hierarchies of directors, shareholders and officers, or delineations of power to amend bylaws, elect managers, or authorize distributions. The members of an LLC are able to determine the entity's management structure (or lack of it) themselves through the operating agreement that initiates the company.

In addition to the limited liability and flexible management offered by the LLC form, there are significant tax advantages as well. While the participants enjoy the limited liability of a corporate structure, the IRS has chosen to treat LLCs in the same way as it treats partnerships, with the advantages of pass-through of income and losses for federal tax purposes.

Most states follow the Uniform Limited Liability Company Act (ULLC). An LLC is formed by filing articles of organization with the secretary of state in the same type manner that articles of incorporation are filed. The articles must contain the name, purpose, duration, registered agent, and principle office of the LLC. The name of the LLC must contain the words ***limited liability company*** or ***LLC.***

A few states also require that a notice of the intention to form an LLC be published in a local newspaper. The members can decide how to operate the business. If there is no agreement, the state LLC statute will govern the outcome, and if there is no statute on the issue, partnership law principles apply.

Management of an LLC is vested in its members. An ***operating agreement*** is executed by the members and operates much the same way a partnership agreement operates. Members may delegate authority to managers who run the LLC much the same way officers of a corporation would run a corporation. Profits and losses are shared according to the terms of the operating agreement.

Dissociation and Dissolution of an LLC

Dissociation occurs when a member ceases to be associated with the carrying on of a business. A member of an LLC has the power, but may not have the right, to dissociate from the firm. Events that trigger dissociation under the Uniform Limited Liability Company Act are the same as those under the Uniform Partnership Act.

Effect of Dissociation

On dissociation, a member's right to participate in the firm's business ends. The duty of loyalty also ends, and the duty of care continues only with respect to events that occurred before dissociation. The member's interest in the firm must be bought out according to the LLC agreement, or for its "fair" value.

Dissolution

A dissociating member does not normally have the right to force the firm to dissolve (although the other members can dissolve the firm if they want and a court might order dissolution). On dissolution, any member can participate in winding up. After liquidation of the assets, the proceeds are distributed first to creditors (which may include members), second to capital contributors, and finally to members according to the operating agreement or in equal shares.

Limited Liability Partnerships

A limited liability partnership (LLP) is a partnership in which the partners have limited liabilities. It therefore exhibits elements of partnerships and corporations. In an LLP, one partner is not responsible or liable for another partner's misconduct or negligence.

All of the owners of an LLP have limited personal liability for business debts. LLPs are particularly well-suited to professional groups, such as lawyers and accountants. In fact, in some states LLPs are only available to professionals.

Professionals often prefer LLPs to general partnerships, corporations, or LLCs because they don't want to be personally liable for another partner's problems - particularly those involving malpractice claims. An LLP protects each partner from debts against the partnership arising from professional malpractice lawsuits against another partner. (A partner who loses a malpractice suit for his own mistakes, however, doesn't escape liability.)

Creating a limited liability partnership is done at the state level. Each state has its own rules, but in general you must pay a fee and file papers with the state, usually a "certificate of limited liability partnership." This document is similar to the articles (or certificate) filed by a corporation or an LLC and includes information about the general partners. Filing fees for LLPs are similar to those for corporations and LLCs.

Advantages and Disadvantages

Liability Protection

One advantage of a limited liability partnership is the liability protection it affords. This type of partnership structure protects individual partners from personal liability for negligent acts of other partners or employees not under their direct control. In addition, individual partners are not personally responsible for company debts or other obligations. This is advantageous for an individual partner when potential lawsuits or claims of negligence against the business are concerned.

Tax Advantages

Individuals in a partnership are normally liable for filing personal income taxes, self-employment taxes and estimated taxes for themselves, according to the Internal Revenue Service. The partnership itself is not responsible for paying taxes. The credits and deductions of the company are passed through to partners to file on their individual tax returns. Credits and deductions are divided by the percentage of individual interest each partner has in the company. This can be beneficial for partners who have a limited interest in the company.

Flexibility

Limited liability partnerships offer participants flexibility in business ownership. Partners have the authority to decide how they will individually contribute to business operations. Managerial duties can be divided equally or separated based on the experience of each partner. In addition, partners who have a financial interest in the company can elect to not have any authority over business decisions but still maintain ownership rights based on their percentage interest in the company.

How Do You Choose between LLCs and LLPs

One of the most important decisions that an entrepreneur makes is the selection of the form in which to do business. To make the best decision, a businessperson should understand all aspects of the various forms, including legal, tax, licensing, and business considerations. It is also important that all of the participants in the business understand their actual relationship, regardless of the organizational structure.

Both LLPs and LLCs can set up whatever management structure the participants desire. Also, all unincorporated business organizations, including LLPs and LLCs, are treated as partnerships for federal income tax purposes (unless an LLC elects to be treated as a corporation). This means that the firms are not taxed at the entity level. Their income is passed through to the partners or members who must report it on their individual income tax returns. The chief benefits of electing corporate status for tax purposes are that the members generally are not subject to self-employment taxes, and fringe benefits may be provided to employee-members on a tax-reduced basis. The tax laws are complicated, however, and a tax professional should be consulted about the details.

FREQUENTLY ASKED QUESTIONS

What is the difference between a limited liability company (LLC) and a limited liability partnership (LLP)? An LLP is similar to an LLC? The difference between them is that an LLP is designed more for professionals who normally do business as partners in a partnership. The major advantage of the LLP is that it allows a partnership to continue as a pass-through entity for tax purposes but limits the personal liability of the partners.

Why are LLCs and LLPs attractive to businesspersons? For many business persons, these business forms combine the tax advantages of partnerships with the limited liability of corporations. The income of the firm is passed through to the members or the partners, rather than being taxed at the organization's level. Even one-member LLCs may realize the tax advantage that accrues from not being taxed as a corporation (unless the LLC elects otherwise). Also, the members or the partners of the firm are not usually liable beyond the extent of their investment in the firm for the debts and other obligations of the firm.

Why should the members of an LLC (or the participants in any forms of business organization discussed in this chapter) prefer to put the terms of their operating agreement in writing? Generally, LLC members should protect their interests by forming a written operating agreement. If there is no written agreement covering an issue in dispute among the members, the state LLC statute will govern the outcome. Typically, the principles of partnership law apply. These statutes and principles may not be to the liking of all, or any, of the members.

What are the characteristics of a limited liability partnership (LLP)? An LLP is similar to an LLC. The difference between them is that an LLP is designed more for professionals who normally do business as partners in a partnership. The major advantage of the LLP is that it allows a partnership to continue as a pass-through entity for tax purposes but limits the personal liability of the partners.

Member Managed Limited Liability Company Operating Agreement

This Agreement, dated *(date),* made and entered into between **XYZ, LLC,** a limited liability company organized pursuant to the *(Name of State)* Limited Liability Company Act, hereinafter called the *Company, (Name of Member One)*, of *(street address, city, county, state, zip code), (Name of Member Two)*, of *(street address, city, county, state, zip code),* and *(Name of Member Three)*, of *(street address, city, county, state, zip code),* hereinafter called the ***Members.***
In consideration of the mutual benefits and obligations set forth in this Agreement, the parties agree as follows:

I. Definition of Terms. Unless the context otherwise requires, the terms defined in this **Section I** shall, for the purposes of this Agreement, have the following meanings:

A. ***(Name of State) Act*** means the *(Name of State)* limited liability company statute, *(citation to statute)*, as amended from time to time.

B. ***Additional Members*** has the meaning set forth in **Section XIII.**

C. ***Affiliate*** means, with respect to a specified Person, any Person that directly or indirectly controls, is controlled by, or is under common control with, the specified Person. As used in this definition, the term *control* means the possession, directly or indirectly, of the power to direct or cause the direction of the management and policies of a Person, whether through ownership of voting securities, by contract or otherwise.

D. ***Agreement*** means this Limited Liability Company Agreement of the Company, as amended, modified, supplemented or restated from time to time.

E. ***Capital Account*** means, with respect to any Member, the account maintained for such Member in accordance with the provisions of **Section IV.**

F. ***Capital Contribution*** means, with respect to any Member, the aggregate amount of money and the fair market value of any property (other than money) contributed to the Company pursuant to **Section IV** with respect to such Member's Interest.

G. ***Certificate*** means the Certificate of Formation of the Company and any and all amendments to the Certificate of Formation and restatements of the same filed on behalf of the Company with the office of the Secretary of State of the State of ***(Name of State)*** pursuant to the ***(Name of State)*** Act.

H. ***Code*** means the Internal Revenue Code of 1986, as amended from time to time, or any corresponding federal tax statute enacted after the date of this Agreement. A reference to a specific section of the Code refers not only to such specific section but also to any corresponding provision of any federal tax statute enacted after the date of this Agreement, as such specific section or corresponding provision is in effect on the date of application of the provisions of this Agreement containing such reference.

I. ***Company*** means **XYZ, LLC,** the limited liability company formed and continued under and pursuant to the *(Name of State)* Act and this Agreement.

J. ***Covered Person*** means a Member, any Affiliate of a Member, any officers, directors, shareholders, partners, employees, representatives or agents of a Member, or their respective Affiliates, or any employee or agent of the Company or its Affiliates.

K. ***Fiscal Year*** means:

1. The period commencing upon the formation of the Company and ending on *(month and day), (year);*

2. Any subsequent 12-month period commencing on *(month and day),* and ending on *(month and day);* or

3. Any portion of the period described in **Clause 2** above which the Company is required to allocate Profits, Losses and other items of Company income, gain, loss or deduction pursuant to **Section VIII.**

L. ***Interest*** means a Member's limited liability company interest in the Company which represents such Member's share of the profits and losses of the Company and a Member's right to receive distributions of the Company's assets in accordance with the provisions of this Agreement and the *(Name of State)* Act.

M. *Member* means each of *(Name of First Member), (Name of Second Member),* and *(Name of Third Member),* and includes any Person admitted as an Additional *Member* pursuant to the provisions of this Agreement, in such Person's capacity as a member of the Company; *Members* means two or more of such Persons when acting in their capacities as members of the Company. For purposes of the *(Name of State)* Act, the *Members* shall constitute one class or group of members.

N. ***Net Cash Flow*** means, for each Fiscal Year or other period of the Company, the gross cash receipts of the Company from all sources, but excluding any amounts, such as gross receipts taxes, that are held by the Company as a collection agent or in trust for others or that are otherwise not unconditionally available to the Company, less all amounts paid by or for the account of the Company during the same Fiscal Year or other period (including, but not limited to, payments of principal and interest on any Company indebtedness and expenses reimbursed to the Members under **Section V-B**, and less any amounts determined by the Members to be necessary to provide a reasonable reserve for working-capital needs or any other contingencies of the Company. Net Cash Flow shall be determined in accordance with the cash receipts and disbursements method of accounting and otherwise in accordance with generally accepted accounting principles, consistently applied. Net Cash Flow shall not be reduced by depreciation, amortization, cost recovery deductions, depletion, similar allowances or other non-cash items, but shall be increased by any reduction of reserves previously established.

O. ***Percentage Interest*** means the Interest of a Member, expressed as a portion of one hundred percent, as shown on **Schedule A**.

P. ***Person*** includes any individual, corporation, association, partnership (general or limited), joint venture, trust, estate, limited liability company, or other legal entity or organization.

Q. ***Profits*** and ***Losses*** means, for each Fiscal Year, an amount equal to the Company's taxable income or loss for such Fiscal Year, determined in accordance with Section 703(a) of the Code.

R. ***Tax Matters Partner*** has the meaning set forth in **Section XI-A.**

S. ***Treasury Regulations*** means the income tax regulations, including temporary regulations, promulgated under the Code, as such regulations may be amended from time to time (including corresponding provisions of succeeding regulations).

II. Formation and Term

A. Formation.

1. The Members have formed the Company as a limited liability company under and pursuant to the provisions of the *(Name of State)* Act and agree that the rights, duties and liabilities of the Members shall be as provided in the *(Name of State)* Act, except as otherwise provided in this Agreement.

2. Upon the execution of this Agreement or a counterpart of this Agreement, *(Name of Member One), (Name of Member Two),* and *(Name of Member Three)* shall be admitted as Members of the Company.

3. The name and mailing address of each Member and the amount contributed to the capital of the Company shall be listed on the attached **Schedule A.** The Members shall be required to update **Schedule A** from time to time as necessary to accurately reflect the information in the schedule. Any amendment or revision to **Schedule A** made in accordance with this Agreement shall not be deemed an amendment to this Agreement. Any reference in this Agreement to **Schedule A** shall be deemed to be a reference to **Schedule A** as amended and in effect from time to time.

4. *(Name of Member One)*, as an authorized person within the meaning of the *(Name of State)* Act, shall execute, deliver and file the Certificate.

B. **Name.** The name of the Company is ***XYZ, LLC.*** The business of the Company may be conducted upon compliance with all applicable laws under any other name designated by the Members.

C. **Term.** The term of the Company shall commence on the date the Certificate is filed in the office of the Secretary of State of the State of *(Name of State)* and shall continue until *(date)*, unless the Company is dissolved before such date in accordance with the provisions of this Agreement. The existence of the Company as a separate legal entity shall continue until cancellation of the Certificate in the manner required by the *(Name of State)* Act.

D. **Registered Agent and Office.** The Company's registered agent and office in the State of shall be *(Name)*, of *(street address, city, county, state, zip code).* At any time, the Members may designate another registered agent or registered office.

E. **Principal Place of Business.** The principal place of business of the Company shall be at *(street address, city, county, state, zip code).* At any time, the Members may change the location of the Company's principal place of business.

F. **Qualification in Other Jurisdictions.** The Members shall, if required by law or if deemed advisable by the Members, cause the Company to be qualified, formed or registered under assumed or fictitious name statutes or similar laws in any jurisdiction in which the Company transacts business. *(Name of Member One)* as an authorized person within the meaning of the *(Name of State)* Act, shall execute, deliver and file any certificates (and any amendments or restatements of such certificates) necessary for the Company to qualify to do business in a jurisdiction in which the Company may wish to conduct business.

III. Purpose and Powers of the Company

A. **Purpose.** The Company is formed for the object and purpose of, and the nature of the business to be conducted and promoted by the Company is, engaging in any lawful act or activity for which limited liability companies may be formed under the *(Name of State)* Act and engaging in any and all activities necessary, convenient, desirable or incidental to the foregoing, including, but not limited to, acquiring, holding, managing, operating and disposing of securities of corporations, partnerships, limited liability companies and trusts.

B. **Powers of the Company.** The Company shall have the power and authority to take any and all actions necessary, appropriate, proper, advisable, incidental or convenient to or for the furtherance of the purpose set forth in **Section III-A,** including, but not limited to, the power:

1. To conduct its business, carry on its operations and have and exercise the powers granted to a limited liability company by the *(Name of State)* Act in any state, territory, district or possession of the United States, or in any foreign country that may be necessary, convenient or incidental to the accomplishment of the purpose of the Company;

2. To acquire by purchase, contribution of property or otherwise, own, hold, operate, maintain, finance, sell, convey, transfer, or dispose of any securities or other personal property that may be necessary, convenient or incidental to the accomplishment of the purpose of the Company;

3. To enter into, perform and carry out contracts of any kind, including, but not limited to, contracts with any Member, any Affiliate of a Member, or any agent of the Company necessary to, in connection with, convenient to, or incidental to the accomplishment of the purpose of the Company;

4. To purchase, take, receive, subscribe for or otherwise acquire, own, hold, vote, use, employ, sell, mortgage, lend, pledge, or otherwise dispose of, and otherwise use and deal in and with, shares or other interests in or obligations of domestic or foreign corporations, associations, general or limited partnerships (including, but not limited to, the power to be admitted as a partner and to exercise the rights and perform the duties created by such partnerships), trusts, limited liability companies (including, but not limited to, the power to be admitted as a member or appointed as a manager and to exercise the rights and perform the duties created by such admission or appointment), or individuals or direct or indirect obligations of the United States or of any government, state, territory, governmental district or municipality or of any instrumentality of any of them;

5. To lend money for its proper purpose, to invest and reinvest its funds, to take and hold real and personal property for the payment of funds so loaned or invested;

6. To sue and be sued, complain and defend, and participate in administrative or other proceedings, in its name;

7. To appoint employees and agents of the Company, and define their duties and fix their compensation;

8. To indemnify any Person in accordance with the *(Name of State)* Act and to obtain any and all types of insurance;

9. To cease its activities and cancel its Certificate;

10. To negotiate, enter into, renegotiate, extend, renew, terminate, modify, amend, waive, execute, acknowledge or take any other action with respect to any lease, contract or security agreement in respect of any assets of the Company;

11. To borrow money and issue evidences of indebtedness, and to secure the same by a mortgage, pledge or other lien on the assets of the Company;

12. To pay, collect, compromise, litigate, arbitrate or otherwise adjust or settle any and all other claims or demands of or against the Company or to hold such proceeds against the payment of contingent liabilities; and

13. To make, execute, acknowledge and file any and all documents or instruments necessary, convenient or incidental to the accomplishment of the purpose of the Company.

14. The Company may merge with, or consolidate into, another *(Name of State)* limited liability company or other business entity as allowed by the limited liability statutes of *(Name of State).*

IV. Capital Contributions; Interests; Capital Accounts; Advances

A. Capital Contributions.

1. Each Member has contributed or is deemed to have contributed to the capital of the Company the amount set forth opposite the Member's name on the attached **Schedule A.** The agreed value of the Capital Contributions made or deemed to have been made by each Member shall be set forth on **Schedule A.**

2. No Member shall be required to make any additional capital contribution to the Company. However, a Member may make additional capital contributions to the Company with the written consent of all of the Members.

B. Member's Interest. A Member's Interest shall for all purposes be personal property. A Member has no interest in specific Company property.

C. Status of Capital Contributions.

1. Except as otherwise provided in this Agreement, the amount of a Member's Capital Contributions may be returned to it, in whole or in part, at any time, but only with the consent of all of the Members. Any such returns of Capital Contributions shall be made to all Members in proportion to the Percentage Interests. Notwithstanding the foregoing, no return of a Member's Capital Contributions shall be made if such distribution would violate applicable state law. Under circumstances requiring a return of any Capital Contribution, no Member shall have the right to demand or receive property other than cash, except as may be specifically provided in this Agreement.

2. No Member shall receive any interest, salary or drawing with respect to its Capital Contributions or its Capital Account or for services rendered on behalf of the Company or otherwise in its capacity as a Member, except as otherwise specifically provided in this Agreement.

3. Except as otherwise provided in this Agreement and by applicable state law, the Members shall be liable only to make their capital contributions pursuant to **Section IV-A,** and no Member shall be required to lend any funds to the Company or, after a Member's Capital Contributions have been fully paid pursuant to **Section IV-A,** to make any additional capital contributions to the Company. No Member shall have any personal liability for the repayment of any Capital Contribution of any other Member.

D. Capital Accounts.

1. An individual Capital Account shall be established and maintained for each Member.

2. The Capital Account of each Member shall be maintained in accordance with the following provisions:

a. To such Member's Capital Account there shall be credited such Member's Capital Contributions (consisting of cash or the fair market value of any property net of any liabilities secured by such contributed property that the Company is considered to assume or take subject to under Section 752 of the Code); such Member's distributive share of Profits; and such Member's distributive share of other items of income, gain or credits; and

b. To such Member's Capital Account there shall be debited the amount of cash and the fair market value of property distributed by the Company to such Member (net of liabilities secured by such distributed property which the Member is considered to assume or take subject to under Section 752 of the Code); such Member's distributive share of Losses; and such Member's distributive share of other items of loss or deduction.

E. Advances. If any Member shall advance any funds to the Company in excess of its Capital Contributions, the amount of such advance shall neither increase its Capital Account nor entitle it to any increase in its share of the distributions of the Company. The amount of any such advance shall be a debt obligation of the Company to such Member and shall be subject to such terms and conditions acceptable to the Company and each Member. Any such advance shall be payable and collectible only out of Company assets, and the other Members shall not be personally obligated to repay any part of such advance. No Person who makes any non-recourse loan to the Company shall have or acquire, as a result of making such loan, any direct or indirect interest in the profits, capital or property of the Company, other than as a creditor.

V. Members

A. Powers of Members. The Members shall have the power to exercise any and all rights or powers granted to the Members pursuant to the express terms of this Agreement and the *(Name of State)* Act.

B. Reimbursements. The Company shall reimburse the Members, for all ordinary and necessary out-of-pocket expenses incurred by the Members on behalf of the Company. Such reimbursement shall be treated as an expense of the Company that shall be deducted in computing the Net Cash Flow and shall not be deemed to constitute a distributive share of Profits or a distribution or return of capital to any Member.

C. Partition. Each Member waives any and all rights that it may have to maintain an action for partition of the Company's property.

D. Resignation. A Member may not resign from the Company without the written consent of all of the other Members.

VI. Management

A. Management of the Company.

1. In accordance with Section ____ of the *(Name of State)* limited liability act, management of the Company shall be vested in the Members. Except as otherwise expressly provided in this Agreement, whenever this Agreement requires or permits actions to be taken by the Members, the decision by Members owning more than ____% of the Percentage Interests shall control.

2. The Members shall have full, exclusive and complete discretion to manage the business and affairs of the Company, to make all decisions affecting the business and affairs of the Company and to take such actions as they deem necessary or appropriate to accomplish the purpose of the Company as set forth in this Agreement. There shall not be a "manager" *[within the meaning of the (Name of State) Limited Liability Company Act]* of the Company.

3. With respect to third parties, each Member is an agent of the Company's business, and each Member may bind the Company. If a Member binds the Company, but did not have the authority to so act under this Agreement (including by failing to obtain necessary consents from other Members), in addition to any other remedy (at law or in equity) that may be available against such Member, such Member shall be liable for all damages caused by breaching this Agreement.

C. Reliance by Third Parties. Any Person dealing with the Company or any Member may rely upon a certificate signed by any Member as to:

1. The identity of a Member;

2. The existence or nonexistence of any fact or facts which constitute a condition precedent to acts by the Members or in any other manner germane to the affairs of the Company;

3. The Persons who are authorized to execute and deliver any instrument or document of, or on behalf of, the Company; or

4. Any act or failure to act by the Company or as to any other matter whatsoever involving the Company or any Member.

VII. Amendments and Meetings

A. Amendments. Any amendment to this Agreement shall be adopted and be effective as an amendment to the Agreement if it receives the affirmative vote of all of the Members, provided that such amendment be in writing and executed by all of the Members.

B. Meetings of the Members.

1. Meetings of the Members may be called at any time by any Member. Notice of any meeting shall be given to all Members not less than ***(number)*** days nor more than ***(number)*** days prior to the date of such meeting. Each Member may authorize any Person to act for it by proxy on all matters in which a Member is entitled to participate, including waiving notice of any meeting, or voting or participating at a meeting. Every proxy must be signed by the Member or its attorney-in-fact.

2. The Members shall establish all other provisions relating to meetings of Members, including notice of the time, place or purpose of any meeting at which any matter is to be voted on by any Members, waiver of any such notice, action by consent without a meeting, the establishment of a record date, quorum requirements, voting in person or by proxy or any other matter with respect to the exercise of any such right to vote.

3. The Company may take any action contemplated by this Agreement as approved by the unanimous written consent of the Members.

VIII. Allocations

A. Profits and Losses.

1. Subject to the allocation rules of **Section VIII-B,** Profits for any Fiscal Year shall be allocated among the Members in proportion to the Percentage Interests.

2. Subject to the allocation rules of **Section VIII-B**, Losses for any Fiscal Year shall be allocated among the Members in proportion to the Percentage Interests.

B. Allocation Rules.

1. For purposes of determining the Profits, Losses or any other items allocable to any period, Profits, Losses and any such other items shall be determined on a daily, monthly or other basis, as determined by the Members using any method that is permissible under Section 706 of the Code and the Treasury Regulations under that Section.

2. Except as otherwise provided in this Agreement, all items of Company income, gain, loss, deduction and any other allocations not otherwise provided for shall be divided among the Members in the same proportions as they share Profits and Losses for the Fiscal Year in question.

3. The Members are aware of the income tax consequences of the allocations made by this **Article VIII** and agree to be bound by the provisions of this **Article VIII** in reporting their shares of Company income and loss for income tax purposes.

4. The Members intend that the allocation provisions set forth in this Agreement are intended to comply with Section 704(b) of the Code and the Treasury Regulations issued under that Section and the provisions are to be interpreted in a manner consistent with those Treasury Regulations.

C. Tax Allocations; Section 704(c) of the Code. In accordance with Section 704(c) of the Code and the Treasury Regulations under that Section, income, gain, loss and deduction with respect to any property contributed to the capital of the Company shall, solely for income tax purposes, be allocated among the Members so as to take account of any variation between the adjusted basis of such property to the Company for federal income tax purposes and its initial fair market value.

IX. Distributions.

A. Net Cash Flow. Except as otherwise provided in **Article XV** (relating to the dissolution of the Company), any distribution of the Net Cash Flow during any Fiscal Year shall be made to the Members in proportion to the Percentage Interests.

B. Distribution Rules. All distributions pursuant to **Section IX-A** shall be at such times and in such amounts as shall be determined by the Members.

C. Limitations on Distribution. Notwithstanding any provision to the contrary contained in this Agreement, the Company shall not make a distribution to any Member on account of its interest in the Company if such distribution would violate the *(Name of State) Limited Liability Company Act* or other applicable law.

X. Books and Records

A. Books, Records and Financial Statements.

1. At all times during the continuance of the Company, the Company shall maintain, at its principal place of business, separate books of account for the Company that shall show a true and accurate record of all costs and expenses incurred, all charges made, all credits made and received and all income derived in connection with the operation of the Company business in accordance with generally accepted accounting principles consistently applied, and, to the extent inconsistent with such principles, in accordance with this Agreement. Such

books of account, together with a copy of this Agreement and of the Certificate, shall at all times be maintained at the principal place of business of the Company and shall be open to inspection and examination at reasonable times by each Member and its duly authorized representative for any purpose reasonably related to such Member's interest in the Company.

2. The Members shall prepare and maintain, or cause to be prepared and maintained, the books of account of the Company. The Members shall prepare and file, or cause to be prepared and filed, all applicable federal and state tax returns.

B. Accounting Method. For both financial and tax reporting purposes and for purposes of determining Profits and Losses, the books and records of the Company shall be kept on the accrual method of accounting applied in a consistent manner and shall reflect all Company transactions and be appropriate and adequate for the Company's business.

C. Annual Audit. At any time at a Member's sole discretion, the financial statements of the Company may be audited by an independent certified public accountant, selected by such Member, with such audit to be accompanied by a report of such accountant containing its opinion. The cost of such audits will be an expense of the Company. A copy of any such audited financial statements and accountant's report will be made available for inspection by the Members.

XI. Tax Matters

A. Tax Matters Partner.

1. *(Name of Member One)* is designated as *Tax Matters Partner* of the Company for purposes of Section 6231(a)(7) of the Code. *(Name of Member One)* may not choose a forum for the resolution of tax matters or extend any statute of limitation without the written consent of all of the Members.

2. The Tax Matters Partner shall, within *(number)* days of the receipt of any notice from the Internal Revenue Service in any administrative proceeding at the Company level relating to the determination of any Company item of income, gain, loss, deduction or credit, mail or otherwise deliver a copy of such notice to each Member.

B. Taxation as Partnership. The Company shall be treated as a partnership for U.S. federal income tax purposes.

XII. Liability; Exculpation; Indemnification

A. Liability. Except as otherwise provided by the ***(Name of State)*** Act, the debts, obligations and liabilities of the Company, whether arising in contract, tort or otherwise, shall be solely the debts, obligations and liabilities of the Company, and no Covered Person shall be obligated personally for any such debt, obligation or liability of the Company solely by reason of being a Covered Person.

B. Exculpation.

1. No Covered Person shall be liable to the Company or any other Covered Person for any loss, damage or claim incurred by reason of any act or omission performed or omitted by such Covered Person in good faith on behalf of the Company and in a manner reasonably believed to be within the scope of authority conferred on such Covered Person by this Agreement, except that a Covered

Person shall be liable for any such loss, damage or claim incurred by reason of such Covered Person's gross negligence or willful misconduct.

2. A Covered Person shall be fully protected in relying in good faith upon the records of the Company and upon such information, opinions, reports or statements presented to the Company by any Person as to matters the Covered Person reasonably believes are within such other Person's professional or expert competence and who has been selected with reasonable care by or on behalf of the Company, including information, opinions, reports or statements as to the value and amount of the assets, liabilities, Profits, Losses or Net Cash Flow or any other facts pertinent to the existence and amount of assets from which distributions to Members might properly be paid.

C. Fiduciary Duty. To the extent that, at law or in equity, a Covered Person has duties (including fiduciary duties) and related liabilities to the Company or to any other Covered Person, a Covered Person acting under this Agreement shall not be liable to the Company or to any Member for its good faith reliance on the provisions of this Agreement. The provisions of this Agreement, to the extent that they restrict the duties and liabilities of a Covered Person otherwise existing at law or in equity, are agreed by the parties to replace such other duties and liabilities of such Covered Person.

D. Indemnification. To the fullest extent permitted by applicable law, a Covered Person shall be entitled to indemnification from the Company for any loss, damage or claim incurred by such Covered Person by reason of any act or omission performed or omitted by such Covered Person in good faith on behalf of the Company and in a manner reasonably believed to be within the scope of authority conferred on such Covered Person by this Agreement, except that no Covered Person shall be entitled to be indemnified in respect of any loss, damage or claim incurred by such Covered Person by reason of gross negligence or willful misconduct with respect to such acts or omissions; provided, however, that any indemnity under this **Section XII-D** shall be provided out of and to the extent of Company assets only, and no Covered Person shall have any personal liability on account of the same.

E. Expenses. To the fullest extent permitted by applicable law, expenses (including legal fees) incurred by a Covered Person in defending any claim, demand, action, suit or proceeding shall, from time to time, be advanced by the Company prior to the final disposition of such claim, demand, action, suit or proceeding upon receipt by the Company of an undertaking by or on behalf of the Covered Person to repay such amount if it shall be determined that the Covered Person is not entitled to be indemnified as authorized in **Section XII-D**.

F. Insurance. The Company may purchase and maintain insurance, to the extent and in such amounts as the Members shall, in its sole discretion, deem reasonable, on behalf of Covered Persons and such other Persons as the Members shall determine, against any liability that may be asserted against or expenses that may be incurred by any such Person in connection with the activities of the Company or such indemnities, regardless of whether the Company would have the power to indemnify such Person against such liability under the provisions of this Agreement. The Members and the Company may enter into indemnity contracts with Covered Persons and such other Persons as the Members shall determine and adopt written procedures pursuant to which arrangements are made for the advancement of expenses and the funding of obligations under **Section XII-E** and containing such other procedures regarding indemnification as are appropriate.

G. Outside Businesses. Any Member or Affiliate of a Member may engage in or possess an interest in other business ventures of any nature or description, independently or with others, similar or dissimilar to the business of the Company, and the Company and the Members shall have no rights by virtue of this Agreement in and to such independent ventures or the income or profits derived therefrom, and the pursuit of any such venture, even if competitive with the business of the Company, shall not be deemed wrongful or improper. No Member or Affiliate of a Member shall be obligated to present any particular investment opportunity to the Company even if such opportunity is of a character that, if presented to the Company, could be taken by the Company, and any Member or Affiliate of a Member shall have the right to take for its own account (individually or as a partner or fiduciary) or to recommend to others any such particular investment opportunity.

XIII. Additional Members.

A. Admission. By approval of all of the Members, the Company is authorized to admit any Person as an additional member of the Company (each, an *Additional Member* and collectively, the *Additional Members*). Each such Person shall be admitted as an Additional Member at the time such Person:

1. Executes this Agreement or a counterpart of this Agreement; and

2. Is named as a Member on the attached **Schedule A.** The legal fees and expenses associated with such admission shall be borne by the Company.

B. Allocations. Additional Members shall not be entitled to any retroactive allocation of the Company's income, gains, losses, deductions, credits or other items; provided that, subject to the restrictions of Section 706(d) of the Code, Additional Members shall be entitled to their respective share of the Company's income, gains, losses, deductions, credits and other items arising under contracts entered into before the effective date of the admission of any Additional Members to the extent that such income, gains, losses, deductions, credits and other items arise after such effective date. To the extent consistent with Section 706(d) of the Code and Treasury Regulations promulgated under that Section, the Company's books may be closed at the time Additional Members are admitted (as though the Company's tax year had ended) or the Company may credit to the Additional Members pro rata allocations of the Company's income, gains, losses, deductions, credits and items for that portion of the Company's Fiscal Year after the effective date of the admission of the Additional Members.

XIV. Assignability and Substitute Members

A. Assignability of Interests. No Member may assign the whole or any part of its Interests.

B. Recognition of Assignment by Company. No assignment or pledge of any Interest, or any part of an Interest, that is in violation of this **Article XIV** shall be valid or effective, and neither the Company nor the Members shall recognize the same for the purpose of making distributions pursuant to this Agreement. Neither the Company nor the Members shall incur any liability as a result of refusing to make any such distributions to the assignee of any such invalid assignment.

C. Pledge. No Member may pledge or otherwise encumber the whole or any part of its Interests.

XV. Dissolution, Liquidation and Termination

A. No Dissolution. The Company shall not be dissolved by the admission of Additional Members in accordance with the terms of this Agreement.

B. Events Causing Dissolution. The Company shall be dissolved and its affairs shall be wound up upon the occurrence of any of the following events:

1. The expiration of the term of the Company, as provided in **Section II-C;**

2. The written consent of all Members;

3. The death, retirement, resignation, expulsion, bankruptcy or dissolution of a Member or the occurrence of any other event under the *(Name of State) Act* that terminates the continued membership of a Member in the Company unless, within *(number)* days after the occurrence of such an event, all of the remaining Members agree in writing to continue the business of the Company; or

4. The entry of a decree of judicial dissolution under Section ___ of the *(Name of State) Limited Liability Company Act).*

C. Liquidation. Upon dissolution of the Company, the Members shall carry out the winding up of the Company and shall immediately commence to wind up the Company's affairs; provided, however, that a reasonable time shall be allowed for the orderly liquidation of the assets of the Company and the satisfaction of liabilities to creditors so as to enable the Members to minimize the normal losses attendant upon a liquidation. The Members shall continue to share Profits and Losses during liquidation in the same proportions, as specified in **Article VIII,** as before liquidation. The proceeds of liquidation shall be distributed in the following order and priority:

1. To creditors of the Company, including Members who are creditors, to the extent otherwise permitted by law, in satisfaction of the liabilities of the Company (whether by payment or the making of reasonable provision for payment); and

2. To the Members in accordance with their Capital Account balances, after giving effect to all contributions, distributions and allocations for all periods.

D. Termination. The Company shall terminate when all of the assets of the Company, after payment of or due provision for all debts, liabilities and obligations of the Company, shall have been distributed to the Members in the manner provided for in this **Article XV** and the Certificate shall have been canceled in the manner required by the *(Name of State)* Act.

E. Claims of the Members. The Members and former Members shall look solely to the Company's assets for the return of their Capital Contributions, and if the assets of the Company remaining after payment of or due provision for all debts, liabilities and obligations of the Company are insufficient to return such Capital Contributions, the Members and former Members shall have no recourse against the Company or any other Member.

XVI. Miscellaneous

A. Notices. All notices provided for in this Agreement shall be in writing, duly signed by the party giving such notice, and shall be delivered, mailed via an overnight courier service, telecopied or mailed by registered or certified mail, as follows:

1. If given to the Company, at the address specified in **Section II-E** of this Agreement; or

2. If given to any Member, at the address set forth opposite its name on the attached **Schedule A,** or at such other address as such Member may designate in the future by written notice to the Company.

3. All such notices shall be deemed to have been given when received.

B. Failure to Pursue Remedies. The failure of any party to seek redress for violation of, or to insist upon the strict performance of, any provision of this Agreement shall not prevent a subsequent act, which would have originally constituted a violation, from having the effect of an original violation.

C. Cumulative Remedies. The rights and remedies provided by this Agreement are cumulative and the use of any one right or remedy by any party shall not preclude or waive its right to use any or all other remedies. The rights and remedies are given in addition to any other rights the parties may have by law, statute, ordinance or otherwise.

D. Binding Effect. This Agreement shall be binding upon and inure to the benefit of all of the parties and, to the extent permitted by this Agreement, their successors, legal representatives and assigns.

E. Severability. The invalidity or unenforceability of any particular provision of this Agreement shall not affect the other provisions of this Agreement, and this Agreement shall be construed in all respects as if such invalid or unenforceable provision was omitted.

F. Counterparts. This Agreement may be executed in any number of counterparts with the same effect as if all parties had signed the same document. All counterparts shall be construed together and shall constitute one instrument.

G. Governing Law. This Agreement and the rights of the parties under this Agreement shall be interpreted in accordance with the laws of the State of *(Name of State)*, and all rights and remedies shall be governed by such laws without regard to principles of conflict of laws.

In witness, the parties have executed this Agreement the day and year first above written.

XYZ, LLC

By:________________________________

(Name of Member One), and Individually

By:________________________________

(Name of Member Two), and Individually

By:________________________________

(Name of Member Three), and Individually

Limited Liability Partnership Agreement of *(Name of Partnership),* L.L.P.

This Limited Liability Partnership Agreement is made and entered into as of the *(date),* by and among **John Doe,** hereinafter called ***Doe,*** **Mary Smith,** hereinafter called ***Smith,*** and **John Roe,** hereinafter called ***Roe,*** each of whom is referred to herein as a *Partner.* The Partners hereby form a limited liability partnership, hereinafter called the *Partnership* under the laws of the State of *(Name of State)* for the purpose of *(describe business of Partnership)* and agree to operate the Partnership pursuant to the terms and provisions hereinafter set forth.

I. Definitions.

A. **Capital Account** means the Capital Account maintained for each Partner pursuant to **Section VII(C).**

B. **Capital Contribution** means, with respect to any Partner, the amount of money and the initial Gross Asset Value of any property (other than money) contributed to the Partnership with respect to the Partnership interest held by such Partner. For purposes of this Paragraph, money contributed to the Partnership does not include increases in any Partner's share of Partnership liabilities pursuant to Code § 752(a).

C. **Code** means the Internal Revenue Code of 1986, as amended from time to time.

D. **Depreciation** means, for each fiscal year or other period, an amount equal to the depreciation, amortization or other cost recovery deduction allowable with respect to an asset for such year or other period, except that if the Gross Asset Value of an asset differs from its adjusted basis for federal income tax purposes at the beginning of such year of other period, Depreciation shall be an amount which bears the same ratio to such beginning Gross Asset Value as the federal income tax depreciation, amortization or other cost recovery deduction for such year or other period bears to such beginning adjusted tax basis; provided, however, that if the federal income tax depreciation, amortization or other cost recovery deductions for such year is zero, Depreciation shall be determined with reference to such beginning Gross Asset Value using any reasonable method selected by a Majority of the Partners.

E. **Gross Asset Value** means, with respect to any asset, the asset's adjusted basis for federal income tax purposes, except as follows:

1. The initial Gross Asset Value of any asset contributed by a Partner to the Partnership shall be the gross fair market value of such asset, as determined by the contributing Partner and the other General Partners;

2. The Gross Asset Values of all Partnership assets shall be adjusted to equal their respective gross fair market values, as determined by the Partners, as of the following times: **(i)** the distribution by the Partnership to a Partner of more than a *de minimis* amount of Partnership Property as consideration for an interest in the Partnership if the Partners shall reasonably determine that such adjustment is necessary or appropriate to reflect the relative economic interests of the Partners in the Partnership; and **(ii)** the liquidation of the Partnership within the meaning of Treas. Regs. § 1.704-1(b)(2)(ii)(g);

3. The Gross Asset Value of any Partnership asset distributed to any Partner shall be the gross fair market value of such asset on the date of distribution as determined by the distributee Partner and the other Partners; and

4. The Gross Asset Values of Partnership assets shall be increased *(or decreased)* to reflect any adjustments to the adjusted basis of such assets pursuant to Code § 734(b) or Code § 743(b), but only to the extent that such adjustments are taken into account in determining Capital Accounts; provided, however, that Gross Asset Values shall not be adjusted pursuant to this paragraph to the extent the Partners determine that an adjustment pursuant to the foregoing Paragraph is necessary or appropriate in connection with a transaction that would otherwise result in an adjustment pursuant to this paragraph. The determination of the Gross Asset Value of an asset shall take into account the premium or discount, if any, of the liabilities associated with such asset. If the Gross Asset Value of an asset has been determined or adjusted pursuant to the foregoing **Subparagraphs B** or **D,** such Gross Asset Value shall thereafter be adjusted by the Depreciation taken into account with respect to such asset for purposes of computing Profits and Losses.

F. **Majority of the Partners** means more than 50% of the Partners.

G. **Net Cash Flow** means for each fiscal year or other period, all revenues *(which do not include refundable deposits or unearned rent)* of the Partnership received in cash during such fiscal period, including Capital Contributions and the net cash proceeds from a sale or other disposition of a Partnership asset, less the sum of **(i)** operating expenses of the Partnership paid in cash during such period, **(ii)** the aggregate of all cash payments during such period with respect to proper liabilities of the Partnership and payments of interest and principal on indebtedness of the Partnership, **(iii)** amounts paid on account of any loans made to the Partnership by any Partner (interest on which shall be at the rate of one (1) percentage point over the then prevailing prime rate of ***(Name and Location of Bank),*** as it varies from time to time, but in no event to exceed the maximum rate permitted by law); and **(iv)** such reserves, if any, as a Majority of the Partners shall agree upon.

H. **Nonrecourse Deductions** has the meaning set forth in § 1.704-2(b)(1) of the Treas.Regs. The amount of Nonrecourse Deductions for a Partnership fiscal year equals the excess of **(i)** net increase, if any, in the amount of partnership minimum gain during that fiscal year over **(ii)** the aggregate amount of any distributions during such fiscal year of proceeds of a nonrecourse liability that are allocated to any increase in partnership minimum gain, determined according to the provisions of § 1.704-2(c) of the Treas.Regs.

I. **Profits and Losses** means, for each fiscal year or other period, an amount equal to the Partnership's taxable income or loss for such year or period, determined in accordance with Code § 703(a) (for this purpose, all items of income, gain, loss or deduction required to be stated separately pursuant to Code § 703(a)(1) shall be included in taxable income or loss), with the following adjustments:

1. Any income of the Partnership that is exempt from federal income tax and not otherwise taken into account in computing Profits or Losses shall be added to such taxable income or loss;

2. Any expenditures of the Partnership described in Code § 705(a)(2)(B) or treated as Code § 705(a)(2)(B) expenditures pursuant to Treas.Regs. § 1.704-1(b)(2)(iv)(b), and not otherwise taken into account in computing Profits or Losses pursuant to this paragraph shall be subtracted from such taxable income or loss;

3. In the event the Gross Asset Value of any Partnership asset is adjusted, the amount of such adjustment shall be taken into account as gain or loss from the disposition of such asset for purposes of computing Profits or Losses;

4. Gain or loss resulting from any disposition of Partnership Property with respect to which gain or loss is recognized for federal income tax purposes shall be computed by reference to the Gross Asset Value of the Property disposed of, notwithstanding that the adjusted tax basis of such property differs from its Gross Asset Value; and

5. In lieu of the depreciation, amortization and other cost recovery deductions taken into account in computing such taxable income or loss, there shall be taken into account Depreciation for such fiscal year or other period.

II. Name. The name of the Partnership shall be **XYZ, LLP.** The business of the Partnership, however, may be conducted under any other name selected unanimously by the Partners.

III. Place of Business; Execution of Lease. The location of the principal place of business of the Partnership, and the place where the records of the Partnership shall be kept, shall be *(street address, city, state, zip code)*, or such other place as may from time to time be designated by a Majority of the Partners. It is agreed that the principal place of business shall be maintained by the Partnership under a lease in the form attached hereto as **Exhibit A,** and each Partner hereby authorizes and ratifies the execution by the Partnership of such lease.

IV. Purpose. The purpose for which the Partnership is organized is to render *(describe),* which shall consist of any and all work or duties within the scope of *(Name of Profession)*, such as *(describe).* Such purposes may not be amended except upon unanimous approval of the Partners.

V. Term. The term of the Partnership shall commence on the date hereof and shall continue until *(date)*, unless earlier terminated in accordance with this Agreement or as otherwise provided by law.

VI. Registration and Renewal. The Partners shall acknowledge and cause to be filed in the Office of the *(Name of State)* Secretary of State a statement of qualification as a limited liability partnership, and annual reports as and when required by applicable law. The Partnership shall cause the publication of the statement of qualification as required by applicable law.

VII. Capital Contributions and Capital Accounts.

A. Capital Contributions. The Partners' Capital Contributions shall consist of:

1. An initial capital contribution of $ ___________ each due immediately upon execution hereof, and

2. Additional Capital Contributions, not to exceed $______________ per Partner in the aggregate, due upon demand therefore by a Majority of the Partners. Any demand for additional Capital Contributions shall be made solely in the discretion of a Majority of the Partners as and when they deem the finances of the Partnership to require such a draw. Further, whenever such a demand is made, an equal amount shall be demanded from each Partner.

B. Default. In the event of a default by any Partner in its contribution obligations, the other Partners shall have the right, but not the obligation, to advance extra capital in accordance with the provisions of **Section XX** hereof.

C. Capital Accounts. The Partnership shall maintain for each Partner a Capital Account in accordance with the rules of Regulations Sections 1.704-1(b) and 1.704-2.

D. Carryover of Capital Account Upon Transfer of Partnership Interest. Upon transfer of all or a part of an interest in the Partnership, the Capital Account of the transferor that is attributable to the transferred interest shall carry over to the transferee partner. Notwithstanding the preceding sentence, if the transfer of an interest in the

Partnership causes a termination of the Partnership under § 708(b)(1)(B) of the Code, the Capital Account that carries over to the transferee partner will be adjusted in accordance with Paragraph (b)(2)(iv)(e) of Treas.Regs. § 1.704-1 in connection with the constructive liquidation of the Partnership under Paragraph (b)(1)(iv) of Treas.Regs. § 1.708-1. The constructive reformation of the Partnership shall, for purposes of this **Section 7** only, be treated as the formation of a new partnership, and the Capital Accounts of the Partners will be determined and maintained accordingly.

VIII. Rights, Powers and Liabilities of the Partners.

A. Management of Partnership Day-to-Day Business. The day-to-day business of the Partnership shall be administered at the direction from time to time of a Majority of the Partners. A Majority of the Partners may effect such administration in any manner deemed appropriate by them in their sole discretion, including, without limitation, the appointment of a Partner as Managing Partner with or without established guidelines for authority and action.

B. Extraordinary Partnership Decisions. All Partnership decisions involving matters other than the day-to-day business of the Partnership, including, without limitation, decisions involving or relating to:

1. The sale, lease or other disposition of any property of the Partnership having a value in excess of $5,000;

2. The purchase or contract to purchase, by the Partnership, of any real property, or any asset or service with a cost to the Partnership in excess of $5,000;

3. The settlement, release or compromise of any claims or debts of or in favor of the Partnership;

4. Any transaction with an affiliate of any Partner;

5. The admission of a new Partner to the Partnership (provided that any new Partner admitted under this subparagraph shall execute a counterpart of this Partnership Agreement and shall agree to be bound by all of the terms and provisions hereof to the same extent as if he or she were an original signatory hereto, except that such new Partner shall have no liability with respect to Partnership liabilities arising prior to such new Partner's admission to the Partnership);

6. Dissolution of the Partnership prior to its stated term; or

7. Any other transaction in connection with which it is anticipated that the Partnership will expend in excess of $5,000, shall, unless a specific provision of this Agreement (such as **Section X** below or **Section IV** above) requires unanimous approval, be made only by the written consent of greater than 75% of the Partners, which consent a Partner may give or withhold in each Partner's sole and absolute discretion. Such consent may be obtained with or without a meeting of all of the Partners.

C. Nonwaiver. Except as expressly set forth in this **Paragraph VIII,** nothing contained herein shall be construed to limit or modify the duty of care, duty of loyalty or obligations of good faith and fair dealing of any partner, provided that:

1. The following categories of activities shall not be construed as a violation of any partner's duty of loyalty: *(describe)*;

2. The following shall prescribe the standard by which the performance of the Partners' duty of care is to be measured: *(describe)*; and

3. The following shall prescribe the standards by which the performance by the partners of the obligations of good faith and fair dealing are to be measured: *(describe)*.

IX. Full Time Service; Competing Activities. Each Partner shall devote all of his or her professional time to the business of the Partnership and shall engage in no competing activity without the written consent of all other Partners. It is agreed that any activity involving *(describe)* or commercial activity substantially related to *(describe)* shall be deemed to be a competing activity. Moreover, it is acknowledged that the pursuit by any Partner of business activities that compete with the business of any client of the Partnership is potentially disadvantageous to the Partnership, and therefore prior to engaging in any such activities, a Partner shall submit a written proposal to the Partnership describing in detail the contemplated activities and shall not pursue such activities without the consent of a Majority of the Partners.

X. Decisions Requiring Unanimous Approval. Notwithstanding any other provision hereof, a decision on any of the following matters shall require the unanimous approval of all of the Partners, which approval a Partner may give or withhold in such Partner's sole and absolute discretion:

A. Amendments of this Agreement, including any amendment to admit a new partner;

B. Any sale or other disposition of substantially all of the assets of the Partnership or disposition of the goodwill of the Partnership's business;

C. Borrowings by the Partnership in excess of $15,000 in the aggregate;

D. Any assignment of the property of the Partnership in trust for creditors or on the assignee's promise to pay the debts of the Partnership;

E. Any act which would make it impossible to carry on the ordinary business of the Partnership; or

F. Any confession of a judgment or submission of a Partnership claim or liability to arbitration or reference.

XI. Income, Gain, Losses and Distributions. All Partnership income, loss, gain and credits for each fiscal year shall be allocated to the Partners in accordance with their **Participation Percentage** as established by the Partnership not later than ninety days following the end of the year in question. The total Participation Percentages shall equal 100%; each Partner shall be assigned a Participation Percentage based on such Partner's contribution to the Partnership for the year in question. The evaluation of each Partner's contribution shall take into consideration, among other things, such Partner's billings and collections for the year in question, the total billed to and collected from clients whose accounts are managed by such Partner, such Partners administrative contribution to the Partnership, and such Partner's years of service to the Partnership. Participation Percentages shall be established by a Majority of the Partners at a meeting held for that purpose. Notwithstanding any other provision hereof, in the absence of willful disregard of Partnership obligations, no Partner shall be assigned a Participation Percentage which, when applied to Partnership income for the year in question would yield income to such Partner in an amount less than such Partner's **Minimum Income Share.** Each Partner's **Minimum Income Share** shall be an amount equal to **(a)** 75% of **(b)** such Partner's income for the previous year multiplied by a fraction, the numerator of which is the Partnership's **Net Income Per Partner** for the year in question and the denominator of which is the

Partnership's **Net Income Per Partner** for the previous year. **Net Income Per Partner** shall be the Partnership's adjusted income for federal income tax purposes divided by the number of Partners for the year in question *(provided that if Partners have been admitted to or left the firm during the year in question, the total number of Partners shall be adjusted appropriately to yield a full time equivalency)*. All distributions by the Partnership shall be made pro rata to the Partners in accordance with Participation Percentages for the year(s) in question.

XII. Books, Records, Accounting, Reports and Certain Tax Matters.

A. Fiscal Year. The fiscal year of the Partnership shall be the calendar year.

B. Books of Account. The Partnership shall keep proper and complete books of account adequate for its purposes. The books of account shall be maintained at its principal place of business and shall be open to inspection and copying by any of the Partners or by their authorized representatives at any reasonable time during business hours. Balance sheets and income reports, audited if requested by any Partner, as well as state and federal income tax returns, shall be prepared at Partnership expense at the end of each fiscal year by *(name of accounting firm)* or such other public accounting firm as hereafter selected by a Majority of the Partners.

C. Basis of Accounting. The Partnership books shall be kept on a cash basis.

D. Bank Accounts. All funds of the Partnership are to be deposited in the Partnership's name in such bank account or money market account or accounts as may be designated by a Majority of the Partners and may be withdrawn for authorized Partnership purposes on the signature of any Partner and such other person or persons as a Majority of the Partners may authorize.

E. Annual Reports. Within seventy-five (75) days after the close of the Partnership's fiscal year, the Partnership shall prepare and mail to each Partner a copy of the Internal Revenue Service Form K-1 as attached to the federal partnership tax return to be filed for the Partnership. Upon request by a Partner, the Partnership will provide such Partner, within ninety (90) days following the end of any fiscal year, a written report setting forth the following:

1. The assets and liabilities of the Partnership;

2. The net income or net loss of the Partnership;

3. Such Partner's Capital Account and the manner of its calculation; and

4. Any other information necessary to enable such Partner to prepare the Partner's individual income tax returns.

F. Meetings. Meetings of the Partners shall be scheduled for mutually convenient times, and each Partner shall have at least twenty-four (24) hours notice of any meeting. Meetings may be called by any Partner. At any meeting, a quorum shall exist only if all Partners are in attendance, either in person or by phone or by written proxy (including a facsimile transmitted proxy) given to a Partner in attendance.

G. Written Minutes. Written minutes of the business transacted at Partnership meetings (if any) shall be made and retained at the Partnership office only if requested by any Partner.

H. Tax Matters Partner. *(Name of Partner)* is hereby appointed as the *tax matters partner* of the Partnership within the meaning of § 6231(a)(7) of the Code.

XIII. Dealing with Affiliates; Business Opportunities. The Partnership shall not enter into any agreements or transactions with, and shall make no payments to, Affiliates of any of the Partners except as otherwise unanimously agreed by the Partners. It is acknowledged that from time to time Partners shall have presented to them, by clients or by third parties, opportunities for investment or active participation in outside business activities. It is further acknowledged that all such opportunities shall initially constitute assets of the Partnership. When presented with any such opportunity, a Partner shall notify the Partnership thereof in writing, and shall include in such notification a recommendation as to whether the Partnership should pursue such opportunity. If the Partnership elects not to pursue the opportunity, the Partner to whom it was presented shall be free to pursue it, subject to the obligations of such Partner hereunder with respect to, among other things, the devotion of substantially all of his or her professional time to the business of the Partnership.

XIV. Transfer of Interests. Except with the prior written consent of all other Partners, no Partner shall sell, assign, convey, hypothecate, encumber or otherwise create in any other party an interest in such Partner's interest in the Partnership, and any attempt to do so shall be void.

XV. Retirement, Withdrawal, Death, Disability, or Bankruptcy of a Partner.

A. Retirement. Each Partner shall be entitled to retire upon reaching the age of 55, and shall be required to retire (unless otherwise agreed in writing by all other Partners) upon reaching age 65. Upon retirement, such Partner's interest in the Partnership shall be redeemed for an amount equal to his or her then-current Capital Account, which amount shall be paid, with interest at 10% per annum, in 120 equal monthly installments.

B. Withdrawal. Any Partner shall have the right to withdraw from the Partnership at any time. If a Partner elects to withdraw prior to age 55, such Partner's interest in the Partnership shall be redeemed for an amount equal to his or her then-current Capital Account, which shall be paid, without interest, as follows: one-half of such balance shall be paid in 60 equal monthly installments; the remaining one-half shall be payable on the fifth anniversary of the date of withdrawal. If a Partner withdraws after age 55, such Partner shall be treated as having retired. Notwithstanding any other provision hereof, a Partner shall be deemed to have withdrawn from the Partnership upon revocation or suspension of his or her license to practice *(Name of Profession)* or the taking of other major disciplinary action against him/her as a *(Name of Profession)* by any governmental or professional authority.

C. Death. Upon the death of a Partner, such Partner's interest in the Partnership shall be redeemed for an amount equal to such Partner's then-current capital account, payable in twenty-four equal monthly installments, with interest at 10% per annum.

D. Disability. If a Partner becomes partially disabled *[i.e., if as a result of injury or illness he or she is unable to engage in the full time practice of (Name of Profession) but is still able to engage in such practice on at least a part-time basis)*, such Partner shall not be required to withdraw from the Partnership, but instead such Partner's interest in Partnership income and loss shall be appropriately adjusted to reflect such Partner's reduced contribution to the Partnership. If a Partner becomes totally disabled (which disability shall be determined by an independent treating physician to prevent the Partner from engaging in the practice of accounting for a period of at least three years) such Partner shall be deemed to have retired from the Partnership on the date of disability, and shall be entitled to payment hereunder for his or her interest in the Partnership as if such retirement had occurred at age 55 or later; provided, however, that if a Partner becomes disabled prior to age 55 and within five years from the date of such disability such Partner shall commence the practice of accounting other than with the Partnership, such payments shall be adjusted so that such Partner shall receive no greater amount than would have been payable had such Partner withdrawn from the Partnership prior to age 55.

XVI. Dissociation and Dissolution

A. Events of Dissociation. A dissociation shall occur upon the occurrence of any event that results in a dissociation with respect to a partner in a partnership at will under *(cite state statute),* or any successor thereto.

B. Effect of Dissociation. If a partner's dissociation does not result in a dissolution under **Section XVI(C)** hereof, then the dissociation shall have the effect set forth in *(cite state statute),* or any successor thereto, and the dissociated partner's interest shall be purchased pursuant to *(cite state statute),* or any successor thereto.

C. Dissolution. The Partnership shall be dissolved:

1. Upon the sale or other disposition of all the assets to which the Partnership has any right, title and interest, and the distribution to the Partners of the cash or cash equivalent proceeds from such sale or other disposition, provided that the Partners acknowledge and agree that upon the sale of substantially all of the Partnership's assets in connection with which the Partnership receives an installment receivable, no such dissolution shall occur until such receivable is paid in full;

2. Upon an order of dissolution by a court of competent jurisdiction or upon any recognized process of dissolution as provided by the laws of the State of *(Name of State);*

3. Upon the occurrence of any event that results in the dissolution of a partnership at will under *(citation of state statute),* or any successor thereto;

4. Upon any partner becoming dissociated by death or for any of the reasons set forth in *(citation of state statute),* or by wrongful dissociation under *(citation of state statute),* unless within 90 days of any such dissociation, a majority of the remaining partners vote to not wind up the Partnership;

5. Upon all of the partners voting to wind up the business of the Partnership;

6. Upon any partner electing to wind up the Partnership after expiration of the term set forth herein; or

7. Upon the occurrence of any event specified in *(citation of state statute).*

XVII. Distribution upon Liquidation. Upon dissolution of the Partnership pursuant to **Section XVI** above and unless, pursuant to **Section XVI(C)** above, the Partnership is not to be liquidated, the Partnership shall be liquidated. Upon liquidation of the Partnership, the assets of the Partnership shall be disposed of pursuant to **Section XVIII** below and the proceeds employed as follows:

A. To liquidate all debts, liabilities and obligations of the Partnership (including debts owed to Partners) and to establish such reserves as a Majority of the Partners deems necessary for the payment of future, contingent or unforeseen liabilities and obligations of the Partnership. If there is a deficit balance in any Partner's capital account upon liquidation of such debts, liabilities and obligations, as determined after taking into account all Capital Account adjustments for the Partnership taxable year during which such liquidation occurs (other than those made pursuant to this **Section XVII**), such Partner shall contribute cash to the Partnership in an amount sufficient to restore such Partner's Capital Account to zero. Such cash contribution shall be made (but in all events prior to the end of the Partnership taxable year in which such liquidation occurred), provided that at the election of a Majority of the Partners (excluding, for purposes of the calculation thereof, the Partner to whom such distribution is to be made) the amount of such distribution may be reduced by the amount to be contributed to restore such Partner's Capital Account to zero, whereupon the full distribution and contribution shall be deemed made. The cash so contributed shall be paid to creditors of the Partnership to the extent necessary to discharge all debts, liabilities and obligations of the Partnership; and then,

B. To distribute the remaining assets or proceeds from the sale thereof to the Partners in proportion to their Capital Account balances, to the extent of any positive balances in such Capital Accounts, as determined after taking into account all Capital Account adjustments for the Partnership taxable year during which such liquidation occurs (other than those made pursuant to this **Section XVII**) (subject, however, to the provisions in **Section XX** hereof). If there is a deficit balance in any Partner's Capital Account following such distribution, such Partner shall contribute cash to the Partnership in an amount sufficient to restore such Partner's Capital Account to zero. Such cash contribution shall be made within ninety (90) days after the date of such liquidation (but in all events prior to the end of the Partnership taxable year in which such liquidation occurred), provided that at the election of a Majority of the Partners (excluding, for purposes of the calculation thereof, the Partner to whom such distribution is to be made) the amount of such distribution may be reduced by the amount to be contributed to restore such Partner's Capital Account to zero, whereupon the full distribution and contribution shall be deemed made. The cash so received by the Partnership shall be distributed to the other Partners in proportion to the positive balances, if any, in their Capital Accounts. During the period of liquidation, the Partnership shall continue to allocate realized income and losses, including those from the disposition of the Partnership properties, in the same manner as before dissolution.

XVIII. Procedures on Liquidation of the Partnership or a Partner's Interest Therein. Promptly following any liquidation of the Partnership, all Partnership receivables and payables shall be liquidated, cash reserves shall be established as agreed by a Majority of the Partners for the payment of unliquidated liabilities, and the Partnership property shall be sold as promptly as possible as is consistent with obtaining the fair value thereof. As soon as practicable thereafter, the then-remaining assets of the Partnership shall be distributed pursuant to **Section XVII** above. The Partnership shall then be terminated, subject only to the execution and filing of any and all necessary instruments required to complete the dissolution, winding up and termination in accordance with the laws of the State of *(name of state)*. Notwithstanding any other provision in this Agreement to the contrary, upon liquidation of any Partner's interest in the Partnership (as defined in Paragraph (b)(2)(ii)(g) of Treas.Regs. § 1.704-1), the liquidating distribution made by the Partnership to such Partner shall be made in accordance with, and shall be equal to, the amount of the positive balance in such Partner's Capital Account, determined after taking into account all Capital Account adjustments for the Partnership taxable year during which such liquidation occurs (other than those made pursuant to this **Section XVIII**) by the end of such taxable year *(or, at the Partnership's election, within 90 days after the date of such liquidation)*.

XIX. Organizational Expenses. All organizational expenses of every kind incurred by the Partnership in connection with the formation of the Partnership (including legal and other expenses but excluding expenses incurred in connection with the formation of any Partner) shall be paid by the Partnership.

XX. Defaulting Partners.

A. Default in Capital Contributions. A defaulting Partner is one who has defaulted in the payment of a Capital Contribution due under the terms of this Agreement and shall be considered as such until the default of such Partner is cured. A Partner shall be considered to have cured the Partner's default only at such time as the Partner has paid to the Partnership the full amount of the Partner's Capital Contributions in default and has paid to all Partners which have advanced extra capital with respect to such default all interest accrued thereon under **Section XXII(D)** hereof. While in default, a Partner shall have no voice or vote whatsoever in the management of the affairs of the Partnership.

B. Right to Advance Extra Capital. In the event any Partner shall fail to advance capital required to be advanced to the Partnership pursuant to the provisions of this Agreement, any or all of the non-defaulting Partner(s) shall have the right (but not the obligation) to advance the capital required to be advanced by the defaulting Partner, pro rata in accordance with the then balances in their Capital Accounts if more than one non-defaulting Partner wishes to make such advances. The sums so advanced to the capital of the Partnership are hereinafter referred to as *extra capital.* The Partner(s) making such advances shall have certain rights against the defaulting Partner as provided below.

C. Extra Drawing Account. A separate drawing account shall be maintained by the Partnership for each Partner which has advanced extra capital, which account shall reflect extra capital advanced by such Partner, the respective date the extra capital is advanced, the date extra capital is withdrawn or otherwise debited to the account, and the identity of the Partner failing to advance the required Capital Contributions. The extra drawing account of any Partner shall not be reduced, changed or affected, except as set forth in **Section XXII(E)** hereof, it being intended that the extra drawing account be kept separate and distinguished from the Capital Account of the Partner maintained in accordance with the provisions of **Section VII** above.

D. Return on Account of Extra Capital. A defaulting Partner shall pay interest on a quarterly basis to any Partner which has advanced extra capital on behalf of the defaulting Partner from the date of the advance until repaid at the higher annual rate from time to time of eighteen percent (18%) per annum or the prime rate of interest charged by *(Name of Bank and Location)*, plus four (4) percentage points, said prime rate to be determined monthly based on the prime rate charged by said bank on the first business day of each month. To the extent the interest is not paid, the distributions to which the defaulting Partner is otherwise entitled under this Agreement shall be paid over to the Partner(s) advancing extra capital on behalf of said defaulting Partner and shall be treated by such non-defaulting Partner(s) as interest income. The defaulting Partner shall treat such payment as interest expense and hereby irrevocably appoints the Managing Partner as the Partner's agent to make such payment. Amounts so distributed to such non-defaulting Partner(s) under this **Subsection (D)** shall be deducted from the Capital Account of the defaulting Partner as a distribution to such defaulting Partner.

E. Extra Capital Distributions. Upon the cure by a defaulting Partner of the Partner's default hereunder, the Capital Contribution made by such defaulting Partner to effect such cure shall be credited to the Partner's Capital Account and shall immediately be distributed to, and charged to the Capital Accounts of, the non-defaulting Partners who advanced extra capital to cure such default, in the same ratio as such non-defaulting Partners advanced such extra capital. Any distributions to which a defaulting Partner is entitled under this Agreement shall, after any payment thereof to the non-defaulting Partner(s) under **Subsection (D)** above, automatically be advanced to the capital of the Partnership to the extent the defaulting Partner is in arrears of amounts required of that Partner. The Partner(s) which advanced extra capital shall thereupon be entitled, at their request to receive distributions of such extra capital in the same ratio as the extra capital was advanced by the non-defaulting Partner(s). In the event the extra capital available for withdrawal is not withdrawn as aforesaid, the extra capital account of the Partners entitled to withdraw the same shall continue to be reflected on the Partnership's books and records and shall remain available for distribution to such Partners upon their request. Such extra capital account shall not bear interest. When distributed, such extra capital shall be charged to the Capital Accounts of the non-defaulting Partners receiving such distribution.

F. **Termination of a Defaulting Partner's Interest.** So long as any Partner shall be in default under the provisions of this Agreement, the non-defaulting Partner(s) may elect to pursue any of the options described below against the defaulting Partner:

1. In the event a defaulting Partner fails, within seven (7) days after receipt of written notice stating that said Partner is in default, to cure said default in full, any non-defaulting Partner(s) may, after five (5) days written notice given to the defaulting Partner and before said default is cured in full, **(A)** expel the defaulting Partner from the Partnership; **(B)** bring suit against the defaulting Partner for the amount in default, together with interest thereon from the day such amount was due at the prime rate of interest charged by *(Name of Bank and Location),* as it varies from time to time, plus four (4) percentage points, and collection expenses, including, without limitation, the fees and disbursements of counsel for the Partnership; and/or **(C)** pursue any other remedy or course of action which the non-defaulting Partners deem to be appropriate.

2. If a Partner is expelled, such expulsion shall be effective without further notice and shall be retroactive to the date the payment was due. A Partner who files a petition in bankruptcy may forthwith be expelled from the Partnership without prior notice or the necessity of any further action by the Partners. Upon the expulsion of any Partner, said Partner shall not have any right to vote or to participate in or receive any net income, net losses, distributions, credits or deductions of the Partnership, commencing with the fiscal year in which such expulsion occurs and thereafter for the term of the Partnership. Notwithstanding any other provision hereof (including the provisions relating to withdrawal from the Partnership) an expelled Partner shall be entitled to the return of its Capital Account in the Partnership, only upon liquidation of the Partnership and after all of the other Partners have received a full distribution of the amount in their Capital Accounts. The rights of an expelled Partner to the return of its Capital Account shall be junior in all respects to those of the remaining Partners.

G. Upon expulsion, the defaulting Partner's interest in the net income and losses of the Partnership shall automatically be reallocated to the non-defaulting Partners in proportion to the balances of their extra capital accounts on the date of expulsion.

H. From and upon the effective date of any expulsion of a Partner hereunder, the Partner(s) who delivered the written notice bringing about such expulsion shall be obligated to make all future Capital Contributions which the expelled Partner would have been obligated to make (provided that such Capital Contributions shall be made pro rata in accordance with the Current Capital Contributions of the Partners so obligated), and such Partner(s) shall be entitled (pro rata in accordance with their Capital Contributions made pursuant to this subsection) to receive all distributions of cash and allocations of income, gain, deduction and loss which the expelled Partner would have been entitled to receive with respect to the Capital Contributions made under this subsection had the expelled Partner not been expelled and had such expelled Partner made such Capital Contributions.

H. No Waiver. Failure of the non-defaulting Partners to promptly exercise any of the rights granted herein for any one default shall not be deemed a waiver of such rights as to such default or any subsequent defaults.

XXI. Employment of the Partners. Each Partner shall be an employee of the Partnership, and with respect to such employment, it is agreed as follows:

A. Salary. No Partner shall receive a salary from the Partnership. Each Partner's compensation shall be limited to his or her share of the income of the Partnership. Each Partnership shall receive a twice-monthly draw of $_________ as an advance against such Partner's share of income for the then-current year. To the extent such draws exceed a Partner's share of income, the excess shall be a charge against such Partner's share of income for the following year.

B. Benefits. The Partnership may from time to time establish various employee benefits, all of which shall apply equally to the Partners. The Partnership shall maintain professional liability insurance in limits of coverage not less than $__________ which shall name each Partner as an additional insured. In the event of any professional liability claim in excess of available insurance coverage, the Partner whose actions gave rise to such claim shall be liable to the Partnership for the full amount of such excess.

C. Vacation. Each Partner shall be entitled to *(number of days)* of vacation per year.

D. Facilities and Support. Each Partner shall be supplied by the Partnership at its expense with reasonable facilities necessary for the effective practice of public accounting, including office facilities, computer and other equipment, access to library and support personnel.

E. Professional Matters. Each Partner shall maintain his or her license to practice public accounting in the State of *(name of state)* in good standing and shall take all actions necessary to ensure that such Partner's professional stature *[including status as a (Name of Profession), which shall be required of all Partners, licensure and any certification or other statement of qualification by a professional organization]* is not impaired. Each Partner shall be entitled to reimbursement from the Partnership for any reasonable expenses incurred in discharging his or her obligations under this Paragraph.

F. Automobile. The Partnership shall provide to each Partner an automobile for such Partner's business and personal use. Each Partner shall be obligated to maintain appropriate automobile insurance, including liability insurance, and shall be obligated to pay the expenses of operating such automobile, including repair expenses.

G. Competition. It is acknowledged that the Partnership will provide to each Partner significant training and will entrust to each Partner significant proprietary information and confidential information regarding its clientele. The Partnership will be irreparably harmed by any Partner who uses such information or benefits from such training in competition with the Partnership within a period of six (6) months after such Partner's withdrawal, resignation or expulsion from the Partnership. Therefore, each Partner covenants and agrees that during his or her time as a Partner and for a period of six months after the termination of his or her time as a Partner for any reason, he or she will not engage in the practice of public accounting anywhere in the State of *(name of state).* In the event of any breach or threatened breach of the foregoing covenant, the Partnership shall have the following remedies, in addition to all other remedies available at law or in equity:

1. The Partnership shall have the right to seek an injunction from any court of competent jurisdiction;

2. The Partnership shall have the right to contact all potential clients of the breaching *(or threatened to be breaching)* Partner and inform such clients of the foregoing covenant and any liability they might have associated with the breach thereof; and

3. The Partnership shall have the right to recover from the breaching party an amount equal to 50% of the gross billings of the breaching Partner generated during the period of his or her breach of the foregoing covenant. Notwithstanding any other provision hereof, if a court should conclude that the foregoing covenant is unenforceable either because of excessive geographic scope or duration, the following shall apply: **(i)** with respect to geographic scope, such covenant shall be deemed to be a severable covenant with respect to each county of the State of *(name of state),* and such covenant shall be reduced in scope by deleting one county at a time (starting with the least populous county and proceeding in inverse order of population) until the covenant is of the greatest permissible geographic scope; and **(ii)** with respect to duration, such covenant shall be deemed to be a severable covenant with respect to each of the 26 weeks following a Partner's withdrawal, resignation or expulsion, and such covenant shall be reduced in scope by deleting one week at a time until the covenant is of the maximum permissible duration.

XXII. Miscellaneous.

A. The invalidity of any portion of this Agreement will not and shall not be deemed to affect the validity of any other provision. If any provision of this Agreement is held to be invalid, the parties agree that the remaining provisions shall be deemed to be in full force and effect as if they had been executed by both parties subsequent to the expungement of the invalid provision.

B. The failure of either party to this Agreement to insist upon the performance of any of the terms and conditions of this Agreement, or the waiver of any breach of any of the terms and conditions of this Agreement, shall not be construed as subsequently waiving any such terms and conditions, but the same shall continue and remain in full force and effect as if no such forbearance or waiver had occurred.

C. This Agreement shall be governed by, construed, and enforced in accordance with the laws of the State of *(name of state).*

D. Unless provided herein to the contrary, any notice provided for or concerning this Agreement shall be in writing and shall be deemed sufficiently given when sent by certified or registered mail if sent to the respective address of each party as set forth at the beginning of this Agreement.

E. In the event that any lawsuit is filed in relation to this Agreement, the unsuccessful party in the action shall pay to the successful party, in addition to all the sums that either party may be called on to pay, a reasonable sum for the successful party's attorney fees.

F. Notwithstanding the foregoing, and anything herein to the contrary, any dispute under this Agreement shall be required to be resolved by binding arbitration of the parties hereto. If the parties cannot agree on an arbitrator, each party shall select one arbitrator and both arbitrators shall then select a third. The third arbitrator so selected shall arbitrate said dispute. The arbitration shall be governed by the rules of the American Arbitration Association then in force and effect.

XXIII. This Agreement shall constitute the entire agreement between the parties and any prior understanding or representation of any kind preceding the date of this Agreement shall not be binding upon either party except to the extent incorporated in this Agreement.

XXIV. Any modification of this Agreement or additional obligation assumed by either party in connection with this Agreement shall be binding only if placed in writing and signed by each party or an authorized representative of each party.

XXV. This Agreement may be executed in any number of counterparts, each of which shall be deemed to be an original, but all of which together shall constitute but one and the same instrument.

XXVI. In performing under this Agreement, all applicable governmental laws, regulations, orders, and other rules of duly-constituted authority will be followed and complied with in all respects by both parties.

XXVII. Incorporation of Documents and Exhibits. All exhibits referred to herein are by this reference made a part hereof as though fully set forth herein.

Witness our signatures this the _____ day of _______________, 20______.

(Signatures of Partners)

Chapter 26

REGULATION OF SECURITIES

Securities were originally regulated at the state level. However, the 1929 Stock Market crash cause Congress to adopt federal statutes which regulated the initial sales of securities *(Securities Act of 1933)* and the secondary trading of stock on the stock markets *(Securities Act of 1934).*

The 1933 Act regulates the initial sale of securities to the public. As will be seen later, some securities are exempt from coverage of the Act. The Act does not specifically define what a security is, but lists approximately 20 items that can be considered to be securities. These include stocks, bonds, mineral interests (like an interest in an oil well), and limited partnership interests.

The landmark case on the definition of a security is the case of *SEC v. Howey Co.* The court in this case defined a security as an *investment* in a common enterprise with *profits* to come from the *efforts* of another. Any investment contract that gives a party to the contract evidence of a debt or a business participation right can be a security covered by the Act. However, the U.S. Supreme Court has excluded pension plans from the definition of a security when employees are not required to contribute to the plan.

Some types of securities are exempt from the extensive registration and filing requirements of the Act. For example:

- Bonds issued by federal, state, county, or municipal governments;
- Commercial paper (e.g., promissory notes) with a maturity of less than nine months;
- Securities issued by banks and charitable organizations;
- Insurance policies;
- Annuities;
- Securities issued by common carriers; The ICC regulates these securities; and
- Stock dividends and stock splits

Certain stock issue transactions are also exempt (i.e., exempt from registration with the *Securities and Exchange Commission)* . The most common exempt transaction that close corporations take advantage of is the *intrastate offering.* To qualify for this exemption, both the investors and the issuer must all be residents of the same state. The issuer must also meet the following requirements:

- 80% of its assets must be located in the state;
- 80% of its income must be earned from operations within the state; and
- 80% of the proceeds from the sale must be used on operations within the state.

Also, for nine months after the issuance, the stock can only be sold to state residents.

Exemptions from SEC registration and filing requirements can save a great deal of accounting and legal expenses.

Some Key Terms: The term "subscription" is applied both to agreements to take stock in a prospective corporation yet to be organized and to agreements to purchase unsold and unissued stock in an organized corporation that is a going concern and that is putting its stock on the market to raise funds. Such subscription agreements are included within the definition of "security" provided by the Securities Act of 1933, as amended, and such securities, as separate and distinct from the securities that may be subsequently delivered pursuant to the terms of such contract, are also subject to all applicable provisions of the Act. The term "issuer," within the meaning of the above definition of underwriter, is expressly stated in such definition to include, in addition to issuer, any person directly or indirectly controlling or controlled by such an issuer, or any person under direct or indirect common control of such an issuer. Underwriting arrangements between an issuer or controlling person of an issuer and any underwriter, or among underwriters prior to the publication and issuance of a security are specifically excluded from the registration requirements of the Securities Act of 1933, as amended

SEC Regulation A is not really an exemption even though it is referred to as a *small offering exemption.* It is really a shortcut method of registering. A short-form registration statement called an S-1 is filed. This regulation applies to issues of $1.5 million or less during any 12-month period. The SEC can group more than one issue within a year. This could cause the exemption to be lost. For example, three registrations of $600,000 each would not qualify for Regulation A if done in a twelve-month period.

Regulation D creates a three-tiered exemption structure that consists of Rules 504, 505, and 506, and permits sales of securities without registration. However, Sellers are required to file a Form D informational statement about the sale. The definition of *accredited investor* is important regarding this exemption as far as a limitation on the number of shareholders allowed (i.e., 35). Accredited investors do not have to be counted as far as the 35 limitation is concerned. An accredited investor includes any investor who at the time of the sale falls into any of the following categories:

- a private business development firm;
- directors, officers, and general partners of issuer;
- banks;
- purchasers of $150,000 or more of the securities;
- natural persons with a net worth greater than $1,000,000; and
- persons with an income of greater than or equal to $200,000 per year.

Regulation D places limits on advertising the securities and restrictions on the sale of the securities to prevent sales within a short period of time after issuance.

The *Rule 504* exemption applies to offerings of $500,000 or less within any 12-month period. Sales to directors, officers, and employees are not counted in the $500,000 limitation. Sales of up to $1,000,000 are allowed if the offering is registered under a state securities statute, commonly called *Blue Sky Laws.* The term *Blue Sky* comes from the purpose of these laws, which is to prevent the sale of speculative schemes that *have no more value than a small area of blue sky.* These statutes commonly contain an antifraud provision which prohibits fraudulent practices and imposes criminal penalties for violations. Also, the statutes contain broker-dealer licensing provisions and provide for the registration of securities, including disclosure statements, with a designated governmental official. This official in Mississippi is the Secretary of State. These Blue Sky Laws apply only to intrastate transactions and do not apply to sales made in interstate commerce.

The *Rule 505* exemption covers sales of up to $7.5 million provided there are no more than 35 non-accredited investors. A *prospectus* must be given to all buyers if both accredited and non-accredited investors are involved. A prospectus is a document given to prospective purchasers of a security that contains information about the issuer of the securities and the securities being issued.

The *Rule 506* exemption has no dollar limitation, but the number of investors and the type of investors are limited. There can be any number of accredited investors, but only 35 or less unaccredited investors. These unaccredited investors must be *sophisticated*, which has been defined as being capable of evaluating the offering and the risks involved.

Stock issued pursuant to a Chapter 11 bankruptcy reorganization are also exempt from registration.

If none of the exemptions apply, then the issuer must go through the registration process. The issuer must first file a *registration statement* and a sample prospectus with the SEC. The SEC has 20 days from the date of filing to act. If no action is taken, then the registration statement automatically becomes effective. However, the SEC always acts within this 20 day period. It does not have to approve or disapprove of the offering within that time period as long as a comment or deficiency letter is issued. This letter requires additional information or clarification on the proposed offering. It generally takes about six months for a new registration to get through the SEC.

The SEC follows a *full disclosure standard* in reviewing the registration materials. This means that the SEC makes no judgment as to the soundness of the investments, but just makes sure that certain information is disclosed.

The information required in a registration consists of:

- a description of the securities;
- an audited financial statement;
- a list of assets of the issuing corporation;
- the nature of the business; and
- identification of the management of the issuer.

Before the registration statement is effective, something called a *tombstone ad* can be run. This is basically an announcement that an issuance will be made, but is not an offer to sale. Also, a sample prospectus call a *red herring* can be issued. There must be a notice in red print that the registration is not effective yet.

Section 11 of the 1933 Act provides for civil liability for inaccurate information in the registration statement. A violation occurs when there is a failure to make a full disclosure or the registration statement contains a material misstatement or omission. People who could possibly be liable under Section 11 include:

- officers,
- directors,
- independent contractors who provided information used in preparing the statement, and
- anyone who signed the registration.

Defenses for Section 11 violations would include:

- immaterial misstatements,
- situations where the investor knew of the misstatement but bought the security anyway,
- due diligence, i.e., the accused party acted with prudence and had no reason to believe that there was a problem. An officer or director would have to show that he had no reason to know of the omission or misstatement.

The Act imposes criminal penalties on anyone who willfully makes untrue statements of material facts or omits required material facts in the registration statement. The maximum criminal penalty is $10,000 and/or five years in jail.

The *Securities Litigation Reform Act of 1995* was passed to stop frivolous suits by "professional plaintiffs." This Act limits attorneys' fees and allows some leeway *(safe harbor protection)* regarding financial predictions in connection with the registration statement.

Section 12 of the 1933 act is a first cousin to Section 11. A Section 12 violation would include:

- selling the securities without registration (unless they are exempt),
- selling before the effective date of the registration statement; and
- false information in the prospectus.

The penalties for Section 12 violations are the same as for Section 11.

The Securities Exchange Act of 1934 is concerned with the secondary distribution of securities on the security exchanges and in over-the-counter markets. Its purpose is to prevent fraudulent practices on the security exchanges and in over-the-counter markets. The exchanges, brokers, and dealers who deal in the securities traded in interstate commerce or on any national security exchange must register with the SEC unless exempted.

All traded securities on exchanges must be registered with the SEC. Also all securities of firms with over $5 million in assets and 750 or more shares must be registered if they are traded in interstate commerce. This registration is somewhat different than 1933 Act registration. The

1933 Act requires issuers to register issuances of securities and these securities are registered only for the term of an issuance. Under the 1934 Act, registered classes of securities remain registered until the issuer takes steps to deregister the securities. The information required in a 1934 registration statement is similar to 1933 Act registration, except the offering information is not included.

In order to maintain a steady flow of material information to investors, the 1934 Act requires public issuers to file periodic reports with the SEC. The *10-K* report is the principal annual report form. This report consists of nonfinancial information about the registrant's activities during the year, such as the nature of the company's business, the property it owns and a statement concerning any legal proceedings by or against the company. The report also includes financial statements with an analysis by management of the financial condition of the company. It also requires a listing of all directors and executive officers and a disclosure of executive compensation information.

If you are required to file a 10-K, the you must also file a *10-Q* on a quarterly basis with quarterly financial information. A monthly report called a *Form 8-K* must be filed when unusual events occur such as spin-offs, bankruptcies and takeovers.

SEC Rule 10b-5 is the principal antifraud rule relating to secondary sales of securities. It is derived from section 10(b) of the 1934 Act which is basically a statutory version of common law fraud. SEC Rule 10b-5 generally prohibit the use of any manipulative, deceptive, or fraudulent scheme or device in connection with the initial issuance or resale of securities in interstate commerce. The 1934 Act antifraud provisions apply to an offer to sell or sale of any security involving the use of the mail, interstate commerce, or a national stock exchange. The 1934 Act applies to both sellers and buyers of securities. A civil action for damages may be brought by any injured party who purchased or sold securities because of false, misleading or undisclosed information. Criminal penalties may be levied because of willful violations.

A failure to give relevant information or giving overly pessimistic information in connection with a sale could result in a violation of Rule 10b-5. The SEC may bring an action against any individual purchasing or selling a security while in the possession of material, inside information. The sanction for trading on inside information can be a civil penalty of up to three times the profit gained or loss avoided as a result of the unlawful sale. Examples of *insiders* would be a director or corporate employee, or a temporary insider retained by the corporation for professional services, such as an attorney, accountant, or investment banker. Insiders are liable for inside trading when the insider fails to disclose material, nonpublic information before trading on it, and thus makes a secret profit. For example in the *SEC v. Texas Gulf Sulphur* case some insiders in a corporation failed to disclose a rich mineral strike prior to buying a chunk of stock. Of course they made a profit. Another example would be buying stock while failing to disclose a pending merger that you as an officer of the company knew about in advance. Any insider who trades based on nonpublic information and makes a profit or avoids a loss because of that information can be liable under 10b-5.

Tippees can also be held liable for trading on inside information. A tippee is a person who is privy to inside information from an insider about a corporation or its securities and uses the information to trade securities and makes a profit as a result of this information.

What should be disclosed? Ask yourself if this is the type of information that would affect a buying or selling decision regarding stock. Examples:

- pending takeovers
- drops in quarterly earnings
- a pending large dividend
- possible major litigation

There must be a breach of fiduciary duty to shareholders before an insider is liable. The tippee does not breach 10b-5 unless he gets information from the insider who breaches a fiduciary duty and the tippee gets financial benefit.

Before a civil action can be brought under 10b-5, the plaintiff must have been an actual purchaser or seller of the stock. The plaintiff must also prove intent to defraud. In a criminal case, the fine can be up to $100,000 and a defendant can be imprisoned for up to five years per violation.

Section 16 of the 1934 Act deals with *insider trading* and *short swing profits.* Corporate officers, directors and shareholders of more than 10% of the stock in a company have greater access to inside information than your average person. These officers, directors and shareholders are liable to the corporation for profits made on sales and purchases during any six month period. There are also certain reporting requirements under the Act.

Section 14 of the 1934 Act deals with the regulation of proxy materials. The idea is to have full disclosure in proxy materials. Proxy materials must be filed with the SEC disclosing:

- who is soliciting the proxy;
- how the materials will be sent;
- who is paying for the solicitation;
- how much is being spent on the solicitation;
- what the purpose of the proxy is, e.g., an annual meeting for an election of directors.

Shareholders can submit proposals to be included in proxy solicitation materials. If the company opposes what the shareholders propose, the shareholders have the right of a 200 word statement on the proposal to be included in the proxy materials. However, proposals are not permitted unless they propose something that is legal and related to the business operations of the company. Social, moral, religious, and political views are not permitted. For example, during the Vietnam war many shareholders wanted to state their views on the war if the company was a supplier of goods or services to the war. This was inappropriate.

Compensation to the executives of corporations has become a major concern of shareholders. The SEC has passed disclosure rules on executive compensation which includes the requirement of a series of charts on the firm's financial performance and a summary of the pay of the top five officers of the company.

If proxies are solicited without following Section 14 guidelines, the proxies are invalid. Actions taken at a meeting where the invalid proxies were used can be set aside.

The *Foreign Corrupt Practices Act* was passed as an amendment to the 1934 Act. It was passed because of bribe activity from U.S. companies to foreign officials. This Act regulates accounting procedures that would make it easy to hide bribes. It prohibits bribes except so-called *grease payments* which is the paying of officials to get them to do their jobs. You are not trying to get them to do anything improper, but are "hurrying them along."

The penalty for violation is a $10,000 fine and/or a five year prison sentence. There is a $100,000 fine available for willful violations by individuals and a $1,000,000 fine available for companies.

Many blue sky laws, like Mississippi's, follow the SEC standard of full disclosure. If the filing is made with a full disclosure of information, then it is lawful regardless of whether or not the investment is any good. States that follow a merit standard basically say that the offering must be "fair, just, and equitable."

States have their own exemptions from registration. Mississippi follows the 1933 Act. States like Mississippi also regulate brokers and dealers.

Chapter 27
MANAGEMENT OF THE CORPORATION

INTRODUCTION
Sometimes, actions that benefit a corporation as a whole do not coincide with the separate interests of the individuals making up the corporation. In considering those situations, it is important for your students to be aware of the rights and duties of the participants in the corporate enterprise.

This chapter focuses on the rights and duties of directors, managers, and shareholders and the ways in which conflicts between and among them are resolved. The duty of care and duty of loyalty owed by directors, the business judgment rule and the immunity it provides directors from honest mistakes, and the duty owed by majority shareholders to the corporation and minority shareholders are among the topics.

ROLES OF DIRECTORS AND OFFICERS
Directors act for and on behalf of their corporation, but no individual director can act as an agent to bind the corporation, and directors collectively control a corporation in a way that no agent can control a principal. Directors hold positions of trust and control over their corporation, but, unlike trustees, they do not own or hold title to property for the use and benefit of others.

ELECTION OF DIRECTORS
The number of directors is stated in the articles or bylaws. Close corporations may eliminate the board altogether. The incorporators, or the corporation in the articles, appoint the first board, which serves until the first shareholders' meeting. A majority vote of the shareholders elects subsequent directors. Directors typically serve for a year or more.

REMOVAL OF DIRECTORS
A director can be removed for cause (and usually not without cause).

VACANCIES ON THE BOARD OF DIRECTORS
A vacancy can occur through a director's death or resignation or if a new position is created.

COMPENSATION OF DIRECTORS
There is no inherent right to compensation, but many states permit the articles or bylaws to authorize it, and in some cases the board can set its own. Directors may set their own compensation [RMBCA 8.11]. A director who is also a corporate officer is an inside director. A director who does not hold a management position is an outside director.

BOARD OF DIRECTORS' MEETINGS
The dates for regular board meetings are set in the articles and bylaws or by board resolution, without further notice. A quorum is generally a majority of the number of authorized directors. Each director has a vote [RMBCA 8.24] Ordinary matters require majority approval; certain extraordinary matters may require more.

RIGHTS OF DIRECTORS

The main right is participation in management, which includes a right to be notified of board meetings, and to have access to all corporate books and records. Most states (and RMBCA 8.51) permit a corporation to indemnify a director for costs, fees, and judgments in defending corporation-related suits.

THE TIMING OF DIRECTORS' ACTIONS IN AN ELECTRONIC AGE

Corporate directors can hold special board meetings to deal with extraordinary matters, provided that they give proper notice to all members of the board. If a special meeting is called without giving sufficient notice to all of the directors, are the resolutions made at that meeting invalid? If so, can the directors validate these resolutions by holding a second special board meeting with proper notice? In today's electronic age, matters of timing can be complicated and can affect a variety of other issues, including the effective date of a director's resignation and the validity of a resolution appointing a new director.

COMMITTEES OF THE BOARD OF DIRECTORS

Executive Committee

Most states permit a board to elect an executive committee from among the directors to handle management between board meetings. The committee is limited to ordinary business matters.

Audit Committee

Selects, compensates, and oversees independent public accountants who audit the firm's financial records under the Sarbanes-Oxley Act of 2002.

NOMINATING COMMITTEE

Chooses candidates on which shareholders vote for the board of directors

COMPENSATION COMMITTEE

Sets salaries and benefits for corporate executives and may determine directors' compensation.

LITIGATION COMMITTEE

Decides whether to pursue litigation on behalf of the corporation.

CORPORATE OFFICERS AND EXECUTIVES

The board normally hires officers; qualifications are set in the articles or bylaws; rights are defined by employment contracts. One person can hold more than one office and be both an officer and a director. Officers' duties are the same as those of directors. Directors and officers are corporate fiduciaries.

DUTY OF CARE

The duty of care includes acting in good faith and in the best interests of the corporation, and exercising the care that an ordinarily prudent person would use in similar circumstances [RMBCA 8.30(a), 8.32(a)]. Breach of the duty may result in liability for negligence.

DUTY TO MAKE INFORMED AND REASONABLE DECISIONS

Directors must be informed on corporate matters and act in accord with their knowledge and training. A director can rely on information furnished by competent officers, or others, without being accused of acting in bad faith or failing to exercise due care. Directors must exercise reasonable supervision when work is delegated. Directors must attend board meetings; if not, he or she should register a dissent to actions taken (to avoid liability for mismanagement).

THE BUSINESS JUDGMENT RULE

Directors and officers are immune from liability when a decision is within managerial authority, as long as the decision complies with management's fiduciary duties, acting on the decision is within the powers of the corporation, there is a reasonable basis for the decision, and no conflict of interest.

DUTY OF LOYALTY

Directors and officers must subordinate their self-interest to the interest of the corporation. This means no self-dealing, no usurping corporate opportunities, etc.

CONFLICTS OF INTEREST

Directors and officers must fully disclose any potential conflict of interest. After full disclosure, the individual may go ahead if the other directors or shareholders approve (assuming the circumstances are otherwise fair and reasonable).

LIABILITY OF DIRECTORS AND OFFICERS

Directors and officers are personally liable for their torts and crimes, and may be liable for those of subordinates (under the "responsible corporate officer" doctrine or the "pervasiveness of control" theory). The corporation is liable for acts done within the scope of employment.

What must directors do to avoid liability for honest mistakes of judgment and poor business decisions? Directors and officers must exercise due care in performing their duties. They are expected to be informed on corporate matters. They are expected to act in accord with their own knowledge and training. Directors are expected to exercise a reasonable amount of supervision when they delegate work to others. Directors are expected to attend board of directors' meetings. In general, directors and officers must act in good faith, in what they consider to be the best interests of the corporation, and with the care that an ordinarily prudent person in a similar position would exercise in similar circumstances. This requires an informed decision, with a rational basis, and with no conflict between the decision maker's personal interest and the interest of the corporation.

ROLE OF SHAREHOLDERS

A shareholder is the owner of the corporation in which he or she holds shares but has no right to manage the firm, and does not have title to its property. There is no legal relationship between a shareholder and a creditor of the corporation (unless, of course, the shareholder is a creditor of the corporation). Shareholders have the power to choose the board of directors, but are owed no special duty individually.

SHAREHOLDERS' POWERS

Shareholders approve fundamental changes to the corporation before the changes are affected. Shareholders elect the board and may remove a director (in some cases, without cause).

SHAREHOLDERS' MEETINGS

NOTICE OF MEETINGS

Shareholders must be notified of shareholders' meetings [RMBCA 7.05]. Special-meeting notices must include a statement of the purpose of the meeting; business transacted at a special meeting is limited to that purpose.

Proxies: Shares are often voted by proxy. Shareholders that own stock worth at least $1,000 can submit proposals to include with proxy materials. The materials may be furnished online.

Why might a company or other party choose to solicit proxies the old-fashioned way, by providing paper documents instead of Internet access despite the added costs? Reasons to provide proxy materials in a paper format include chiefly the personal preference of the shareholders and other corporate participants. There may have at one time been a technological impediment—the company or its owners may not have had access to, or known how to use, compatible technology.

CONDUCTING SHAREHOLDERS' MEETINGS

Corporate articles or bylaws may provide for the conduct of shareholders' meetings. Typically, the company president or the chairperson of the board of directors presides, and the corporate secretary records the minutes of the meeting. The agenda may include reports of management, the amendment or repeal of bylaws, resolutions submitted on behalf of management or shareholders, extraordinary corporate matters or decisions that require shareholder approval, and other subjects. Shareholders can offer and respond to proposals and resolutions. For example, shareholders concerned about social and political issues have used shareholders meetings to propose changes in corporate activities that relate to the issues.

SEC Rule 14a-8 – SEC RULE 14A-8 requires that when a company sends proxy materials to its shareholders, the company must include whatever proposals will be considered at the meeting. Section 14(a) of the 1934 act regulates management's solicitation of proxies from shareholders of section 12 companies. There must be full and accurate disclosure. Sec rule 14a-9 is similar to the antifraud provisions of rule 10b-5. Remedies for violation range from enjoining a shareholder vote to damages.

SHAREHOLDER VOTING

QUORUM REQUIREMENTS

A shareholder quorum is generally more than 50 percent. (Unanimous written, shareholder consent is, in some states, a permissible alternative to a shareholders' meeting.) A majority vote of the shares at the meeting is usually required to pass resolutions. Extraordinary corporate matters, require the approval of a higher percentage of shares entitled to vote, not just a majority of those present at a meeting.

VOTING LISTS

Persons whose names appear on the corporation's records as owners, as of a record date, are entitled to vote.

CUMULATIVE VOTING

In most states, shareholders elect directors by cumulative voting; otherwise, the vote is by a majority of shares at the meeting.

OTHER VOTING TECHNIQUES

Shares can be voted in accord with a shareholder voting agreement or voting trust.

Why is disclosure to the shareholders considered significant? Disclosure in any fiduciary situation is considered important and is emphasized repeatedly in the duties that, for example, an agent is said to owe a principal. Shareholders are the owners of their corporations. Without disclosure, a shareholder (or any party to whom disclosure is due) is making a decision that he or she might decide another way if the "full story" were revealed.

What is a voting proxy? A proxy is written authorization given by a shareholder to a third party to vote the shareholder's shares at a shareholders' meeting.

What is cumulative voting? Cumulative voting is a method of voting designed to allow minority shareholders representation on the board of directors. The number of members of the board to be elected is multiplied by the number of voting shares a shareholder owns.

RIGHTS AND LIABILITIES OF SHAREHOLDERS

RIGHTS OF SHAREHOLDERS

STOCK CERTIFICATES

In jurisdictions that require the issuance of stock certificates, shareholders can demand a certificate and demand that their names and addresses be recorded in the corporate record books. In most states, shares can be uncertified. Notice of shareholder meetings, dividends, and reports are distributed according to the ownership listed in the corporation's books, not on the basis of possession of a certificate.

PREEMPTIVE RIGHTS

The articles of incorporation determine the existence and scope of preemptive rights. Generally, they apply only to additional, newly issued stock sold for cash and must be exercised within a specified time period. Preemptive rights are most significant in a close corporation because of the relatively few number of shares and the substantial interest each shareholder controls.

STOCK WARRANTS

When preemptive rights exist and a corporation is issuing additional shares, each shareholder is given transferable options to acquire a given number of shares from the corporation at a stated price. Warrants are often publicly traded on securities exchanges.

Dividends: Dividends can be paid in cash, property, stock of the corporation that is paying the dividends, or stock of other corporations.

ILLEGAL DIVIDENDS

A dividend paid while a corporation is insolvent is illegal and must be repaid if the shareholders knew that it was illegal when they received it. Directors may be personally liable for paying such a dividend.

From what sources may dividends be paid legally? In what circumstances is a dividend illegal? What happens if a dividend is illegally paid? Depending on state law, dividends may be paid from retained earnings, current net profits, and any surplus. A dividend paid while the corporation is insolvent is an illegal dividend. Dividends improperly paid from an unauthorized account are illegal. Shareholders must return illegal dividends if they knew that the dividends were illegal when they received them. Whenever dividends are illegal or improper, the board of directors can be held personally liable for the amount of the payment.

Directors' Failure to Declare a Dividend

That corporate earnings or surplus is available to pay a dividend is not enough for a court to compel directors to distribute funds that, in the board's opinion, should not be paid. Abuse of discretion must be clearly shown.

Directors' Failure to Declare a Dividend

In Dodge v. Ford Motor Co., 204 Mich. 459, 170 N.W. 668 (1919), in the interest of setting aside money for future investment and expansion, the Ford Motor Co. announced that it would pay no special dividends after October 1915, even though surplus capital in 1916 exceeded $111 million. The minority stockholders, who owned one-tenth of the shares of the corporation, petitioned a Michigan state court to compel the directors to declare a dividend. The court ordered the payment, and the defendants appealed. The Supreme Court of Michigan affirmed. The court determined that a declaration of dividends would not be a detriment to Ford's business and that continued failure to declare such a dividend in view of the large capital surplus could amount to such an abuse of discretion as to constitute fraud. The court, however, refused to specify an amount, perhaps recognizing that it was getting too deeply involved in a matter beyond its scope of expertise. In any event, the court concluded that there was some unspecified point beyond which a corporation could not continue hoarding its cash but instead had to pay out a dividend.

This case is a striking exception to the general rule that directors should not ordinarily be forced to declare dividends to stockholders. Courts are usually very reluctant to become involved in such issues because there is no clear answer as to when the capital surplus of the corporation is so large that the board of directors should be required to declare a dividend. Certainly the contents of this opinion do not suggest that the court engaged in extensive calculations in determining the proper dividend payable to shareholders. In the absence of some evidence of fraud, would it be better to give the directors complete discretion in deciding when to declare dividends to shareholders (assuming that there is adequate capitalization)?

INSPECTION RIGHTS

The shareholder's right of inspection is limited to the inspection and copying of corporate books and records for a proper purpose, provided the request is made in advance. A shareholder can be denied access to prevent harassment or to protect trade secrets or other confidential corporate information.

TRANSFER OF SHARES

Although stock certificates are negotiable and freely transferable, transfer of stock in closely held corporations is generally restricted by contract, the bylaws, or a restriction stamped on the certificate. Any restrictions on transferability (which typically include a right of first refusal) must be noted on the face of the certificate.

RIGHTS ON DISSOLUTION

When a corporation is dissolved and its debts and the claims of its creditors have been satisfied, the remaining assets are distributed on a pro rata basis among the shareholders. Certain classes of preferred stock can be given priority.

THE SHAREHOLDER'S DERIVATIVE SUIT

If directors fail to sue in the corporate name to redress a wrong suffered by the corporation, shareholders can bring a suit. Some wrong must have been done to the corporation, and any damages recovered usually go into the corporation's treasury.

A BRIEF HISTORY OF DERIVATIVE SUITS

The right of shareholders to sue derivatively on the behalf of their corporation was indicated as early as the 1830s. In 1855, the United States Supreme Court upheld a shareholder's right to sue on behalf of a corporation whose officer had paid a tax that the shareholder claimed was unconstitutional [Dodge v. Woolsey, 59 U.S. 331, 15 L.Ed. 401 (1855)].

The derivative suit developed more fully in the second half of the nineteenth century. Procedural restrictions on derivative suits also developed in the federal courts late in the nineteenth century and in the state courts in the first half of the twentieth century. In 1980, at least one study found that during the 1970s, there was only a slight increase in the amount of shareholder litigation.[24] During the 1980s, however, the amount of shareholder derivative litigation for alleged breaches of management duties was extensive. Today, most of the claims brought against directors and officers in the United States are those alleged in shareholders' derivative suits. Other nations, however, put more restrictions on the use of such suits. German law, for example, does not provide for derivative litigation, and a corporation's duty to its employees is just as significant as its duty to the shareholder-owners of the company. The United Kingdom has no statute authorizing derivative actions, which are permitted only to challenge directors' actions that the shareholders could not legally ratify. Japan authorizes derivative actions but also permits a company to sue the plaintiff-shareholder for damages if the action is unsuccessful.

---

[24] Jones, "An Empirical Examination of the Incidence of Shareholder Derivative and Class Action Lawsuits, 1971–1978," 60 Boston University Law Review 306 (1980).

If a group of shareholders perceives that the corporation has suffered a wrong and the directors refuse to take action, can the shareholders compel the directors to act? If so, how? The shareholders cannot compel the directors to act to redress a wrong suffered by the corporation, but if the directors refuse to act, the shareholders can act on behalf of the firm by filing what is known as a shareholder's derivative suit. Any damages recovered by the suit normally go into the corporation's treasury, not to the shareholders personally.

LIABILITIES OF SHAREHOLDERS
Shareholders are not usually personally liable for the debts of a corporation.

WATERED STOCK
A shareholder may be liable if he or she receives watered stock without paying the share's stated value. In that case, the shareholder may be liable to the corporation for the difference between the price paid and the stock's stated value, and to creditors for corporate debts.

DUTIES OF MAJORITY SHAREHOLDERS
A majority shareholder has a fiduciary duty to the corporation and to the minority shareholders when he or she (or a few shareholders acting together) owns enough shares to exercise de facto control over the corporation.

MAJOR BUSINESS FORMS COMPARED
The most appropriate form for doing business depends on the characteristics, tax status, and goals of an enterprise.

REVIEW

Why is it incorrect to characterize a director as either an agent or a trustee of a corporation? Even though directors act for and on behalf of the corporation, no individual director can act as an agent to bind the corporation. Moreover, directors, as a group, collectively control the corporation in a way that no agent can control a principal. Directors are also often incorrectly characterized as trustees because they occupy positions of trust and control over the corporation. Unlike trustees, however, directors do not own or hold title to property for the use and benefit of others.

What are the most common situations in which directors allegedly violate their duty of loyalty? A director typically breaches his or her duty of loyalty when he or she (1) competes with the corporation; (2) usurps a corporate opportunity; (3) has an interest that conflicts with the interest of the corporation; (4) engages in insider trading; (5) authorizes a corporate transaction that is detrimental to minority shareholders; and (6) sells control over the corporation.

What actions must a director or officer take to avoid liability when a corporation enters into a contract or engages in a transaction in which an officer or director has a material interest? The director or officer must make a full disclosure of the interest and must abstain from voting on the proposed transaction. Although standards vary from state to state, a contract will generally not be voidable if it was fair and reasonable to the corporation at the time the contract was made, there was a full disclosure of the interest of the officers or directors involved in the transaction, and the contract is approved by a majority of the disinterested directors or shareholders.

What sort of legal protection is offered to directors and officers by the business judgment rule? The business judgment rule immunizes directors and officers from liability when a decision is within managerial authority, as long as the decision complies with management's fiduciary duties and as long as acting on the decision is in the power of the corporation. To benefit from the rule, directors and officers must act in good faith, in what they consider to be the best interests of the corporation, and with the care that an ordinarily prudent person in a like position would exercise in similar circumstances. This requires a rational, informed decision having no conflict between the decision-maker's personal interest and the interest of the corporation.

Are directors entitled to be indemnified for any legal costs they incur in defending suits against the corporation? Because directors are often named as defendants in suits filed against their respective corporations, most states permit corporations to indemnify directors for any reasonable legal costs, fees and judgments involved in defending corporation-related suits. Many states expressly allow a corporation to purchase liability insurance for its directors and officers to indemnify them for any costs or damages. When statutes are silent on this matter, the power to purchase such insurance is usually considered to be part of the corporation's implied power.

What are some of the more important powers that may be exercised by shareholders? Shareholders must approve fundamental changes affecting the corporation before the changes can be effected. Hence, shareholders are empowered to amend the articles of incorporation (charter) and bylaws, approve the merger or dissolution of the corporation, and approve the sale of all or substantially all of the corporation's assets. The shareholders also elect and remove the board of directors. Some states require that the removal of directors be for cause but other states will allow a director to be removed without cause.

Describe how cumulative voting works. Most states permit or require shareholders to elect directors by cumulative voting - a method of voting designed to allow minority shareholders representation on the board of directors. The number of members of the board to be elected is multiplied by the total number of voting shares held. The result equals the number of votes a shareholder may cast. This total can be cast for one or more nominees for director.

What are the limits on the shareholder's right to inspect corporate records and books? A shareholder is limited to inspecting and copying corporate records and books for a proper purpose if the request is made in advance. The shareholder can properly be denied access to corporate records to prevent harassment or to protect trade secrets or other confidential information. Furthermore, the right of inspection may be conditioned on the shareholder possessing his or her shares for a minimum period of time prior to his making the demand to inspect the records.

What are some of the ways in which a corporation or its shareholders can restrict the transferability of shares? A corporation or its shareholders can restrict transferability by reserving the option to purchase any shares offered for resale by a shareholder. This right of first refusal remains with the corporation or the shareholders for only a specified or reasonable time. Alternatively, a shareholder could be required to offer the shares to other shareholders or to the corporation first.

Can a shareholder institute an action to dissolve a corporation and liquidate its assets?
Yes. In some states, a shareholder has the right to petition a court to appoint a receiver and to liquidate the business assets of the corporation in certain specified situations. A shareholder may institute a dissolution action if (1) the directors are deadlocked in the management of corporate affairs, shareholders are unable to break that deadlock, and irreparable injury to the corporation is being suffered or threatened; (2) the acts of the directors or those in control of the corporation are illegal, oppressive, or fraudulent; (3) corporate assets are being misapplied or wasted; or (4) the shareholders are deadlocked in voting power and have failed to elect successors to directors whose terms have expired or would have expired with the election of successors.

How do the duty of care and the duty of loyalty govern the conduct of directors and officers in a corporation?

Duty of Care. In exercising their duty of care, directors are obligated to be honest and to use prudent business judgment in the conduct of corporate affairs. Directors must exercise the same degree of care that reasonably prudent people use in the conduct of their own personal business affairs. As such, directors can be held liable to the corporation and its shareholders for breaching their duty of care. When directors delegate work to corporate officers and employees, the directors are required to make reasonable efforts to supervise them or else the directors will normally be held liable for negligence or mismanagement of corporate personnel. Furthermore, if a director fails to attend board meetings and takes no actions to prevent illegal actions undertaken by the board, then that director could be held liable for any losses suffered by the company even though that director was not actively involved in the illegal actions. Although the standard of care has been variously described in many court decisions, it essentially requires that directors carry out their responsibilities in an informed, businesslike manner. Directors and officers are expected to act in accordance with their own knowledge and training but they are also usually permitted to make decisions based on information provided by competent officers or employees without being accused of acting in bad faith or failing to exercise due care if such information turns out to be faulty. As the directors oversee the operation of the corporation, they are expected to attend board of directors' meetings—as noted above—and their votes should be entered into the minutes of corporate meetings. Unless a dissent is entered, the director is presumed to have assented to a particular decision. Directors who dissent are rarely held individually liable for mismanagement of the corporation. When a director does vote on matters at board meetings, however, he or she is expected to be informed on corporate matters and to understand legal and other professional advice rendered to the board. A director who is unable to carry out such responsibilities must resign. Even when the required duty of care has not been exercised, directors and officers are liable only for the damages caused to the corporation by their negligence.

Duty of Loyalty. The duty of loyalty of a director to a corporation is grounded in the idea that directors should be faithful to their obligations and duties. In essence, the duty of loyalty is a fiduciary duty requiring the subordination of self-interest to the interest of the entity to which the duty is owed. It presumes constant loyalty to the corporation on the part of the directors and officers. The duty of loyalty prohibits directors from using corporate funds or confidential corporate information for their personal advantage. It requires officers and directors to disclose fully any corporate opportunity or any possible conflict of interest that might occur in a transaction involving the directors of the corporation. Most cases involving breaches of the duty of loyalty typically occur when a director or officer:

- competes with the corporation;
- usurps a corporate opportunity;
- has an interest that conflicts with the interest of the corporation;
- engages in insider trading;
- authorizes a corporate transaction that is detrimental to minority shareholders; or
- sells control over the corporation.

What are the rights of the shareholders of a corporation? Shareholders own the corporation. Although they have no legal title to corporate property vested in the corporation, they do have an equitable interest in the firm. The rights of shareholders are established in the articles of incorporation and under the state's general incorporation laws.

Stock Certificates.
In jurisdictions that require the issuance of stock certificates, shareholders have the right to demand that the corporation issue a certificate and record their names and addresses in the corporate stock record books. Notice of shareholding meetings, dividends and operational and financial reports are all distributed according to the recorded ownership listed in the corporation's books, not on the basis of possession of the certificate.

Preemptive Rights. A preemptive right is a preference given to a shareholder over all other purchasers to subscribe to or purchase a prorated share of a new issue of stock; this right allows the shareholder to maintain his or her portion of control, voting power, or financial interest in the corporation. In general, the articles of incorporation determine the existence and scope of preemptive rights. Preemptive rights apply only to additional, newly issued stock sold for cash and must be exercised within a specified time period. Such rights are far more significant in a close corporation because of the relatively few number of shares and the substantial interest each shareholder controls.

Stock Warrant Rights. When preemptive rights exist and a corporation is issuing additional shares, each shareholder is usually given stock warrants, which are transferable options to acquire a given number of shares from the corporation at a stated price. When the warrant option is for a short period of time, the stock warrants are usually referred to as rights.

Dividend Rights. A dividend is a distribution of corporate profits or income ordered by the directors and paid to the shareholders in proportion to their respective shares in the corporation. Dividends can be paid in cash, property, or corporate stock. Once declared, a cash dividend becomes a corporate debt enforceable at law like any other debt. In general, corporations can only use certain funds, such as retained earnings, net profits, or surplus, for paying dividends.

Voting Rights. Shareholders exercise ownership control through the power of their votes. Each shareholder is entitled to one vote per share. The articles of incorporation, however, can exclude or otherwise limit voting rights, particularly to certain classes of stock.

Inspection Rights. Shareholders in a corporation enjoy both common law and statutory inspection rights. The shareholder's right of inspection, however, is limited to the inspection and copying of corporate books and records for a proper purpose, provided the request is made in advance. A shareholder can properly be denied access to corporate records to prevent harassment or to protect trade secrets or other confidential corporate information. Some states require that a shareholder must have held his or her shares for a minimum period of time immediately preceding the demand to inspect or must hold a minimum number of outstanding shares.

Stock Transfer Rights. Although stock certificates are negotiable and freely transferable by endorsement and delivery, the transfer of stock in closely held corporations is generally restricted by contract, the bylaws, or a restriction stamped on the stock certificate. The existence of any restrictions on transferability must always be noted on the face of the stock certificate and these restrictions must be reasonable. When shares are transferred, a new entry is made in the corporate book to indicate the new owner. Until the corporation is notified and the entry is complete, voting rights, notice of shareholders meetings, dividends, etc., are all given to the current record owner.

Rights on Dissolution. When a corporation is dissolved and its outstanding debts and the claims of its creditors have been satisfied, the remaining assets are distributed on a pro rata basis among the shareholders. Certain classes of preferred stock can be given priority to the extent of the contractual preference.

Shareholder's Derivative Suit. When the corporate directors fail to sue in the corporate name to redress a wrong suffered by the corporation, shareholders may file a derivative suit on behalf of the corporation. The injury must have been suffered by the corporation and any recovery will generally be paid into the corporate treasury. Many states require that shareholders hold a minimum number of shares or have been shareholders for a minimum period of time to file a derivative suit.

Chapter 28

REAL PROPERTY LAW

NATURE OF REAL PROPERTY

Real property includes:

- land,
- buildings and fixtures, and
- rights in the land of another.

LAND

Land means more than the surface of the earth. It includes the soil and all things of a permanent nature attached to the ground such as trees. Land also includes the waters on the ground and things beneath the surface such as minerals. Technically, land is considered as extended downward to the center of the earth and upward indefinitely. However, while the owner of land owns the space above, this ownership right is subject to the right of aircraft to use the air space in such a way that is not dangerous to persons or property lawfully on the land.

A building includes any structure placed on the land or beneath the surface of the land. A fixture is personal property that has been attached to the property or placed in a building in such a way or under such circumstances that it is deemed to be part of the real property. Examples would be a central air conditioning system or a radio tower.

EASEMENTS

An easement is a right in the land of another. An oral promise to create an easement is not binding because of the statute of frauds since this involves a contract regarding the sale or transfer of land. An easement may be created in several ways. The clearest and simplest way to create an easement is by deed. An easement may also be created by implication when part of land is conveyed. For example, if water or drain pipes run from the property conveyed through the property that is retained, there is an implied right to have the use continued. In other words, it is implied that the person selling the land did not mean for the new owner to have the right to dam up the water.

An easement may also be created by implication when it is necessary to the use of the land conveyed. This is the case when property is "landlocked." In many states, you can petition the governing body of the county to grant an easement by necessity when your property is landlocked. An easement may also be created by adverse possession (prescription) which is covered below.

Once an easement has been granted, it cannot be revoked by the grantor without the easement owner's consent. However, an easement may be lost by lack of use when circumstances show an intent to abandon the easement. An example could be a transit system which had an easement to maintain trolley tracks. If the tracks were removed, this would be evidence that the easement had been abandoned.

PROFITS

Profits are the rights to remove something from another person's land, such as the right to remove timber or coal or use the water from another' land.

LICENSES

A license is not an interest in land, but is a privilege to do something on the land of another person. For example, an advertising company that has permission to paint a sign on the side of a barn near a highway has a license. A license can be terminated at any time by the person giving the license (unless a license agreement states otherwise) and will continue only as long as the person giving the license is the owner of the land. Upon the sale of the property, the license terminates unless the new owner agrees to continue the license.

LIENS

Real property may be subject to liens such as the lien of a mortgage that is created when the owner borrows money. The land is made security for the repayment of the debt. Liens may also come into being involuntarily, such as judgment liens, mechanic's liens, and tax liens. In the case of tax and judgment liens, suit can be brought pursuant to these liens and force the owner to satisfy the taxes or the judgment, or his property will be sold to satisfy the taxes or judgment. Mechanic's liens give similar such rights to have a Court-ordered sale. Mechanic's liens involve liens of persons furnishing labor or materials, or both, regarding the improvement of real estate (for example, a contractor's lien).

FIXTURES

A fixture is personal property that is attached to the earth or placed in a building in such a way or under such circumstances that it is deemed to be part of the real property. The question of whether an item is a fixture and, therefore, part of a building can arise in a variety of situations. For example, suppose a person buys an air conditioner or a furnace and has this item installed. The tax assessor may assess the building and add in the value of the item on the theory that it is part of the building. Another situation would be if the buyer of the item owns a building and then sells the building, the new owner may claim that the item stays with the building. Another example would be if the owner places a mortgage on the building and the mortgagee then claims that the item is covered by the mortgage. A final example could be if the buyer of the item is a tenant in the building in which the item is installed, and the landlord claims that the item must stay in the building when the tenant leaves. The buyer of a window air conditioner would argue that this item was not a fixture, but was personal property. The determination of whether or not something is a fixture depends on the common law of fixtures, which is sometimes modified by statute.

Tests of a Fixture

Unless there is an express agreement between the parties, the Courts will apply three basic tests to determine whether personal property has become a fixture.

- **Annexation:** Generally, personal property will become a fixture if it is so attached to the realty that it cannot be removed without materially damaging the realty or destroying the personal property itself. For example, wall-to-wall carpet would be a fixture since removing the carpet would destroy the carpeting.
- **Adaptation:** Personal property which is especially adapted to the use made of the building may constitute a fixture. For example, a custom-made door would be such a fixture.
- **Intent:** The true test is the intention of the person who installs or has the fixture installed. The Wisconsin case of Premonstratensian Fathers v. Badger Mutual Insurance Company is an example of this principle. In this case, the question was whether or not five walk-in coolers or refrigerators were fixtures or personal property. The Court held that they were fixtures since it was obvious that the intent was that they be permanently attached to the building.

Another example is when machinery is installed in a plant in such a way that it would be very difficult and expensive to move, and the moving would cause damage to the machinery. However, machinery and equipment that is movable is ordinarily held to not constitute fixtures. This is true even though it may be necessary to unbolt the machinery or equipment from the floor or disconnect the electrical wires. Ordinarily, refrigerators and freezers, as well as gas and electric ranges, are not fixtures. Portable air conditioners are usually not fixtures.

Trade Fixtures

Equipment that is attached by a tenant to a rented building and used in connection with a business is ordinarily removable by the tenant when the tenant vacates the premises. This type of equipment is called a trade fixture.

Cindy owned and operated a jewelry store and moved the store into a new building which she rented for five years. She moved her showcases, lighting fixtures, and other equipment from her original store to the new store. When the lease expired, she moved out and was about to take these showcases, lighting fixtures, and other equipment with her. The landlord objected, claiming that these items had become fixtures, and therefore Cindy was required to leave them. The court held that since these items were used by Cindy in the trade or business of running a jewelry store, they were considered trade fixtures. They could therefore be removed by her when her lease expired. The ordinary rules governing fixtures do not apply to trade fixtures. However, it is best to specify in a lease what does and what does not constitute trade fixtures.

NATURE AND FORM OF REAL PROPERTY OWNERSHIP

A person's interest in real property can be defined in terms of the period of time for which the person will remain the owner of the property.

Fee Simple Estate

A fee simple estate lasts "forever" in the sense that it lasts until it is sold and then the grantee has the fee. The owner of a fee simple title (also known as fee simple absolute) has the absolute and total interest in the land, although it may be subject to liens. The important characteristics of this estate are:

- Ownership may be transferred during the owner's lifetime;
- Ownership may be transferred by will;
- If it is not transferred by a will, ownership passes to the heirs of a deceased owner;
- It is subject to the rights of the owner's surviving spouse upon the death of the owner; and
- It can be sold by creditors to satisfy the debts of the owner.

A fee simple defeasible is the same as a fee simple interest except that ownership can be lost if restrictions placed on the use of the property are not followed. For example, if you convey property to First Baptist Church as long as the property is used as a church, the church will lose ownership if the property is ever used for anything other than a church. The property would revert back to the grantor. The grantor's interest is called a possibility of reverter.

Life Estate

A life estate (or life tenancy) lasts only during the life of a person, ordinarily its owner. For example, a man may convey a life estate in property to his wife, with the property to pass to his children upon his death. The children's interest would be called a remainder interest. The person with the life estate cannot pass ownership of the property pursuant to a will. However, the life estate and the remainder interest can be sold. But an owner would lose the property upon the death of person on whose life the estate is based. The life estate owner can lease the property, but the lease will terminate on the death of the person on whose life the estate is based.

Future Interests

A future interest is an interest in land that will vest at some time in the future. Both a remainder interest and a possibility of reverter are examples of future interests.

Liability to Third Persons for Condition of Real Property

In the case of real estate, liability is ordinarily based on who is occupying the property. The person in possession may be liable for harm to a third person caused by the condition of the property even though the person in possession is not the owner, but is merely renting the property.

Status of Plaintiff – Common Law Rule

Under common law, the liability to a person injured on real estate is controlled by the status of the injured person. A different duty is owed by the occupier of the land depending upon whether or not the injured person was a trespasser, a licensee, or an invitee.

As far as trespassers are concerned, the occupier ordinarily only owes the duty of refraining from causing intentional harm to the trespasser. The occupier is under no duty to warn the trespasser of dangers or make the property safe to protect trespassers from harm. The main exception to this rule arises in the case of small children, who, although trespassing, are provided greater protection through the attractive nuisance doctrine. Under this doctrine, the owner of a private residential swimming pool could possibly be held liable for the drowning of a five-year-old trespasser if the owner did not maintain adequate fencing around the pool.

Regarding licensees, they are on the premises with the permission of the occupier. The occupier therefore owes them a duty of warning them of dangers which are not obvious and which are known to the occupier. A host must warn a guest of danger, such as a sliding glass door which is "invisible" if the patio lights are on and the house lights are off. The occupier, however, does not owe a duty to the licensee to take any steps to learn the presence of unknown dangers and is under no duty to foresee and guard against every possible hazard.

Invitees are such people as customers whose presence is sought by the occupier to further the business interests of the occupier. Another good definition of invitee is a person who goes on the premises of another in answer to an expressed or an implied invitation of the owner for their mutual advantage. There is a duty in this case to take reasonable steps to discover any danger, and there is a duty to warn the invitee or correct the danger. For example, a store must make a reasonable inspection of the premises to make sure there is nothing on the floor that would be dangerous such as a slippery substance that might cause a customer to fall. The store should either correct the condition or rope off the area, or, at least, give a warning of a wet floor.

In most States, the Courts have expanded the concept of invitees to include people who are invited when it is apparent that they could not be reasonably expected to do their jobs without coming on the premises. A letter carrier would be an example.

Status of Changes – Modern Changes

A number of courts have begun to ignore these common law distinctions and hold the occupier liable according to ordinary negligence standards. In other words, if the occupier, as a reasonable person, should foresee from the circumstances that harm would be caused to a third person, the occupier has the duty to take reasonable steps to prevent this harm. Some courts have taken a middle-of-the-road position and have abolished the distinction between licensees and invitees so that the occupier owes the same duty of care to all lawful visitors.

Recreation Use Statutes

Most States have adopted a statute commonly referred to as a recreational use statute. These statutes basically say that a landowner has no duty to warn others of dangers or keep property safe for persons who are allowed to use the property for recreational purposes without charge.

Co-Ownership of Real Property

Co-ownership of real property can be in the following forms:

- Tenancy in common, in which the interest of each owner may be transferred or inherited;
- Joint tenancy, in which the tenants each have a right of survivorship;
- Tenants by the entirety, in which a husband and wife own property and have a right of survivorship; or
- Community property, which applies in some States to property acquired during the period of a marriage.

Condominiums and Cooperatives

A condominium is a combination of co-ownership and individual ownership. Those who own an apartment house or buy a condominium are co-owners of the land and of the halls, lobby, and other common areas, but each apartment in the building is individually owned by its occupant. In some States, the owners of the various units in the condominium have equal voice in the management and share an equal part of the expenses. In other States, control and liability for expenses are shared by a unit owner in the same ratio as the value of the unit bears to the value of the entire condominium project. The bigger condominium owners would have more say-so than the smaller condominium owners.

A cooperative is different from a condominium. An apartment cooperative will typically be a corporation renting apartments to people who are also owners of stock in the corporation. The apartment complex is owned by the corporation.

Transfer of Title and Deeds

A deed is an instrument by which an owner (the grantor) transfers an interest in land to a new owner (the grantee). No consideration is required to make the deed effective. The deed is necessary to transfer title to land even if it is a gift. It has no effect, and title does not pass until the deed has been delivered. The recording of the deed is not required to make the deed effective to pass title between the buyer and the seller. However, recording is necessary so that the public will know that the buyer is the present owner.

Classification of Deeds

A quitclaim deed transfers whatever interest, if any, a grantor may have in the property, without specifying the interest in any way. No warranty of ownership is given. This type of deed is commonly used to clear title to property. A warranty deed transfers a specified interest and warrants or guarantees that this interest is transferred. The grantor warrants that the title is good, that the transfer is proper, and that there are no liens other than stated in the deed. The grantee can sue if the warranty is breached.

Execution of Deeds

A deed must be signed, and, in order to have a deed recorded, statutes generally require that two or more witnesses also sign the deed or that the grantor acknowledge the deed before a notary public or other officer. This is very important since in most States, if the deed is not properly witnessed or acknowledged, even if you record it, it does not give notice. The law treats the deed as if it were not of record. It is binding between the grantor and the grantee, but it is not notice to bona fide purchasers or lienholders who do not have actual notice of the transfer.

A deed must be executed and delivered by a person having capacity. For example, a minor child cannot execute and deliver a valid deed.

Delivery and Acceptance of Deeds

A deed has no effect, and title does not pass, until the deed has been delivered. Delivery can be shown by words and conduct. The grantor must deliver the deed with the intent that it should take effect as a deed and convey an interest in the property. A deed is ordinarily made effective by handing it to the grantee. A delivery may also be made by placing the deed in the mail addressed to the grantee or giving it to a third person with directions to hand it to the grantee. A delivery in escrow occurs when a deed is delivered to a third person (e.g., an escrow agent) for the purpose of the agent delivering the deed to the grantee after an event or contingency occurs.

No title passes until the event or contingency occurs. For example, a deed may be handed to an attorney to hold in escrow until a prior lien has been satisfied. When the lien has been satisfied, by payment of the underlying debt, the deed can be transferred to the new owner.

Recording of Deeds

The owner of the land may record the deed in the office of the appropriate public official. The name of this official varies from state to state. In some states, like Mississippi, it is the Chancery Clerk. In other States it may be the Recorder of Deeds or the Commissioner of Deeds. Recording is not required to make the deed effective to pass title, but it must be done so that the public will know that the grantee is the present owner. The former owner is therefore prevented from making any other transaction regarding the property. A person purchasing land from the last record title owner will take title free from any unrecorded claim to the land as long as the purchaser did not have notice or knowledge of this claim. The fact that a deed is recorded is notice to the world, even though a person did not know of the deed because they failed to examine the public records. As earlier mentioned, the recording of a deed is notice to the world only if it is properly executed. An improper acknowledgment before a notary public will cause the deed to not have the effective notice. For example, in Mississippi, if the words "signed and sealed" are used rather than the words signed and delivered or executed in the acknowledgment, this can cause the acknowledgment to be invalid.

Additional Protection of Buyers

A buyer may generally also protected from title defects by acquiring title insurance from a reputable title insurance company or a title opinion of an attorney certifying ownership of the property (e.g., who owns the property and what liens, if any, are on the property).

Grantor's Warranties

The warranties of the grantor relate to the title transferred by the grantor. The more important of these covenants or warranties of title that a grantor may make are (1) a guarantee that the grantor owns the estate (fee simple or life) conveyed; (2) a guarantee that the grantor has the authority to make the conveyance (either personally or, for example, by power of attorney); and (3) a guarantee that the land is not subject to any right or interest of a third person, such as a lien or an easement.

Courts in most States hold that when a builder or real estate developer sells a new house to a home buyer, an implied warranty arises that the house and foundation are fit for occupancy. This warranty will not usually be implied against the first buyer when the house is resold, but there is authority that the second buyer can sue the original contractor for breach of implied warranty.

Grantee's Covenants

In a deed, a grantee may agree to do something or refrain from doing certain acts. This agreement will become a binding contract between the grantor and the grantee. An example would be an agreement to maintain fences on the property or that the property will only be used for residential purposes. This kind of covenant is binding, not only between the grantor and the grantee, but it also runs with the land. This means that anyone acquiring the land from the grantee is also bound by the covenant of the grantee. A covenant that provides that the grantee will refrain from certain conduct is called a restrictive covenant. For example, there may be a covenant that no mobile home shall be placed on the property.

A restrictive covenant may limit the kind of structure that can be placed on the property and may also restrict the use that can be made of the land. When a tract of land is developed for individual lots and homes to be built, it is common to use the same restrictive covenants in all of the deeds in order to cause uniform restrictions and patterns on the property. For example, the developer may provide that no home may be built under a certain number of square feet. Any person acquiring a lot within the tract will be bound by the restrictions if they are placed in the deed or a prior recorded deed. Also, these restrictive covenants may be placed in a document at the outset of the development entitled "Restrictive Covenants," and list all the restrictive covenants that will apply to the tracts of land being developed. Any subsequent deed can then refer back to the book and page number where these restrictive covenants are recorded. Any person owning one of the lots in the tract may bring suit against another lot owner to enforce the restrictive covenants. However, restrictive covenants may be deemed abandoned or unenforceable due to estoppel if the restrictive covenants are violated openly for a sufficient period of time for a Court to declare that the restriction has been abandoned.

Other Methods of Transferring Real Property
Title to real property can also be acquired by eminent domain and by adverse possession.

Eminent Domain
By eminent domain, property is taken from its owner and title is acquired by the government or some other public authority. For example, property may be condemned by this State in order to build a highway. The legality of taking property by eminent domain turns upon two questions: (1) whether there is a taking of the property, and (2) whether the property is taken for public use. Regarding the first question, it is not necessary to show that the owner has been physically deprived of the property. It is sufficient to show that the normal use of the property has been seriously impaired or lost. For example, if land is taken for a highway, and the side of the highway runs within one foot of the door of someone's house, the normal use of the property will have been seriously impaired, and the owner is entitled to compensation.

Regarding whether or not the property has been taken for public use, it is usually sufficient to just show that the property has been taken for the public benefit.

Any property taken by eminent domain must be paid for by the governmental body. The owner must receive the fair market value for the property, and this is the question that is often litigated - what constitutes fair market value.

Adverse Possession
Title to land can be acquired by holding it adversely to the true owner for a certain period of time. In this case, the person in possession gains title by adverse possession. The person in possession automatically becomes the owner of the property even though the person had no lawful claim to the land. In order to acquire title in this manner, possession must be actual, visible, exclusive, and continuous for a period of time. In many states, the period of time is ten years. State statutes vary with regard to this period of time.

MORTGAGES

An agreement that creates an interest in real property as security for an obligation, such as the payment of a note, and that is to cease upon the performance of the obligation, is called a mortgage. The person whose interest in the property is given as security is the mortgagor. The person who receives the security is the mortgagee (e.g., lender). Deeds of trust are used mostly in many states, and these are similar to mortgages.

Characteristics of a Mortgage

Two key characteristics of a mortgage are (a) the mortgagee's interest terminates upon the performance of the obligation secured by the mortgage such as payment of the note secured by the mortgage; and (b) the mortgagee has the right to enforce the mortgage by foreclosure if the mortgagor fails to perform the obligation (such as defaulting on the note payments). Any interest in real property can be mortgaged, even a leasehold interest. A mortgage must be in writing because of the statute of frauds since it is, technically, a conveyance of an interest in land.

Creative Forms of Financing

In the past, the only available home mortgages were based on loans charging simple interest amortized over a certain period of time like 20 or 30 years. A new type of mortgage developed 15 to 20 years ago called an adjustable rate mortgage (ARM). A lower interest rate than market rates is usually available for the first few years, but then the rate adjusts at certain intervals to the market rates. This type of financing carries some risk, e.g., the market rate may rise sharply.

A reverse mortgage allows a person who has paid off their mortgage loan to get their equity back over a period of time. This is done by having a mortgage company take a mortgage out on the property and pay the owner over a period of time. Upon the owner's death, the house will revert to the mortgagor unless the loan is paid.

Balloon financing is having payments amortized over a longer period of time than the actual loan. This causes the monthly payments to be lower. For example, a 10 year loan could have is payments amortized over a 25 year period (as if it were a 25 year loan), with a balloon payment of the gross amount due at the end of 10 years. This type of loan also carries the risk of being financially able to make a lump sum payment at the end of the loan term or refinance the loan.

Recording or Filing a Mortgage

An unrecorded mortgage is valid and binding between the parties to it. However, recording statutes in most States provide that the purchasers or creditors who act in good faith and ignorance of an unrecorded mortgage can enforce their rights against the property regardless of the existence of the unrecorded mortgage. The purchaser of land in good faith for value from a mortgagor holds the land free of an unrecorded mortgage. Mortgages and deeds of trust should always be recorded, and deeds of trust and mortgages must be properly acknowledged, or the recording will not constitute notice.

Responsibilities of the Parties

Unless otherwise agreed, a mortgagor has no duty to make improvements. The mortgagor/owner has the duty to pay taxes and assessments. Neither the mortgagor nor the mortgagee has the duty to insure the property unless the mortgage provides otherwise. It is common practice for the mortgagor to obtain a single policy on the property which is payable to the mortgagee and the mortgagor as their interests may appear. This is a common requirement of mortgages.

A mortgagor may be liable to the mortgagee if the mortgagor damages the mortgaged property in such a way as to make the value of the property go down. Then a mortgagor would have a duty to repair.

Transfer of Interest
The mortgagor may ordinarily transfer the land without the consent of the mortgagee. However, consent often is required by language in the mortgage or the deed of trust. A transfer of property upon which there is a mortgage does not do away with the mortgage if it has been properly recorded. The transfer of the property does not affect the liability of the mortgagor to the mortgagee. Unless the mortgagee has agreed to substitute the new owner for the mortgagor's debt, the original mortgagor remains liable. The purchaser of the mortgaged property does not become personally liable for the mortgage debt to the mortgagee unless the purchaser expressly assumes the debt. An assumption of the debt does not release the mortgagor from liability to the mortgagee unless the mortgagee agrees to substitute the new party. Unless there is a substitution, the mortgagee can sue the original debtor for any deficiency after foreclosure.

In most States, a mortgage may be assigned by the mortgagee, and this is often done by one financial institution assigns the note and mortgage to another financial institution.

Rights of Mortgagee after Default
Upon the mortgagor's default, the mortgagee may enforce the mortgage by foreclosure which involves making a public sale of the property. The mortgagee may also sue to enforce the mortgage debt by suing on the promissory note. Generally it is provided that upon any default under the terms of the mortgage, the mortgagee has the right to declare the entire mortgage debt due, even though default relates only to one installment or the doing of some particular act such as failure to maintain insurance on the property. A foreclosure does not destroy the debt that was secured by the mortgage. The mortgagor remains liable for any unpaid balance or deficiency. After default, the mortgagor may seek to stop foreclosure by paying the arrearage on the note. There is a time limitation on doing this. For example, in some states, the mortgagor must pay the deficiency prior to the property actually being sold.

Rights of Mortgagor after Default
In some states, a mortgagor may redeem the property after foreclosure for a certain period of time by paying the arrearage and any costs of foreclosing. This is not true in all states.

LEASES

DEFINITION AND NATURE
The agreement by which one party holds possession of the real property owned by another is a lease. The person who owns the real property is known as the lessor or landlord. The lessee, or tenant, is the one who occupies the property.

CREATION OF THE LEASE RELATIONSHIP

The relationship of landlord and tenant is created by contract. An oral lease is valid at common law, but statutes in most States require written leases for certain tenancies. Many States provide that a lease for a term exceeding three years must be in writing. Statutes in other States require written leases when the term exceeds one year.

ESSENTIAL ELEMENTS

The following elements are necessary to the establishment of the relationship of landlord and tenant:

- The occupying of the land must be with the consent of the landlord.
- A reversionary interest in the land must remain in the landlord. That is, the landlord must be entitled to retake the possession of the land upon the expiration of the lease.
- The tenant must have present possession in the land. This means a right to be in possession of the land now.

CLASSIFICATION OF TENANCIES

Tenancies are classified by duration as tenancies for years, from year to year, at will, and by sufferance.

A tenancy for years is one under which the tenant has an estate of definite duration. The term "for years" is used to describe such a tenancy even though the duration of the tenancy is for only one year or for less than a year.

A tenancy from year to year is one under which a tenant, holding an estate in land for an indefinite duration, pays an annual, monthly, or weekly rent. A distinguishing feature of this tenancy is the fact that it does not terminate except upon proper notice. In almost all States a tenancy from year to year is implied if the tenant holds over after a tenancy for years with the consent of the landlord.

When land is held for an indefinite period, which may be terminated at any time by the landlord or the tenant, a tenancy at will exists. A person who enters into possession of land for an indefinite period with the owner's permission, but without any agreement as to rent, is a tenant at will. (Normally there will be a rental agreement between the parties.) Some States require advance notice of termination of this kind of tenancy.

When a tenant holds over without permission of the landlord, the landlord may treat the tenant as a trespasser or as a tenant. Until the landlord elects to do one or the other, a tenancy by sufferance exists.

TERMINATION OF LEASE

Leases may be terminated in the following ways:

- **Termination by notice.** A lease may give the tenant the power to terminate it by giving notice to the tenant.

- **Expiration of term in a tenancy for years.** When a tenancy for years exists, the relationship of landlord and tenant ceases upon the expiration of the term, without any requirement that one party give the other any notice of termination. Express notice to end the term may be required by provisions of the lease.
- **Notice in a tenancy from year to year**. In the absence of an agreement of the parties, notice is now usually given by statute. It is common practice for the parties to require 30 or 60 days' notice to end a tenancy from year to year. As to tenancies for periods of less than a year, the provisions of the statutes commonly require notice of only one week.
- **Surrender.** A surrender or giving up of the tenant's estate to the landlord terminates the tenancy if the surrender is accepted by the landlord.
- **Forfeiture.** The landlord or tenant may terminate the lease by forfeiting the relationship because of misconduct or breach of a condition of the lease. Forfeiture is not favored by the Courts. In other words, Courts do not like to declare leases to be forfeited.
- **Destruction of Property. If** a lot and building on it are leased, either an express provision in the lease or a statute generally releases the tenant from liability when the building is destroyed, or reduces the amount of rent in proportion to the loss sustained.
- **Transfer of the Tenant.** Residential leases may contain a provision for termination upon the tenant's being transferred by an employee to another city.

NOTICE OF TERMINATION

When notice of termination is required, no particular words are necessary to constitute a sufficient notice, provided the words used clearly indicate the intention of the party. Statutes sometimes require that the notice be in writing.

RENEWAL OF LEASE

When a lease terminates for any reason, it is ordinarily a matter for the landlord and the tenant to enter into a new agreement if they wish to extend or renew the lease. The power to renew the lease may be stated in the original lease by declaring that the lease runs indefinitely, as from year to year, subject to being terminated by either party by giving written notice a specified number of days or months before the termination date.

In the case of **Kilbourne v. Forrester[25],** a 1971 Missouri case, Forrester leased an apartment to Kilbourne for one year in June of 1966. The lease stated, "The lease is renewable at the end of the year." Kilbourne renewed the lease for the year 1967-1968. She again gave notice of renewal for the year 1968-1969, but Forrester refused to recognize such renewal and brought an action to recover possession of the premises. The Court held in favor of Forrester. The statement that the lease was renewable at the end of the year's period meant exactly that. It could therefore only be renewed once at the termination of the original term and could not be renewed a second or subsequent time.

The lease may require the tenant to give written notice of the intention to renew the lease. In such case, there is no renewal if the tenant does not give the required notice.

---

[25] **464 SW 2d 770**

POSSESSION
Most written leases today contain an express promise by the landlord to respect the possession of the tenant. This promise is called a covenant for quiet enjoyment. Such a provision protects the tenant from interference with possession by the landlord.

An eviction may be actual or constructive. It is a constructive eviction when some act or omission of the landlord substantially deprives the tenant of the use and enjoyment of the premises.

It is essential in a constructive eviction that the landlord intended to deprive the tenant of the use and enjoyment of the premises. This intent may, however, be inferred from conduct. There is no constructive eviction unless the tenant leaves the premises. If the tenant continues to occupy the premises for more than a reasonable time after the acts claimed to constitute a constructive eviction, the tenant waives or loses the right to object to the conduct of the landlord.

USE OF PREMISES
The lease generally specifies the use to which the tenant may put the property. In the absence of express or implied restrictions, a tenant is entitled to use the premises for any lawful purpose.

RENT
The tenant is under a duty to pay rent to the landlord. The time of payment of rent is ordinarily fixed by the lease. If the lease is assigned, the assignee is liable to the landlord for the rent. The assignment, however, does not in itself discharge the tenant from the duty to pay the rent. The landlord thus may bring an action for the rent against either the original tenant or the assignee, or both. A sublessee ordinarily is not liable to the original lessor for rent, unless that liability has been expressly assumed. Such a sublessee would only be liable to the sublessor unless the liability has been assumed.

When property is rented for a long term, it is common to include some provision for the automatic increase of the rent at periodic intervals. Such a provision is often tied to increases in the cost of living or in the landlord's operating costs. Such a provision is called an escalation clause.

REPAIRS AND CONDITION OF PREMISES
In the absence of an agreement to the contrary, the tenant has the duty to make those repairs that are necessary to prevent waste and decay of the premises, and is liable for permissive waste on failing to do so. The tenant is ordinarily liable for any damage to the premises caused by willful or negligent acts of the tenant. It is customary for leases to reserve to the landlord the right to enter to inspect the premises and to make repairs.

Various laws protect tenants of apartments or houses by requiring landlords to observe specified safety, health, and fire prevention standards. Some statutes require that a landlord who leases a building for dwelling purposes must keep it in a condition fit for habitation.

Most jurisdictions infer from residential leases of furnished and unfurnished property a warranty that the premises are habitable. If the landlord breaches this warranty, the tenant is entitled to damages. These damages may be set off against the rent.

IMPROVEMENTS
In the absence of special agreement, neither the tenant nor the landlord is under the duty to make improvements, as he normally is under a duty to make repairs. Either party may, as a term of the original lease, make improvements. In the absence of an agreement to the contrary, improvements that are attached to the land become part of the realty and belong to the landlord.

TAXES AND ASSESSMENTS
In the absence of an agreement to the contrary, the landlord, and not the tenant, is usually under a duty to pay ad valorem taxes (e.g., taxes on the land). The lease may provide for an increase in rent if taxes on the rented property are increased.

TENANT'S DEPOSIT
A landlord may require a tenant to make a deposit to protect the landlord from any default on the part of the tenant.

REMEDIES OF LANDLORD
The parties may create by contract a lien in favor of the landlord for rent or damages for failure to make repairs.

The landlord may sue the tenant on the tenant's obligation to pay rent as set forth in the lease. In some jurisdictions, the landlord is permitted to bring a combined action to recover the possession of the land and the overdue rent at the same time.

The lease commonly provides that upon the breach of any of its provisions by the tenant, such as the failure to pay rent, the lease shall terminate or the landlord may exercise the option to declare the lease terminated. When the lease is terminated for any reason, the landlord then has the right to evict the tenant and retake possession of the property.

The landlord may have to resort to legal process to evict the tenant in order to enforce the right to possession of the premises. The action of ejectment is ordinarily used.

If the tenant leaves the premises before the expiration of the lease, is the landlord under an obligation to rent the premises again in order to reduce the rent for which the tenant would be liable? By the common law and majority rule, there is no duty on the landlord to seek to find a new tenant for the premises. However, a growing minority view places greater emphasis on the contractual aspects of the lease so that, when the tenant breaks the contract, the landlord is under the duty to seek to mitigate the damages caused by the tenant's breach and must make a reasonable effort to rent the abandoned property.

A safe policy to follow if you are a landlord is that when a tenant breaks a lease, you should make reasonable efforts to rent the tenant's apartment to someone else.

LANDLORD'S LIABILITY TO TENANT FOR INJURIES ON THE PREMISES

In the absence of an agreement to keep the premises in repair, the landlord is ordinarily not liable to the tenant for injuries caused by the defective condition of the premises that are under the control of the tenant. The landlord is ordinarily not liable for the harm caused by an obvious condition that was known to the tenant at the time the lease was made.

The landlord is ordinarily liable to the tenant for injuries caused by latent defects, or defects that are not apparent, and which the landlord had knowledge of. A new trend is beginning to appear that makes foreseeability of harm the test of the landlord's liability.

Ordinarily, the landlord is not liable to the tenant for crimes committed on the premises by third persons, as when a third person enters the premises and commits larceny or murder. The landlord is ordinarily not required to establish any security system to protect the tenant from crimes of third persons. However, the landlord should take great pains to put this in the lease.

However, when the criminal acts of third persons are reasonably foreseeable, the landlord may be held liable for the harm caused to a tenant. For example, when a tenant has repeatedly reported that the dead bolt on the apartment door is broken, the landlord is liable for the tenant's loss when a thief enters through the door because this type of criminal conduct was foreseeable. Also, when the landlord of a large apartment complex does not take reasonable steps to prevent repeated criminal acts, the landlord is liable to the tenant for the harm caused by the foreseeable criminal acts of a third person.

A provision in a lease which excuses the landlord from liability is generally valid, regardless of the cause of the tenant's loss. A number of Courts, however, have restricted the landlord's power to limit liability in the case of residential leasing (as compared to commercial leasing). A modern trend holds that clauses limiting liability of the landlord are void with respect to harm caused by the negligence of the landlord when the tenant is a residential tenant.

Leases commonly contain a provision declaring that the tenant will indemnify the landlord for any liability (of the landlord to a third person) that arises in connection with the rented premises.

LANDLORD'S LIABILITY TO THIRD PERSONS

The landlord is ordinarily not liable to third persons injured because of the condition of any part of the rented premises that is in the possession of a tenant by virtue of a lease. The landlord, however, should require the tenant to carry liability insurance in a commercial lease and carry it himself in a residential lease if the tenant is not required to carry the insurance.

If the landlord retains control over a portion of the premises, such as hallways or stairways, the landlord is ordinarily liable for injuries to third persons caused by failure to exercise proper care in connection with that part of the premises under his control. The modern trend of cases makes the landlord liable when a third person is harmed by a condition that the landlord was obligated under the lease to correct or when the landlord was obligated to keep the premises causing the harm in repair.

TENANT'S LIABILITY TO THIRD PERSONS

A tenant in complete possession has control of the property and is therefore liable when the tenant's failure to use due care cause harm to (a) licensees, such as persons allowed to use a telephone, and (b) invitees, such as customers entering a store. With respect to both licensees and invitees, the tenant is liable as if he were the owner.

The liability of the tenant to third persons is not affected by the fact the landlord may have contracted in the lease to make repairs, which, if made, would avoid the injury. The tenant could be sued in such a situation and then turn around and sue the landlord. The injured party would normally sue both the tenant and the landlord.

TRANSFER OF LANDLORD'S REVERSIONARY INTEREST

The reversionary interest of the landlord may be transferred voluntarily by the landlord or involuntarily by a judicial or execution sale. The tenant then becomes the tenant of the new owner of the reversionary interest, and the new owner is bound by the terms of the lease.

The landlord has the right to assign the rent independent of the lease. For example, the rent may be assigned as collateral for a loan.

TENANT'S ASSIGNMENT OF LEASE AND SUBLEASE

An assignment of a lease is a transfer by the tenant of his entire interest in the premises to a third person. A tenancy for years may be assigned by the tenant unless the tenant is restricted from doing so by the terms of the lease. A sublease is a transfer to a third person (the sublessee) of less than the tenant's entire interest. An example of this: Smith rented a farm from Dale for 20 years. He rented the south part of the land to Jones for five of the 20 years. Was Jones an assignee or sublessee? Jones was sublessee because Smith had transferred only part of the premises for part of the term for which he held the premises as lessee. In order to be an assignee, Jones would have to have received the entire interest under the lease.

If the entire interest of the tenant is transferred to a third person, the transaction is an assignment of the lease, without regard to whether the parties have described the transaction as a sublease or as an assignment.

The lease may contain provisions denying the right to assign or sublease, or may contain provisions restricting the privilege of assigning or subleasing. These restrictions allow the landlord to obtain protection from new tenants who would damage the property or who were financially irresponsible.

An express promise by the sublessee is necessary to make the sublessee liable for the obligations of the lease to the original lessor. However, when a lease is assigned, the assignee becomes bound by the terms of the lease as soon as he takes possession of the property.

Neither the act of subletting nor the landlord's consent to the subletting releases the original tenant from liability under the terms of the original lease unless expressly stated so by the landlord. When a lease is assigned, the original tenant remains liable for the rent that becomes due.

It is customary for the tenant to require the sublessee to promise to perform all obligations under the original lease and to indemnify the tenant for any loss caused by the default of the sublessee. If the sublessee promises to assume the obligations of the original lease, the landlord, as a third-party beneficiary, may sue the sublessee for breach of the terms of the original lease.

Landlord-tenant law varies by state, but typically covers the rights and obligations resulting from the landlord-tenant relationship, including the lease or rental agreement itself, termination, abandonment, eviction, renewal, rent, security deposit and improvements and repairs to the property. A landlord is a person who contracts through a lease or rental agreement to fully or partially rent his or her real property to another for a specific time period and for a set payment of rent. The person who rents such property from a landlord is referred as a tenant.

Two or more persons who enter into a rental or lease agreement with a landlord are referred to as cotenants. Although cotenants have the same legal obligations under a rental or lease agreement, each cotenant may be independently liable to the landlord for failure to comply with the agreement, including rental obligations. A typical rental or lease agreement cotenant provision states that the cotenants are jointly and severally liable for compliance with the agreement. Any agreements between cotenants regarding rental or lease obligations are not binding on a landlord, but cotenants may seek to enforce such agreements against one another in the same way other types of contracts are enforced. When a single tenant seeks to add a roommate, he or she must follow the landlord's application process, and the landlord may request that a new rental or lease agreement be signed. The new agreement may include increases in the amount of rent and security deposit required.

LANDLORD AND TENANT LAW

FREQUENTLY ASKED QUESTIONS

Is an oral lease enforceable?
A lease can be an oral agreement, or it can be in writing. If the lease extends beyond one year, most states require that it be in writing. An oral lease has the disadvantage of future misunderstandings over terms of the agreement, and potential problems regarding enforcement of terms between the landlord and the tenant.

What is a landlord?
A *landlord is* the owner of piece of real property who leases it to another person. The landlord is also referred to as the *lessor* of rental property. The landlord *lets* a tenant use and occupy his/her rental property in exchange for the monthly payment of rent.

What is a tenant?
A *tenant* is a person who has the right to use and occupy rental property in accordance with a rental agreement or *lease.* The tenant is also referred to as the *lessee* of rental property. The tenant may use and occupy the rental property as long as he complies with the terms and conditions of the rental agreement, including, but not limited to, the payment of rent.

What is a subtenant?

A *subtenant* or *sublessee* is a person who has the right to use and occupy rental property leased by a tenant from a landlord. A subtenant has responsibilities to both the landlord and the tenant. A tenant can sublet rental property to a subtenant, but often must obtain the prior agreement of the landlord. In a sublease, the tenant still remains responsible for the payment of rent to the landlord and any damages to the property caused by the subtenant.

What is a lease or rental agreement?

A *lease,* sometimes also referred to as a *rental agreement,* is an agreement between a landlord and a tenant which gives the tenant the right to use and occupy rental property for a period of time.

What is the difference between a residential and a commercial lease?

When a person leases rental property from a landlord for use as a residence, the arrangement is called a *residential lease.* When a business leases rental property, the arrangement is called a *commercial lease.* While there are many similarities between residential and commercial leases, state and local law more often regulates the relationship between a tenant and a landlord under a residential lease. Since commercial leases are viewed as being contracts between knowledgeable business people, less governmental protection is needed, as knowledgeable business people should be able to negotiate the terms of the lease to their respective satisfaction.

What does it mean that a tenant shall not commit *waste?*

This means that the tenant has the responsibility to keep the rental property clean, to properly dispose of trash, and shall not deliberately or negligently allow damage to the property. Further, most leases require the tenant to return the rental property to the landlord in a clean and habitable condition, except for *reasonable wear and tear,* at the end of the lease term.

What is does the phrase *repair and deduct* mean in a rental agreement?

To keep residential real property in habitable condition, some local jurisdictions (and some standard lease forms) allow a tenant to give written notice to the landlord that there is a defect in the property. The notice to the landlord typically must provide the landlord with a reasonable amount of time to make the repair (*i.e., cure the defect*). After waiting the required amount of time and after providing the written notice to the landlord, the tenant may then go out and hire a professional to make the necessary repair, pay the repairman, and then deduct the reasonable cost of the repair from the rent paid to the landlord.

What is constructive eviction?

Constructive eviction is a term used in the law of real property to describe a circumstance in which a landlord either does something or fails to do something that he has a legal duty to provide (*e.g.* the landlord refuses to provide heat or water to the apartment), rendering the property *uninhabitable.* A tenant who is constructively evicted may terminate the lease and seek damages. To maintain an action for damages, the tenant must show that the uninhabitable conditions were a result of the landlord's actions (not the actions of some third party) and that the tenant vacated the premises in a reasonable time. A tenant who suffers from a constructive eviction can claim all of the legal remedies available to a tenant who was unjustly told to leave.

When can a landlord terminate a tenant's right to use and possess the rental property?
The more common reasons why a landlord may terminate a tenant's right to use and possess residential rental property include:

- failure of the tenant to pay rent when due;
- *waste* to the rental property caused by the tenant;
- possession of pets in violation of the rental agreement;
- occupancy of the rental property by persons not named on the lease;
- significant disturbances of other tenants (such as extreme noise);

What can happen in a situation where the landlord has terminated the tenant's right to use and possess the rental property?
Before a landlord forces a tenant out of residential rental property, the landlord must provide written notice to the tenant and provide a reasonable amount of time for the tenant to cure the default (if time is allowed by the lease). If the tenant does not cure the default within a reasonable amount of time, and does not voluntarily vacate the rental property, the landlord must then initiate a formal *eviction* proceeding or *unlawful detainer* action. The law looks with disfavor on *self-help* evictions, in which the landlord or the landlord's agents show up and physically take the tenant and the tenant's possessions out of the rental property, change the locks on the doors to the rental property, or shut off water/electricity in an effort to force the tenant to leave. Formal court orders are usually required to get a reluctant tenant out of residential rental property.

Can a tenant ever terminate their legal obligations of a lease during its term?
Yes, there are generally three ways:

- termination due to the legal misconduct of the landlord;
- replacement in the premises by a new tenant, or
- by mutual agreement between the landlord and tenant.

If another tenant has moved in and is paying the full amount of rent, the first tenant's obligation is ended. A landlord cannot legally collect rent from more than one tenant for the same premises.

What is the difference between a security deposit and an advance payment of rent?
The security deposit is held by the landlord (or held in trust in a bank account maintained by the landlord) in the event that there is any damage to the rental property that has been caused by the tenant while he had possession. An advance payment of rent sometimes is collected at the inception of the rental agreement to assure the landlord that he will be paid the last month of rent before the tenant vacates the rental property. A security deposit usually may not be used toward the payment of the last month's rent unless the rental agreement states otherwise. When a tenant has paid the equivalent of a month's rent as a security deposit, the tenant must pay the last month's rent to the landlord and then wait for the landlord to return the security deposit (as opposed to defaulting on the rental agreement by defaulting in the payment of the last month's rent).

Some states and local jurisdictions have laws specifying how the landlord is to hold the security deposit (such as in a separate account at a bank) and who is entitled to the interest earned on a security deposit. Both state and local laws and ordinances can be very specific on the handling of security deposits.

I put a deposit down on an apartment, had an approved application, and was set to sign a lease. At the last minute, I was told the apartment was no longer available. Do I have any recourse?
Until you have a signed lease, you do not have any contractual rights to the property. Unless the refusal was on prohibited grounds such as race, color, creed, etc., you probably have no recourse against the apartment owner.

We signed a year's lease on a rental unit for our college-bound son, with the understanding that his roommates would pay their share of the rent. One roommate left without paying his third of the rent. The landlord has filed eviction papers and we are expected to pay the unpaid rent. How can we get out of this lease?
Read the lease and see if there is a provision for terminating the lease on 30 days notice and paying extra months' rent or some other amount of money to break the lease early. If not, you are probably liable for the entire rent for the rest of the lease. If you want your son to stay, you should pay the "demand amount" in the eviction papers to the court immediately. This will stop the eviction, but you'll still have to pay the entire rent for the rest of the lease. You can sue the roommate and his parents if they cosigned for contribution (his share of the rent/utilities).

Can a tenant refuse to let an agent onto property after receiving 24 hours notice? The lease does not cover the issue.
During the term of the lease, the home and the land it sits on "belongs" to your tenant, and you have no right to invade your tenant's "quiet enjoyment" of the property. The tenant may allow, or disallow, anyone he or she wants to come upon the land or into the home. This also depends on what the lease says and the terms of any state statutes. Many lease forms give the landlord the right to come onto the premises under certain conditions whether the tenant agrees or not.

My roommate and I are co-signors on a lease of a house. She wants out before the lease expires, leaving me liable for rent and utilities. Can she do this?
She cannot legally breach the contract and leave you liable for all of the rent and utilities. You can sue her for her share of the lease expenses.

We went from a 1-year lease to a month-to-month tenancy. Our landlady gave us a 30-day notice in the middle of a month. I thought 30-day notices had to be given on the first of each month. What's the law?
The 30-day notice can be given on any day, not necessarily on the 1st or any particular day. It is effective 30 days thereafter with the tenant responsible for the rent to the end of the 30th day.

The sign-out sheet given to me by the manager of our apartments following a walkthrough indicated everything was fine except for dusty blinds. The landlord, however, now wants to charge for dusty blinds and pet odor. There was no mention in the walkthrough or on the sign-out sheet of foul pet odors. Can they do this?

The landlord is not limited to what they notice during the walk through. Some defects cannot be seen without a thorough inspection. Pet odor may not be noticeable when the windows are open, but show up when they're closed and the air conditioning unit on. States have different rules as to the time period the landlord can hold the deposit and the procedure for inspection, return of the deposit, etc.

I have 7 months remaining on my home lease. The owner defaulted on the mortgage and the mortgage holder has instituted foreclosure proceedings. What are my rights as a tenant with regard to the mortgage company?
You can send a letter to the mortgage holder with a copy of the lease saying you are in occupancy and that your lease must be honored. Send the letter certified, return receipt required. Normally they have constructive notice of your occupancy if it is obvious and will have to honor your lease. You might also check the laws of your jurisdiction. Some jurisdictions have very specific landlord tenant laws.

I have been paying rent on a home owned by my mom for the last 16 months. There is no rental agreement between us. Now she wants to evict me and has threaten to bring the marshals if I don't remove myself and belongings in 1.5 months. Can she do this?
When you do not have a written lease and have been paying rent monthly, most states will declare that you have a month-to-month rental agreement. A landlord can terminate a month-to-month rental on 20-30 days notice. However, state law varies on what type of notice is necessary. Usually it has to be written notice delivered to the tenant. Then the landlord has to wait 30 days until you are illegally holding over before she can start eviction proceedings. The landlord cannot lock the house until a court grants her a writ and the sheriff evicts you. Even then, she cannot keep your belongings unless you owe her money. If she tries, you get to sue her for conversion (theft).

What is the Uniform Residential Landlord and Tenant Act
In the 1960s, the federal government funded a legal aid project to write a model landlord and tenant act. The model code drafted at that time was given to the National Conference of Commissioners on Uniform State Laws, who drafted the *Uniform Residential Landlord and Tenant Act (URLTA)* in 1972. This code was approved by the American Bar Association in 1974. Since that time many states like Alaska, Arizona, Florida, Hawaii, Iowa, Kansas, Kentucky, Montana, Nebraska, New Mexico, Oregon, Rhode Island, South Carolina, Tennessee, and Virginia have adopted residential landlord and tenant laws based on this model, though there are variations.

The URLTA favors neither landlords nor tenants. It was intended to make residential landlord and tenant laws more fair to all parties and more relevant to rentals in a modern urban setting.

There are a few issues often covered in state laws or local ordinances that are not addressed by the URLTA. These include rent increases or rent control and the handling of security deposits. The URLTA does not specify whether landlords must keep security deposit money separate from his or her own money, whether interest must be paid on security deposits, or whether deposit funds must be placed in interest-bearing accounts.

Is there a difference between a residential and a commercial lease?
When a person leases rental property from a landlord for use as a residence, the arrangement is called a residential lease. When a business leases rental property, the arrangement is called a commercial lease.

While there are many similarities between residential and commercial leases, state and local law more often regulates the relationship between a tenant and a landlord under a residential lease than the parties to a commercial lease. Since commercial leases are viewed as being contracts between knowledgeable business people, less governmental protection is needed, as knowledgeable business people should be able to negotiate the terms of the lease to their respective satisfaction. Therefore many more terms of a commercial lease can be negotiated and statutes waived than in the residential context.

A building I am considering is occupied by several commercial tenants. If I buy the building, can I evict them?
Generally no. If a tenant has a legally valid tenancy, i.e., a written lease, and is current on the rent and all other lease obligations, the law usually lets the tenant remain in possession until the end of the lease, regardless of who owns the building.

Your should ask the owner for the legal status of each tenant since your ownership of the building will be subject to those leases. It is a good idea to get the seller to get an "estoppel certificate" from each tenant. A *tenant estoppel certificate* is used to verify the current status of the tenant and landlord's rights and obligations under an existing lease when a landlord is seeking a loan on the leased property or selling the property. The estoppel certificate identifies the tenant and landlord; the leased property location; the lease commencement date, termination date and option period, if any; the status of rent, prepaid rents and security deposits; status of any defaults by the landlord, among other information. It usually contains a statement by the borrower indicating the amount owed on their mortgage loan along with the interest rate.

Are there housing laws against discrimination?
The Federal Fair Housing Act prevents discrimination on the basis of race in the sale or renting of housing. This law applies to anyone who is selling or renting real estate or housing. It is also unlawful to "steer" residents of a certain race to a neighborhood in which people of the same race live.

Some state and local laws have added impermissible grounds for discrimination. For example, some prohibit landlords from refusing to rent to prospective tenants with children or an animal(s) or below a set age. Others have legislated extra protection for those who are blind, disabled or students.

Is the landlord responsible for maintaining rental property and complying with local housing codes?
Landlords have the responsibility to maintain residential rental property and repair any defects or problems. Under most state law, there is an implied warranty of habitability; that is, a landlord not only must deliver residential rental property to the tenant in a habitable condition, but he remains responsible for maintaining the property in a habitable condition during the term of the

lease. Habitability is usually defined as the minimum standard for decent, safe, sanitary housing suitable for residential purposes.

Most communities have local housing codes. The codes are local ordinances or laws that require owners of real property, including landlords, to maintain the property and make any necessary repairs. These codes typically require that any residential rental property offered by a landlord must meet the minimum standards established in the code. The landlord's responsibility is not only to deliver the rental property to the tenant in compliance with the housing codes but also to maintain compliance with the housing codes throughout the term that the tenant has use and possession of the rental property.

Who is responsible for making repairs to the premises in a residential lease?
Your lease or rental agreement may say whether you or your landlord is responsible for making a repair. Generally, a landlord is responsible for making major repairs, particularly those caused by the weather or natural forces (such as rain, flood, or a brush fire), and repairs caused by ordinary wear and tear from use of the unit (the clogged drain and faucet). The tenant is responsible for making repairs for damage he caused.

You should tell a landlord that a repair is needed and allow him to come and see the damage. If your landlord doesn't come or refuses to make the repair, you should write a letter to the landlord stating what repair is needed, when the damage occurred, when you notified the landlord that a repair was needed, and ask the landlord again to make the repair. Keep a copy of this letter; you might need it later.

If the damage to the unit might violate a building or health code, you can call the relevant local authorities and ask for an inspection. For example, health and building codes require a landlord to provide adequate heat, a roof that doesn't leak, and to deal with unwanted pests like mice, rats, and cockroaches.

If the landlord still doesn't make the repair or if the damage doesn't violate a code, you may be able to make the repair yourself and deduct the cost from your rent. You should notify the landlord in writing that you intend to do that in order to give the landlord an opportunity to make the repairs. Keep a copy of the letter. You should check your state law and local codes to see if there are limits on withholding rent is such a situation. For example, some states limit the amount of the repairs and allow the tenant to make repairs only once in six months.

If the conditions in the rental unit are very serious, you may be able to stop paying rent at all until the unit is repaired. For example, if the roof leaks, half the heaters don't heat, and the oven doesn't work, that's serious. If one light fixture is out and air is coming in around a window, that's not serious enough to stop paying rent. Some states recognize an implied warranty of habitability, which means that a landlord is legally held to have promised to keep the unit in a livable condition, even when the lease or rental agreement doesn't say that.

If I do not own property, but only rent a house or apartment, do I still have a need for insurance?
Even if you do not own the building where you live, it is likely you have valuable personal items which would be expensive to replace if they are stolen or damaged by fire or some other cause. Also, you still have potential legal liability to someone who is injured on property you occupy, even if you are not the property owner. A "Renters Policy" is essentially like a Homeowners Policy but without coverage for the buildings or structures. Because of this, Renters Policies usually cost far less than Homeowners Policies. Sometimes the lease will require the tenant to carry insurance.

What is Rent Control?
Rent control refers to laws that limit the amounts of rent and the amounts that rent can be increased in any year. There is no nationwide or statewide rent control in the U.S., and all the rent control laws and regulation are passed by cities. Most of the cities with rent control are located in New York, California, and New Jersey. Washington, D.C. also has rent control.

Rent control laws don't just concern rent limits or rent increases. They usually also deal with the landlord's responsibility to make repairs, lease renewals, evictions, and special rules for groups like senior citizens. In some cities senior citizens are protected from any rent increase, even when increases are allowed for younger tenants.

How do you determine the rent in a commercial lease?
In many cases the rent in a commercial lease will be expressed as so many dollars per square foot. This is the annualized price for the unit, so the monthly rent is determined by multiplying the rent per square foot by the total number of square feet in the unit and dividing by twelve months. For comparative purposes with other suitable rental units, you need to know whether the rent includes or excludes taxes, insurance on the building, and utilities. To the extent it excludes them, you will have to pay these items in addition to the rent. Sometimes rent escalation clauses permit the owner to raise the rent because of inflation or when taxes or utilities go up during the year. Finally, many retail and restaurant leases will include clauses that require the tenant to pay either a flat monthly rental or a rental based on a set percentage of sales in the store or restaurant, whichever is higher.

What is an option to renew?
An important issue in commercial leases involves an option to renew the lease at the end of the lease term for an additional term. Without an option to renew, you may be forced to move or to pay an extraordinarily high rent to remain where you are just at the time the business is becoming very profitable. To provide maximum protection, the rent, or at least a formula for determining the rent during the renewed period, should be specified.

Can the lease protect my business from competitors?
Commercial leases may prohibit the lessor from leasing space to a competitor, or if the lessor will not agree to this, a provision may provide that space leased to any competitor must be located on a different floor or in a different wing of a shopping center.

What should a residential lease or rental agreement include?

- the name of the landlord, tenant, and any others who will occupy the rental property;
- a description of the rental property subject to the lease;
- the term of the lease (*e.g.,* month-to-month, 1 year lease, 5 year lease, etc.);
- the amount of rent that the tenant must pay the landlord, and when that rent is due;
- the terms of the agreement regarding the *security deposit* (*e.g.,* how much, whether it is held at interest, and when it will be returned at the end of the lease);
- what can happen in the event of *default,* which is the failure of either party to live up to the terms of the agreement (such as the failure of the tenant to pay rent or the landlord to keep the rental property in habitable condition);
- whether or not the tenant must pay the landlord a *late fee* if the rent is not paid on time;
- that the tenant will be in default in the event that the tenant disturbs other tenants' *right of quiet enjoyment;*
- the respective duties and responsibilities of the landlord and tenant regarding the maintenance (*e.g.,* repairs) of the rental property;
- what happens at the end of the term of the lease (*e.g.,* option to renew, conversion of lease to a lesser term, notice of termination by the tenant to the landlord, etc.);
- under what conditions may the landlord enter the rental property;
- whether the tenant must pay the attorney fees and costs incurred in a lawsuit, in the event that a lawsuit is filed and the tenant loses;
- whether the landlord must pay the attorney fees and costs incurred in a lawsuit, in the event that a lawsuit is filed and the landlord loses; and
- whether the tenant may have a pet, and if so, whether an additional deposit is required.

What can happen in an unlawful detainer or eviction action?
When a landlord wants to have a tenant removed from rental property, either due to the tenant's default or because a tenant refuses to leave at the expiration of the lease term, the landlord must generally get the assistance of a court of law if the tenant refuses to leave voluntarily. *Self-help* eviction, as explained above, is not favored by courts and could result in the landlord having to pay damages to the tenant, and possibly be convicted of a crime.

The first step is for the landlord to file a complaint with the court and pay the required filing fee. Then the tenant must be served with a copy of the complaint and a notice that he/she is being sued *(e.g., served with process).* The process or *summons* explains to the defendant.

- That he is being sued;
- The name of the court in which he is being sued.
- When he must file an answer.
- The fact that a default judgment will be entered if no answer is filed.

In the event that the tenant loses the lawsuit, the landlord may be given a monetary judgment (such as for damages to the premises, the amount of money owed for rent, plus attorney fees and costs) plus a *writ* of possession or execution. A writ of possession may then be executed by the local constable or sheriff so that the tenant is removed from the rental property and the landlord is once again given possession. In some jurisdictions, it is possible that the landlord is given possession of the rental property but the tenant continues to be responsible for the payment of rent to the end of the lease term (although the landlord would have an obligation to make a good faith effort to re-rent the rental property so as to mitigate the damages sustained due to the tenant's default).

What happens to the security deposit at the end of the lease?
Some states set forth specific laws governing the return of security deposits. The landlord is required to return the security deposit within a set period of time (for example, in some states a landlord must return the security deposit to the tenant within 21 days). In the event that less than the full amount of the security deposit is returned, the landlord must provide the tenant with a written statement regarding any deductions made from the security deposit.

If a tenant has not been around for over 6 months and not paid any rent, can I clean out the apartment and re-rent it?
You should be able to get an eviction order for non-payment. The sheriff will move the tenant's belongings out. In some cases you must first give a statutory notice of abandonment for 15-20 days to the last known address before changing the locks. Also if the tenant's property has a material value (*e.g.,* over $300) the landlord generally cannot throw it away at the time of the eviction.

Are Landlord's liable for injuries that occur on their property?
Landlords are liable for *dangerous conditions* on the property they own if they knew or should have known about the danger. For example, if the concrete blocks in the sidewalk leading up to an apartment building are uneven and the landlord has visited the building and had the opportunity to see the sidewalk or if the tenants have complained, the landlord knows or should know of the problem and must fix it. If he does not fix it, and an elderly guest of a tenant trips and breaks a hip, the landlord will be liable. It is always a good idea for tenants to inform the landlord in writing of any possibly dangerous conditions either in the rented unit or in the common areas of a number of rentals, and to keep copies of those letters. Landlords should make repairs as quickly as possible.

To be held liable for injuries or damage the landlord has to have been negligent in some way. For example, if there is a snowstorm followed by a thaw and a quick freeze, so that the sidewalks are covered with ice, the landlord won't normally be responsible if a tenant slips and falls. The landlord can't control the weather. If the tenant's child runs the hose during a freeze to make a skating rink and mom falls and breaks a leg, that isn't the landlord's fault. On the other hand, if there is some problem with the slope of a sidewalk that makes it dangerous in normal winter weather for the area, the landlord will be liable if he or she doesn't repair the problem and someone is injured. Also, allowing the sidewalks on the premises to remain frozen for several days and taking no action could cause the landlord to be liable for a slip and fall type injury.

A landlord may sometimes be held liable for dangers he had no actual knowledge of if he should have known of the danger. For example, if the wiring of a house is very old and the owner doesn't ever have it checked, he might be held liable to someone who is injured by a shock or a fire. If the owner doesn't have a chimney cleaned for many years and the tenant is damaged or injured by a flue fire, the landlord will probably be liable, even if he didn't actually know the chimney was clogged. A reasonable person would check old wiring and clean a chimney.

What process does a landlord have to go through to evict a tenant?
A landlord who wants to evict a tenant must follow the relevant state and local laws to the letter. The process of eviction is a very fast one compared to other kinds of legal actions. The trade off is that the landlord must do everything exactly right. If the landlord makes mistakes in giving eviction notices, for example, the case can be thrown out and the landlord will have to begin again.

The first thing as landlord has to do to begin an eviction is to end the tenancy. This is done by giving an eviction notice. There are several kinds of notices a landlord might use:

- **Nonpayment of rent**: If the tenant doesn't pay the rent when it's due, the landlord can serve a notice that the rent is due and give the tenant a certain time (usually 3–5 days) in which to pay the rent (and any late fees specifically listed in a written rental agreement) or move out. If the tenant pays the full amount in the time stated, there can be no eviction on that notice.

- **Fixing a violation**: In some states a landlord can give a tenant a notice to fix some violation of a rental agreement, such as a junk car in the front yard, a pet that's forbidden by the lease, or more people living in the unit than is allowed in the agreement. The notice must state the amount of time the tenant has to correct this. For example, state law may give the tenant 5 or 10 days. If the tenant corrects the violation within the time, there can be no eviction on that notice.

- **Unconditional notice**: In some states a landlord may give a notice for a tenant to move without any possibility of correcting something. In most places this can only be done if the tenant has seriously violated the rental agreement. Example would be if the tenant has repeatedly been late with the rent or has caused major damage to the premises. The time given to move depends on state law. If the tenant has done what the landlord claims, he or she must move or be evicted.

- **30-day or 60-day notices**: In most states, in a month to month tenancy, a landlord can give an eviction notice for a tenant to move without giving any reason. The time allowed under state law for such a notice is usually 30 or 60 days, but it may be as short as 20 days or as long as 90 days. There may be different time periods if the tenant has lived in the unit for a long time, is a senior citizen or disabled, or is receiving federal housing assistance. A landlord can't give this kind of notice to a tenant with a lease until the lease period is over. He or she also can't give such a notice for illegal reasons such as discrimination or retaliation against a tenant for reporting violations or insisting on repairs. This kind of notice may also be forbidden in places with rent control or rent stabilization laws.

At the end of a notice period, if the tenant hasn't corrected the problem (like paying the rent or finding a new home for the cat) or moved out, the landlord can file an eviction action in the appropriate local court. The pleadings evidencing the action have to be served in a way defined by the law on the tenant. After receiving eviction papers the tenant has a chance to answer. The time for the tenant to answer will be on the papers that are served. An answer must be in the form required by the local court rules and state law, so a tenant might get help with drafting an answer. This is the time for the tenant to raise defenses such as that no rent is owed because the tenant properly deducted the amount of necessary repairs from the rent, the landlord didn't give proper notice of a rent increase, a rent increase was for the purpose of illegal discrimination, or a 30-day notice was given because the tenant reported a health code violation in the unit.

If the tenant doesn't file an answer with the court, the court will enter what is called a default judgment for eviction if the landlord can show that the court papers were served properly on the tenant. The tenant may have a default judgment set aside if there was a good reason why he or she wasn't able to answer on time.

If the tenant raises a valid defense, the case will be set for a hearing or trial on the facts. This is the time for the tenant to produce proof, including inadequate notices given by the landlord and letters written by the tenant.

If the court rules that the landlord can evict the tenant, the landlord must take the court order to the sheriff and the sheriff will come and post a notice, usually on the tenant's door, telling the tenant that if she or he does not move out by the date and time given, the sheriff will come and remove the tenant and the tenant's belongings from the unit.

The entire eviction procedure can take as little as 20 days if the landlord does everything right and the tenant has no defense, to several months if the tenant raises a valid defense that has to go to trial.

What are some of the most important elements of a commercial lease?
Generally, the elements of a lease agreement are the parties, the premises to be demised (i.e., leased), the term of the lease agreement, and the consideration or rent. The parties to a lease of commercial property or office space must be identified with particularity. The property to be demised must be identified sufficiently, and, generally, the principles of interpretation applicable to deeds apply to leases in determining the question of sufficiency. A lease of premises that consists of less than an entire building should be especially specific, setting forth measurements, descriptions, floors, rooms, and walls to be included. The lease of an entire building will generally include the land on which the building is situated. Additionally, certain easements or rights to parts of structures generally are inherent in a lease for a portion of a building or an office space, including a right of access and exit; right to the use of common hallways, stairs, and elevators; and entitlement to light, air, and utility connections.

An outline of the most important elements of a commercial lease would be as follows:

1. Name and Address of Lessor.
2. Name and Address of Lessee.
3. Description of leased premises.

4. Term of lease, including the date the term commences and the date and hour it expires.
5. Rental.
    A. Agreement by lessee to pay specified rent.
    B. Total amount of rent for entire lease term.
    C. Amount of each periodic installment.
    D. Time and place of payment.
    E. Percentage instead of or in addition to fixed rent.
    F. Minimum rent under percentage lease.
    G. Provisions for abatement of rent.
6. Delineation of rights and responsibilities with respect to repairs, alterations, and modifications.
7. Designation of liability for real and personal property taxes.
8. Designation of liability for utilities.
9. Restrictions on use of premises.
10. Access to premises and parking facilities.
11. Advertising restrictions.
12. Right of lessor to enter premises for inspection and repairs.
13. Rules and regulations to be followed by lessee and by guests and invitees of lessee.
14. Responsibilities of parties for maintaining casualty, fire, property damage, and personal injury insurance.
15. Assignment and sublease provisions.
16. Effect of partial or total destruction of premises.
17. Effect of partial or total condemnation.
18. Option to renew lease.
    A. Term of renewal.
    B. Rental during renewal term.
    C. Time and manner of exercising option.
19. Option to purchase demised premises.
    A. Purchase price.
    B. Time and manner of exercising option.
20. Termination provisions.
21. Default or breach by lessee.
    A. Lessor's right of reentry and re-letting.
    B. Termination and forfeiture.
    C. Legal and equitable remedies available to parties.
    D. Attorney's fees and costs.
22. Surrender of premises; effect of holdover.
23. Date.
24. Signatures.

Chapter 29

ENVIRONMENTAL LAW

COMMON LAW REMEDIES AND THE ENVIRONMENT

A nuisance exists when the activities of one landowner interferes with the use and enjoyment of the property of another landowner or the community. Nuisances can be such things as bad smells, polluted air, or excessive noise. A court can issue an injunction to stop or get rid of the nuisance or can assess damages. The courts attempt to balance the social utility of the protection of a plaintiff with the social utility of the activity of the defendant. The mere fact that the plaintiff shows harm does not establish that the defendant's conduct is a nuisance. When the community's welfare outweighs the interest of the plaintiff, the activity of the defendant is not deemed a nuisance. For example, it has been held that smoke, fumes, and noise from public utilities and power plants were not nuisances, although they harmed the plaintiffs. The court believed that the interests of the community in the activity of the defendants outweighed the interests of the plaintiffs that were affected.

AIR POLLUTION REGULATION

The *Clean Air Act of 1963* had not been a very effective Act until 1970 when some substantial amendments were adopted. This was the first legislation which had some authority for federal enforcement. The *Environmental Protection Agency* (EPA) was authorized to establish air quality standards and the states were required to implement these standards. These standards included such things as controlling the amount of certain substances in the air like carbon monoxide.

The 1977 Amendments to the Clean Air Act gave authority to the EPA to regulate business growth in order to achieve air quality standards. The EPA was given authority to designate nonattainment areas. These would be areas which had significant air quality problems. A new facility cannot be built in one of these areas unless the new plant has the greatest possible emission controls.

The Clean Air Act was again substantially amended in 1990. These amendments focused on such things as acid rain, smog, and chemicals that would deplete the ozone layer. Acid rain is rain that has acid in it from coal smoke. Other aspects of these amendments:

- Cities were given deadlines to meet antipollution standards.
- What constituted a source of pollution was tightened up so as to include many small businesses which had not been previously covered such as dry cleaners, paint shops and bakeries.
- Regulations on car emission control systems were tightened.
- Plants that have the potential of being major polluters now have to get operating permits from the EPA and are required to use what is called *maximum achievable control technology* (MACT) in their operations regarding toxic emissions. This is a standard for controlling air emissions that is stricter that the previous standards.
- This Act carries both civil and criminal penalties.

WATER POLLUTION REGULATION

The *Federal Water Pollution Act of 1972* was the first meaningful and enforceable federal legislation in this area. This Act is now known as the *Clean Water Act.* Some highlights of this Act:

- Federal standards for discharges by factories into waterways, like rivers, are now enforced on an industry-wide basis.
- The EPA establishes a range of permissible discharge which differs depending on what kind of industry is involved. For example, the ranges for pulp mills are different than those for textile manufacturers.
- A business must obtain a permit from the EPA in order to discharge waste products into a waterway. This does not include discharges into sewer systems. Permits are difficult to obtain. The EPA may require the waste to be treated prior to release.

The *Safe Drinking Water Act* is a federal statute allows the EPA to establish national standards for contaminant levels in drinking water.

The *Oil Pollution Act of 1990* was passed in response to huge spills like the *Exxon Valdez.* Pursuant to this Act, companies must either clean up the spill or pay the federal government its costs for the clean-up. This Act applies to all navigable waters up to 200 miles offshore. Those responsible for spills are liable for penalties of up to $25,000 per day or $1,000 per barrel spilled. If negligence or willful misconduct is involved, penalty is increased to $3,000 per day. Failure to report a spill can bring a $250,000 fine for an individual plus imprisonment. Corporations can be fined up to $500,000.

SOLID WASTE DISPOSAL REGULATION

The *Toxic Substances Control Act of 1976* was passed by Congress in response to the dumping of chemicals by businesses. Pursuant to this Act, the EPA is authorized to control the manufacture, use, and disposal of toxic substances.

The *Resource Conservation and Recovery Act of 1976* (RCRA) regulates the disposal of potentially harmful substances by requiring permits for storage or transfer of these substances. These permits tell the EPA where these substances are located.

CERCLA

The *Comprehensive Environmental Response, Compensation, and Liability Act of 1980* (CERCLA) authorizes the President to issue funds for the cleanup of areas that were once disposal sites for hazardous wastes. The funds are held in a trust fund often called the *Superfund.* If funds are expended from the trust fund to clean up a site, the company can be sued by the EPA for money to reimburse the fund. Seven hundred hazardous substances are now covered.

CERCLA is triggered when a hazardous substance has been spilled, leaked, pumped, poured, discharged, dumped, or disposed into the environment from a *facility.* A *facility* includes a building, structure, equipment, pipe, well, storage container or motor vehicle. CERCLA places liability on past and present owners and operators of a facility and transporters of a hazardous substance to a facility. To prove liability under CERCLA, a plaintiff seeking to recover clean-up costs only needs to prove that the site is a facility, that the defendant is a responsible party, that a release or threatened release of a hazardous substance has occurred, and that the release or threatened release caused the plaintiff to incur costs in response to the release or threatened release. Negligence of the plaintiff does not have to be proven.

A current property owner is liable under CERCLA, even though the owner did not contribute to the pollution. Prior owners are liable under CERCLA if they owned the site at the time of the disposal of the hazardous substance.

CERCLA does provide some defenses to a suit for cost recovery. The *third party defense* allows a defendant to avoid liability for releases caused *solely* by the *act or omission of a third party* unless the third party is an employee or agent of the defendant or where the act or omission occurs in connection with some sort of *contractual relationship* between the third party and the defendant.

Another defense is the *innocent landowner defense.* CERCLA was amended by the *Superfund Amendments and Reauthorization Act of 1986* (SARA). SARA defines the term *contractual relationship* to include a land transfer or deed unless the defendant acquired the property in question *after the disposal or placement of the hazardous substance on, in, or at the facility.* To take advantage of this defense, a property owner must establish either that when it acquired the property it *did not know and had no reason to know* that any hazardous substance had been disposed of on the land, or that it acquired the land by *inheritance or bequest.* To establish that he *did not know or have reason to know,* the landowner must show that at the time of acquisition, he made an appropriate investigation into the previous ownership and uses of the property. A relative high standard of investigation is required in commercial transactions.

ENVIRONMENTAL QUALITY REGULATION

The *National Environmental Policy Act of 1969* requires federal agencies to file an environment impact statement for proposed actions that may affect the environment. The EIS is to contain:

- The proposed action's environmental impact.
- Adverse environmental effects, if any.
- Alternative methods.
- Short term and long term effects.
- Any irreversible effects.

OTHER FEDERAL ENVIRONMENTAL REGULATIONS

Under the *Federal Environmental Pesticide Control Act*, the use of pesticides is controlled. Pursuant to this Act, all pesticides must be registered with the EPA before they can be shipped or distributed. They also can be classified by EPA according to their dangers.

Under the *Asbestos Hazard Emergency Response Act,* schools must inspect for asbestos and take containment or removal action. Asbestos is a toxic pollutant and any buyers or tenants of buildings must be informed of its presence pursuant to the Superfund Act. Employees also must be notified.

The Endangered Species Act was enacted to protect species that are in danger of extinction. The Secretary of Interior names non-marine species and the Secretary of Commerce names marine wildlife. Pursuant to this Act the habitat of endangered species cannot be disturbed.

STATE ENVIRONMENTAL LAWS

Not only must businesses be aware of federal environmental laws, individual states have their own set of environmental laws. In an article in the July/August issue of *The Mississippi Lawyer* entitled *Environmental Law and Property Rights: Lurking Danger,* the authors demonstrate how Mississippi environmental laws and federal environmental laws can effect even a small family business. The following is a hypothetical fact situation prepared by the authors of the article which is based in part on an actual case.

Assume that a small family business began in a fairly populated rural area several years ago in a small shop making barbecue grills. Due to the reputation of the quality of the product, the business grew, thus requiring the business to construct a metal building with a concrete floor. The building was solely used for the manufacture of barbecue grills. The manufacture process was simple and included punching, forming, and welding metal. The grills were painted in paint booths, dried off and then packed for delivery. As the business continued to grow, the owners constructed electrostatic spray paint booths, an oven booth and a cleaning furnace. A natural gas boiler was also installed as a heat and energy source. The building had to be enlarged to accommodate the additional spray booths. Debris from construction was disposed of in the back of the property in a waste pile. At times it was necessary to wash out the building, and the wastewater ran into a ditch by the building. The ditch eventually ran into a creek.

Eventually, a manufacturer of barbecue grills learned of the quality production of the family business and approaches the owners about buying them out. A site inspection does not reveal any possible contamination of the property. However, the day before the purchase is made, the manufacturer learns that the family business has never held any environmental permits. The owners are surprised to learn that a small family business like theirs would need any environmental permits. What permits should the owners have obtained, and what is the exposure of the manufacturer in purchasing this business?

ENFORCEMENT OF ENVIRONMENTAL LAWS

The *Environmental Protection Agency* is the main agency responsible for policing the major environmental problems of air and water pollution, solid waste disposal, toxic substance management, and noise pollution.

The Council on Environmental Quality is a part of the executive branch of the federal government and is responsible for formulating environmental policy and making recommendations to Congress.

Other agencies involved in enforcement of environmental issue include:

- The Atomic Energy Commission;
- The Federal Power Commission;
- The Department of Housing and Urban Development (HUD);
- The Department of Interior;
- The Forest Service;
- The Bureau of Land Management; and
- The Department of Commerce.

CRIMINAL SANCTIONS FOR VIOLATIONS
The Clean Air Act, the Clean Water Act, and the Resource Conservation and Recovery Act all have criminal and civil sanctions.

GROUP SUITS — THE EFFECT OF ENVIRONMENTALISTS
Environmental groups can, and often do, bring law suits to enforce federal and state environmental laws. These groups often have the organizational structure and funding to handle these types of suits. Some of these groups include:

- the Sierra Club;
- the Environmental Defense Fund; and
- League of Conservation Voters.

INTERNATIONAL ENVIRONMENTAL ISSUES
By the end of 1992 the *European Union* (EU) had passed more than 200 environmental directives that focus on noise restrictions, protection of endangered species, energy efficiency and air and water quality. The EU created the *European Environment Agency* as a clearinghouse for environmental information and hope that this agency can eventually act like the EPA.

Chapter 30

WILLS, ESTATES AND TRUSTS

A last will and testament is a declaration by which a person, the testator, names a person to manage his estate (an executor) and provides for the transfer of his property at death. A will does not control all of a testator's assets. Most jointly owned assets and those with beneficiary designations, such as life insurance and retirement accounts, are not controlled by a testator's will. When one dies these assets automatically go to the surviving joint owner or person named as a beneficiary.

By completing a will, a person directs how to distribute personal property, real property, money, and particular items to the intended beneficiaries. A will also allows a person to choose trusted individuals to act as their personal representatives, who will take charge of the estate, wind it up, and distribute it according to stated wishes. In the absence of a will, a person risks having their property distributed by a court-appointed stranger according to their state's laws of intestacy or escheating (forfeiting) to the state. This may result in a longer and more expensive administration process than a will would require, and the property may wind up being distributed against the deceased's wishes.

Other benefits of preparing a will include:

- The ability to name a guardian for minor children to ensure they are cared for as the parent would wish. If both parents of a child or children die without a will, a court-appointed guardian takes custody of any minor children and of the parents' estate;
- People often use a will to express their final wishes for burial, cremation, and/or organ donation;
- A properly written will may result in significant estate tax savings, allowing a person's loved ones to benefit even more from their generosity; and
- Clearly stated wishes in a will can minimize family disputes and the burden of intestate administration.

An attorney is not needed to prepare a will. Requirements vary by state, but most states require two witnesses to sign the will at the direction of the maker. Statutes commonly allow anyone 18 or older to make a will. The will maker must have testamentary capacity, meaning that he/she is of sound mind and acting under free will, understands the nature and situation of his/her property and his/her relations to those persons who would naturally inherit, and understands the nature of the actions taken. Wills are not required to be filed with the court prior to death, although some states allow a will to be filed with a probate court of recorder's office.
Common terminology regarding wills includes:

- ***Testator,*** who is the person who died after making a will. A female will maker is often called a testatrix;

- ***Executor or Administrator,*** who is the person named in the will responsible for administering and settling the estate. A female is often called an executrix or adminstratrix;
- ***Bequeath,*** which means to give by way of a will and is often used to refer to personal property;
- ***Devise,*** which means to give by way of a will and is often used to refer to real property.
- ***Residue,*** which is property remaining after all specific gifts have been disposed of. A will often contains a residuary clause that leaves to all property of the deceased not otherwise disposed of to a residuary beneficiary.
- ***Self-proving affidavit,*** which is allowed by some states to be used at the time of the execution of the will to verify the valid signing of the will. It may simplify the probate process by dispensing with the need for the witnesses to be called to court to testify that the will was properly executed. The affidavit should be sworn to before a notary public.
- ***Codicil,*** which refers to an amendment to a will or a modification of the terms of the original will. The codicil is subject to the same legal requirements as the will itself in order to be valid, and must make a reference to the will it amends.

Types of Gifts. Gifts may be specific or general. The residuary (assets remaining after specific gifts have been made and debts paid) are distributed to the surviving spouse, descendants, or others. If the assets are insufficient to pay all general bequests, the legatees receive reduced benefits.

Requirements for a Valid Will – Testamentary Capacity and Intent. The elements for a general test for capacity are basically the same as having the capacity to enter into a contract. Contractual capacity is the ability to understand that a contract is being made and to understand its general nature. The fact that a person does not fully understand the meaning and all ramifications of a contract does not mean that the person lacks contractual capacity.
A will may be set aside if it were not in fact entered into voluntarily by the testator. If it were entered into because of undue influence or physical or economic duress, it may be set aside. ***Undue influence*** arises in a situation where a confidential type relationship exists and one party has such influence over the other party that the other party's free will is dominated to the benefit of the influencing party. ***Confidential relationships*** which may result in undue influence can be such things as the relationship of an elderly parent and an adult child, a physician and patient, an attorney and client, or any other relationship of trust and confidence in which one party exercises a control or influence over another. Because of the possibility that a person in such a confidential relationship may dominate the will of another and take unfair advantage, if such a confidential relationship exists, the law presumes that undue influence has occurred if the dominating party obtains any benefit from a will made with the person alleged to be dominated. The will is then voidable and may be set aside unless it can be proven that no such domination took place.

Witness Requirements. Two, and sometimes three, witnesses are required. The number, their qualifications, and the manner in which witnessing must be done varies. Some states [(though not the Uniform Probate Code (UPC)] prohibit interested parties from witnessing. A witness does not have to read the will. Sometimes, witnesses must sign in the sight or presence of each other, but the UPC requires only that the testator acknowledge his or her signature to the witnesses (UPC 2–502).

Publication Requirements. Some states require a testator to declare to the witnesses that the will is his or her "last will or testament."

Revocation by a Physical Act of the Maker. A testator may revoke a will by intentionally burning, tearing, canceling, obliterating, or destroying it or by having someone else do so in the presence of the maker and at the maker's direction. In some states, partial revocation is recognized. Of course, where provided, statutorily prescribed methods must be followed.

Revocation by a Subsequent Writing. A codicil can amend or revoke provisions in a will. A new will may (or may not) revoke a prior will, depending on the language. If an express declaration of revocation is missing, the wills are read together; if there are inconsistent dispositions, the second will controls.

Revocation by Operation of Law. A marriage, divorce or annulment, or the birth of children after a will has been executed generally revokes the will (at least as regards the new spouse, ex-spouse, or new children). Generally, depending on the testator's intent and applicable state law, a new spouse and new children get intestate shares, and an ex-spouse gets nothing.

Probate Procedures – Informal Probate. The assets of small estates may be distributed without formal probate. Title to cars, bank accounts, and other property can sometimes be passed by filling out forms, particularly when it is held in joint tenancy or there is only one heir. Once a will is admitted to probate, family members can settle among themselves the distribution of a decedent's assets, although a court order is needed to protect the estate from future creditors and to clear title.

Estate Administration: The orderly procedure used to collect assets, settle debts, and distribute the remaining assets when a person dies is the subject matter of estate administration. The rules and procedures for managing the estate of a deceased are controlled by statute and, consequently, vary from state to state. In every state, there is a special court, often called a probate court that oversees the management of estates of decedents.

The first step is: Is there a Will? After a person dies is usually to determine whether or not the decedent left a will. In most cases, the decedent's attorney will have that information. If there is uncertainty as to whether a valid will exists, the personal papers of the deceased must be reviewed. If a will exists, it probably names a personal representative (executor) to administer the estate. If there is no will, or if the will fails to name a personal representative, then the court must appoint an administrator.

Personal Representative's Duties. The personal representative has a number of duties. His or her first duty is to inventory and collect the assets of the decedent. If necessary, the assets are appraised to determine their value. Both the rights of creditors and the rights of beneficiaries must be protected during the estate administration proceedings. In addition, the personal representative is responsible for managing the assets of the estate during the administration period and for not allowing them to be wasted or unnecessarily depleted.

The personal representative receives and pays valid claims of creditors and arranges for the estate to pay federal and state income taxes and estate taxes (or inheritance taxes, depending on the state). A personal representative is required to post a bond to ensure honest and faithful performance. Usually, the bond exceeds the estimated value of the personal estate of the decedent. Under most state statutes, the will can specify that the personal representative need not post a bond.

When the ultimate distribution of assets to the beneficiaries is determined, the personal representative is responsible for distributing the estate pursuant to the court order. Once the assets have been distributed, an accounting is rendered to the court, the estate is closed, and the personal representative is relieved of any further responsibility or liability for the estate.

Estate Taxes. The death of an individual may result in tax liabilities at both the federal and state levels. At the federal level, a tax is levied on the total value of the estate after debts and expenses for administration have been deducted and after various exemptions have been allowed. The tax is on the estate rather than on the beneficiaries. Therefore, it does not depend on the character of any bequests or on the relationship of the beneficiary to the decedent, unless a gift to charity that is recognized by the Internal Revenue Service as deductible from the total estate for tax purposes is involved. Estate planning for larger estates also considers other deductions available under federal law. An entire estate can pass free of estate tax if the estate is left to the surviving spouse.

The majority of states assess a death tax in the form of an inheritance tax imposed on the recipient of a bequest rather than on the estate. Some states also have a state estate tax similar to the federal estate tax. In general, inheritance tax rates are graduated according to the type of relationship between the beneficiary and decedent. The lowest rates and largest exemptions are applied to a surviving spouse and the children of the decedent.

Intestacy Laws. Laws of intestacy pass a decedent's estate to his or her spouse and blood relatives (those descended from common ancestors). The only exception to this general statement is that legally adopted persons are also treated as blood relatives. One share of the decedent's estate is allocated for each child of the decedent and one share is allotted to the spouse of the decedent, if any. For example, the estate of a man who dies with a wife and three children would be split between the wife and children in equal fourths. This allocation is made *per stirpes*, meaning that the share of any deceased child is split between that child's children (the decedent's grandchildren), and so on at subsequent generational levels. If the decedent leaves no spouse or children, his estate is split among descendants of his ancestors, beginning with father, mother, siblings, and children of siblings who predecease the decedent. If the decedent leaves no children and a spouse, his or her spouse will inherit the entire estate.

Stepchildren, Adopted Children, and Illegitimate Children. Legally adopted children are heirs; stepchildren are not. An illegitimate child is an heir of the mother, but not of the father, unless paternity is established before death. The property of a person who dies intestate, and without heirs, passes to the state. A will must follow exactly the requirements of the appropriate state's statutes to be effective. Besides distributing property, a will can appoint a guardian and a personal representative.

Types of Gifts. Gifts may be specific or general. The residuary (assets remaining after specific gifts have been made and debts paid) are distributed to the surviving spouse, descendants, or others. If the assets are insufficient to pay all general bequests, the legatees receive reduced benefits.

In *Shaw Family Archives, Ltd. v. CMG Worldwide, Inc.*,[26] Marilyn Monroe, a New York resident, had died in 1962. Eventually, her estate's residuary assets were transferred to Marilyn Monroe, LLC (MMLLC). During Monroe's life, photographer Sam Shaw took photos of her. After his death, the photos descended to the Shaw Family Archives (SFA), which licensed Monroe's picture, image, and likeness for commercial use. In Indiana, in 2006, t-shirts that bore her picture and SFA's inscription on the label were available for sale. MMLLC asserted that under Indiana's Right of Publicity Act (which creates a right of publicity that survives for 100 years after a person's death) it owned a right of publicity bequeathed by the residuary clause of Monroe's will, and that SFA had violated this right. SFA and others filed a suit in a federal district court against MMLLC and CMG Worldwide, Inc., contending that MMLLC did not own such a right.

The court issued a summary judgment in SFA's favor, holding that MMLLC had not become the owner of a right of publicity in Marilyn Monroe's name, likeness, and persona through her will. Monroe had not had the testamentary capacity to bequeath such a right because she had not owned it – such rights had not existed – at the time of her death. "New York law does not recognize any common law right of publicity and limits its statutory publicity rights to living persons." Thus "any publicity rights (Monroe) enjoyed during her lifetime were extinguished at her death." No case or statute "stands for the proposition that any intent on the part of the testator can overcome his testamentary incapacity to devise property he does not own at the time of his death."

Naming Guardians for minor children. The following is a fairly typical statute dealing with this issue: Any parent, even though under twenty-one (21) years of age, may, by an instrument to take effect at the parent's death and wholly written and signed by him or her, or attested by two (2) or more credible witnesses . . . . appoint some suitable person as guardian of his motherless or her fatherless child . . . . subject to the approval of the court.

If a single parent dies intestate, or both parents die in a common accident without a will, the court will appoint the guardian of the children of the parents.

Other benefits of executing a will include:

- People often use a will to express their final wishes for burial, cremation, and/or organ donation;

[26] 486 F. Supp. 2d 309 (D. C. N. Y. 2007)

- A properly written can result in significant estate tax savings, depending upon the federal and state tax laws.

- An unfortunate fact of life is that settling an estate oftentimes brings out the worst in people. Families can be forever torn apart. Many people acknowledge that this is true - for others - but believe that their kids would respect the parents' wishes and never stoop to fighting over the estate. Even if this were correct, what about the kids' spouses? In-laws (sons and daughters, particularly) can be a problem. Unless you spell out your wishes in a Will, you may cause your family to tear apart after your death. On the other hand, a will that clearly states the testator's desires can minimize family disputes.

FREQUENTLY ASKED QUESTIONS

What happens if a person dies without a will? The laws of each state vary slightly in some case and a great deal in others; but generally follow these guidelines:

- If decedent is married without children, the spouse inherits the whole estate.

- If decedent is married with children, the spouse and each child share in the estate equally.

- If the decedent has child and is not married, the estate shall descend to his or her children, and their descendants, in equal parts, the descendants of the deceased child or grandchild to take the share of the deceased parent in equal parts among them.

- When there shall not be a child or children of the intestate nor descendants of such children, then the brothers and sisters and father and mother of the intestate and the descendants of such brothers and sisters shall inherit the estate in equal parts, the descendants of a sister or brother of the intestate to have in equal parts among them their deceased parent's share.

- If there shall not be a child or children of the intestate, or descendants of such children, or

- brothers or sisters, or descendants of them, or father or mother, then such estate shall descend, in equal parts, to the grandparents and uncles and aunts, if any.

- If none of the above situations is applicable, such estate shall descend in equal parts to the next of kin of the intestate in equal degree, computing by the rules of the civil law.

Degrees of Kinship by the Rules of Common Law

		Great Grandparent (3)		Great-Great Uncle/Aunt (5)
Great Aunt/Uncle (4)		Grandparent (2)		First Cousin Twice-Removed (6)
First Cousin Once Removed (5)		Parent (1)	Aunt/Uncle (3)	Second Cousin Once Removed (7)
Second Cousin (6)	Sibling (2)	Decedent	First Cousin (4)	Third Cousin (8)
Second Cousin Once- Removed (7)	Niece/Nephew (3)	Child (1)	First Cousin Once Removed (5)	Third Cousin Once- Removed (9)
Second Cousin Twice-Removed (8)	Great Niece/Nephew (4)	Grandchild (2)	First Cousin Twice Removed (6)	Third Cousin Twice Removed (10)
Second Cousin Thrice-Removed (9)	Great-Great Niece/Nephew (5)	Great Grandchild (3)	First Cousin Thrice Removed (7)	Third Cousin Thrice Removed (11)

How large does a person's estate have to be to justify making a last will and testament? A will can be important regardless of the size of your estate. With a will, you can be sure that your estate is distributed the way you want it to be. You can designate a guardian to care for your children if both spouses are deceased. Finally, by choosing an executor, you can choose someone you are comfortable with handling your estate.

Is it expensive to have a will done? That depends on how complicated your will is and how much advance information about assets and conveyances you provide your attorney.

What happens if a person dies without a will? The laws of each state vary slightly in some case and a great deal in others; but generally follow these guidelines:

- If decedent is married without children, the spouse inherits the whole estate.
- If decedent is married with children, the spouse and each child share in the estate equally.
- If the decedent has child and is not married, the estate shall descend to his or her children, and their descendants, in equal parts, the descendants of the deceased child or grandchild to take the share of the deceased parent in equal parts among them.

- When there shall not be a child or children of the intestate nor descendants of such children, then the brothers and sisters and father and mother of the intestate and the descendants of such brothers and sisters shall inherit the estate in equal parts, the descendants of a sister or brother of the intestate to have in equal parts among them their deceased parent's share.
- If there shall not be a child or children of the intestate, or descendants of such children, or brothers or sisters, or descendants of them, or father or mother, then such estate shall descend, in equal parts, to the grandparents and uncles and aunts, if any.
- If none of the above situations is applicable, such estate shall descend in equal parts to the next of kin of the intestate in equal degree, computing by the rules of the civil law.

Can I change my Last Will And Testament? You can make and execute a new will as often as you desire. Do not try to change it by using strikeouts and/or written additions. This can cause many problems in interpretation and possibly void your will. A codicil can be used to amend or revoke provisions in a will. The codicil is subject to the same legal requirements as the will itself as far as its execution and the capacity of the testator. With the use of word processors, it is just as easy to do a new will adopting the changes. Be sure to put in your new will language such as "I, *(Name of Testator)* . . . do hereby make, publish and declare this to be my Last Will and Testament, **hereby revoking any previous Wills and/or Codicils heretofore made by me.**

Trusts

When the legal title to certain property is held by one person while another has the use and benefit of it, a relationship known as a trust has been created. The trust developed centuries ago to get around various nuances and complexities, including taxes, of English real property law. The trustee has legal title and the beneficiary has "equitable title," since the courts of equity would enforce the obligations of the trustee to honor the terms by which the property was conveyed to him. A typical trust might provide for the trustee to manage an estate for the grantor's children, paying out income to the children until they are, say, twenty-one, at which time they would become legal owners of the property.

Trusts may be created by bequest in a will, by agreement of the parties, or by a court decree. However created, the trust is governed by a set of rules that grew out of the courts of equity. Every trust involves specific property, known as the res (res; Latin for "thing"), and three parties, though the parties may be the same person.

Settlor or Grantor: Anyone who has legal capacity to make a contract may create a trust. The creator is known as the settlor or grantor. Trusts are created for many reasons; for example, so that a minor can have the use of assets without being able to dissipate them or so that a person can have a professional manage his money.

Trustee: The trustee is the person or legal entity that holds the legal title to the res. Banks do considerable business as trustees. If the settlor should neglect to name a trustee, the court may name one. The trustee is a fiduciary of the trust beneficiary and will be held to the highest standard of loyalty. Not even an appearance of impropriety toward the trust property will be permitted. Thus a trustee may not loan trust property to friends, to a corporation of which he is a principal, or to himself, even if he is scrupulous to account for every penny and pays the principal back with interest. The trustee must act prudently in administering the trust.

Beneficiary:
The beneficiary is the person, institution, or other thing for which the trust has been created. Beneficiaries are not limited to one's children or close friends; an institution, a corporation, or some other organization, such as a charity, can be a beneficiary of a trust, as can one's pet dogs, cats, and the like. The beneficiary may usually sell or otherwise dispose of his interest in a trust, and that interest likewise can usually be reached by creditors. Note that the settlor may create a trust of which he is the beneficiary, just as he may create a trust of which he is the trustee.

Express Trusts. Trusts are divided into two main categories: express and implied. Express trusts include testamentary trusts and inter vivos (or living) trusts. The testamentary trust is one created by will. It becomes effective on the testator's death. The inter vivos trust is one created during the lifetime of the grantor. It can be revocable or irrevocable. A revocable trust is one that the settlor can terminate at his option. On termination, legal title to the trust assets returns to the settlor. Because the settlor can reassert control over the assets whenever he wishes, the income they generate is taxed
to him.

By contrast, an **irrevocable trust** is permanent, and the settlor may not revoke or modify its terms. All income to the trust must be accumulated in the trust or be paid to the beneficiaries in accordance with the trust agreement. Because income does not go to the settlor, the irrevocable trust has important income tax advantages, even though it means permanent loss of control over the assets (beyond the instructions for its use and disposition that the settlor may lay out in the trust agreement). A hybrid form is the reversionary trust: until the end of a fixed period, the trust is irrevocable and the settlor may not modify its terms, but thereafter the trust assets revert to the settlor. The reversionary trust combines tax advantages with ultimate possession of the assets.

Of the possible types of express trusts, five are worth examining briefly: (1) Totten trusts, (2), blind trusts, (3) Clifford trusts, (4) charitable trusts, and (5) spendthrift trusts.

Totten Trust: The Totten trust, which gets its name from a New York case, *In re Totten*[27]*is* a tentative trust created when someone deposits funds in a bank as trustee for another person as beneficiary. (Usually, the account will be named in the following form: "Mary, in trust for Ed.") During the beneficiary's lifetime, the grantor-depositor may withdraw funds at his discretion or revoke the trust altogether. But if the grantor-depositor dies before the beneficiary and had not revoked the trust, then the beneficiary is entitled to whatever remains in the account at the time of the depositor's death.

Blind Trust
In a blind trust, the grantor transfers assets—usually stocks and bonds—to trustees who hold and manage them for the grantor as beneficiary. The trustees are not permitted to tell the grantor how they are managing the portfolio. The blind trust is used by high government officials who are required by the Ethics in Government Act of 1978 to put their assets in blind trusts or abstain from making decisions that affect any companies in which they have a financial stake. Once the trust is created, the grantor-beneficiary is forbidden from discussing financial matters with the

---

[27] **179 N.Y. 112 (1904)**

trustees or even to give the trustees advice. All that the grantor-beneficiary sees is a quarterly statement indicating by how much the trust net worth has increased or decreased.

Clifford Trust. Clifford Trusts, named after the settlor in a Supreme Court case, *Helvering v. Clifford,*[28] are reversionary. The grantor establishes a trust irrevocable for at least ten years and a day. By so doing, the grantor shifts the tax burden to the beneficiary. So a person in a higher bracket can save considerable money by establishing a Clifford Trust to benefit, say, his or her children. The tax savings will apply as long as the income from the trust is not devoted to needs of the children that the grantor is legally required to supply. At the expiration of the express period in the trust, legal title to the res reverts to the grantor. However, the Tax Reform Act of 1986 removed the tax advantages for Clifford trusts established after March 1986. As a result, all income from such trusts is taxed to the grantor. Existing Clifford trusts were not affected by the 1986 tax law.

Charitable Trust. A charitable trust is one devoted to any public purpose. The definition is broad; it can encompass funds for research to conquer disease, to aid battered wives, to add to museum collections, or to permit a group to proselytize on behalf of a particular political or religious doctrine. The law in all states recognizes the benefits to be derived from encouraging charitable trusts, and states use the cy pres[29] doctrine to further the intent of the grantor. The most common type of trust is the charitable remainder trust. You would donate property – usually intangible property such as stock – in trust to an approved charitable organization, usually one that has tax-exempt 501(c)(3) status from the IRS. The organization serves as trustee during your life and provides you or someone you designate with a specified level of income from the property that you donated. This could be for a number of years or for your lifetime. After your death or the period that you set, the trust ends and the charitable organization owns the assets that were in the trust.

There are important tax reasons why people set up charitable trusts. The Trustor gets five years' worth of tax deductions for the value of the assets in the charitable trust. Capital gains are treated favorably, as well: charitable trusts are irrevocable, which means that the person setting up the trust (the "Trustor") permanently gives up control of the assets to the charitable organization. Thus, the charitable organization could sell an asset in the trust that would ordinarily incur significant capital gains taxes, but since the Trustor no longer owns the asset, there is no capital gains tax: as a tax-exempt organization, the charity will not pay capital gains, either.

Spendthrift Trust. A spendthrift trust is established when the settlor believes that the beneficiary is not to be trusted with whatever rights she might possess to assign the income or assets of the trust. By express provision in a trust instrument, the settlor may ensure that the trustees are legally obligated to pay only income to the beneficiary; no assignment of the assets may be made, either voluntarily by the beneficiary or involuntarily by operation of law. Hence the spendthrift beneficiary cannot gamble away the trust assets nor can they be reached by creditors to pay her gambling (or other) debts.

---

[28] **309 US 331 (1940)**

[29] ***as near as possible to the testator's or donor's intentions when these cannot be precisely followed.***

Express Trusts in Business. In addition to their use in estate planning, express trusts are also created for business purposes. The business trust was popular late in the nineteenth century as a way of getting around state limitations on the corporate form and is still used today. By giving their shares to a voting trust, shareholders can ensure that their agreement to vote as a bloc will be carried out. But voting trusts can be dangerous. Agreements that result in price fixing or other restraints of trade violate the antitrust laws; for example, companies are in violation when they act collusively to fix prices by pooling voting stock under a trust agreement, as happened frequently at the turn of the century.

Implied Trusts. Trusts can be created by courts without any intent by a settlor to do so. For various reasons, a court will declare that particular property is to be held by its owner in trust for someone else. Such trusts are implied trusts and are usually divided into two types: constructive trusts and resulting trusts. A constructive trust is one created usually to redress a fraud or to prevent unjust enrichment. Suppose you give $1 to an agent to purchase a lottery ticket for you, but the agent buys the ticket in his own name instead and wins $1,000,000, payable into an account in amounts of $50,000 per year for twenty years. Since the agent had violated his fiduciary obligation and unjustly enriched himself, the court would impose a constructive trust on the account, and the agent would find himself holding the funds as trustee for you as beneficiary. By contrast, a resulting trust is one imposed to carry out the supposed intent of the parties. You give an agent $100,000 to purchase a house for you. Title is put in your agent's name at the closing, although it is clear that since she was paid for her services, you did not intend to give the house to her as a gift. The court would declare that the house was to be held by the agent as trustee for you during the time that it takes to have the title put in your name.

Factors Affecting Estates and Trusts – Principal and Income

Often, one person is to receive income from a trust or an estate and another person, the remainderman, is to receive the remaining property when the trust or estate is terminated. In thirty-six states, a uniform act, the Uniform Principal and Income Act (UPIA), defines principal and income and specifies how expenses are to be paid. If the trust agreement expressly gives the trustee power to determine what income is and what is principal, then his decision is usually unreviewable. If the agreement is silent, the trustee is bound by the provisions of the UPIA.

The general rule is that ordinary receipts are income, whereas extraordinary receipts are additions to principal. Ordinary receipts are defined as the return of money or property derived from the use of the principal, including rent, interest, and cash dividends. Extraordinary receipts include stock dividends, revenues or other proceeds from the sale or exchange of trust assets, proceeds from insurance on assets, all income accrued at the testator's death, proceeds from the sale or redemption of bonds, and awards or judgments received in satisfaction of injuries to the trust property. Expenses or obligations incurred in producing or preserving income – including ordinary repairs and ordinary taxes – are chargeable to income. Expenses incurred in making permanent improvements to the property, in investing the assets, and in selling or purchasing trust property are chargeable to principal, as are all obligations incurred before the decedent's death.

Taxation. Estates and trusts are taxable entities under the federal income tax statute. The general rule is that all income paid out to the beneficiaries is taxable to the beneficiaries and may be deducted from the trust's or estate's gross income in arriving at its net taxable income. The trust or estate is then taxed on the balance left over—that is, on any amounts accumulated. This is known as the conduit rule, because the trust or estate is seen as a conduit for the income.

Power of Appointment. A power of appointment is the authority given by one person (the donor) to another (the donee) to dispose of the donor's property according to whatever instructions the donor provides. A power of appointment can be created in a will, in a trust, or in some other writing. The writing may imply the power of appointment rather than specifically calling it a power of appointment. For example, a devise or bequest of property to a person that allows that person to receive it or transfer it gives that person a power of appointment. The person giving the power is the donor, and the person receiving it is the donee.

There are three classes of powers of appointment. General powers of appointment give donees the power to dispose of the property in any way they see fit. Limited powers of appointment, also known as special powers of appointment, give donees the power to transfer the property to a specified class of persons identified in the instrument creating the power. Testamentary powers of appointment are powers of appointment that typically are created by wills.

If properly used, the power of appointment is an important tool, because it permits the donee to react flexibly to circumstances that the donor could not have foreseen. Suppose you desire to benefit your children when they are thirty-five or forty according to whether they are wealthy or poor. The poorer children will be given more from the estate or trust than the wealthier ones. Since you will not know when you write the will or establish the trust which children will be poorer, a donee with a power of appointment

Summary

Estate planning is the process by which an owner decides how her property is to be passed on to others. The four basic estate planning tools are wills, trusts, gifts, and joint ownership. In this chapter, we examined wills and trusts. A will is the declaration of a person's wishes about the disposition of her assets on her death. The law of each state sets forth certain formalities, such as the number of witnesses, to which written wills must adhere. Wills are managed through the probate process, which varies from state to state, although many states have now adopted the Uniform Probate Code. In general, anyone over eighteen and of sound mind may make a will. It must be signed by the testator, and two or three others must witness the signature. A will may always be modified or revoked during the testator's lifetime, either expressly through a codicil or through certain actions, such as a subsequent marriage and the birth of children, not contemplated by the will. Wills must be carefully drafted to avoid abatement and ademption. The law provides for distribution in the case of intestacy. The rules vary from state to state and depend on whether the decedent was married when she died, had children or parents who survived her, or had collateral heirs.

Once a will is admitted to probate, the personal representative must assemble and inventory all assets, have them appraised, handle claims against the estate, pay taxes, prepare a final accounting, and only then distribute the assets according to the will.

A trust is a relationship in which one person holds legal title to certain property and another person has the use and benefit of it. The settlor or grantor creates the trust, giving specific property (the res) to the trustee for the benefit of the beneficiary. Trusts may be living or testamentary, revocable or irrevocable. Express trusts come in many forms, including Totten trusts, blind trusts, Clifford trusts, charitable trusts, and spendthrift trusts. Trusts may also be imposed by law; constructive and resulting trusts are designed to redress frauds, prevent unjust enrichment, or see to it that the intent of the parties is carried out.

FREQUENTLY ASKED QUESTIONS

What is a Trust? A Trust is an entity which owns assets for the benefit of a third person (beneficiary). A Living Trust is an effective way to provide lifetime and after-death property management and estate planning. When you set up a Living Trust, you are the Grantor; anyone you name within the Trust who will benefit from the assets in the Trust is a beneficiary. In addition to being the Grantor, you can also serve as your own Trustee (Original Trustee). As the Original Trustee, you can transfer legal ownership of your property to the Trust. This can save your estate from estate taxes when you die. Just remember that it does not alleviate your current income tax obligations.

What is an Irrevocable Trust? A trust created during the maker's lifetime that does not allow the maker to change it.

What is a Revocable Trust? A trust that can be amended and revoked, usually by the person who established the trust. This trust may become irrevocable and unamendable when the only person who can amend or revoke the trust dies or becomes incompetent.

What is a Living Trust? A living trust is a trust established during a person's lifetime in which a person's assets and property are placed within the trust, usually for the purpose of estate planning. The trust then owns and manages the property held by the trust through a trustee for the benefit of named beneficiary, usually the creator of the trust (settlor). The settlor, trustee and beneficiary may all be the same person. In this way, a person may set up a trust with his or her own assets and maintain complete control and management of the assets by acting as his or her own trustee. Upon the death of the person who created the trust, the property of the trust does not go through probate proceedings, but rather passes according to provisions of the trust as set up by the creator of the trust.

Will a Living Trust avoid probate? Perhaps the biggest advantage of a living trust is that it does not have to go through probate, as does a will. However, there are other estate planning devices which avoid probate, such as a joint tenancy, a life insurance policy, and others.

Can a Living Trust be Contested? Yes. A trust can be contested in a special proceeding. There is no blanket rule that a living trust cannot be contested.

What are the Pros and Cons of using a Living Trust rather than a Will? A Last Will and Testament enables you to do the following:

- You are able to name an executor of your will to handle your wishes as expressed in your will. He or she also will work through the probate process with the aid of an attorney and handle the distributions of your property and assets following court costs, taxes and payment of debts.

- You are able to list specific items or percentages of your assets as bequests to certain people or organizations.
- You are able to select a guardian for your minor children should both spouses die before the children are grown. This guardian can also handle the assets passed to the children by you and distribute the assets to the children upon their reaching the age of majority.

A Living Trust has the following attributes:

- You may also make bequests to specific parties with a living trust. You may elect to distribute your property and accounts immediately following your death or you can set up a plan for distribution over a span of time with conditions to be sure your bequest is being used wisely.
- You are able to select a guardian for your children until they are of legal age and for their assets.
- Your living trust will be managed during your lifetime and transferred to another trustee designated by you following your death with no court publicity.
- **Keeping Things Private** - Probate is a public proceeding. This means that anyone can go to the court house and take a look at what has been filed on your behalf. A Revocable Living Trust does not need to be filed with a court; therefore it will not be a public record.

Cons of Using a Revocable Living Trust.

- **Up Front Costs are High** - In general, it will cost more money to set up and fund a Revocable Living Trust than simply execute a Last Will and Testament. But in the long run the overall time and money spent on a living trust is usually
- **Funding a Trust can be a lot of Trouble** - Once your trust has been signed, you are not finished. You will need to contact your banks, investment and insurance companies, and transfer agents to change account and stock ownership and update beneficiaries. You also may have to have new stock certificates issued or assign a partnership or LLC interest to the Trust, If your car is in the trust, you will have to change the title. The same is true for real estate you own. You should carefully consider what kind of assets you have before using a Revocable Living Trust.
- **You most likely will Still Need a Last Will and Testament** – You may not have time to continue to transfer every asset that comes into your name into the trust. You will need a **Pour Over Will** to regarding your assets that have not been transferred. Your Pour Over Will will probably need to be probated.

Chapter 31
E-COMMERCE

The term e-commerce or e-business basically means doing business on the Internet. The laws regulating the Internet and doing business online are still evolving.

Electronic transactions fall into two general categories: *pure electronic* and *hybrid.* Pure electronic transactions are transactions conducted entirely online, without the use of any traditional writings. An example is the point-and-click agreement found on many Web sites. The visitor to the Web site is presented with an online agreement and asked to click on a button to accept its terms. Hybrid transactions involve the use of written agreements, frequently called *trading partner agreements,* which are entered into before any electronic transactions take place. The parties draft these written agreements to specify the manner in which they anticipate electronic transactions are to be conducted.

The legal analysis of online transactions is basically the same as for traditional written agreements. Consideration, warranties, and other basic legal issues are analyzed in substantially the same way as with written agreements. The two biggest issues regarding e-contracts are: (1) Whether an electronic contract is a writing for purposes of the statute of frauds; and (2) Whether the agreement can be properly authenticated.

Under the Uniform Commercial Code ("UCC"), a contract for the sale of goods may be made in any manner sufficient to show agreement, which includes conduct by both parties that recognizes the existence of the contract. The statute of frauds requires certain types of agreements to be in writing and to be signed by the party sought to be bound by the agreement. The purpose behind the rule is to prevent a nonexistent agreement, allegedly made by one of the parties, to be proven by fraud or perjury.

The statute of frauds normally does not apply if it is possible under the terms of the agreement to perform the contract within one year. If a contract provides for the sale of goods with a price of $500.00 or more, this type of contract must ordinarily be in writing. Of the contracts statutorily required to be in writing, those most likely to be encountered online are agreements that cannot be performed within 1 year and agreements for the sale of goods costing more than $500. However, the majority of daily transactions on the Internet are one-time purchases for substantially less than $500 (for example, purchase of a music compact disc or a book). These transactions need not be in writing.

The statute of frauds requires a writing to evidence the contracts which it states must be in writing. This does not necessarily have to be a formal contract signed by both parties. It can be a letter signed by only one party setting forth the terms of the oral agreement. However, the writing, whether it be a letter or memorandum, must be signed by the person "to be charged." This means it must be signed by the person against whom you are seeking to enforce the contract. The writing must contain all of the material terms of the contract. However, the UCC provides that transactions between merchants involving the sale of goods need not be signed by the party to be charged as long as a written confirmation of the contract is sent within a reasonable time. The written confirmation will satisfy the statute unless written notice of objection to its contents is given within 10 days after the confirmation is received.

It is uncertain how the applicable law will be applied in the context of online agreements since there is no clear guidance as to whether a purely electronic transaction will constitute a writing for purposes of the statute of frauds. Part of the uncertainty is attributable to the definition of writing contained in the UCC. Writing includes printing, typewriting, or any other intentional reduction to tangible form. The UCC's definition did not contemplate a technology in which data is stored in a computer memory and not on paper. An argument can be made that data stored in computer memory is not considered sufficiently tangible to satisfy the statute of frauds. However, the data can be printed at any time. If storage in a computer's memory is not sufficiently tangible, the electronic information can be produced in tangible form by simply printing it. In addition, electronic transactions are really no different than telegrams and telexes, both of which have been held to satisfy the writing requirement of the statute of frauds.

Once it has met the standards for a writing, the online agreement must meet the subscription requirement. The subscription (signature) requirement of the statute of frauds can be satisfied by a single writing or by a series of writings. For purposes of the statute, if one of a series of papers relating to the same matter is signed by the party to be charged, that is sufficient, as all the papers are to be considered together in evidencing one contract or memorandum. The UCC has no formal requirements for a signature, only that it appears for the purpose to authenticate the writing. Instead of a name, the signature arguably can be an initial or a symbol.

If an e-mail is sent, the sender identification in the header of an e-mail will be sufficient to show authentication. However, will use of the individual's initials or name at the end of the message satisfy the signature requirement? E-mail software can create a signature that includes name, job title, and phone number. A digital signature provides a means of authenticating both the content and creator of an electronic document through use of public key encryption. With public key encryption, each user is assigned two keys or passwords: one private, the other public. The public key is distributed freely. The owner may post its public key on its World Wide Web site or may make the key available through one of the public key databases maintained by third parties on the Internet. As for the private key, only its owner knows the password. As long as a user's private key remains secure, public key encryption allows for the delivery of confidential and verifiably authentic documents.

Trading partner agreements

Largely because of the uncertain state of the statute of frauds in the online environment, there is a growing trend for parties to enter into written trading partner agreements before they engage in electronic transactions. Trading partner agreements attempt to resolve unsettled legal issues, such as the application of the statute of frauds, through written contractual provisions.

Some trading partner agreements include waiver clauses in which the parties expressly agree not to raise the statute of frauds as a defense in a dispute over the enforceability of subsequent electronic transactions. Other agreements include definitions of writings and signatures specifically directed to the type of electronic communications the parties will use in forming their online agreements.

Article 2B of the Uniform Commercial Code will likely resolve many of the issues surrounding the statute of frauds in online contracts. Originally designed to address only software licenses, Article 2B has grown to include online licenses, subscription agreements, and other forms of electronic contracts.

Many of the transactions conducted online relate to the sale or lease of consumer goods. State and federal consumer protection laws (e.g., Magnuson-Moss Warranty Act) govern these transactions, which regulate advertising, warranties, and disclaimers. These laws also provide consumers with remedies not normally available under common law or the UCC. In addition to general consumer protection laws, many states have adopted or are in the process of adopting specific laws directed at electronic transactions to protect consumers. It is important to check for the latest development of consumer protection law intended to cover Internet transactions.

The *Electronic Signatures in Global and National Commerce Act* validates contracts executed by electronic signature and serves to protect consumers by requiring consumers to provide adequate consent to an electronic transaction. The Act establishes the validity of certain transactions in or affecting interstate or foreign commerce. Specifically, it provides that a signature, contract, or other record relating to such transactions may not be denied legal effect, validity or enforceability solely because it is in electronic form. A contract relating to *interstate or foreign transactions* may not be denied legal effect, validity or enforceability solely because an electronic signature or electronic record was used in its formation. The Act defines an electronic record as a contract or other record created, generated, sent, communicated, received, or stored by electronic means. An electronic signature means an electronic sound, symbol, or process, attached to or logically associated with a contract or other record and executed by or adopted with the intent to sign the record. However, this act only applies to interstate and international commerce. It would therefore only affect transactions between buyers & sellers in different states, or in different countries.

The *Uniform Computer Information Transactions Act* (UCITA) was proposed for state adoption to eliminate the requirement for tangible writings and signatures in the purchase of "computer information". Unfortunately, only about 2 states have actually enacted a version of this proposed act. Most state legislatures are not expected to create or adopt a version of that law; therefore, it is not likely to provide much of a uniform solution.

The *Uniform Electronic Transactions Act* (UETA) was proposed for amendment of state commercial codes to eliminate the requirement for tangible writings and signatures in the purchase and sale of "goods". Some version of this legislation has been adopted in 47 states and the US Virgin Islands. Even if it is adopted in all 50 states, it will only govern transactions for procurement of goods, and *not* services or computer information.

UCC Article 2B revisions, as proposed for adoption by National Conference of Commissioners for Uniform State Law, would change some of the requirements for a writing and a signature. Contracts formed electronically would therefore be enforceable. It will be years before that recommendation is universally adopted and incorporated into state commercial codes. There is also little case law interpreting such legislation. Therefore, it may be some time before this UCC revision provides a viable solution to address the requirements for a writing and for a signature.

It should also be reiterated that UCC and state commercial code requirements are not applicable to services. Therefore, an electronic contract may be binding to a services transaction, even though it might not have been enforceable for a commodity purchase.

Advertising in E-Commerce – Section five of the *Federal Trade Commission Act,* prohibits "unfair or deceptive acts or practices." This prohibition covers:

- Advertising claims;
- Marketing and promotional activities; and
- General sales methods

This Act ensures consumer protection online as well as in traditional print, television and other communication modes. In fact, since about 1999, the commission has taken a number of actions to prevent online fraud and deception.

The contents of an advertisement must comply with three basic principles:

- **An ad must be truthful and not misleading.** So, if an ad is likely to mislead an average consumer and that misperception influences a customer's decision to buy or use the product, it is considered deceptive.
- **Advertisers must be able to substantiate their claims.** If you're going to run an ad, you must have support for the claims the ad conveys. For example, if your ad claims that tests show *xyz.com* is a better search engine than *abcd.com*, you should have some test results to back that up. If there is more than one reasonable interpretation a consumer can make, the ad has to substantiate each interpretation.
- **An ad cannot be unfair.** It's unfair if, according to the FTC, it causes (or is likely to cause) serious consumer injury that couldn't have been reasonably avoided, and isn't justified by the potential benefit to consumers or competition. For example, you must disclose all hidden fees. It's also considered unfair if you don't admit that you paid individuals for endorsements.

Make It Clear and Conspicuous: Much of the FTC's *Dot Com Disclosures Guide* is devoted to a discussion of what constitutes a "clear and conspicuous" disclosure. The requirements depend on the nature of the advertisement. To determine if your ad complies, the FTC recommends adopting the perspective of a reasonable consumer and then asking yourself if the disclosure is presented in a way that you would both notice and understand.

There are a number of factors to consider, including:

- Whether a single disclosure is sufficient or whether the disclosure needs to be posted at various points throughout the site;

- Whether anything on the site distracts attention from the disclosure;
- The location of the disclosure, including where it is in relation to the advertisement; and
- The prominence of the disclosure.

The FTC emphasizes that its rules and guides using the terms "written" or "writing" apply online as well as offline. The FTC also cautions that certain advertisements sent by e-mail may be considered "direct mail advertisements" and thus be subject to certain prohibitions under the direct mail solicitation rules. Ultimately, if you run an ad on your Web site that a reasonable consumer will understand and that will not deceive that consumer, you should be fine. If, however, you run an ad that is even slightly deceptive or somewhat confusing, and you fail to "clearly and conspicuously" disclose, you may have a problem.

Site Use Agreement – Do you know those agreements on Websites, which no one reads, but on which we all click, “I agree?” Those agreements are called *clickwrap agreements*, terms and conditions, and site user agreements. They all serve a similar purpose. The term "clickwrap" has evolved from the word "shrinkwrap" which describes the agreements in shrunken font size that are often wrapped around software disk boxes or envelopes.

A contract is an agreement between two parties. The parties can agree to almost anything that isn't illegal. So in a clickwrap agreement, you can set forth all the possible restrictions on the use of your Website, and the purchase of products or services through it. You can lower your business risks by limiting your liability for things that you might be sued for, and you can accomplish other helpful objectives, such as waiving warranties that are implied by law into the purchase of products, and choosing the location for litigating disputes.

The law generally presumes that everyone has the capacity to contract. Parties to an agreement must have contractual capacity before the agreement will be binding on both parties. Contractual capacity is the ability to understand that a contract is being made and to understand its general nature. The fact that a person does not fully understand the meaning and all ramifications of a contract does not mean that the person lacks contractual capacity. But if a party does lack capacity, then the contract is usually avoidable (or voidable) and the party without capacity may avoid the contract.

Some classes of persons such as people under the age of 21, or in most states, under the age of 18, are deemed by law to lack contractual capacity. People under 18 are considered to be minors. With some exceptions, a contract made by a minor is voidable. The minor, in other words, may avoid the legal liability under a contract. Upon reaching the age of majority, a minor may affirm or ratify the contract and therefore make it contractually binding on him. Any expression of the minor's intention to avoid the contract will accomplish avoidance. Because of this age issue, you may want to restrict the use of your site to persons over 18.

You must also consider persons in other countries. Keep in mind that there is a good chance that you will not be able to get a foreigner into court in the U.S. Also, if you're sued abroad by a user, the foreign judicial system may not uphold the U.S. contract, and may apply their own law instead – even if the contract says that U.S. law applies. Keep in mind that US law restricts us from doing business with certain countries like Cuba, Iraq, Syria and others – in fact, it's illegal to do business with some of them. Having persons in these nations make purchases or download software from your Website would almost certainly be considered "doing business" with these countries. It's also considered exporting, which is in some cases completely prohibited, while in others, it just requires an export license.

Clickwrap Agreement Terms or Clauses

Parties – As with any contract, it is essential to know who the parties are to the agreement. The user is the person clicking onto the site and downloading it onto his or her computer. Since the provider wants the contract to be binding, any definition of user should include a representation that the user can legally enter into the agreement.

For example, is the user a person individually or an agent for others, including a corporation? Does the user have the ability to enter into a contract or is he or she a legal minor or otherwise incapable of entering into a binding contract? An affirmation by the user that he or she is legally capable of entering into a contract or license agreement should be included. On the other hand, the provider must be identified as well. The Web site may be a subsidiary or agent of another company that may hold the copyright, trademark, or other rights, so it is important to name the correct party. This may mean making sure that a subsidiary or agent has been properly given the rights to use copyrighted material, trademarks and the like on the site.

Agreement that the users are over 18: This can help ensure that the user is either over 18 and bound by the contract, or supervised by a parent who agrees to the contract and the minor's use.

Agreement that the user is truthful in information disclosed on the site, agrees to what he or she is buying, and agrees to pay for it: This can provide a remedy against the user if fraudulent credit card information, contact information or other information is provided, or if the user disputes the charge later. Threat of litigation regarding the agreement can sometimes result in faster resolution of payment disputes.

Agreement that the user agrees not to copy materials on the site. Agreement not to reverse engineer or break into the site, and not to use the Website materials, products or services to violate law.

Agreement that the user will use the site in accordance with the instructions, and will not to disclose his password to others for use, and that the site has a license (permission) for use of anything the user submits or posts to the site.

Agreement that the use of the site is at the discretion of the company, and that any use may be terminated by the company at any time.

Terms of Purchases or Services Provided – The clickwrap agreement should obtain the user's agreement to any policies regarding the purchase, including warranty, shipping, returns or otherwise, of products and/or services. It is important to be aware that FTC regulations and other laws govern sales of products over the Internet, as they do mail order and store purchases.

The clickwrap agreement should include language that waives legal warranties that are implied by law regarding the sale of products (goods) under the Uniform Commercial Code. The UCC implied warranties include the following.

Warranty of Title – Every seller, by the mere act of selling, makes a warranty that the seller's title is good and that the transfer is lawful as to passage of title.

Warranty Against Encumbrances – Every seller, by the mere act of selling, makes a warranty that the goods shall be delivered free from any lien of which the buyer at the time of the sales transaction had no knowledge.

Warranty of Fitness for a Particular Purpose – A buyer may intend to use the goods for a particular or unusual purpose, compared to the ordinary use for which the goods are customarily sold. If so, the seller makes an implied warranty that the goods will be fit for that purpose when:

- the buyer relies on the seller 's skill or judgment to select or furnish suitable goods, and
- when the seller at the time of contracting knows or has reason to know the buyer's particular purpose and of the buyer's reliance on the seller's judgment.

When the buyer makes the purchase without relying on the seller's skill and judgment, no warranty of fitness for a particular purpose arises.

Warranty against Infringement (merchant seller).
Unless otherwise agreed, every merchant seller warrants that the goods will be delivered free of the rightful claim of any third person by way of patent infringement, trademark infringement, or any other intellectual property law infringement.

Warranty of fitness for normal use (merchant seller).
A merchant seller makes an implied warranty of the **merchantability** of the goods sold. This warranty is in fact a group of warranties, the most important of which is that the goods are fit for the ordinary purposes for which they are sold.

Disclaimer of Warranties – The seller will want to disclaim all warranties, expressed or implied, as to merchantability, fitness for a particular purpose, or non-infringement. These disclaimers should be in the form required for disclaimers under the UCC and other applicable laws – i.e., they should be conspicuous, (all caps, bold, etc.). These warranties apply to the sales unless they are appropriately waived or disclaimed in writing.

Copyright – This term should state that the materials on the Web site are copyrighted. As such, they may not be modified, published, transmitted, reproduced, posted, or displayed in any media, including but not limited to electronic, print, mechanical and photocopying, other than for the personal use of the user while he or she visits the site.

Trademark – If the web site contains any of the provider's trademarks, logos, and/or service marks, their use must be restricted. To the extent that the various marks can be identified and listed, they should be. Users should be put on notice that they are not being granted any license or right to use any of the trademarks, logos and/or service marks, other than to download them for personal use while visiting the Web site.

Other Laws. The agreement should state that the user agrees to be bound by all applicable laws and regulations that may pertain to the site, including U.S. export and reimport laws and regulations.

Accuracy. The provider should disclaim any representations or warranties as to the accuracy of information on the site or any omissions or other errors in the content.

Limitation of Liability. The seller will want to put the user at risk for use of the site. This would include disclaiming liability for damages, direct or indirect and actual, consequential, or punitive, arising out of or in connection with the use of the site.

Viruses. The seller will want to disclaim any representations that the site as downloaded by user is virus free. At most, the provider may want to state that it has taken reasonable efforts to ensure that its site is virus free but that it cannot guarantee or warrant that it is virus free when it is downloaded by the user.

Activity on the site. To the extent that a site user is able to post information on the site, the provider of the site should state that it does not monitor, but reserves the right to monitor, the site for the content of postings. The provider should assume no responsibility for or liability for such monitoring. It should prohibit the user from placing or posting on the site any statement that is defamatory, libelous, false, obscene, pornographic, profane, or inaccurate.

Privacy. The site should post a public policy concerning privacy on the site. The agreement, or a separate policy statement, should disclose to what extent the site collects information on users, the type of information collected, whether the individual user can be identified, what the information collected is used for, who has access to the information, whether the information is sold or otherwise made available to third parties, and how the user can restrict the use of the information.

Confidentiality. The provider should inform the user that information the user posts on the site is deemed non-confidential and nonproprietary.

Indemnification. The user should be required to defend, indemnify, and hold harmless the provider from and against all claims and expenses, including attorney fees, arising out of the use of the Web site.

Choice of law. The agreement should include a choice-of-law provision.

Venue. The agreement should include a provision as to where venue would be proper. It also should include language identifying where the service is being performed or other similar information to bolster the venue choice.

Termination. The provider should be able to terminate the agreement if the user violates any provision of the use agreement or any laws or other regulations.

Acceptance. That the site is covered by a use agreement should be made clear to the user in a conspicuous manner. The user should be required to acknowledge that he or she has read the terms of the agreement, understands them and agrees to be bound by them. Ideally, the user should acknowledge agreement by being required to type in a phrase such as "I accept."

FREQUENTLY ASKED QUESTIONS E-COMMERCE

What is E-Commerce?

The term *e-commerce* or *e-business* basically means doing business on the Internet. The laws regulating the Internet and doing business online are still evolving.

What other laws specifically govern E-Commerce?

A number of new laws have been enacted that pertain specifically to the Internet. For example, federal laws such as the **Digital Millennium Copyright Act** provide stiff **civil and criminal penalties** for pirating and other unauthorized use of software. If a licensor brings a civil action against you, for example, it may be possible to obtain an injunction and monetary damages. The licensor may then choose between actual damages, which includes the amount lost because of infringement, plus any profits attributable to the infringement. In addition, the government can criminally prosecute you for copyright infringement. If convicted, penalties can include up to five years in prison and a fine of up to $500,000. Second-time offenders risk 10 years of prison and a $1,000,000 fine.

Many of the transactions conducted online relate to the sale or lease of consumer goods. State and federal consumer protection laws (*e.g.,* **Magnuson-Moss Warranty Act**) govern these transactions, which regulate advertising, warranties, and disclaimers. These laws also provide consumers with remedies not normally available under common law or the Uniform Commercial Code (UCC). In addition to general consumer protection laws, many states have adopted or are in the process of adopting specific laws directed at electronic transactions to protect consumers.

The **Electronic Signatures in Global and National Commerce Act** validates contracts executed by electronic signature and serves to protect consumers by requiring consumers to provide adequate consent to an electronic transaction. The Act establishes the validity of certain transactions in or affecting interstate or foreign commerce. Specifically, it provides that a signature, contract, or other record relating to such transactions may not be denied legal effect, validity or enforceability solely because it is in electronic form. A contract relating to *interstate or foreign transactions* may not be denied legal effect, validity or enforceability solely because an electronic signature or electronic record was used in its formation. The Act defines an electronic record as a contract or other record created, generated, sent, communicated, received, or stored by electronic means. An electronic signature means an electronic sound, symbol, or process, attached to or logically associated with a contract or other record and executed by or adopted with the intent to sign the record. However, this act only applies to interstate and international commerce. It would therefore only affect transactions between buyers & sellers in different states, or in different countries.

The **Uniform Computer Information Transactions Act (UCITA)** was proposed for state adoption to eliminate the requirement for tangible writings and signatures in the purchase of "computer information". Unfortunately, only about 2 states have actually enacted a version of this proposed act. Most state legislatures are not expected to create or adopt a version of that law; therefore, it is not likely to provide much of a uniform solution.

The **Uniform Electronic Transactions Act (UETA)** was proposed for amendment of state commercial codes to eliminate the requirement for tangible writings and signatures in the purchase and sale of "goods." Some version of this legislation has been adopted in 47 states and the US Virgin Islands. Even if it is adopted in all 50 states, it will only govern transactions for procurement of goods, and *not* services or computer information.

UCC Article 2B revisions, as proposed for adoption by National Conference of Commissioners for Uniform State Law, would change some of the requirements for a writing and a signature. Contracts formed electronically would therefore be enforceable. It will be years before that recommendation is universally adopted and incorporated into state commercial codes.

I understand that certain types of contracts must be in writing to enforceable. How does that affect the enforceability of making contracts on the Internet?
You are correct. The law does require that certain contracts must be in writing in order to be enforceable by a Court. The state statutes that require certain contracts to be in writing are called *statutes of fraud.* Statutes of fraud require that either the contract itself be in writing and signed by both parties or there must be a sufficient memorandum of the agreement *signed by the party being sued for breach of contract.*

- The statute of frauds normally does not apply if it is possible under the terms of the agreement to perform the contract within one year. If no time for performance is specified in the oral agreement and the performance will not necessarily take more than one year, the statute of frauds would not apply.
- An agreement that cannot be performed within one year after the agreement is made must be in writing.
- Contracts involving the sale of land must be evidenced by a writing.
- Another type of contract that must be in writing is the promise to answer for the debt of another person.
- A promise by the executor or administrator of an estate to use personal funds to pay a debt of the estate must be in writing.
- A promise made in consideration of marriage must be in writing. An example of this would be a prenuptial agreement.
- If a contract provides for the sale of goods with a price of $500.00 or more, it must ordinarily be in writing.

It is uncertain how the applicable law will be applied in the context of online agreements since there is no clear guidance as to whether a purely electronic transaction will constitute a writing for purposes of the statute of frauds. Part of the uncertainty is attributable to the definition of writing contained in the UCC. Writing includes printing, typewriting, or any other intentional reduction to tangible form. The UCC's definition did not contemplate a technology in which data is stored in a computer memory and not on paper. An argument can be made that data stored in computer memory is not considered sufficiently tangible to satisfy the statute of frauds. However, the data can be printed at any time. If storage in a computer's memory is not sufficiently tangible, the electronic information can be produced in tangible form by simply printing it. In addition, electronic transactions are really no different than telegrams and telexes, both of which have been held to satisfy the writing requirement of the statute of frauds.

Once it has met the standards for a writing, the online agreement must meet the subscription requirement. The subscription (signature) requirement of the statute of frauds can be satisfied by a single writing or by a series of writings. For purposes of the statute, if one of a series of papers relating to the same matter is signed by the party to be charged, that is sufficient, as all the papers are to be considered together in evidencing one contract or memorandum. The UCC has no formal requirements for a signature, only that it appears for the purpose to authenticate the writing. Instead of a name, the signature arguably can be an initial or a symbol.

If an e-mail is sent, the sender identification in the header of an e-mail will be sufficient to show authentication. However, will use of the individual's initials or name at the end of the message satisfy the signature requirement? E-mail software can create a signature that includes name, job title, and phone number.

Proposed Article 2B of the Uniform Commercial Code will likely resolve many of the issues surrounding the statute of frauds in online contracts regarding the sale of good. Originally designed to address only software licenses, Article 2B has grown to include online licenses, subscription agreements, and other forms of electronic contracts.

Other Acts that will provide some relief from the statute of frauds and which are discussed above are:

- The **Electronic Signatures in Global and National Commerce Act**;
- The **Uniform Computer Information Transactions Act; and**
- The **Uniform Electronic Transactions Act.**

What are the legal requirements for creating a Web page?
There are really very few legal requirements in creating a Web page. The first thing you have to do is to secure the rights to use the domain name that you choose. This requires registering the name with a domain administrator. There are a number of domain name registration services around the world. The one you use should be accredited by the **Internet Corporation for Assigned Names and Numbers** ("**ICANN**"). ICANN is a nonprofit corporation that has been delegated responsibility by the U.S. government to coordinate Internet technical functions, including management of the Internet domain name system.

Once you are able to secure domain name registration, the process of starting an e-commerce business will be much the same as any other business enterprise. For example, you may want to incorporate your business. You will also need to enter into numerous contractual relationships in order to secure the services and products that are required to get the business up and running.

You should pay close attention to any contracts that you are asked to sign, as they may have long-reaching effects. You should also be very careful about the scope and extent to which you use various products.

You also have to be very careful about intellectual property rights. One question to ask yourself, for example, is whether or not it is appropriate to incorporate source code into your Web site that you have taken from a commercial software company. It is oftentimes contemplated by a software license that the user is allowed to reproduce and distribute a software product as part of its own product, provided that usage is adding significant and primary value to the underlying software, along with numerous other limitations and restrictions.

Licensing your business can also be problematic. Wherever you have a home office, it is almost a certainty that you will need to obtain a business license. There may be other requirements in the ***locale where you are located***. You must also undertake due diligence to see what requirements may be on the other end where your customers are. This is sometimes called part of the "fulfillment" process, which could be exceedingly complex depending upon the nature of your business and where your customers are located.

Once your business is up and operating, compliance issues are ongoing. A business activity that is illegal in one medium is not going to become legal simply because you are doing it over the Internet. Given the lack of restrictions in accessing and using the Internet, it is also sometimes easier to fall into traps for the unwary. Examples would include posting unauthorized materials on a Web site, infringing upon intellectual property rights, or engaging in unlawful solicitations (for example, spamming). In some instances, it is also much easier to get ripped off over the Internet by, for example, sending money to someone via an online auction to purchase an item that is never sent to you.

What is "spamming" and is it illegal?
Spamming can take on many forms and is difficult to precisely define. Generally speaking, though, it consists of mass posting or cross-posting of unsolicited e-mail for commercial purposes. Under federal law, it's unlawful to send junk mail by facsimile, with the possibility of civil liability of up to $500 per copy. Efforts have been made to extend this law to spam sent over the Internet, but isn't clear if this law applies to spamming.

Some states like California have gone further. Under legislation approved in September 1998, unsolicited commercial e-mail messages must include opt-out instructions and contact information. An opt-out request must also be honored. Certain messages must also be identified in their subject lines as being advertisements. A service provider may also sue a sender of unsolicited commercial e-mail for violating the provider's policies if the sender has actual notice of such policies and if the spam is sent out through the provider's facilities located in California.

Chapter 32
GLOBAL AND INTERNATIONAL PERSPECTIVES

GLOBAL ECONOMIC PERSPECTIVES
Economics is a social discipline which encapsulates human behaviors. Globally, all humans have some association with the producing or consuming of goods and services. Any contemplation of economics involves considerations of both the art and science of resource allocation. The primary inquiry of economics is stated as: How does one satisfy the unlimited wants and needs of humans with respect to the availability, accessibility, and allocation of scarce, limited resources through time? In addition, supplementary questions of economics among all societies are: What to produce? What quantity to produce? For whom to produce?

Many businesses pursue international endeavors whereby they must interact with different countries and cultures. Doing so necessitates operations among different economies in foreign nations where laws may differ. Thus, businesses seeking international endeavors must have some understanding of economic systems and legal challenges internationally.

ECONOMIC SYSTEMS
The primary economics question and its supportive inquiries must be addressed by all economic systems and markets. Around the world, myriads of markets exist among various economic systems. Generally, worldwide, four categories of economic systems exist: 1) capitalism, 2) communism, 3) socialism, and 4) bartering, and 5) hybrid (mixed).

Capitalism – Capitalism facilitates the free exchanging of goods and services, spawns and facilitates competition, and provides for private, individual property ownership. The pricing of goods and services is governed by market forces. Individuals, groups, and organizations may participate openly in a capitalistic economic system whereby all have some chance of success or failure.

Communism – Communism is characterized by collectivism, labor regulation, regulation of the production of goods and services, societal classlessness, indoctrinating and controlling of masses of people, and government control of the economic system. Private ownership of property is disallowed in favor of governmental possession, ownership, and control. Similarly, open market competition is quashed in favor of government control within the economic system. It also typically exhibits authoritarian, totalitarian dictatorships that advocate and encourage the utter eliminating of capitalism.

Socialism – Socialism involves government possession and control of some, but not all, societal institutions. Some private ownership and private profit exists within the socialist economic system. Socialism is a milder form of communism. Some folks may use the terms socialism and communism interchangeably, but communism is the more excessive of the two concepts.

Barter – Bartering represents an exchanging of commodities. Basically, something of value is traded for another entity that is deemed to have some sort of value. For instance, someone may trade 50 chickens for masonry services.

Mixed/Hybrid – A hybrid or mixed system exhibits various characteristics of multiple economic systems. It exhibits neither the radical, extreme control of absolute communism nor the individual and freedoms of capitalism. Many Asian nations have incorporated some forms of mixed or hybrid economic systems.

GLOBAL BUSINESS

Businesses may transcend national boundaries thereby representing international functions and activities. In doing so, international business endeavors may involve numerous economic systems.

INTERNATIONAL LAW AND TRANSACTIONS

International law may be defined as a body of law formed as a result of international customs, treaties, and organizations that governs relations among or between nations. International Customs are customs evolved over the centuries. Treaties and International Agreements are agreements between or among nations. International Organizations and Conferences are composed mainly of nations and usually established by treaty – for example, the 1980 Convention on Contracts for the International Sale of Goods, or CISG.

Legal systems are generally divided into common law and civil law systems. Common law systems are based on case law. These systems exist in countries that were once a part of the British Empire (such as Australia, India, and the United States). **Stare decisis** requires following precedent unless otherwise necessary. Civil law systems are based on codified law (statutes). Courts interpret the code and apply the rules without developing their own laws. Civil law systems exist in most European nations, in Latin American, African, and Asian countries that were colonies of those nations; Japan; South Africa; and Muslim countries.

There are three important legal principles based largely on notions of courtesy and respect:

- the Principle of Comity,
- the Act of State Doctrine, and
- the Doctrine of Sovereign Immunity.

The Principle of Comity: Comity is legal reciprocity – the principle that one jurisdiction will extend certain courtesies to other nations (or other jurisdictions within the same nation), particularly by recognizing the validity and effect of their executive, legislative, and judicial acts. The term refers to the idea that courts should not act in a way that demeans the jurisdiction, laws, or judicial decisions of another jurisdiction. Part of the presumption of comity is that other jurisdictions will reciprocate the courtesy shown to them.

The Act of State Doctrine: The judicial branch of one country will not examine the validity of public acts committed by a recognized foreign government within its own territory. This doctrine avoids disturbing diplomatic relations. The act of state doctrine and the doctrine of sovereign immunity tend to immunize foreign nations from the jurisdiction of U.S. courts so that, in general, U.S. firms or individuals who own property overseas have little U.S. legal protection against government actions in the countries in which they operate. The act of state doctrine is a judicially created doctrine that provides the judicial branch of one country will not examine the validity of public acts committed by a recognized foreign government within its own territory. This doctrine is often employed in cases involving expropriation or confiscation.

The Doctrine of Sovereign Immunity: The Foreign Sovereign Immunities Act (FSIA) of 1976 governs the circumstances in which an action may be brought in the United States against a foreign nation, including attempts to attach a foreign nation's property. A foreign state is not immune from the jurisdiction of U.S. courts if:

- The state has waived its immunity;
- The action is based on a commercial activity carried on in the United States by the foreign state. A "foreign state" includes a political subdivision and an instrumentality of the state. A "commercial activity" is a mercantile activity that has substantial contact with the United States.
- The state has committed a tort in the United States or violated certain international laws. Under the Foreign Sovereign Immunities Act, a foreign state may be subject to the jurisdiction of U.S. courts when the state has "waived its immunity either explicitly or by implication" or when the action is "based upon a commercial activity carried on in the United States by the foreign state."

Doing Business Internationally: International business transactions include selling products (or services) in foreign markets. There are basically two ways to sell products in foreign markets: export goods manufactured domestically or manufacture goods there. Manufacturing goods in foreign countries may have the advantages of lower costs, taxes, and trade barriers, as well as less government regulation.

Exporting: There are two ways to export: direct and indirect. Direct exporting does not involve third parties. Indirect exporting involves the use of a third party to sell a product in a foreign market for a domestic manufacturer. When that party is in a foreign market, it's an agent. If that party, located in a foreign market, takes title to the goods, it's a distributor.

MANUFACTURING ABROAD

There are several ways to manufacture goods abroad:

- Licensing, which involves payment of royalties;
- Franchising, which is a grant of the right to operate and share in the profits of a business or sell goods or services under a brand or chain name. Franchise may mean the right one has to operate a store or sell goods or services under a franchise agreement. In a franchise business relationship, the owner (the franchisor) licenses others (the franchisees) to operate outlets using business concepts, property, trademarks and trade names owned by the franchisor; and

- Investing in a Wholly Owned Subsidiary or a Joint Venture. When a U.S. firm establishes a wholly-owned foreign subsidiary, the parent company often retains complete ownership of the facilities and complete control over all phases of the operation. In a joint venture, a U.S. firm shares ownership, control, profits, and liabilities.

Regulation of Specific Business Activities: National laws and international agreements impose controls on international business transactions.

Investing – Government regulation of expropriation and confiscation of investment property. Essentially, expropriation involves compensation for what is taken; confiscation does not. International law principles are violated when property is confiscated. Some countries provide constitutional or statutory guaranties against it, or insurance for their citizens' investments abroad. Few remedies are available, however.

Export Controls – Under the Constitution, Congress cannot impose export taxes, but Congress controls exports by setting quotas or other restrictions on the flow of commodities, products, and data. Congress stimulates exports through tax incentives (exempting income) and encouraging investment in and loans to U.S. export companies. Under the Export Administration Act of 1979, restrictions can be imposed on the flow of technologically advanced products and technical data.

Import Controls – The production and sale of domestic products may also be stimulated by import restrictions, which include prohibitions, quotas, and tariffs. Prohibitions are imposed on illegal drugs, books that urge insurrection against the U.S. government, agricultural products that pose dangers to domestic crops or animals, goods coming from enemies of the United States.

Quotas and Tariffs are imposed on such products as oil. The procedure for imposing antidumping duties involves two U.S. government agencies: the International Trade Commission (ITC) and the International Trade Administration (ITA). The ITC is an independent agency that makes recommendations to the president concerning temporary import restrictions. The ITC assesses the effects of dumping on domestic businesses. The ITA is part of the Department of Commerce and decides whether import sales were at less than fair market value. The ITA determination establishes the amount of antidumping duties, which are set to equal the difference between the price charged in the United States and the price charged in the exporting country. A duty may be retroactive to cover past dumping incidents.

Dumping – Specific laws deal with what the United States regards as unfair international trade practices (dumping is an example).

Minimizing Trade Barriers – To minimize international trade barriers, most of the world's leading trade nations abide by the World Trade Organization (WTO). Each member country agrees to treat other members at least as well as it treats the country that receives its most favorable treatment (normal trade relations (NTR) status). Regional trade agreements that help to minimize barriers include the European Union (EU), the North American Free Trade Agreement (NAFTA), and the Central America–Dominican Republic–United States Free Trade Agreement (CAFTA-DR).

Bribing Foreign Officials – Congress attempts to reduce the amount of bribes given foreign government officials by representatives of U.S. corporations through the Foreign Corrupt

Practices Act of 1977. The Foreign Corrupt Practices Act (FCPA) is designed to prevent the bribing of foreign officials in order to obtain foreign government contracts. Payments to foreign officials for **facilitation**, often referred to as **grease payments,** are not prohibited under FCPA so long as these payments are made only to get officials to do their normal jobs that they might not do, or would do slowly, without some payment. These payments can be made only to secure a permit or license; obtain paper processing; secure police protection; provide phone, water, or power supply; or similar such actions.

COMMERCIAL CONTRACTS IN AN INTERNATIONAL SETTING

Problems arising from language and legal differences may be avoided by including provisions designating the official language of the contract, the legal forum for resolving contract disputes, the substantive law that will be applied, whether disputes will be arbitrated or litigated, and what acts or events will excuse the parties from performance under the contract.

Choice of Language – Besides designating the official language by which the contract will be interpreted, this clause may allow for a translation that can be authoritative if it is ratified by all parties.

Choice of Forum – This clause should identify the specific court that will have jurisdiction over a dispute. The choice cannot deny a party an effective remedy, be the product of fraud or unconscionable conduct, cause substantial inconvenience to a party to the contract, or violate public policy.

Choice of Law – As with language and forum, the parties to an international contract can choose whatever law they wish to govern their contract (at least under international agreements—the UCC restricts the choice to whatever is "reasonable"). Under the 1986 Hague Convention on the Law Applicable to Contracts for the International Sale of Goods, if a choice-of-law is not specified, the governing law is that of the country in which the seller's business is located.

Force Majeure Clause – Force majeure clauses commonly stipulate eventualities in addition to acts of God that may excuse a party from liability for nonperformance.

Civil Dispute Resolution – Arbitration clauses are common in contracts governing international sales. The arbitrator of choice is sometimes a neutral entity (the International Chamber of Commerce, for instance). The United Nations Convention on the Recognition and Enforcement of Foreign Arbitral Awards assists in enforcing arbitration clauses, as do provisions in other treaties.

PAYMENT METHODS FOR INTERNATIONAL TRANSACTIONS

Monetary Systems –Firms engaged in international transactions rely on the convertibility of currencies. Exchange rates are set by the forces of supply and demand. Correspondent banking makes it possible to transfer funds internationally. Most interbank transfers are handled electronically.

Letters of Credit – Letters of credit facilitate international transactions. In a simple letter of credit transaction, the issuer (a bank) agrees to pay the beneficiary (seller) when the beneficiary has complied with the terms of the letter (which typically requires delivery of a bill of lading to prove that a shipment has been made). In return, the account party (buyer) promises to reimburse the issuer for the amount paid to the beneficiary. The issuer does not police the underlying contract: a letter of credit is independent of the underlying contract between the buyer and the seller.

U.S. Laws in a Global Context

International Tort Claims – All nations have laws governing torts, but there are significant variations in the application and effect of the laws. The Alien Tort Claims Act of 1789 allows foreign citizens to bring suits in U.S. courts for injuries allegedly caused by violations of international tort law. Some cases have involved violations of human rights. Some have alleged environmental crimes.

Antidiscrimination Laws – Under the Civil Rights Act of 1991, Title VII of the Civil Rights Act of 1964 covers U.S. citizens working abroad for U.S. employers, unless compliance with Title VII would violate the laws of the country in which they work.

www.ingramcontent.com/pod-product-compliance
Lightning Source LLC
LaVergne TN
LVHW060021210926
848481LV00013B/3762